The Supreme Court in the Federal Judicial System

Second Edition

STEPHEN L. WASBY
State University of New York at Albany

Holt, Rinehart and Winston
New York Chicago San Francisco Philadelphia
Montreal Toronto London Sydney
Tokyo Mexico City Rio de Janeiro Madrid

Library of Congress Cataloging in Publication Data

Wasby, Stephen L., 1937–
The Supreme Court in the federal judicial system.

Includes index.
1. United States. Supreme Court. 2. Courts—United States. I. Title.
KF8742.W38 1984 347.73'6 83-13009
347.30735
ISBN 0-03-062078-3

Address correspondence to:
383 Madison Avenue
New York, N.Y. 10017

Printed in the United States of America
Published simultaneously in Canada
4 5 6 7 059 9 8 7 6 5 4 3 2

CBS COLLEGE PUBLISHING
Holt, Rinehart and Winston
The Dryden Press
Saunders College Publishing

To the memory of my grandparents,

Frances and Benjamin Bunshaft,

and

Harold ("Hal") Chase,
Constitutional law scholar, teacher,
Marine, but more important: friend,
and the person who made my first book possible.

The good people do is not interred with their bones,
but lives in the hearts
of those who cherish their memory.

Preface

The United States Supreme Court receives much attention, adulation, and criticism. Yet the American public knows far less about it than about Congress or the president. Our national legislators and particularly the president, aided by media coverage, work at making themselves highly visible. The Court, however, has no public relations apparatus and remains generally secretive about its internal processes; its rulings are supposed to speak for themselves. Moreover, there has been little public education about the Court's functioning or its place in our government, a result of the "mystery of the law," lack of attention in the educational system and in the media, and lawyers' failure to inform the lay public. Our knowledge of the Court thus depends to a particularly large degree on what others have explained about the institution.

In the last half-dozen years, the Supreme Court's work and the justices' activities became more visible as a result of a journalistic expose of strategic maneuvering in the Burger Court and a study of two famous justices' extrajudicial political activities. Although these add a significant dimension to our knowledge of the Supreme Court's workings, neither provides the general reader with adequate information about the Court or a sufficient context in which to evaluate its work. This book is written in the hope of remedying such deficiencies in knowledge about the Supreme Court. My intent is to provide not only understanding of what the Court has done thus far but also a basis for understanding its future actions. Justices come and go, and the doctrine announced by the Court may change, but the Court's basic method of deciding cases and the considerations that influence its decisions remain relatively stable.

Scholars who have devoted their attention to the Court provide much of the basis for what appears here. Some data on the Court has been prepared for this volume, and I have also drawn on my own prior work while trying to avoid inflicting too much of it on the reader, but this book is basically a synthesis of others' studies. It reflects both emphases and gaps in the existing literature on the Supreme Court, and thus is hardly the last word. Although the most recent studies have been used, detailed analyses of the Court's most recent terms appear only after several years. Salient information through the end of the Supreme Court's 1981 Term (ending in June 1982) has been presented, with the most important cases of the 1982 Term noted.

To understand the Supreme Court, one must know about its internal procedures, including how cases are accepted for review and how those cases are decided; the Court's role at the top of our nation's judiciary—how it fits into our dual court system of separate national and state courts; and its role in the overall political system. We must therefore look not only at the Supreme Court but also at the entire national court system, the relations between federal and state courts, the Court's relations with Congress and the executive branch, and the impact of the Court's decisions. All these matters are discussed in this book, with primary emphasis throughout on the Court's operation rather than on the doctrines that the justices announce. However, in addition to the illustrative use of cases, particular attention is given to the Court's rulings on access to federal courts and on congressional and presidential actions.

The book is divided into ten chapters. Chapter 1 presents a general discussion of the Supreme Court's role in the American government, legal and political system, with some attention paid both to history and to contemporary political controversy concerning the Court. This is followed by discussion of the structure and administration of the federal court system (Chapter 2) and the selection of federal judges (Chapter 3). Chapter 4 deals with the role of lawyers and interest groups in pursuing litigation; Chapter 5 with rules for getting into courts and the relation between federal and state courts; and Chapter 6 with the Court's exercise of choice in determining what cases to decide. Chapters 7 and 8 provide an extended consideration of the way in which the Court handles cases accepted for review, judicial interaction in deciding cases, and considerations, including the exercise of judicial review, affecting the Court's opinions. After an examination of the Court's review of congressional and executive branch actions in Chapter 9, the book concludes with a discussion of the communication of decisions to those affected and the impact of those rulings in Chapter 10.

Those familiar with the first edition of this book will find that it has been restructured. In order to provide discussion of basic institutional matters before turning to what the justices have done within those institutional confines, I have moved material on structure of the courts and on judicial selection closer to the front of the book. Discussion of judicial review has been tied more directly to treatment of the Supreme Court's role and to the development of the Court's opinions. Material on public opinion concerning the Court is now considered in connection with the Court's impact. Besides the use of newly available sources and the updating of examples, there is consideration of two new topics—the controversy over the role of federal courts in "social policy" litigation and use of judicial selection commissions during the Carter administration—and significant expansion of material on interest group litigation activity, now the subject of a separate chapter. No bibliography is included in this edition, but anyone who wishes to read further can easily do so by following up items in the footnotes at the end of each chapter. As before, a Table of Cases is provided where the reader can find citations to cases discussed in the text.

In a work of this sort, acknowledgments are many. Over time many ideas and much information have been provided by helpful and generous colleagues, not all of whom can be mentioned here. I wish particularly to thank for their help with particular sections of this manuscript David Adamany, Wayne State University; Jerry Goldman, Northwestern University; Maeva Marcus, Supreme Court of the United States; Karen O'Connor, Emory University; D. Marie Provine, Syracuse University; and Elliot

Slotnick, Ohio State University. The fine editorial hand of sometime coauthor Joel Grossman, University of Wisconsin, Madison, is still evident from earlier endeavors. Keith O. Boyum, California State University, Fullerton, and George F. Cole, University of Connecticut, read the entire manuscript and made exceptionally helpful comments, the results of which I hope they will recognize. I wish especially to express my gratitude to the late Harold Chase for his support and continuing interest. It is to his memory that this edition is in part dedicated. I wish he had lived to see its publication.

Thanks also go to Denise Rathbun, formerly of Praeger Publishers, who first asked me to write this book, and to Marie Schappert, my editor at Holt, Rinehart and Winston, who encouraged the writing of this revised edition. Students in my Spring 1982 Supreme Court course were the first to be exposed to the sequence used in this edition. That sequence was persuasively suggested by my wife Karen, who also read the basic draft of this revision and forced me to make matters clear(er). She helped me to keep my sanity, absorbed an author's usual midwriting grumping, and refused to take any responsibility for the final product, nicely (?) leaving that all to me; I accept the responsibility, and will not even blame Suzanne Hagen, who effectively transformed my total lack of artistry into diagrams of the court system's structure, or Addie Napolitano, who did a superb job of manuscript preparation.

S.L.W.

Contents

CHAPTER **3**

Judicial Selection 67

CHAPTER **4**

Lawyers, Interest Groups, and Appeals 100

CHAPTER **5**

Getting Into Court 121

CHAPTER 9

CHAPTER 10

Chapter 1

The Supreme Court's Roles

The Supreme Court of the United States is seen in many different ways by the American public. To some the Court is lawgiver, the nation's high tribunal and protector of the Constitution—and perhaps upholder of our liberties. To others the Court is not the finder of the law but a policy maker perhaps usurping the legislative prerogative or acting as an obstacle to change. Whether they evaluate the Supreme Court positively or negatively, many people see it as different both from other courts in the United States and from the highest courts of other nations.

After World War II, courts in an increasing number of nations were granted a power previously possessed by few courts outside the United States—the power of *judicial review*, the power to invalidate acts of other branches of the government as violating the Constitution. The U.S. Supreme Court remains unusual among highest courts of the world in being not solely a *constitutional court*, one created to hear only questions of the validity of legislative and executive actions and questions of the Constitution's meaning. Instead it has both the power of judicial review *and* the authority to handle all types of litigation, including cases involving interpretation of statutes and application of already-developed policy to particular fact situations (norm enforcement), such as determinations in employee injury cases under federal law. The Supreme Court also differs from most other courts—which *must* accept and decide most cases brought to them—in being able to choose the cases it hears.

If this were not enough to make the Supreme Court exceptional, it is the highest court in the national judicial system, not only the highest among the federal courts but also the court of last resort for cases from the judicial systems of all the states. It thus has the final judicial word in any case involving the U.S. Constitution, which is binding on state courts as well as on federal judges. The Court's ability to choose its cases, coupled with its paramount position, gives its rulings the widest possible influence. Although Alexander Hamilton wrote in *The Federalist* that because it did not possess "either the sword or the purse" the Supreme Court would be the "least dangerous" branch, the Court has become very important—and powerful—indeed.

Although the Supreme Court may have the final judicial word, its statements are final only after Congress, the executive, state officials, and even the public have been able to respond; in short, the law is what the judges say it is, after everyone else has had their say. To the extent that the Court's interpretation of a statute or a constitutional provision is accepted as appropriate, it is perhaps only because the Court is the *highest* court. As Justice Jackson admonished, "We are not final because we are infallible, we are infallible only because we are final."[1]

People expect the Supreme Court to act like a court—or like what they think a court is. Indeed, like any other court, the Supreme Court acts within a particular legal system. In the United States, the legal system is supposedly adversary in nature, and judges are expected to rely on *precedent,* that is, decisions in past cases. However, people react to the Court not only in terms of its procedures but in terms of its results as well. They treat it not only as a legal institution deciding specific cases but also as another agency of government, making policy by its decisions just as legislatures make policy by enacting statutes and executive agencies by promulgating regulations. All courts—even trial courts sentencing defendants after accepting a guilty plea—are policy makers. However, the Supreme Court's policy making is far more visible than the actions of most lower courts, such as state supreme courts' decisions in the business cases that constitute a larger proportion of their caseload. Because Supreme Court rulings potentially apply to the entire nation, they have far greater significance than those of most other courts. Public reaction to the Court's decisions (its policy statements) forces the Court to become an actor in the political system: if the Court's actions are to have an effect and if, in the long run, the Court is to survive, the justices must take the Court's environment into account.

This chapter provides some context for our subsequent, more detailed examination of the Supreme Court in the federal judicial system. We begin with a discussion of the current controversy about the courts and the reach of their decisions. This is followed by a description of changes in the Court's importance in our political system over the course of our nation's history and then by an examination of the shift from the Warren Court of the 1950s and 1960s to the present Burger Court and the trends in the Burger Court's rulings. We conclude the chapter by returning to the theme of this introduction—the roles of the Supreme Court.

THE COURTS AND CURRENT CONTROVERSY[2]

Judicial Imperialism

Courts, we have been told repeatedly since the late 1970s, are "activist" rather than "self-restrained." Judges, we are told, are an "imperial judiciary" making decisions on "social policy" issues that judges should not decide. Moreover, we are told of "judicial incapacity"—that courts lack the skill, competence, or capacity to resolve such social policy issues.[3] Complaints of this sort have come even from within the judiciary. Justice Rehnquist has asserted, "It is basically unhealthy to have so much authority concentrated in a small group of lawyers who have been appointed to the Supreme Court and enjoy virtual life tenure." Justice Powell has characterized lower court busing orders as "typify[ing] intrusions on local and professional authorities that affect the quality of education" so as to constitute a "wholesale substitution of judicial legislation for the judgments of elected officials and professional educators" and a "social engineering that hardly is appropriate for the federal judiciary."[4]

In the 1980s the courts, particularly the federal courts and most specifically, the Supreme Court, were attacked more seriously and on a broader front than at any time since the late 1950s and early 1960s, when the Court's internal security rulings produced cries of "Impeach Earl Warren!" and efforts to limit the Court's jurisdiction, and probably even since 1937, when Roosevelt tried to pack the Supreme Court. Decisions on abortion, school prayer, and school desegregation ("forced busing") have particularly provoked intense reaction and efforts to remove the Court's appellate jurisdiction or the jurisdiction of all federal courts (see pages 246–248) over the subjects of those cases. Rulings by lower federal courts on conditions in state prisons and mental hospitals—in which some judges have specified in considerable detail how the institutions should be restructured and administered—have also produced considerable hostility. Litigation on school desegregation and institutional conditions is particularly complex and drawn-out. Because considerable time is needed to prove a constitutional violation and then, once the violation is proved, to develop a remedy, a court tends to remain involved in overseeing the implementation of its decree for an extended period, perhaps many years. Such cases, because they involve multiple parties and numerous issues, are said to be far different from traditional litigation pitting an individual or company against another individual or company over a specific past act; they are referred to as "public law litigation."[5] Judges in such cases are seen as particularly intrusive, displacing state and local officials and becoming administrators of school systems or state institutions.

The fact that federal judges are appointed for life increases the frustration of the critics of their actions: judges are seen as not only intrusive but also unaccountable. Undoubtedly adding to the feeling that judges are beyond accountability was the Supreme Court's 1978 ruling in *Stump v. Sparkman** that judges were immune from lawsuits for damages resulting from actions they had undertaken as judges. A judge

*Citations to cases mentioned in the text may be found in the Table of Cases, page 317.

who had ordered the sterilization of a 15-year-old female at the request of the girl's mother was sued for his part in the sterilization when the daughter and her husband learned years later why she could not have children. The Supreme Court refused to say the judge's act—normally one not performed by judges—was not "judicial." However, dissenting Justice Stewart argued that "the conduct of a judge surely does not become a judicial act merely on his own say-so. A judge is not free, like a loose cannon, to inflict indiscriminate damage whenever he announces that he is acting in his judicial capacity."

Criticism of the courts is deeply felt; it is intellectually appealing in a political system in which the elected branches of government are expected to be dominant; and it carries considerable political weight. In evaluating the criticism, one must keep several matters in mind. One is that, like previous attacks on the courts, current criticism is largely prompted by critics' dislike of the courts' *results*. The attack on the Supreme Court in the 1930s resulted from a preference for the program of economic regulation the Court struck down. The liberals who criticized the Court's "activism" then did not also criticize it in the 1950s and 1960s when the Court supported civil liberties. Another point is that "social policy" issues, such as labor-management relations, taxation, and economic regulation of business, have long been brought to the courts for disposition. However, the users of the courts—those raising current social policy questions—have changed: those representing racial minorities, women, and the poor or disadvantaged have joined the advantaged elements of society, such as major commercial interests, in using courts to seek redress of grievances. Thus courts have been faced with many more civil rights cases.

The "imperial judiciary" and "judicial incapacity" arguments also tend to focus on the courts to the exclusion of other political actors. Much recent litigation concerning rights of the disadvantaged is based on congressional statutes, not on the Constitution, and such litigation results from the need to have judges interpret and enforce vague and ambiguous statutory provisions and the regulations developed to implement the statutes. (The same is true of efforts to clean up the environment.) Judges did not enact the statutes and regulations on which people base their cases nor are they to blame for the lack of clarity. As Justice Powell reminds us, "Congress' failure to make policy judgments can distort our system of separation of powers by encouraging other branches to make essentially legislative decisions."[6] Yet it is the courts, not Congress or executive agencies, that are blamed.

Similarly it is judges, not the officials whose actions (or nonactions) have led to litigation, who are criticized. Critics have attacked a judge's involvement in administering the Boston school system to produce desegregation, but not the Boston School Committee's adamant refusal to obey *state* laws on school desegregation. Long-standing prison and mental hospital conditions, often so appalling that even conservative federal judges find the conditions in violation of the Constitution, are given less attention than judges' orders to remedy the violation. Critics of the "imperial judiciary" also seem to forget that, although judges have been willing to provide officials with considerable leeway in remedying conditions on their own, more severe remedial orders often result from officials' resistance to the initial judicial rulings.

Even if judges do not shirk their duty when cases are brought before them, they may remain *reluctant* to become deeply involved in such litigation. Moreover, they cannot impose their views concerning schools or prisons until someone brings a case to court, often as a last resort after complaints to unresponsive legislators and executives. This use of courts as a "last resort" is evidence of courts' connections to, rather than isolation from, the political process. As this indicates, it is litigants, not judges, who initiate cases and thus establish courts' agendas.

According to contemporary critics of judges' lack of capacity to handle complex social policy issues, courts "carve up and . . . treat as separate" transactions that "are intertwined in social life."[7] To such critics the issues presented by any one case may provide an unrepresentative slice of a larger problem that is better addressed as a whole. Preoccupied with individual cases, judges are said not to think about whether the cases represent typical situations from which precedents for later cases might be properly derived. The resultant judicial policy making is thus piecemeal, with correction of problems only intermittent rather than continuous. Perhaps this is an accurate description of judicial policy making, but it is an accurate description of policy making in the other branches of government as well.[8]

Legislators, administrators, *and* judges generally begin developing policy with a problem presented by particular instances. Most legislative action, for example, occurs only after a series of complaints by constituents or interest groups, not unlike litigants' filing of cases. To some degree, however, officials in all three branches contemplate other situations to which the policy they announce is intended to apply. Judges, who are expected to be subject-matter generalists, may have difficulty dealing with new areas of the law, but so do legislators, who are also generalists not always adequately informed who also lack an adequate basis for choosing experts to assist them. Time and preparation can, however, overcome these difficulties for both judges and legislators. Judges' supervision of institutions can also be facilitated by required periodic reports, reliance on complainants' attorneys to return to court if something is amiss, and appointment of judicial masters who can "compensate for judges' lack of familiarity with organizational routines and procedures in defendant institutions."[9]

Judicial Accountability[10]

The intensity of contemporary criticism of "imperial" judges insufficiently responsive to current political sentiment should not make us forget the strongly and widely held view that judges *should* be independent. Although independence can result in judges' exercising discretion in ways we dislike, we do not wish judges' decisions to be purchased nor to have their decisions reflect partisan political considerations. Similarly, there is a strong argument that because of the substantial pressures against the rights of the disadvantaged, the courts, particularly the Supreme Court, need to serve as a beacon light for such rights.

The wish by many people that judges be independent does not eliminate influences that help to keep them at least somewhat accountable, if we define accountability to mean "keeping an institution's decisions in line with community political and social values and otherwise imposing constraints on the exercise of discretion."[11] Indeed, Shapiro argues that the "universal pattern" is that judging is "an integral part of the mainstream of political authority rather than . . . a separate entity,"[12] thus suggesting clear connections with—and accountability to—the political system.

Judges are accountable *within* the legal system (legal accountability) and *to* the broader political system (political accountability), similar to the "legal subculture" and "democratic subculture" in which all judges operate.[13] Legal accountability includes judges' socialization, their exposure to and learning of norms; legal precedents and the public nature of judicial action; reversal of judges' decisions by higher courts; and constraints imposed by courts' organizational needs. Political accountability derives from the role of public opinion—including resistance—in the judicial process, in addition to the selection and removal of judges. Within the legal system, judges are accountable primarily to lawyers or other judges, while political accountability propels judges toward the broader public or at least its more attentive members. Overlap and convergence between the types of accountability occur both because lawyers participate in judicial selection and because they are part of the political elite.

In the United States, judges receive no formal judicial training before they become judges and only limited formal judicial training after they reach the bench. Before they become judges their most extensive relevant socialization is to their roles as lawyers. As judges, they learn most from contact with other judges, not from nonjudges and even less from nonlawyers. Legal education and training produce thorough exposure to the norm of judicial independence; to the expectation that decisions should be derived from precedent; to the idea that, when applicable precedent is lacking, they should look to "the law" as the source of decisions; and to the norm that decisions should be explained in written opinions. Precedent (see pages 210–214) affects the process by which judges arrive at the reasoned decisions expected of them; the requirement of written (or at least public) opinions, in addition to making the judicial process more open, assists in producing accountability because others can examine the justifications that judges have offered for their actions.

Cutting against accountability is the increasing proportion of unpublished opinions in the lower courts, the fact that the Supreme Court does not provide —and does not have to provide—reasons for denying review of cases, and courts' secrecy about their own internal operations. Although there is considerable freedom of action for lower courts, the potential sanction of reversal by higher courts helps produce accountability, at least to the higher courts, in those cases litigants choose to appeal; litigants thus become an important part of the process of producing judicial accountability. Within any court, trial or appellate, as part of the dynamics that within any organization have a strong effect on everyone's everyday actions, there is accountability (lateral or horizontal accountability) to other judges of the court, to other court officials, and to the lawyers who regularly practice there.

We are more likely to think of the effect of judicial decisions on public opinion (see pages 274–283) than of the reverse. Nonetheless, political accountability may take place through the effect of public opinion on judges, many of whom became accustomed to responding to it while holding elective public office before their judicial appointment, and we can see the continuing pull of constituency particularly in controversial cases such as those involving race relations.[14] Certain aspects of public opinion are also increasingly pressed upon judges by single-issue interest groups. Even in the absence of such activity, judges are not unaware of the political environment relevant to their decisions; the comment has been made that the judges "follow the election returns." Judges certainly are aware of public opinion in the form of resistance to their decisions. Because such resistance certainly lessens the effects of "judicial imperialism"— when disliked decisions are not fully implemented or when they are ignored, resisted, attacked, and overturned in other arenas (see Chapters 9 and 10)—such action may be an important way of holding courts accountable to the views held by significant segments of the public.

A key principal means by which judges might be held accountable, one directly at the intersection of legal and political accountability, is the process by which they are selected. A particular method of judicial selection can affect which political actors play a dominant role and can help to establish the value to which judges may be accountable: partisan election is likely to magnify the importance of political party leaders, but appointive methods—such as that used in the federal judiciary (see pages 74–80)—and "merit systems" increase the relative importance played by the organized bar. Accountability may be built in before a judge takes the bench through the choice of appropriate nominees and through participation by lawyers' groups and other interested individuals and groups in the selection process, thus potentially reducing the need for continuing mechanisms of accountability. On the other hand, there has been increased development of means for disciplining judges and even removing them (see pages 71–74).

THE PRESENT COURT AND THE HISTORICAL PATTERN: THE COURT'S RELATIVE IMPORTANCE

Historical perspective is important when one examines the Supreme Court's place in our political system. In order to evaluate competing claims that, from a critic's perspective, the Court is too "conservative" (or too "liberal"), too "activist" (or too "restrained"), one must first be able to penetrate such rhetorical terms as "strict construction," "self-restraint," and "activism"—terms that refer to adherence to precedent, injection of personal values, and willingness to intervene in controversial matters (see pages 224–228). Second, one must also understand how the Court's performance at any one time compares with its performance in other periods.

Statements that the Burger Court is conservative on civil liberties issues, for example, are based on a comparison with the Warren Court, which decided a substantial majority (upward of 80 percent) of civil liberties cases in favor of the civil liberties claim, while the Burger Court, by contrast, has decided over half against the claim. A comparison of the Burger Court with the Vinson Court (1946–1953) would produce a different result; the former's support of civil liberties would look relatively liberal because of the latter's lower support for civil liberties. One's evaluation might also be affected by the realization that the period of the Warren Court was the first time that the Court gave substantial attention to civil liberties and civil rights claims. In the long view of the Court's history, that attention, coupled with the Warren Court's *support* of civil liberties claims, made the Warren Court something of an aberration. In this section, we therefore present a brief historical recapitulation of the Court's work; our focus is on the Court's importance as a major political actor and how that importance has varied over time. In the succeeding section, we look at the transition from the Warren Court to the Burger Court and examine major trends in the latter's decisions.

The Warren Court's position on civil liberties and civil rights and the controversy surrounding its decisions made it a central force in the American political system. At the least it was highly involved in key policy issues, even if it was not as important as the president and Congress, and the public became accustomed to the Court's being in that position. This, coupled with considerable attention paid to the Burger Court's rulings because of a preference that there should be no retreat from important Warren Court precedents, makes it easy to forget that the Supreme Court's relative position in our political constellation has changed over time.

The Court has not always been as central or important as it now appears. It may come as somewhat of a shock, for example, to realize that when, early in the Court's history, partisan conflict between Congress and the Court led to cancellation of a term of Court (something quite unlikely to happen now), the nation's business went on without interruption. The Supreme Court did not even have its own building until the 1930s: the Court met in the basement of the Capitol, and the justices did much of their work in their Washington, D.C., homes. Although the Supreme Court edifice across from the Capitol (brought in under cost, a miracle not likely to recur) is properly impressive: one of the first justices to work in it said that he and his colleagues felt like "Nine Black Beetles in the Temple of Karnak."

The significance of the Supreme Court's role in the American system has varied, across time and between issues. At times, the Court has seemed central to the nation's development; at other times, it has been more in the background. One of the periods of the Court's greatest centrality came in the early nineteenth century under Chief Justice John Marshall, who helped the Court achieve its earliest prominence. Through Marshall, the Court established its power to invalidate acts of Congress. Through decisions such as *Gibbons v. Ogden*, establishing Congress's power over interstate commerce broadly defined, and *McCulloch v. Maryland*, striking down a state tax on the National Bank, the Court played a major role in establishing the national government's place in our scheme of federalism. Under Chief Justice Roger Taney, the Supreme Court was perhaps less obtrusive. In that period, the Court allowed the states more authority over commerce, ruling in *Cooley v. Board of Port Wardens* that where diversity was needed, states could act where the federal government had not done so. Unfortunately for Taney's reputation, in the *Dred Scott* case—the Court's second exercise of judicial review at the national level—the Court seriously exacerbated the tensions that led to the Civil War by upsetting Congress's regulation of slavery in the territories and ruling that a slave was not a person who could sue in the courts. Prior to the Civil War, there was a much closer link between the Court's rulings and party policy than would be found later. This link reduced the Court's independence and thus the centrality of its role. During and after the Civil War, the Court also played a subordinate role—its usual posture with respect to war efforts—generally sustaining Lincoln's actions and his theory of the relation between Union and Confederacy.

The Court's general prestige in the late nineteenth century was great, but the Court did not play a positive leadership role. The Court undercut post–Civil War civil rights legislation, for example, in the *Civil Rights Cases,* and then, in *Plessy v. Ferguson,* sustained state legislation requiring Negroes to ride in separate railroad cars. At the same time, the justices were saying that the Fourteenth Amendment's Due Process Clause did not include the Bill of Rights' procedural protections for criminal defendants.[15] Later the Court's conservatism led it to uphold convictions of "subversives" in cases brought in the atmosphere of World War I.[16] The Court's importance in the late nineteenth and early twentieth century also resulted from its striking down most state attempts to regulate the economy even when Congress had not acted. This was the period when "substantive due process"was at its height—with the judges reading into the Constitution their views of what was "reasonable" for the states to legislate. The Court also undid Congress's attempts to regulate the economy, defining the commerce and taxing powers narrowly and even saying that powers not expressly delegated to the federal government were reserved to the states—language like that of the Articles of Confederation.[17]

During the New Deal period, the Court became a principal political actor as a result of its actions striking down much early New Deal legislation.[18] These decisions ran contrary to the political realignment reflected in President Roosevelt's election. (It was during this time that in calling a Supreme Court session to order, the court crier is alleged to have said, "May God save the United States from this Honorable Court.") The president made the Court an issue in his 1936 campaign and then in 1937 proposed that for every justice over the age of seventy who did not retire, an additional justice could be named. Although Roosevelt said that this change was needed in the interest of judicial efficiency, it was clear that the president wished to use the new appointments to neutralize the justices opposed to his program. The "Court-packing" plan provoked a storm of disapproval even among Roosevelt's own supporters and was not adopted. However, FDR really won the the "war" against the Court when, as a result of some changes in judges' positions and the retirement of several conservative justices, the Court sustained a wide variety of economic regulatory measures.[19] (Perhaps the battle of 1937 would never have occurred had FDR been able to name one or more members of the Court during his first term; rumors of Justice VanDevanter's impending retirement came when the Court-packing plan was under heavy fire.)

After 1937 the Court regularly accepted Congress' determinations as to the reach of the Commerce Clause, even as applied to racial discrimination,[20] although in

1976, in *National League of Cities v. Usery*, the Court did invalidate Congress' extension of the minimum wage to state employees. After 1937 the Court also adopted a restrained stance toward state economic regulation, as long as such regulation did not directly interfere with national regulatory programs or impinge on civil rights.

The Court's post-1937 restraint concerning economic regulation was not immediately accompanied by judicial protection for civil liberties. During World War II, the Court again showed its unwillingness to protect civil liberties during wartime. The Court showed its deference to the president in sustaining the relocation of Japanese-Americans in the *Korematsu* case, deciding against the executive only in ruling that a relocated citizen had to be released once the citizen's loyalty had been verified.[21] After World War II, blacks began to win some support for their rights in housing and graduate education,[22] but, as noted previously, the Vinson Court had a generally conservative record on civil liberties.

Only with the Warren Court were minorities able to win victories they had not been able to obtain from reluctant legislatures and executives. Through its civil liberties "activism," most of it evident in decisions striking down state restrictions on individual rights, the Court again became extremely prominent and central in the nation's life. The Court was also pretty much "the only game in town" for civil liberties and civil rights policy until Congress enacted the Civil Rights Act of 1964 and the Voting Rights Act of 1965 and the executive branch developed implementing regulations for those statutes, leading to a sharing of civil rights policy making among the three branches but only slightly diminishing the Court's centrality.

The Warren Court's first major step was the invalidation of racial segregation ("separate but equal") in education in *Brown v. Board of Education* (1954), followed in 1956 and 1957 by protection for political dissidents caught up in government internal security investigations aimed at suspected Communists and other radicals. The Warren Court also required that both houses of each state legislature be apportioned on the basis of population; expanded free speech in the areas of obscenity and libel; invalidated prayers in public schools; and overturned convictions of those protesting against racial discrimination in transportation and places of public accommodations, also regularly sustaining Congress' actions to protect civil rights with respect to public accommodations, voting, and housing.[23] The justices also turned their attention to the poor, invalidating the poll tax and durational residence requirements for receiving welfare benefits.[24]

In what produced probably the greatest controversy, the Court adopted a series of broad rules protecting criminal defendants and suspects. Of these the most notable were *Mapp v. Ohio* (improperly seized evidence inadmissible at trial—the "exclusionary rule"), *Gideon v. Wainwright* (right to counsel for indigents at trials for felonies and major misdemeanors), and *Miranda v. Arizona* (no confession admissible without suspect being warned of rights). That the Court also approved "stop and frisk" practices, lifted restrictions on material that could be taken in a search, approved the use of informants, and supplied the basis for electronic surveillance with a warrant received far less attention.[25] So did the Court's avoidance of some problems, such as the implementation of school desegregation for over a decade after the *Brown* decision and the basic constitutional question of the right of a private proprietor to refuse service on the basis of race—never reached despite all the sit-in convictions the Court reversed. Furthermore, the Court was criticized for having subordinated the interests of racial minorities to the concerns of whites and having too closely followed public opinion. The Court, it was said, had "struck down only the symbols of racism," leaving racist practices intact, and "had waltzed in time to the music of the white majority—one step forward, one step backward and sidestep, sidestep."[26]

The Warren Court's civil liberties record, reinforced by its easing of access to the courts for those wishing to challenge government action, led to a considerable dependence on the federal courts for the protection of civil liberties. The Court's favorable reception for civil liberties claimants led groups increasingly to turn first to the federal courts for redress for their grievances, particularly against state and local officials, instead of using the courts as a last resort. This development, which a federal judge has characterized by saying that an entire generation of lawyers were taught to "seek ye first the kingdom of the federal courts," gave pause even to supporters of the Court's decisions. They wondered whether reliance on the courts might lead to atrophy of the legislative process, central to a democratic political system. As Judge J. Skelly Wright stated:

> It would be a very serious matter for the people to come to rely on the Court as the most important force for change in our society. That the legislature might come to enact laws without adequately considering their constitutionality, leaving it to the Court to correct its mistakes, would be very unfortunate; but if the people and legislatures were to come to expect the Court to do their work for them, it would be far worse.[27]

Perhaps because strong action provokes reaction, this situation was not to continue undisturbed.

At the end of the nation's second century, the Supreme Court experienced a period of considerable change. There were major changes in personnel. Unlike FDR, Richard Nixon had immediate opportunities to select justices. Nixon was able to select a Chief Justice and another justice in his first year in office—although the Senate's defeat of two nominations delayed the second appointment—and two more two years later. Chief Justice Earl Warren and Justice Abe Fortas left the Court in 1969, followed in 1971 by Hugo Black and John Marshall Harlan and in 1975 by William O. Douglas, who had joined the Court in 1939 and served on it longer than anyone else. Warren Burger became Chief Justice and was joined first by Harry Blackmun, then by Lewis Powell and William Rehnquist. Later John Paul Stevens replaced Douglas, and in 1981 the first woman justice, Sandra O'Connor, replaced Potter Stewart. Having made the Court, and particularly its criminal procedure rulings, a subject of campaign controversy—thereby increasing expectations that the new Court would indeed change Warren Court policy—Nixon gave particular attention to his nominees' ideology. Thus it should be no surprise that the changes in personnel brought changes in doctrine (discussed below), and in the Court's relationship to public opinion. The new Court's decisions responded to criticism of judicial "activism" and moved the Court closer to the more conservative public opinion on civil liberties that had developed in the late 1960s.

The Court's change in position—both its real changes and the considerable change perceived by those who had become accustomed to the Warren Court's liberalism—led some to turn for resolution of their grievances to state courts in states where such courts were liberal; such suggestions even came from liberal members of the Court such as Justice Brennan.[28] Civil liberties activity was also mounted on other fronts; this included the extended if unsuccessful effort to obtain ratification of the Equal Rights Amendment (ERA). Events surrounding Watergate further deflected attention from the Court toward the president and Congress. The balance of influence between the courts and the elected branches of government thus moved toward the situation predating the Warren Court, making the Court not as predominant or central a political actor as it had been during the 1950s and 1960s. However, the high "surprise level" in its actions —as the Court showed itself to be not consistently conservative or self-restrained—and political activity, provoked by the Court's own policies, to eliminate or reduce "forced busing" and to limit abortions indicated that the Court had by no means left the political arena, and it remained more central than the Court of the 1940s. The continuing validity of some Warren Court precedents and the Burger Court's own early decisions on employment discrimination and women's rights (areas not explored by the Warren Court) continued to give the Court a greater prominence concerning civil liberties—and a more liberal complexion—than it had before Earl Warren became Chief Justice. With a growing public conservatism on civil rights matters, people continued to turn to the judiciary and the Supreme Court for whatever assistance they could obtain; after all, said a civil rights lawyer, "It's the only Supreme Court we have."

THE COURT IN TRANSITION AND THE BURGER COURT

Shifts, both real and perceived, between the Warren Court and the Burger Court focused attention on transitional periods in the Supreme Court's history. Perhaps all courts pass through transitional periods. As they change personnel, their policy direction changes and, as noted earlier, so does the relationship of the Court to public sentiment—at times moving closer to public opinion, at times appearing to lead that opinion. Such changes also involve shifts in the predominant role the courts assume, whether as restrained discoverers of the law or more actively as developers or makers of policy. During a transitional period, several years may elapse before a pattern is clear. Moreover, different patterns may characterize different policy areas. The "new" Court may extend earlier rulings; maintain, consolidate, or clarify those rulings; or curtail or erode the precedents of previous years—often with substantial cumulative effect. Direct reversal of precedent may occur, but usually only after several years have elapsed. As one observer put it: "After the Marshall era, a period of great constitutional creativity, the Court experienced a period characterized by limitation and modification but not by major departure from established precedent."[29] In some ways that was the Burger Court's position vis-à-vis the Warren Court.

The transition to the Roosevelt Court, which began prior to a change in personnel and then was reinforced by new justices such as Hugo Black and William O. Douglas, did not take place until FDR's second term, when his first opportunities to nominate justices occurred. The transition from the Vinson Court to the Warren Court was immediately visible in the 1954 ruling in *Brown v. Board of Education* on school desegregation. However, a few terms passed before the Court "succeeded impressively in freeing itself from the self-doubts that deterred constitutional development during the 1940–1953 period."[30] For example, after its liberal internal security decisions of 1956 and 1957, the Court retreated in the face of a concerted congressional attack on its jurisdiction, with the Court supporting civil liberties claims less than half the time in 1958–1960. The Court's support of such claims at rates of close to 80 percent came only when Justice Felix Frankfurter retired in 1962 and was replaced by Justice Arthur Goldberg, the Court's fifth reliable civil liberties vote. Even with Goldberg present, in 1964 there was a noticeable drop in the percentage of civil liberties claims supported. However, the Warren Court did "finish strong," providing an extremely clear contrast with what was to follow.

The transition from the Marshall Court (1801–1835) to the Taney Court (1836–1863) also illustrates another aspect of some transitions; they may begin before the end of one Chief Justice's tenure. Thus the Marshall Court "spoke with less authority and gave ground before the dynamic forces of Jacksonianism and particularism. Most notably it adopted a more permissive attitude toward state legislative power."[31] On the other hand, the transition to the Burger Court did not begin before Earl Warren's departure; the Warren Court's strongest support for civil liberties came in its last terms. Another aspect of the Marshall to Taney transition—considerable continuity accompanying change—can be said to characterize the most recent transition.

Beginnings of the Burger Court

The Burger Court's first several years of rulings indicated a Court that reinforced or advanced some Warren Court doctrine and developed rights in some previously unexplored areas. More important, the Burger Court seemed generally unwilling to go beyond the Warren Court and took action eroding major Warren Court rulings, particularly concerning search and seizure and the Fifth Amendment. By limiting access to the courts, the justices also made it considerably more difficult to bring federal court suits challenging alleged deprivations of civil liberties.

Initially, Chief Justice Burger produced no great across-the-board policy change, although some areas saw more change than others. The Court limited expansion of Warren Court doctrine, but the basic picture for several years was one of marginal change and a generally unsettled pattern. The Burger Court did not at first directly overrule precedent; instead it whittled away at prior rulings. However, in the 1975 Term the Court overruled the 1968 Warren Court precedents that had allowed picketing of a store in a shopping center and had upheld Congress's extension of the minimum wage law to state employees.[32]

The 1974 Term left a picture of a "reluctant Court" that

> tries to make potentially important cases stand for as little as possible; a Court whose theme song is the refrain "we *only* decide"; a Court that loves to decide issues "in these particular circumstances," that performs contortions to avoid announcing new principles even when new principles are inescapably needed, and that pretends not to be announcing them even while it is announcing them.[33]

Nonetheless, even before the Burger Court consolidated its position, its decisions demonstrated considerable withdrawal from and undercutting of Warren Court policies affecting the entire range of civil liberties problems. Such change was particularly noticeable in the areas of criminal procedure and free speech.

In Burger's first term, support for civil liberties claims fell from 80 percent at the end of the Warren Court to 55 percent. By the 1972 Term, it was down to 43.5 percent, the lowest since 1957. Indicative of the change is that, in the 1974 Term, when the Court was divided, the justices rejected civil liberties claims 29 of 46 times. As Schubert has shown, on political liberalism (civil liberties), the early Nixon Court ranked behind both the middle years of the Warren Court and the Roosevelt Court. This put the Court at "about the point where it was when [Nixon] became vice-president and Earl Warren was in his first term or two."[34] Concerning economic liberalism (support for government regulation), the Nixon Court demonstrated even greater change, ranking just above the Hughes Court (1930–1941) that FDR had battled.

The Burger Court gave greater weight to claims by both national and state government, and less to claims by the individual citizen, than had the Warren Court, and subjected challenged state laws and action to less strict tests. The Court also was less willing to have the federal courts serve as a forum for resolving complaints against the government. When a policeman complained that he had been improperly discharged without a hearing, the Court said, "The federal court is not the appropriate forum in which to review the multitude of personnel decisions that are made daily by public agencies. . . . The United States Constitution cannot feasibly be construed to require federal judicial review for every such error."[35]

Although such a ruling indicated judicial self-restraint, overall the Court's record of invalidating federal and state legislative acts provides evidence to the contrary. Decisions on both types of legislation produced sharp breaks from a pattern of more than thirty years:

> In no decision did the Warren Court—nor, for that matter, did any Supreme Court since the mid-1930's—hold that an act of Congress was invalid on the ground that the lawmaking branch had exceeded its delegated powers and invaded ground reserved to the States by the tenth amendment. The Burger Court has done so twice. . . . In no decision did the Warren Court—nor, for that matter, did the Supreme Court for a period

> of over thirty-five years—hold any state law in violation of the contract clause of the Constitution. In the last two years, the Burger Court has done so twice. . . . In no decision did the Warren Court—nor, for that matter, did any Supreme Court in nearly twenty-five years—invalidate an act of Congress or an act of the President on the ground that it usurped the other branch's constitutional powers.[36]

yet the Burger Court had done so.

The Court moved forward with Warren Court doctrines in some areas and broke new ground in other areas not considered by the Warren Court. The justices upheld lower court judges' authority to order broad remedies for school segregation, including busing; invalidated schemes for evading desegregation; and told private schools they could not discriminate on the basis of race.[37] The Court took a strong stand against discrimination in employment. It reinforced Congress' action in passing Title VII of the 1964 Civil Rights Act, by ruling in the *Griggs* case that non-job-related employment tests with a discriminatory effect could not be used even though no discrimination was intended; the justices also supported back pay and seniority remedies for job discrimination.

In the area of women's rights, the Court invalidated an automatic preference for men as executors of estates, statutes making it easier for men than women to obtain dependents' benefits, automatic exemptions of women from jury duty, and forced maternity leave requirements for school teachers.[38] However, the justices allowed employers to exclude pregnancy from disability insurance coverage—a decision eventually reversed by Congress.[39] Perhaps most significant as well as most controversial was the Court's invalidation, in *Roe v. Wade* and *Doe v. Bolton* (1973), of laws interfering with the right to obtain an abortion, particularly during the first semester of pregnancy.

On the other hand, the Court limited the scope of the Fourteenth Amendment's protections. The justices ruled that a private club did not have to serve a black guest merely because it had a state liquor license and that Jackson, Mississippi, could close all its swimming pools for economic reasons, even though the dissenters said it was being done to avoid desegregation.[40] The Court's attitude toward welfare recipients was quite unfavorable. The Court did say in 1970 that welfare benefits could not be discontinued without a hearing, but sustained "maximum grant" provisions despite their effects on large families and upheld removal of benefits when a welfare recipient would not allow a social worker in her home without a warrant.[41] The Court also affected minorities by retreating from the Warren Court's reapportionment rulings. Greater flexibility was allowed for state legislative districts than for congressional districts, and the Court refused to set aside multimember legislative districts that provided less opportunity for blacks to be elected.[42]

In First Amendment cases, the Court continued—and advanced—a strong position on separation of church and state. Although permitting construction financing and broader aid for secular functions at the college level and free textbooks for parochial schools, the justices outlawed virtually every other form of aid to elementary and secondary parochial schools.[43] The Court also upheld property tax exemptions for churches in *Walz v. Tax Commission* (1970), and in *Wisconsin v. Yoder* (1972) sustained the right of Amish parents to limit their children's schooling.

The Court's free speech posture was mixed. In *New York Times v. United States* (1971) the justices refused to allow the government an injunction against publication of the "Pentagon Papers" and struck down "gag orders" on the press in criminal trials. However, grand juries were allowed to question reporters about their confidential sources, and free speech by military officers and on military bases was restricted.[44] The Court distinctly moved away from the Warren Court's position on obscenity in *Miller v. California* (1973), rewriting the definition of the concept to give greater scope to local community values.

The Burger Court's greatest retrenchment from Warren Court doctrine occurred with respect to criminal procedure, particularly searches and confessions. The rule excluding improperly seized evidence was held inapplicable to grand jury proceedings.[45] In *Stone v. Powell* (1976) the Court limited federal court review of claims about improper searches. Some car searches by the Border Patrol were invalidated. However, searches of people and cars were generally made easier, and by allowing seizure of business records the Court abandoned the ninety-year-old doctrine of *Boyd v. United States* (1886) that private papers could not be subpoenaed because they might contain incriminatory statements.[46] *Miranda* was not overturned but was weakened by a ruling that confessions obtained without warnings could be used to impeach a witness's testimony at trial.[47] The Court also limited the immunity necessary before a person could be compelled to testify.[48]

The Court extended the right to counsel at trial to all cases where a person was to be jailed (*Argersinger v. Hamlin*, 1972). However, the right to counsel at police line-ups and on appeal was limited, and the justices also refused to make counsel automatically available for those whose probation or parole was being revoked or to provide counsel in prison proceedings for rule violations; procedural protections were, however, established in those situations.[49] The Court's legitimizing and encouraging of plea bargaining and its strict limiting of challenges to a conviction once a defendant, with assistance of counsel, had entered a guilty plea was of particular importance.[50] So was the ruling striking down the death penalty as then applied (*Furman v. Georgia*, 1972). However, four years later, in *Gregg v. Georgia* (1976), the Court ruled that the death penalty did not violate the Eighth Amendment prohibition on cruel and unusual punishment, at least if it was not mandatory and aggravating *and* mitigating circumstances were considered in sentencing. The Court later ruled that the death penalty for rape was excessive and grossly disproportionate to the crime (*Coker v. Georgia*, 1977) and required procedural protections for imposition of the death sentence.[51]

Civil Liberties in the Later Burger Court

The headline, "Pragmatism, Compromise Marks Court: Tricky Track Record Harder to Categorize Than Pundits Predicted," effectively captures the Supreme Court's posture in 1980, with "the Warren Court's legacy . . . more intact today than many would have predicted 10 years ago."[52] This characterization continues to be true. The Court continues to issue some major rulings favoring civil liberties claims, such as *Plyler v. Doe* (1981) sustaining the right of children of aliens illegally present in the country to attend public school. Nonetheless, the Burger Court has generally continued its conservative-leaning record on civil liberties. Its support of civil liberties claims decreased into the 30 percent range in the 1980 and 1981 Terms after the Court had supported somewhat over 40 percent of civil liberties claims decided in 1976–1978. A specific indication of Burger Court trends is the progressive decline, from the 1969 through 1979 Terms, in the rate at which interests of poor people prevailed in the Supreme Court—from 65 percent at the beginning of the period to only 30 percent in the post-1975 period.[53]

An additional indication that state officials who challenged assertions of rights had replaced civil liberties claimants as the principal victors in civil liberties cases can be seen in the Court's treatment of cases brought directly from state court where one party was a state official and the other a private rights claimant. Roughly *one-fourth* of all state-initiated petitions were successful in some way, with challenged lower court rulings being reversed, vacated, or granted full review; the same was true of *less than 10 percent* of petitions from civil liberties claimants.[54] Closely related was the Court's willingness to upset state court decisions interpreting rights expansively. Furthermore, although during the heyday of the Warren Court *no* state civil liberties ruling was overturned for exceeding the Supreme Court's civil liberties standards, the Burger Court did so both directly and, more frequently, by sending cases back to state courts for clarification of the constitutional basis of prorights rulings.

After 1975, First Amendment rulings were less prominent than earlier. In the church-state area, the Court was willing to approve more forms of aid to parochial schools.[55] "Commercial speech" (advertising) was given protection by the Court, for example, by striking down restrictions on lawyers' advertising (*Bates v. Arizona State Bar*, 1977). The Court also tried to deal with the relation between freedom of the press and defendants' rights. After first saying, in a case involving *pretrial* proceedings, that judges could close the courtroom in *trials*, the Court did find a First Amendment right to open trials.[56] The Court—which does not permit radio or television coverage of its own proceedings—also ruled that states could allow live electronic media coverage of trials even if defendants objected.[57]

With ratification of the Equal Rights Amendment pending until mid-1982, cases on women's rights and gender discrimination received considerable attention. In the continuing controversy over the Court's 1973 abortion ruling, the Court struck down a variety of requirements that interfered with a woman's right to obtain an abortion. However, efforts by federal, state, and local governments to impose severe restrictions on abortion funding were upheld.[58] Although the Court upheld Congress' adoption of male-only draft registration, the justices did assist women who were fighting employment discrimination in programs receiving federal funds and did expand the basis for sex discrimination pay complaints, although the justices declined to adopt the controversial "comparable worth" theory.[59]

Apart from this assistance, the Court moved in a more conservative direction on employment discrimination by imposing tests for proving such discrimination that were far more difficult to satisfy and by sustaining seniority provisions despite the claim that they locked in past discrimination.[60] The Court also handed down three major cases on affirmative action, the most troublesome topic in the employment discrimination area—indeed, in the whole race relations field. The first, and perhaps best-known, is the *Bakke* case (1978), where one five-judge majority narrowly invalidated a medical school's action in setting aside a specific number of seats for minorities, but another five-judge majority said that race *could* be taken into account in remedying past discrimination. The Court then, in the *Weber* case, upheld an apprenticeship program voluntarily established by a company and a union, in which places were equally divided between blacks and whites. Finally, in *Fullilove v. Klutznick* (1980), the justices approved Congress' action in setting aside a certain proportion of federal funds for public works projects for minority business enterprises.

Where schools instead of jobs were at issue, the Court's pattern was mixed. In *Milliken v. Bradley*, a 1974 ruling in a case from Detroit—seen by some as the end of the road for desegregation—the Court struck down busing across school district lines because districts outside the center city had not been shown to have discriminated. The Court also limited lower court judges' discretion to order desegregation, requiring that remedies for school segregation be tailored more narrowly than in the past. Showing its lack of predictability, the Court ruled that northern cities like Dayton and Columbus, Ohio, were subject to the full range of desegregation remedies for having maintained segregated school systems since before the Court's 1954 *Brown* ruling.[61]

Criminal procedure continued to be the area in which the Court most strongly supported government officials—police, prosecutors, and prison administrators, to whom deference was shown through a seeming return to the idea that courts should keep "hands off" prison matters; the Court turned aside attacks on conditions for pretrial detainees (those not yet convicted) and on double-celling and other deficiencies in prison conditions.[62] (The Court also made it more difficult to use the writ of habeas corpus in federal courts to challenge alleged constitutional violations in state trials; see pages 141–142.)

In its Fourth Amendment rulings, the Court extended protections when it ruled that arrest warrants were necessary before police could make a felony arrest in the suspect's home and that search warrants were required where the person was in someone else's home.[63] However, in addition to making it more difficult for defendants to challenge a search, the Court continued to support law enforcement efforts by allowing unannounced searches of newspaper offices for evidence relating to a crime and warrantless covert entry of property to install a "bug."[64] The Court also, after limiting the authority of police to search, without a warrant, items taken from properly stopped cars, ultimately extended warrantless searches of cars by ruling, in *United States v. Ross* (1982), that when police properly stop an automobile, they may search not only the passenger compartment of the car but also items found within the car.

Continuing to confound observers' expectations, the Court left standing both the

Miranda requirements and the exclusionary rule, despite the campaign by the Chief Justice and Justice Rehnquist against the latter. Although a majority of the justices continued to rule that giving a defendant *Miranda* warnings did not cure the taint of an illegal detention (bad stop), the effect of *Miranda* was weakened: questioning of a suspect could be resumed several hours after it had initially been terminated and grand jury testimony and tax investigations could be carried out without persons being warned of their *Miranda* rights.[65] The two most important "*Miranda* cases" of this period involved confessions obtained by subtle techniques. In *Brewer v. Williams* (1977), officers transporting a murder defendant, who had a lawyer, played upon his religious concerns and mental state by speaking of the need for the murdered child to have a "Christian burial" before snow made it impossible to find the child's body; defendant then directed the officers to the body. Prosecutors tried to use this case to overturn *Miranda*, but the Court, avoiding that issue, ruled that the officers had interfered with defendant's right to counsel. In *Rhode Island v. Innis* (1980), officers taking a suspect to the police station engaged in a conversation ostensibly between themselves in which they referred to the possibility that a child would get hurt if a gun (used in a murder) were not found; the suspect thereupon took them to the gun. The Court, although defining "interrogation" broadly—to extend beyond direct questions—said the defendant had *not* been interrogated in violation of *Miranda*.

The Burger Court's decisions on civil liberties, in particular those on criminal procedure, have moved the Court closer to public opinion than was the Warren Court at the height of its support for civil liberties claims. However, the Burger Court has not cut back on Warren Court rulings as much as had been expected, in part because of their strength as precedent and the civil liberties education they provided. The Court, less than fully predictable as a policy-making body, remains embroiled in controversy because of Warren Court rulings as well as some of its own, although it is no longer so regularly at the cutting edge in establishing civil liberties and civil rights policy.

THE SUPREME COURT'S ROLES

Out of this look at the controversy in which courts are often embroiled, at the Supreme Court's changing place in the American political system, and at the Court's recent pattern of decisions, we can begin to get some sense of the roles the Court has played, does play, and is expected to play.

Article III of the Constitution mentions "judicial power" and indicates the reach of that power. "Judicial power" is not otherwise explained, nor are the Supreme Court's expected tasks otherwise indicated. We can, however, identify such tasks from expectations held of the highest appellate court in any legal system. These include:

- marking boundaries between national power and state power;
- maintaining boundaries between decision-making units at any level of government;

- interpreting and clarifying statutory law and common (judge-made) law;
- delineating limits of governmental authority against claims of individual liberty;
- insuring its place as final interpreter of the Constitution and laws; and
- overseeing lower courts' interpretation and application of legal rules.[66]

> The judicial power shall extend to all cases, in law and equity, arising under this Constitution, the laws of the United States, and treaties made, or which shall be made, under their authority; to all cases affecting ambassadors, other public ministers and consuls; to all cases of admiralty and maritime jurisdiction; to controversies to which the United States shall be party; to controversies between two or more states; between a state and citizens of another state; between citizens of different states; between citizens of the same state claiming lands under grants of different states; and between a state, or the citizens thereof, and foreign states, citizens or subjects. (Art. III, Sec. 2)

These multiple tasks do not necessarily fit together well and may in fact conflict with each other. Thus the Supreme Court, "a court of law operating within a malleable but recognizable set of rules," is both "a tribunal dispensing justice between litigants" and "a coequal branch of the federal government with a responsibility for formulating national policy while deciding specific cases."[67]

These principal tasks just identified for a highest appellate court are part of the Supreme Court's role as a principal national policy maker. That broad role has not, however, been fully or easily accepted by many other actors in the American governmental system. For many years the principal belief about the Supreme Court—still believed by many—was that the Court did not make, but only found, the law. The idea that there was an external, immutable truth that could be found through "right reason" (an idea that is part of the philosophical view known as *natural law*) took the form that judges found preestablished law in statutes, regulations, and particularly the Constitution, applying in specific cases the intentions of the authors of those documents. Reverence for the Supreme Court, which was thought to be "above politics," reinforced this view: the Constitution became our Bible and the Supreme Court justices our high priests, and the public transferred "our sense of the definitive and timeless character of the Constitution to the judges who expound it."[68]

The belief that courts found rather than made the law has had considerable force and has been enunciated by the justices themselves. It was stated perhaps most starkly by Justice Owen Roberts just one year before President Franklin Roosevelt attempted to "pack" the Court because of its obstruction of the New Deal:

> When an Act of Congress is appropriately challenged in the courts as not conforming to the constitutional mandate the judicial branch of the Government has only one duty—to lay the article of the Constitution which is invoked beside the statute which is challenged and to decide whether the latter squares with the former. All the court does, or can do, is to announce its considered judgment upon the question. The only power it has, if such

> it may be called, is the power of judgment. This court neither approves nor condemns any legislative policy. Its delicate and difficult office is to ascertain and declare whether the legislation is in accordance with, or in contravention of, the provisions of the Constitution; and, having done that, its duty ends.[69]

This disingenuous statement—by a justice who was soon to shift his vote on the validity of economic regulation in the famous "Switch in Time That Saved Nine" (by blunting FDR's 1937 attack on the Court)—has been called the *slot machine theory of judicial interpretation*: if you get two apples and a lemon, you lose; if three oranges appear, you win. Despite its amazingly simplistic character, this myth of what judges do has been perpetuated even by some who realize it to be a myth because they believe that the myth makes the Court's decisions legitimate in the eyes of those affected by them.

Myth or no myth, the Supreme Court is without doubt a policy maker, "not an impartial arbiter but a participant in social conflict [seeking] to serve twin goals of system stability and responsible government through conflict management."[70] The Court helps manage conflict by providing an arena in which major national issues can be debated. As de Tocqueville noted long ago, most political, economic, and social issues in the United States are transformed into legal questions that end up in court. When legislative and executive arenas are not open to debate on major issues, such as racial equality before the 1960s, those issues are particularly likely to be moved to the courts for resolution. Even when elected officials do consider important issues, they may prefer to allow ultimate resolution of those issues to be made by the justices rather than assuming responsibility themselves.

The Supreme Court's policy-making role was made clear by the Judges' Bill of 1925 in which Congress gave the Court its present power to select the cases it would hear. A court required to decide all cases brought to it could be more easily seen as a regular "court of law." Such a court would decide a smaller proportion of controversial cases and would engage in "error-correction" in a large proportion of routine cases. However, it is hard to say that a court is not making policy when it chooses cases affecting broad classes of people and uses them to announce rules intended to have general application. Indeed, justices of the Supreme Court themselves have made clear that the Court's function is not "to correct every perceived error coming from the lower . . . courts" but is instead to decide "cases of broad significance."[71] Because such cases more often than not produce division in the Court, indicating that the law can hardly be clear or obvious, it is quite difficult to maintain the view that the justices are only finding the law. If a trial judge decides a case one way, only to be reversed by an appellate court by a vote of, say, 6–5, and the Supreme Court reverses in turn by a 5–4 vote, can one claim the law is being "found"? (One is reminded of the joke, "There stands the Supreme Court like a rock, 5–4.")

The law-finding myth may not have been difficult to believe when the Court's rulings conformed closely to the nation's predominant ideology, as in the probusiness era of the late nineteenth century before the Court obtained the authority to choose its cases. However, the conflict between President Franklin Roosevelt and the Court over New Deal programs helped considerably both to alter the view that the Court found law and to produce a realization that, as one wag put it, Supreme Court decisions are not brought by constitutional storks. Chief Justice Charles Evans Hughes' statement that the law is what the judges say it is, a recognition that judges exercise discretion in interpreting ambiguous language in statutes and the Constitution, further confirmed the realization. Although debate continued about what the Supreme Court *should* do, doubt about its policy-making role and the political effects of its decisions was further extinguished by resistance to and attacks on rulings of the Warren Court (1953–1969) on such subjects as internal security, reapportionment, school prayer, and criminal procedure. The hold of the myth of the Court as law-finder may be further reduced by the portrayal in *The Brethren* of the very human traits of the justices of the Burger Court (1969–) and of their bargaining and negotiation over the Court's opinions, and from revelations about continuing involvement in extrajudicial political activity by Justices Louis Brandeis and Felix Frankfurter.[72]

Virtually all who follow the Court's work now admit that the Court does make policy and cannot avoid doing so. Some of the judges have even openly acknowledged that this is the case. Justice Byron White, dissenting in *Miranda v. Arizona,* argued that the majority's ruling, while not exceeding the Court's powers, served to "underscore the obvious—that the Court has not discovered or found the law in making today's decision, nor has it derived it from irrefutable sources." Instead it had made new law "in much the same way that it has done in the course of interpreting other great clauses of the Constitution. This is what the Court historically has done. Indeed, *it is what it must do* and will continue to do until and unless there is some fundamental change in the constitutional distribution of governmental powers."[73]

Yet from time to time judges try to say that they do not engage in policy making based on their personal values—that they act differently as judges from the way they would act in other situations. As Justice Frankfurter put it in 1943 while dissenting when the Court invalidated the compulsory flag salute for school children:

> As judges we are neither Jew nor Gentile, neither Catholic nor agnostic. As a member of this Court I am not justified in writing my private notions of policy into the Constitution. . . . The duty of a judge who must decide which of two claims before the Court shall prevail . . . is not that of the ordinary person.[74]

Justice Blackmun, dissenting in 1972 when the majority invalidated the death penalty as then applied, said the punishment "violates childhood's training and life's experience" and that as a legislator he would sponsor legislation to repeal the penalty and as a governor he would use executive clemency to prevent people from being executed. But, he said, "There—on the Legislative Branch of the State or Federal Government, and secondarily, on the Executive Branch—is where the authority and responsibility for this kind of action lies."[75]

Such statements may continue to provide support for those who continue to believe that the Court finds the law and that it should act in special, nonpolitical ways.

These beliefs are part of the context within which the Court, like any other policy maker, must act and which serve to constrain its actions. Indeed, the Supreme Court must continue to act like a court if it is to be effective. However, such statements, even if deeply felt by the person making them, may not only distract us from seeing the political values supported by the justices' votes but may well be irrelevant for those most directly affected by the Court's decisions. Whatever a judge's anguish and however moving the statement of that anguish, the ultimate consumer is interested in the judge's votes, in the specific outcome of the case, not in the judge's rhetoric, no matter how much that rhetoric interests other judges and lawyers. Thus someone on Death Row would be more interested in Justice Blackmun's vote to uphold capital punishment than in the justice's personal unhappiness about the death penalty.

Judges cannot put past experience and personal values, particularly their policy views, fully to one side, particularly if they are members of a high appellate court that decides controversial cases. It has been argued that judges are readily interchangeable one for another (fungible). Were that true, however, senators and interest groups would not display such concern about the values of the potential members of the High Court, as Right-to-Life advocates did about Sandra Day O'Connor's votes in the Arizona Senate on abortion issues and as civil rights groups did about William Rehnquist's opposition to a public accommodations ordinance in Phoenix.

Personal values do not, however, always dominate judges' decisions (see pages 192–202). Judges vary in the degree to which they can put their personal views of policy to one side rather than making themselves as highly predictable as was William O. Douglas at the liberal end of the political spectrum and is William Rehnquist at the conservative end. *Judicial role conceptions*—expectations, based on others' views, of what a judge should do—can affect judges' actions, as can other factors, including the Court's internal institutional norms. This is true even in a court like the U.S. Supreme Court, which can choose the cases it hears, although the presence of a high proportion of the most controversial cases will result in judges' policy positions being more evident. Because the justices' policy positions do play a major part in the Supreme Court's decisions, the Court is thus quite clearly a policy maker, although the political *effects* of its decisions would make it one even if judges kept personal views fully under wraps.

As a policy maker, the Supreme Court does not play a single uniform policy-making role. There are differences from one policy area to the next in the degree to which the Court makes policy. At times policy making is evident in major single decisions; at other times policy develops cumulatively through several decisions in a policy area. In some areas, the Court may be a "policy leader"; in others, it may avoid such leadership. It may accept Congress' statement of the need for a statute or an administrative agency's rationale for a regulation, or it may make its own determination of the need and evaluation of the rationale. Such variation "might seem rather strange in an isolated and insulated court administering The Law by processes of rigorous legal logic" but is not unusual "in a political agency faced with a wide range of problems, each entailing a different constellation of political forces."[76] However, although the Court is a policy maker, it is not just any old political actor. It wears special garb, proceeds by means of special forms, and uses specialized language. It is *both* a political institution and, because of its format, procedures, and language, a legal one.

NOTES

1. *Brown v. Allen*, 344 U.S. 443 at 540 (1953).
2. This section is drawn from Stephen L. Wasby, "Arrogation of Power or Accountability: 'Judicial Imperialism' Revisited," *Judicature* 65 (October 1981):209–219.
3. See Donald Horowitz, *The Courts and Social Policy* (Washington, D.C.: The Brookings Institution, 1977); Nathan Glazer, "Toward an Imperial Judiciary," *The Public Interest* 40 (Fall 1975):104–123; Raoul Berger, *Government by the Judiciary: The Transformation of the Fourteenth Amendment* (Cambridge, Mass.: Harvard University Press, 1977).
4. *Richmond Newspapers v. Virginia*, 448 U.S. 555 at 607 n. 35 (1980); *Columbus Board of Education v. Penick*, 443 U.S. 449 at 484, 487 (1979).
5. See Abram Chayes, "The Role of the Judge in Public Law Litigation," *Harvard Law Review* 89 (May 1976):1281–1325.
6. *Schweiker v. Wilson*, 450 U.S. 221 at 244 n. 5 (1981).
7. 449 U.S. 560.
8. For a well-developed set of criteria for examining the relative capacity of policy-making institutions, see Lief Carter, "When Courts Should Make Policy: An Institutional Approach," *Public Law and Public Policy*, ed. John Gardiner (New York: Praeger, 1977), pp. 141–157.
9. Ralph Cavanagh and Austin Sarat, "Thinking About Courts: Toward and Beyond a Jurisprudence of Judicial Competence," *Law & Society Review* 14 (Winter 1980):406. See also Vincent M. Nathan, "The Use of Masters in Institutional Reform Litigation," *Toledo Law Review* 10 (Winter 1979):419–464, and Special Project, "The Remedial Process in Institutional Reform Litigation," *Columbia Law Review* 78 (May 1978):785–929.
10. For a more complete discussion, see Stephen L. Wasby, "Accountability of the Courts," *Accountability in Urban Society*, ed. Scott Greer et al. (Beverly Hills, Calif.: Sage, 1978), pp. 143–168.
11. Ibid., p. 145.
12. Martin Shapiro, *Courts: A Comparative and Political Analysis* (Chicago: University of Chicago Press, 1981), p. 20.
13. Richard J. Richardson and Kenneth N. Vines, *The Politics of Federal Courts: Lower Courts in the United States* (Boston: Little, Brown, 1970), pp. 8–11.
14. See Jack Peltason, *Fifty-Eight Lonely Men* (New York: Harcourt, Brace and World, 1961); Kenneth N. Vines, "Southern State Supreme Courts and Race Relations," *Western Political Quarterly* 13 (March 1965):5–18; Charles Hamilton, *The Bench and the Ballot: Southern Federal Judges and Black Voters* (New York: Oxford University Press, 1973); Micheal Giles and Thomas Walker, "Judicial Policy-Making and Southern School Segregation," *Journal of Politics* 37 (November 1975):917–936.
15. For example, *Hurtado v. California*, 110 U.S. 516 (1884) (grand jury indictment), and *Twining v. New Jersey*, 211 U.S. 78 (1908) (Fifth Amendment).
16. *Abrams v. United States*, 250 U.S. 616 (1919), and *Schenck v. United States*, 249 U.S. 47 (1919). See also *Gitlow v. New York*, 268 U.S. 652 (1925).

17. On child labor legislation, see *Hammer v. Dagenhart*, 247 U.S. 251 (1918) (commerce), and *Bailey v. Drexel Furniture*, 259 U.S. 20 (1922) (taxation).
18. For example, *Schechter Poultry Corp. v. United States*, 295 U.S. 495 (1935); *United States v. Butler*, 297 U.S. 1 (1936); *Carter v. Carter Coal Co.*, 298 U.S. 238 (1936).
19. *National Labor Relations Board v. Jones & Laughlin Steel Corp.*, 301 U.S. 1 (1937); *United States v. Darby*, 312 U.S. 100 (1941).
20. *Heart of Atlanta Motel v. United States*, 371 U.S. 241 (1964); *Katzenbach v. McClung*, 379 U.S. 294 (1964).
21. *Ex Parte Endo*, 323 U.S. 293 (1944). The Court also sustained use of a military commission to try German saboteurs who had landed in the United States, *Ex Parte Quirin*, 317 U.S. 1 (1942), and when the war was over the Court refused to extend due process protections to a Japanese general charged with atrocities committed by his soldiers, *Yamashita v. United States*, 327 U.S. 1 (1946).
22. *Shelley v. Kraemer*, 334 U.S. 1 (1948) (restrictive covenants); *Sweatt v. Painter*, 339 U.S. 629 (1950) and *McLaurin v. Board of Regents*, 339 U.S. 637 (1950) (law school and graduate education). Whites-only primary elections had been invalidated during the war: *Smith v. Allwright*, 321 U.S. 649 (1944).
23. Reapportionment: *Reynolds v. Sims*, 377 U.S. 533 (1964); obscenity: *Roth v. United States/Alberts v. California*, 354 U.S. 476 (1957); libel: *New York Times v. Sullivan*, 376 U.S. 254 (1964); school prayer: *Engel v. Vitale*, 370 U.S. 421 (1962) and *Abington School District v. Schempp*, 374 U.S. 203 (1963); public accommodations: *Heart of Atlanta Motel v. United States*, 371 U.S. 241 (1964) and *Katzenbach v. McClung*, 379 U.S. 294 (1964); voting: *South Carolina v. Katzenbach*, 383 U.S. 301 (1966); housing: *Jones v. Mayer*, 392 U.S. 409 (1968). See generally Stephen L. Wasby, *Continuity and Change: From the Warren Court to the Burger Court* (Pacific Palisades, Calif.: Goodyear, 1976), pp. 71–77.
24. *Harper v. Virginia Board of Elections*, 383 U.S. 663 (1963); *Shapiro v. Thompson*, 394 U.S. 618 (1960).
25. *Terry v. Ohio*, 392 U.S. 1 (1968); *Warden v. Hayden*, 387 U.S. 294 (1967); *Lewis v. United States*, 385 U.S. 206 (1966) and *Hoffa v. United States*, 385 U.S. 293 (1966); *Berger v. New York*, 388 U.S. 41 (1967).
26. Lewis M. Steel, "Nine Men in Black Who Think White," *New York Times Magazine*, October 13, 1968, pp. 56, 117.
27. "The Role of the Supreme Court in a Democratic Society—Judicial Activism or Restraint?" *Cornell Law Quarterly* 54 (November 1968):8.
28. See William Brennan, "State Constitutions and the Protection of Individual Rights," *Harvard Law Review* 90 (January 1977):489–504.
29. Richard Funston, "Foreword: The Burger Court: New Directions in Judicial Policy-making," *Emory Law Journal* 23 (Summer 1974):656.
30. Robert G. McCloskey, "Reflections on the Warren Court," *Virginia Law Review* 51 (November 1965):1234.
31. Don E. Fehrenbacher, *The Dred Scott Case: Its Significance In American Law & Politics* (New York: Oxford University Press, 1978), p. 226.
32. *Hudgens v. National Labor Relations Board*, 424 U.S. 507 (1976), overruling *Food Employees v. Logan Valley Plaza*, 391 U.S. 308 (1968); *National League of Cities v. Usery*, 426 U.S. 833 (1976), overruling *Maryland v. Wirtz*, 392 U.S. 183 (1968). In 1983, the Court in turn came close to overruling the *National League of Cities*, when it sustained application of the federal age discrimination law to state and local government employees.

E.E.O.C. v. Wyoming, 103 S.Ct. 1054 (1983). In the same year, in reconsidering (but not overturning) the exclusionary rule in search cases, the Court did overturn two Warren Court rulings on the use of informants' tips as the basis for obtaining a warrant. *Illinois v. Gates*, 103 S.Ct. 2317 (1983), overruling *Spinelli v. United States*, 393 U.S. 410 (1969), and *Aguilar v. Texas*, 378 U.S. 108 (1964).

33. Paul Bender, "The Reluctant Court," *Civil Liberties Review* 2 (Fall 1975):101.
34. Glendon Schubert, "The Future of the Nixon Court," University Lecture, University of Hawaii, May 9, 1972, p. 12.
35. *Bishop v. Wood*, 426 U.S. 341 (1976).
36. Jesse Choper, "The Burger Court: Misconceptions Regarding Judicial Restraint and Insensitivity to Individual Rights," *Syracuse Law Review* 30 (Spring 1979):771–772. The first two cases are *Oregon v. Mitchell*, 400 U.S. 112 (1970) (18-year-olds' right to vote) and *National League of Cities v. Usery*, 426 U.S. 833 (1976) (application of the minimum wage to state and local employees); the last case is *Buckley v. Valeo*, 424 U.S. 1 (1976) (method of selecting the Federal Election Commission).
37. *Swann v. Charlotte-Mecklenberg School District*, 402 U.S. 1 (1971) (busing); *Norwood v. Harrison*, 413 U.S. 455 (1973) (free textbooks to racially exclusive private schools); *Runyon v. McCrary*, 427 U.S. 160 (1976) (admission to racially discriminatory private schools). See also *Bob Jones University v. United States*, 103 S.Ct. 2017 (1983).
38. *Reed v. Reed*, 404 U.S. 71 (1971); *Frontiero v. Richardson*, 411 U.S. 676 (1973); *Taylor v. Louisiana*, 419 U.S. 522 (1975); *Cleveland Board of Education v. LaFleur*, 414 U.S. 632 (1974).
39. *Geduldig v. Aiello*, 417 U.S. 484 (1974). Congress' action came after *General Electric Co. v. Gilbert*, 429 U.S. 125 (1976).
40. *Moose Lodge v. Irvis*, 407 U.S. 163 (1973); *Palmer v. Thompson*, 403 U.S. 217 (1971).
41. *Goldberg v. Kelly*, 397 U.S. 254 (1970) and *Wheeler v. Montgomery*, 397 U.S. 280 (1970) (notice and hearing); *Dandridge v. Williams*, 397 U.S. 471 (1970) (maximum grants); *Wyman v. James*, 400 U.S. 309 (1971) (home visits).
42. *Mahan v. Howell*, 410 U.S. 315 (1973); *Whitcomb v. Chavis*, 403 U.S. 124 (1974).
43. See *Tilton v. Richardson*, 403 U.S. 673 (1971) (higher education); *Lemon v. Kurtzman*, 403 U.S. 602 (1971) and *Meek v. Pittenger*, 431 U.S. 349 (1975) (elementary and secondary education).
44. *Nebraska Press Association v. Stuart*, 427 U.S. 539 (1976) (gag order); *Branzburg v. Hayes*, 408 U.S. 665 (1972) (journalists' testimony about sources); *Parker v. Levy*, 417 U.S. 733 (1974) (military officers' free speech); *Greer v. Spock*, 424 U.S. 828 (1971) (military bases).
45. *United States v. Mandujano*, 425 U.S. 564 (1976).
46. See *Almeida-Sanchez v. United States*, 413 U.S. 266 (1973) (roving border searches); *United States v. Robinson*, 414 U.S. 218 (1973), *Cady v. Dombrowski*, 413 U.S. 433 (1973), and *Schneckloth v. Bustamonte*, 412 U.S. 218 (1973) (car-related searches); *Andresen v. Maryland*, 427 U.S. 463 (1976) (records).
47. *Harris v. New York*, 401 U.S. 222 (1971), reinforced by *Oregon v. Hass*, 420 U.S. 714 (1975).
48. *Kastigar v. United States*, 406 U.S. 441 (1972).
49. *Kirby v. Illinois*, 406 U.S. 682 (1972) (line-up); *Ross v. Moffitt*, 417 U.S. 600 (1974) (discretionary appeals); *Morrissey v. Brewer*, 408 U.S. 471 (1972) (parole); *Gagnon v. Scarpelli*, 411 U.S. 778 (1973) (probation); *Wolff v. McDonnell*, 418 U.S. 539 (1974) (prison discipline).

50. *North Carolina v. Alford*, 400 U.S. 25 (1970) and *Santobello v. New York*, 404 U.S. 527 (1971); *Brady v. United States*, 397 U.S. 542 (1970).
51. See *Gardner v. Florida*, 430 U.S. 349 (1977) (material available to judge for sentencing had to be made available to the defense); *Estelle v. Smith*, 451 U.S. 454 (1981) (limiting testimony of psychiatrist who had examined defendant to determine competence to stand trial); and *Bullington v. Missouri*, 451 U.S. 430 (1981) (defendant who had received life sentence in murder trial could not receive death penalty when retried).
52. A. E. Dick Howard, *National Law Journal* (February 18, 1980):17, 28.
53. Gayle Binion, "The Disadvantaged Before the Burger Court: The New Unequal Protection," *Law & Policy Quarterly* 4 (January 1982):39–41. For examinations of specific terms of Court, see John P. MacKenzie, "The Lost Court," *Civil Liberties Review* 3 (October/November 1976):36–53, and Stephen L. Wasby, "Certain Conservatism or Surprise: Civil Liberties in the 1976 Term," *Civil Liberties Review* 4 (November/December 1977):33–51.
54. Robert C. Welsh, "Federalism and the Burger Court's Review of State Civil Liberties Judgments," paper presented to American Political Science Association, 1982, p. 4. The data is based on "paid" cases only.
55. See *Wolman v. Walter*, 433 U.S. 229 (1977). Allowed: books, standardized testing and scoring, diagnostic services, therapeutic and remedial services; not allowed: instructional materials, equipment, field trips.
56. *Gannett v. DePasquale*, 443 U.S. 368 (1979); *Richmond Newspapers v. Virginia*, 448 U.S. 555 (1980).
57. *Chandler v. Florida*, 449 U.S. 560 (1982).
58. See *Planned Parenthood of Central Missouri v. Danforth*, 428 U.S. 52 (1976) (spousal consent); *Bellotti v. Baird*, 443 U.S. 622 (1979) (parental consent); and *City of Akron v. Akron Center for Reproductive Health*, 103 S.Ct. 2481 (1983); *Harris v. McRae*, 448 U.S. 297 (1980) (funding).
59. *Rostker v. Goldberg*, 453 U.S. 57 (1981) (draft registration); *North Haven Board of Education v. Bell*, 102 S.Ct. 1912 (1982) (employment in programs receiving federal funds); *County of Washington v. Gunther*, 452 U.S. 161 (1981) (pay).
60. *Washington v. Davis*, 426 U.S. 229 (1976) ("intent" rather than effect required to show a constitutional violation); *Teamsters v. United States*, 431 U.S. 324 (1977) and *American Tobacco Co. v. Patterson*, 102 S.Ct. 1534 (1982) (seniority).
61. *Dayton Board of Education v. Brinkman*, 443 U.S. 526 (1979) and *Columbus Board of Education v. Penick*, 443 U.S. 449 (1979).
62. *Bell v. Wolfish*, 441 U.S. 520 (1979) (pretrial detainees); *Rhodes v. Chapman*, 452 U.S. 337 (1981) (state prison).
63. *Payton v. New York*, 445 U.S. 573 (1980); *Steagald v. United States*, 451 U.S. 204 (1981).
64. *Zurcher v. Stanford Daily*, 436 U.S. 547 (1978); *Dalia v. United States*, 441 U.S. 236 (1979). The *Zurcher* decision was overturned in part by Congress. The Privacy Protection Act of 1980 limited government searches and seizures of documentary material in the possession of journalists not themselves suspected of being involved in a crime; some states enacted similar laws.
65. *Dunaway v. New York*, 442 U.S. 200 (1979) (illegal stop); *Michigan v. Mosley*, 423 U.S. 96 (1975) (resumption of questioning); *United States v. Mandujano*, 425 U.S. 564 (1976) (grand jury); *Beckwith v. United States*, 425 U.S. 341 (1976) (tax investigation).
66. Arthur D. Hellman, "The Business of the Supreme Court Under the Judiciary Act of 1925:

The Plenary Docket in the 1970's," *Harvard Law Review* 91 (June 1978):1716; D. Marie Provine, *Case Selection in the Supreme Court* (Chicago: University of Chicago Press, 1980), p. 101.

67. Walter F. Murphy, *Elements of Judicial Strategy* (Chicago: University of Chicago Press, 1964), pp. 208–209.
68. Max Lerner, "Constitution and Court as Symbols," *Yale Law Journal* 46 (1939):1294–1295.
69. *United States v. Butler*, 297 U.S. 1 at 62–63 (1936).
70. S. Sidney Ulmer, "Researching the Supreme Court in a Democratic Pluralist System: Some Thoughts on New Directions," *Law & Policy Quarterly* 1 (January 1979):55.
71. *Boag v. MacDougall*, 102 S.Ct. 700 at 701 (1982) (Justice O'Connor, concurring).
72. Robert Woodward and Scott Armstrong, *The Brethren: Inside the Supreme Court* (New York: Simon and Schuster, 1979); Bruce Allen Murphy, *The Brandeis/Frankfurter Connection: The Secret Political Activities of Two Supreme Court Justices* (New York: Oxford University Press, 1982).
73. 384 U.S. 436 at 531–532 (1966); emphasis supplied.
74. *West Virginia State Board of Education v. Barnette*, 319 U.S. 624 at 647 (1943).
75. *Furman v. Georgia*, 408 U.S. 238 at 405–406, 410–411 (1972).
76. Martin Shapiro, *Law and Politics in the Supreme Court* (New York: Free Press, 1964), p. 328.

Chapter 2

Elements of the Federal Judicial System

This chapter is intended to provide a picture of the federal court system's overall structure. We look at the basic levels of the national court system and at associated specialized courts, starting with the district courts and moving to the courts of appeals, followed by a discussion of judicial administration. An examination of the Supreme Court and its position in the federal judicial system concludes the chapter.

The United States has a dual court system of separate national and state courts, a result of our system of federalism. There is a set of national courts including territorial courts, and each state has its own courts, giving us fifty-one separate court systems (fifty-two if one counts the District of Columbia's courts separately). Each state has trial courts of general jurisdiction, that is, courts with legal authority to hear all civil and criminal cases; they are usually called district or circuit courts. All states also have specialized courts of one or more types, for example, for probate (wills and estates) or juvenile and family proceedings. Most states have an intermediate appellate court, to which all or most appeals are taken first, and a supreme court (in some states, called the court of appeals). Many states retain a fourth level of limited jurisdiction courts—the "inferior" (meaning lower) or "petty" courts—including justice-of-the-peace courts, mayors' courts, police courts, and some municipal courts established to assist with the higher volume of litigation in large urban areas. Appeals from decisions of these courts are directed to the general jurisdiction trial courts for a new trial (trial *de novo*) instead of going directly to an appellate court.

Although the Supreme Court of the United States, the only court specifically designated in the Constitution, is our principal interest as the apex of the federal judicial system, we must also pay attention to the lower federal courts. The national judicial structure—the Supreme Court, courts of appeals, district courts, and magistrates (connected to and generally subordinate to the district courts), as well as some specialized courts such as the bankruptcy courts—is similar to most states' court systems. The Supreme Court cannot initiate cases but must rely on the lower federal courts (and the state courts) as the source of its business, the place where cases are initiated and in which they take the shape in which they arrive at the Supreme Court and with which the justices must then work. The lower federal courts are also where most federal litigation terminates, so that they make much law in areas of litigation not reviewed or seldom reviewed by the Supreme Court. The basic relations among federal courts, to be discussed in this chapter, are portrayed in Figure 2.1. (Those between state courts and federal courts are portrayed and discussed in Chapter 5.) Arrows indicate paths that cases follow from one level of court to another. (Except for bankruptcy courts, the specialized courts discussed in the text do not appear in the diagram.)

DEVELOPMENT OF THE FEDERAL COURT SYSTEM

The federal court system as we now know it assumed its present basic form only late in the nineteenth century. The system of federal courts established by Congress in the Judiciary Act of 1789 was relatively elementary. In addition to the Supreme Court, specified by the Constitution itself (see Art. III, Sec. 1), the Congress created district courts and circuit courts. The district courts' jurisdiction was not broad, and

> The judicial power of the United States shall be vested in one Supreme Court, and in such inferior Courts as the Congress may from time to time ordain and establish. (Art. III, Sec. 1)

they dealt mainly with admiralty cases. The circuit courts, although they had some appellate jurisdiction over the district courts, were primarily trial courts for diversity of citizenship cases (suits between citizens of different states). In the circuit courts,

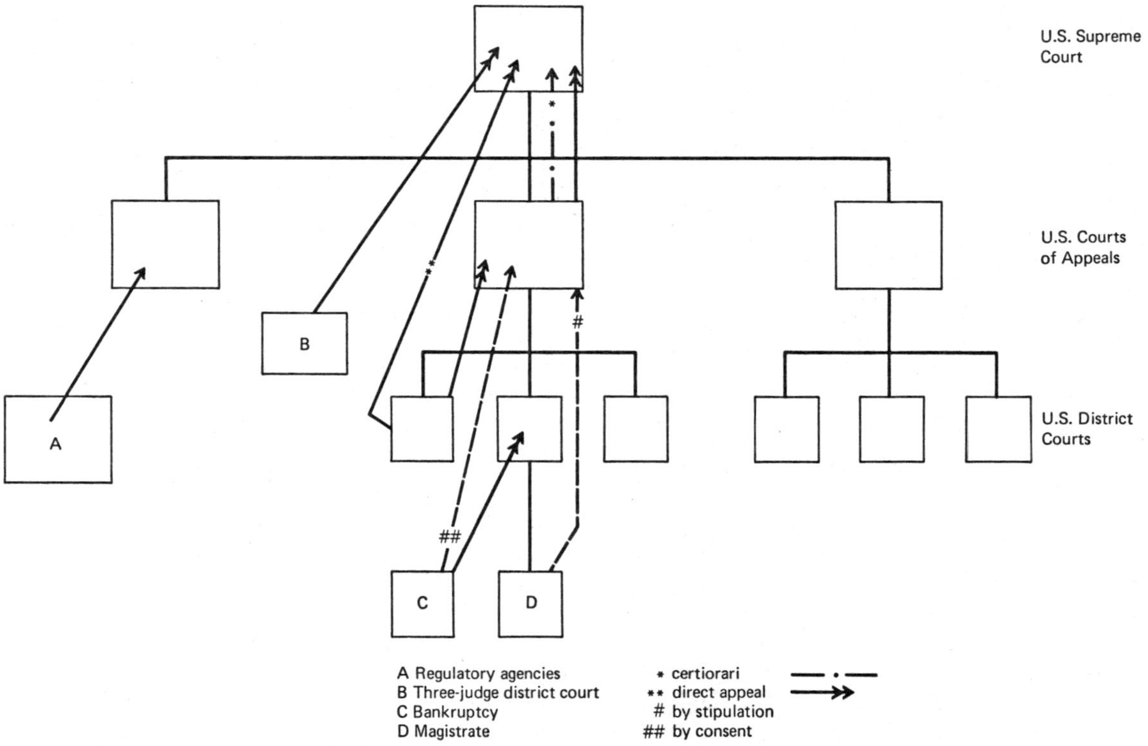

FIGURE 2.1 The Federal Court System

which did not have their own judges, a district judge and two Supreme Court justices were to sit twice a year in each district of the circuit. Almost immediately (in 1793), Congress reduced the burden on Supreme Court justices of attending court in the districts so that each year only one justice would have to sit once in each district. In 1801, sixteen circuit court judgeships for six circuits were created, but in 1802 the Jeffersonian Democrats promptly repealed this action by the Federalists.

District judges were used increasingly in the circuit courts until after the Civil War, and the Supreme Court justice assigned to the circuit (the *circuit justice*) often did not visit certain parts of large western circuits. Because of the extreme distance from the East Coast to California, a separate circuit court—with its own circuit judges—was established for California. In 1869, nine judgeships were created specially for the circuit courts: these circuit judges had the same authority as the Supreme Court justices assigned to the circuit, who were now required to attend only one term of circuit court in each district of the circuit every two years. A circuit justice, circuit judge, or district judge could hold circuit court, or any two could sit as a panel. Nonetheless, district judges held circuit court most of the time, creating a dual role in which they sat in review over their own district court decisions. Supreme Court justices also had this dual role when they sat on circuit and later had to review their rulings appealed to the Supreme Court.

Supreme Court justices are no longer subject to the rigors of riding circuit. In the early days, they had to put up with "the dangers and miseries of overturned vehicles, runaway horses, rivers in full flood, or icebound and scruffy taverns."[1] There were even more serious dangers: the life of Justice Stephen Field, on circuit in California, was threatened by a disgruntled litigant who was shot and killed by the U.S. marshal assigned to guard the justice. After the state indicted the marshal for murder, he was transferred to the federal court's jurisdiction and was exonerated. The Supreme Court itself ruled in *In Re Neagle* that his action was part of properly enforcing the nation's laws. (In 1982, a man angry at the Supreme Court's decisions struck Justice Byron White several times while White was about to deliver a speech to a bar association meeting in Utah, but the justice was not injured.) Circuit duty was continued for many years because the lower courts needed help with their caseload and because the Supreme Court's caseload was not overwhelming; in addition, Congress felt that if the justices stayed in Washington, they might be dominated by the capital's lawyers, with whom they often shared rooming houses.

In the Judiciary Act of 1875, the district courts for the first time received general federal question jurisdiction, allowing them to hear civil suits involving at least $500 if the case arose "under the Constitution, laws, or treaties of the United States." (At the same time, the jurisdictional minimum for cases coming to the Supreme Court from the circuit courts was $5,000.) Congress did not provide for review of capital (death sentence) cases until 1889 and for all cases involving "infamous crimes"—those where a sentence of imprisonment was possible—until 1891.

The failure to create any lower federal courts in the Constitution, and the limited jurisdiction given them in the early years, resulted from arguments that the state courts, bound by the Supremacy Clause (Art. VI) could be expected to enforce the Constitution. Whatever the force of such arguments in connection with the Constitution's ratification, competing considerations later came to the fore. Particularly important were the feelings of those wanting a strong national government that because the state courts were not enforcing federal law adequately, a federal judicial mechanism was necessary for that purpose.

In 1891, the U.S. Courts of Appeals (as they are now called) were established, to be staffed by two circuit judges and a Supreme Court justice, for whom a district judge could substitute. The old circuit courts, which thus became courts without full-time judges, were finally abolished in 1911, at last making district courts the dominant federal court of original jurisdiction. The presence of a regular set of intermediate appellate courts meant that the Supreme Court no longer had to accept all the cases in which its decision was sought, and the movement toward giving the Court control over what cases it would hear then began. This process of providing the Supreme Court with discretionary jurisdiction began in 1914, continued in 1916, and was fully consummated in the Judges Bill of 1925, which provided authority to hear large categories of cases on petition for a writ of certiorari (see pages 158–167).

THE DISTRICT COURTS

District courts are the federal judicial system's general jurisdiction trial courts; thus they can hear all civil and criminal cases for which Congress has provided, and it is here that federal jury trials take place. Each of the nation's ninety-four district courts, which sit at locations designated by statute, is located in a single state or territory, except for the District of Wyoming, which includes the Montana and Idaho portions of Yellowstone National Park. Twenty-six states, the District of Columbia, and the nation's four territories each constitute one district; the remaining states have two to four districts each. Congress added 117 district judgeships in the Omnibus Judgeship Act of 1978, so there are now 516 district judgeships, an increase of 128 percent from 1960. (All district judges are appointed by the president with the advice and consent of the Senate.) District courts vary considerably in the number of judgeships. Several districts (Rhode Island and the Northern District of West Virginia) have only one judge; a few others have one full-time judge and share a "floater" with another district. On the other hand, the Southern District of New York, which includes Manhattan, has twenty-five judges. Several other districts have more than a dozen judges: the Northern and Central Districts of California, centered at San Francisco and Los Angeles, respectively; the Northern District of Illinois (Chicago); and the Eastern District of Pennsylvania (Philadelphia).

The district courts have a large caseload (almost 200,000 cases a year in recent years) covering both a wide range of criminal offenses and diverse types of civil cases, including antitrust, commerce, patent and copyright, contract, and tort suits. Most district court civil cases involve private individuals or businesses raising federal questions or bringing suit under diversity of citizenship jurisdiction; the United States is a party in only roughly one-fourth of the civil cases. New congressional statutes, resulting from shifts in the national political agenda, have led to increases in district court cases on such subjects as environmental protection, job discrimination, and education of the handicapped. As these examples indicate, there has been not only an increase in district court caseload but a shift within that caseload from private litigation to litigation involving actions of national, state, and local government agencies.

District court caseloads have increased substantially in recent years. Filings per year, which have not necessarily run parallel to increases in population or economic growth,[2] increased well over 100 percent from 1960 to 1980. Growth in the number of criminal cases has resulted not only from increases in crime and from increased public pressures on prosecutors to "do something," but also from new federal criminal statutes. An increase in related cases concerning criminal procedure resulted from the Supreme Court's decisions in the 1960s protecting defendants' rights and facilitating state prisoners' access to federal courts; there was also an increase in cases raising prison confinement issues. Some of these cases have been deflected from the district courts as a result of decisions by the Burger Court restricting state prisoners' use of federal court, coupled with use of new prison grievance mechanisms.

The Speedy Trial Act directed district court *attention* to criminal cases by imposing a strict calendar on the stages of a federal criminal case from arrest and indictment through trial and by providing dismissal of the case for failure to meet these deadlines. Congress has also specified numerous categories of civil cases to be given priority or expedited, but has not ranked the various priorities. Such actions have strained the capacity of busier district courts to keep up with routine civil cases. Although district judgeships were added in 1978 to help reduce backlog, filings may increase if potential litigants think that judges will be able to decide cases more promptly. Although the Court ruled in 1976 that district judges may *not* use workload as a reason for refusing to accept cases that are within their jurisdiction,[3] Chief Justice Burger and some of his colleagues, as well as many other other lawyers, have advocated having Congress eliminate diversity of citizenship cases as one way of reducing caseload.

Most district court decisions are final. They are either not appealed, or if appealed, are settled prior to an appellate ruling, or, in the vast proportion of cases reviewed by the courts of appeals, they are sustained—often in brief affirmances without opinion. In 1965–1967, for example, roughly one-third of completed district court cases were taken to the appellate courts, but because of terminations before final submission, the proportion finally reviewed was only about one-fifth.[4] When we add the fact that by no means all court of appeals rulings are carried to the Supreme Court, which grants review to only a very small percentage of those cases in which review is sought, "the great majority of district court decisions are neither reviewed nor reversed."[5] Thus district court decisions are *the* rulings in all but a very small percentage of cases decided there.

Moreover, appellate court review of district court output is not uniform across the districts within each circuit or across subject matters; indeed courts of appeals provide "sustained supervision" of district court decisions "in only a few areas of public policy."[6] In part because district court rulings on various subjects are appealed in differing proportions, appellate review is not necessarily concentrated so as to produce uniformity on questions of federal law or protection of important federal interests. For example, rates of appeal were among the lowest where appellate supervision of district judges in civil rights cases was most needed because the district judges resisted appellate rulings. The low rate of review and appellate court reversal means that district courts follow appropriate legal doctrine through informal controls rather than as a result of the explicit sanction of reversal by superiors. The informal controls include precedent, professional socialization including service with the court of appeals, anticipation of appellate judicial action, and ideological unity provided by shared regional and political backgrounds.[7]

District court cases are ordinarily heard by one judge. However, in special situations, three-judge district courts, composed of two district judges and a court of appeals judge, have been convened. These courts were first established in 1903 to deal with requests for injunctions against Interstate Commerce Commission (ICC) orders. The jurisdiction of these courts was extended in 1910 to cases involving state laws when it was felt that allowing single district judges to invalidate state laws gave them too much power, particularly over state economic regulation. Their jurisdiction was further extended in 1913 to requests for injunctions against state administrative actions and to federal statutes in 1937. Appeals from decisions of three-judge district courts go directly to the Supreme Court—in part because of the importance of the cases, in part because an appeals court judge has already participated in hearing them.

Starting in the 1950s, and particularly from the mid-1960s through the early 1970s, there was greater use of three-judge courts, as litigants increasingly sought injunctions against state laws alleged to interfere with civil rights. As a result, more cases came directly to the Supreme Court—without benefit of prior treatment by the courts of appeals. Moreover, these cases fell within the Court's mandatory jurisdiction (those it must hear). The cases accounted for a significant portion of the Court's decisions (nearly one-fourth in one year), although the Court disposed of most of them summarily. The justices felt that these mandatory appeals hindered the Court's ability to choose the cases it would consider fully, a development that ran counter to the purpose of giving the Court its certiorari (discretionary) jurisdiction. Under Chief Justice Burger, the Court developed doctrines to limit the use of three-judge courts, and the Chief Justice called upon Congress to eliminate three-judge district courts and to eliminate other direct appeals as well. Such appeals were first eliminated with respect to ICC orders and government civil antitrust cases.

Then in 1976 a law was passed to eliminate three-judge courts except in congressional and state legislative reapportionment cases or unless specifically provided for in congressional statutes like the Civil Rights Act of 1964 and the Voting Rights Act of 1976. Henceforth, requests for injunctions against state laws would be handled by single judges; even when three-judge courts were required, a single judge was to handle all preliminary matters, although direct appeal to the Supreme Court would still occur.

District of Columbia and the Territories

The District of Columbia is governed both under laws covering the entire nation and those passed by its governing body and by Congress that apply specifically to the District. In addition to the usual national courts—a district court and a court of appeals—the District has another set of courts, closer in function to state courts and established under Congress's authority to make laws for the nation's capital (Art. I, Sec. 8, cl. 17). Prior to 1971, cases from the District of Columbia Court of Appeals went not directly to the U.S. Supreme Court, as they would from the highest state courts, but to the U.S. Court of Appeals for the District of Columbia. In 1970 a new District of Columbia Superior Court assumed most local jurisdiction, including some cases formerly in the U.S. District Court. Most cases from the District of Columbia Court of Appeals now go directly to the U.S. Supreme Court, but appeals involving a law "not applicable exclusively to the District of Columbia" still go to the U.S. Court of Appeals.

The territorial courts in the Canal Zone, Guam, the Virgin Islands, and the Northern Mariannas (the newest federal judicial district) were established under Congress's power to regulate the territories. They hear cases under local as well as federal laws. Decisions concerning the district court's authority to hear appeals from local courts—for example, whether that authority should be transferred to local supreme courts—must be made by Congress because such review at times turns on questions of federal law.[8] In earlier years, the territorial courts were treated much like regular district courts; although the judges sometimes had legislative as well as judicial duties, they had tenure "during good behavior," that is, for life, under Article III of the Constitution. By the midnineteenth century, however, Congress shifted the basis for creating their positions to Article IV concerning governing of the territories, so the territorial judges lost their lifetime positions. Presidents beginning with Millard Fillmore even treated the judges as removable summarily. Judges of the territorial courts now have terms of from four to eight years. Since 1966, those in Puerto Rico, which has commonwealth status, have had lifetime appointments. When a territory becomes a state, the territorial court is abolished and is replaced by a regular Article III court with lifetime judgeships. In 1982, the District Court for the Canal Zone also went out of existence as a result of the Panama Canal Treaty transferring authority over the Zone to the Panamanian government.

Magistrates

The position of U.S. magistrate resulted from the reorganization of the U.S. commissioner system.[9] The commissioners' authority was largely restricted to trying petty criminal offenses (no more than six months in jail, a $500 fine, or both) committed in federal enclaves such as military bases and national parks, where they were often the only federal judicial "presence." Commissioners could also issue search and arrest warrants, conduct preliminary hearings and bail proceedings, and file criminal complaints in more serious cases. Despite these tasks, the commissioners often did not have a clear idea of their authority or functions, and there was considerable variation from district to district in how commissioners were to deal with basic problems. The commissioners, about one-third of whom were not lawyers, were paid by a fee system with a $10,500 limit, quickly reached by the busiest commissioners.

Under the Federal Magistrates Act, fully effective in 1971, there are both full-time magistrates, who serve for eight years, and part-time magistrates, who serve for four years. All, except for some part-time magistrates serving under special circumstances, must be lawyers. In 1980, reflecting a shift to full-time positions, there were almost 200 full-time and almost 300 part-time magistrates. More than two-thirds of the full-time magistrates serve in the nation's twenty-five largest federal court districts, assigned there by the U.S. Judicial Conference.

Magistrates started with all the commissioners' former duties. As district court caseload increased substantially, magistrates were given additional duties by statute or have been assigned them by district judges in order to relieve the district judges of some of their caseload. Such additional duties have accounted for an increasing proportion of the magistrates' work each year. The Federal Magistrates Act of 1979 provided that magistrates may now hear, and impose sentence in, all jury and nonjury misdemeanor criminal cases, if the defendant waives the right to trial by a district judge; previously they could hear only cases involving minor offenses (those with a maximum fine of $1,000, a year's prison sentence, or both) and could not hear jury trials. Their juvenile jurisdiction is still limited to petty cases and depends on the juvenile's consent; they may not impose any term of imprisonment on juveniles.

Magistrates also conduct pretrial criminal proceedings and conduct preliminary review of applications for posttrial relief. In 1974 the Supreme Court, interpreting Congress' intent, refused to allow even full-time magistrates to conduct evidentiary hearings on federal habeas corpus petitions, limiting them to submitting reports to the district judge.[10] In 1976 Congress overruled this decision and gave magistrates authority to conduct such hearings upon referral by the district judge. Subsequently, a divided Supreme Court held that a district judge did not need to rehear testimony from a hearing to suppress evidence on which a magistrate had based findings and recommendations; there was no violation of Article III, said Chief Justice Burger, in delegating authority to hear such testimony to a magistrate so long as the district judge is the ultimate decision maker.[11]

Magistrates' civil jurisdiction has also been expanded. Before the passage of the 1979 act, they could conduct civil pretrial and discovery proceedings, act as special masters in civil cases, and review administrative records in Social Security cases. The Supreme Court upheld district judges' referrals to magistrates of Social Security Act benefit entitlement cases as "substantially assist[ing] the district judge in the performance of his judicial function, and benefit[ing] both him and the parties"; the district judge had the opportunity to review—and object to—the magistrate's findings of fact and conclusions of law and could hear the matter *de novo* if he wished.[12] With the consent of both parties, magistrates could also conduct civil trials; appeal to the district courts for a trial *de novo* protected an individual's right to be tried by an Article III judge, although the district judge usually based a ruling on the magistrate's report. The 1979 statute confirmed existing practice in civil cases; any full-time and some part-time magistrates who had been so designated by the district court could hear and confer judgment in any jury or nonjury civil cases with the consent of all the parties. (Reference to the magistrates was to be made through the court clerk, not a judge, to avoid the potential problem of the judge's inducing the reference in order to reduce his own workload.) Appeals in such cases were shifted to the court of appeals, unless the parties agreed at the time a case was referred to the magistrate that the appeal would go to the district judge.

Bankruptcy Court

Those presiding over bankruptcy proceedings, formerly called referees in bankruptcy, as of 1973 have been called bankruptcy judges; there were 222 of them in 1982, with an increasing proportion serving on a full-time rather than part-time basis. Prior to 1946, they were paid by fees they collected, but now are salaried, with their salaries subject to adjustment by Congress. They were appointed by district judges for six-year terms up to the passage of the Bankruptcy Reform Act of 1978. That statute, which widened the scope of substantive bankruptcy law, retained the bankruptcy courts as "adjuncts" of the district courts, but changed bankruptcy judges' status in important ways. The judges' terms were increased to fourteen years, and they were now to be appointed not by the district judges but by the president. (Before 1984, merit screening committees would have the power to recommend termination of bankruptcy judges whose terms expired, and the chief judges of the circuits could terminate those judges and appoint replacements.)

Under the new statute, bankruptcy courts' jurisdiction was also expanded. Instead of being limited to so-called summary matters, involving property in the court's possession, they could now deal with "plenary" disputes involving third-party property, which previously they could do only by consent. They were given jurisdiction over *all* civil proceedings related to cases in bankruptcy, including state law as well as federal law questions. Bankruptcy courts were also to have a somewhat different relationship to the district courts from that of magistrates. The courts of appeals could appoint three-member bankruptcy judge panels to hear appeals; without such a panel, the district court would hear appeals, but, if both parties consented, the appeals could go directly to the courts of appeals. (In another important change, most supervision of the assets of bankrupts was to be placed in the hands of bankruptcy trustees appointed by the attorney general rather than in the hands of individuals appointed for particular cases by the judges; this part of the legislation was to be implemented gradually, starting with pilot projects in eighteen federal districts.)

The scope of bankruptcy judges' new authority led to legal challenges. In 1982, in a case involving a matter typically within state court jurisdiction (a contract by a company that was in the bankruptcy court's jurisdiction), a badly divided Supreme Court ruled that Congress had unconstitutionally granted too much authority to these judges who did not have lifetime tenure.[13] The Court's prevailing opinion was not restricted to a ruling that the extension of jurisdiction to cases not directly related to federal law was improper, but invalidated Congress' broad extension of jurisdiction. Justice Brennan found constitutional justification for having territorial (and District of Columbia) courts, courts-martial, and courts and administrative agencies with judges of limited terms (Article I judges) established to adjudicate cases involving "public rights" (those granted by the government against itself, such as pensions). However, when most of the attributes of "judicial power"—including authority over matters normally handled through the common law—were vested in judges, those judges had to be Article III judges with the necessary independence provided by their lifetime appointments and the corollary protection against salary reduction. Otherwise lack of independence might cause the judges to slant their decisions in order to increase their chances of reappointment. Chief Justice Burger voted to sustain Congress' actions, although he had earlier strenuously disagreed with a congressional proposal to give bankruptcy judges Article III status, a proposal opposed by the Judicial Conference of the United States as well.

To avoid invalidating decisions already reached by bankruptcy judges who carried over from the earlier statute but were exercising new authority, the Court did not make its ruling retroactive. It also gave Congress several months to change the statute either by curtailing the bankruptcy judges' jurisdiction or by giving them Article III status. After extending this stay of its decision for several months when Congress was unable to agree on a new bankruptcy court statute, the Supreme Court refused to extend the stay further at the end of 1982. Congressional inaction in that year's lame-duck session resulted not only from disagreement over bankruptcy judges' proper status—and over the political issue of whether one president should be able to name a large number of lifetime judges at one time—but also from disagreement over whether changes should be made in the substantive provisions of the bankruptcy statute, which had facilitated bankruptcies by individuals. Confusion over the status of the existing bankruptcy courts resulted from this stalemate, which continued well into 1983. There were also challenges to their jurisdiction to hear cases, although the Judicial Conference provided guidelines for dividing jurisdiction between the bankruptcy courts and district courts until a new statute could be enacted, and emergency interim rules were adopted by the judicial districts.

Other Specialized Courts

There are a number of other specialized trial-level courts. Despite the preference for general jurisdiction courts, specialized courts have been established throughout our history, when particular problems have been thought to require focused attention or there has been a large number of cases on a particular issue at one time. In the mid-nineteenth century, for example, a special court was established to settle the status of Spanish and Mexican land grants in the territory ceded by Mexico to the United States in the Treaties of 1848 and 1853. Similarly, the U.S. Court of Claims (now the U.S. Claims Court) was established in 1855 to provide for suits against the United States government and to relieve the pressure on Congress from requests for private bills to deal with claims against the government.

When it was first established, the only claims the Court of Claims could hear were those referred by the House of Representatives or the Senate; it did not have authority to award judgments against the government and could only report its findings to Congress along with a proposed bill authorizing payment. In the 1860s, however, its judgments were made final. Originally an Article I court whose judges had limited terms, the Court of Claims was made an Article III court in 1953, and the Supreme Court rejected challenges to the change.[14] Prior to its 1982 reorganization, the Court of Claims had original jurisdiction over contractual, tax, injury, and other nontort claims against the United States; public contract cases constituted the largest part of its work. It also had limited concurrent jurisdiction with the courts of appeals over tort actions initiated against the federal government in the district courts. The district courts have concurrent jurisdiction with the Claims Court over all civil actions against the government in which damages of $10,000 or less are sought, but the Claims Court has sole jurisdiction over certain contract claims involving larger sums.

Initial determinations in the Court of Claims were made by one of sixteen judges (trial commissioners), who, in addition to adjudicating cases referred by Congress, had functions analogous to those of U.S. magistrates or special masters. Only the court's five Article III judges, who sat together in Washington, D.C., could enter dispositive orders; they decided major motions and appeals from the trial judges' findings of fact and handled appeals from decisions of government contract boards. The Federal Court Improvement Act of 1982 created a clearer separation between the work done by the trial judges and that done by the Article III judges: the U.S. Claims Court again became an Article I court (with 16 judges) with trial jurisdiction over nontort claims against the U.S. government. Its appellate jurisdiction was lodged in the new Court of Appeals for the Federal Circuit (see pages 45–46).

The U.S. Tax Court was created in 1924 as the Board of Tax Appeals; it was renamed the Tax Court of the United States in 1942. It was an independent agency in the executive branch until 1969, when it became a legislative court. Based in Washington, D.C., its 19 judges—who serve 15-year terms—and masters (special trial judges appointed by the court) can hold hearings at other locations. The Tax Court, where over 30,000 cases are filed each year, has a present caseload of over 50,000 cases. It shares jurisdiction over tax litigation with the Claims Court and the district courts, but is the only one to which a taxpayer can bring a case before making full payment of taxes instead of having to pay under protest and then sue to recover. Its basic jurisdiction is over cases in which the taxpayer contests the government's assertions of tax liability in excise tax cases or with respect to income, estate, or gift taxes. In 1974 and 1979, the Tax Court also was given the authority to issue declaratory judgments (statements of litigants' rights before the government takes action against them) on such matters as the tax status of organizations, employee retirement plans, and government bonds. The taxpayer who has overpaid and wishes to recover some of those funds may go either to the Claims Court or to the district courts, which also have jurisdiction over enforcement of tax levies and over liens; the district courts, moreover, are the exclusive forum (court) for criminal tax proceedings.

The U.S. Court of International Trade was created in 1980 from the Customs Court, an administrative body that had evolved into an Article III court. Its nine judges, no more than five of whom may be from one political party, are appointed by the president with the advice and consent of the Senate. It has appellate jurisdiction over rulings and appraisals on imported goods made by the collectors of customs. When it was transformed into the Court of International Trade, its jurisdiction was broadened somewhat to give it exclusive jurisdiction over conflicts arising under the Tariff Act of 1930, the Trade Act of 1974, and the Trade Agreements Act of 1979.

Perhaps the most intriguing special court, recently established, is the Foreign Intelligence Surveillance Court. It is a result of the provision of the 1978 Wiretap Act that court orders must be obtained for telephone and other electronic taps of foreign agents (individuals and embassies) in the United States—including, in exceptional cases, American citizens with information thought essential to the national security. The seven members of the court are to be appointed—to staggered terms—by the Chief Justice after consultation with the chief judges of the circuits; they are regular judges of other courts serving on the FIS Court as well when needed. What makes the court unusual is that it meets in a "secure" courtroom and conducts its work in secret, not writing opinions or publishing rulings, except in a recent decision saying that the court's jurisdiction did not extend to searches of private property.

THE COURTS OF APPEALS

The U.S. Courts of Appeals are the general appellate courts for the federal judicial system. They handle cases on all types of federal law—"traditional" areas of litigation such as admiralty, bankruptcy, and antitrust; constitutional issues that are more prominent in the Supreme Court's work; and cases appealed from federal regulatory agencies, which are in effect the trial courts for matters within their jurisdictions. The U.S. Courts of Appeals (formerly called the Circuit Courts of Appeals) were created in their present form in 1891, as a result of increased federal court caseload and the recognition of the impracticality of having Supreme Court justices sit on circuit. The establishment of these courts—creating a basic appellate court for the federal judiciary—began the process of providing the Supreme Court with the ability to control which cases it would hear. The courts of appeals bring some degree of uniformity to national law, providing some oversight of activities once considered primarily local. They are, however, a decentralized mechanism, exhibiting considerable diversity; they thus can reflect regional variations in needs and values. As a result of their location in the judicial system,

> they enforce national policies [but] also mediate between national law and various political and professional constituencies in regional communities. . . . As intermediates in many dimensions of responsibility, they look down to district courts and agencies, up to the Supreme Court and the central goverment, in to themselves, their colleagues and staffs, across to rival appellate courts, and all around to various groups and individuals who compose their attentive publics.[15]

There are now twelve U.S. Courts of Appeals—eleven numbered circuits and one for the District of Columbia—with general appellate jurisdiction, in addition to the specialized Court of Appeals for the Federal Circuit and a Temporary National Emergency Court of Appeals (see page 46). Except for the District of Columbia Circuit, each court of appeals covers several states. The courts range in size from the First Circuit (Massachusetts, New Hampshire, Maine, Rhode Island, and Puerto Rico), the smallest with four judgeships, to the Ninth (Alaska, Hawaii, California, Oregon, Washington, Idaho, Montana, Nevada, and Arizona, plus Guam and the Northern Marianas), with 23 judgeships. Until 1980, when the Fifth Circuit (the Deep South) was divided into the Fifth and Eleventh Circuits, no new circuit had been created since the mid-1920s, when the Tenth Circuit (the Rocky Mountain states) was carved out of the Eighth Circuit, which at the time extended westward from the Mississippi River.

Division of the Fifth Circuit and failure to divide the Ninth Circuit both illustrate political aspects of structuring our judicial system. Prior to 1978, the Fifth Circuit had the largest number of judgeships (15) and it was to receive eleven more in 1978. Because a court of 26 judges was thought much too large, proposals were made to divide the circuit. However, enactment was delayed for several years—in fact, delaying passage of the Omnibus Judgeship Act until 1978—by resistance from the NAACP, concerned that a relatively liberal civil rights court would be broken up, and particularly from Senator James Eastland of Mississippi, then chairman of the Senate Committee on the Judiciary. Eastland insisted on having one circuit composed only of Texas and Louisiana, with Mississippi, Georgia, Alabama, and Florida in the other. Then came Eastland's announcement of retirement from the Senate, the appointment of some black judges, withdrawal of NAACP opposition, and support by Senator Edward Kennedy, the incoming committee chair, for a different division (adding Mississippi to Texas and Louisiana); this change of circumstance allowed the circuit division to occur.

The problem in the Ninth Circuit was, and is, how to divide the circuit to provide balanced caseloads without the unprecedented acts of splitting of a single state or leaving a one-state circuit. Because California generates roughly two-thirds of the Ninth Circuit's caseload and because dividing California between two circuits further raises the sticky political question of whether northern and southern California should become separate states, dividing the circuit has proved impossible. The circuit was, however, allowed to establish administrative units (divisions) to facilitate its work.

There are now 132 authorized judgeships for the courts of appeals, with 35 having been added by the 1978 Judgeship Act. (There are also 12 judges for the Court of Appeals for the Federal Circuit, a specialized court discussed later.) Assisting the circuit judges in deciding cases are the courts' *senior* (semiretired) *judges*, as well as district judges and judges from other circuits who sit "by designation." Most court of appeals cases are heard by three-judge panels of changing membership; a panel *is* the court of appeals for the cases it decides. A court of appeals sits *en banc*—that is, all of the court's judges sitting together—to hear particularly important cases, usually after a panel has heard the case. (A "short" *en banc* of some number less than the entire court is used in the Ninth Circuit because of its size.) A panel's ruling is supposed not to be overruled by another panel but only by the *en banc* court.

En banc sittings, which are relatively new, developed when the Supreme Court gave the appeals courts the responsibility for producing uniformity in legal matters within a circuit. Because bringing all members of an appeals court together prevents the judges from hearing cases in panels, thus slowing down the court's work, and may increase rather than decrease conflict, *en banc* sittings are not used frequently.

All the courts of appeals operate under the same Federal Rules of Appellate Procedure, but adopt separate Local Rules. This "power to define subsidiary rules lends surprisingly little standardization to internal decision making or administrative practice."[16] For example, the circuits vary in reliance on oral argument (the Second Circuit uses it in almost every case while other circuits dispense with it in a significant portion of cases) and use of summary dispositions (decisions without opinions or only very brief orders) to deal with their heavy caseloads.

Although all members of the Supreme Court live in one metropolitan area and work in the same courthouse, this is true for only two circuits (the Seventh and District of Columbia); judges in the other courts of appeals reside at various and often widely dispersed locations throughout the circuit, meeting face-to-face when hearing oral argument and discussing cases immediately thereafter, while relying heavily on mail and telephone for further discussion of cases and developing of opinions. This geographic dispersion, coupled with rotation of panel membership, large caseloads, and ideological differences, can contribute to inconsistency *within* a court of appeals, limiting the courts' ability to produce uniformity in national law.[17]

The recent growth in appeals court caseload has been phenomenal and disproportionate to the growth in district court caseload. More than 20,000 cases are docketed in the U.S. Courts of Appeals each year, an increase of over *400* percent from 1960 to 1980. Because of increased protection for defendants' rights, and the resultant availability of counsel for indigent defendants, in the courts of appeals, as in the district courts, criminal cases have accounted for the greatest growth in recent years; they now account for roughly one-third of the caseload in appeals courts. Because criminal appeals are expected to be handled expeditiously, greater attention to them may mean a delay in reaching and deciding other types of appeals. The recent increase in judges may help certain courts of appeals reduce backlogs temporarily. However, as a result of the additional district judgeships created at the same time, more decisions will be appealed; in addition, proportionately more cases may be appealed by litigants whose trials are more promptly terminated. The result will be a continuing heavy caseload for the appeals courts.

Cases from some federal agencies may go either to the appeals court in the circuit containing the site of the controversy or to the Court of Appeals for the District of Columbia, the site of agency headquarters. Certain other cases—for example, radio and television station license renewal cases from the Federal Communications Commission (FCC) and certain Environmental Protection Agency (EPA) cases—must by statute be taken only to the District of Columbia Circuit, which thus has developed a particularly important role in reviewing agency decisions. This is but one example of a more general phenomenon seen also in the emphases on commercial litigation in the Second Circuit (New York) and on civil rights in the old Fifth Circuit: each court of appeals becomes "a magnet for certain subjects of federal law by virtue of location, special jurisdiction, and predilections," as well as differing propensities of attorneys and litigants to appeal different types of cases.[18]

Cases in the courts of appeals vary substantially in their complexity. Certain appeals are thought to be "frivolous," having little substance and not raising new issues. Many others are routine, and still other appeals are "ritualistic," brought because of the litigants' demands even when the likelihood of reversal of the district court is low. Only a relatively small proportion of cases involve "nonconsensual" appeals "which raise major questions of public policy and upon which there is considerable disagreement."[19] Among the nonconsensual appeals may be those in which "issue transformation" has taken place in the appeals court. Among those would be instances in which civil liberties issues were not an important part of the case at trial but became central in the appeal. Through such issue transformation, found in civil liberties cases and particularly in race relations cases in the Third, Fifth, and Eighth Circuits from 1956 through 1961, the appeals courts, which granted liberties denied in the district courts, enforced a more "national" and less local perspective.[20] However, an examination of all cases from the district courts up in the Second, Fifth, and District of Columbia Circuits in Fiscal Years 1965–1967 led to the conclusion that there was very little issue transformation. Only seven percent of the cases provided an indication that the two levels of judges defined the issues in cases differently. However, the appellate judges filtered issues as they moved up to the Supreme Court. This was part of the intermediate courts' "important functions as gatekeepers, directing traffic in the stream of federal appeals."[21]

The courts of appeals must hear all cases brought to them. The finality of decisions by these courts is particularly significant. Because very few cases are appealed to the Supreme Court and the Court rejects most certiorari petitions, in the great bulk of cases appeals court rulings are left as the final judicial statement. For example, in the Second, Fifth, and District of Columbia Circuits, only one in five decisions was appealed, with the Supreme Court granting review to only one-tenth of those—leaving over 98 percent of appeals court rulings as final. Because most of their actions are not disturbed, the appeals courts "*make* national law," although "residually and regionally," and the Supreme Court remains largely dependent on them to "enforce the supremacy and uniformity of national law," particularly in those areas of law in which undisturbed cases tend to cluster.[22] These include such important subjects as workmen's compensation and minimum wage, social security, insurance contracts, and even school desegregation. This means that "Courts of Appeals are mini-Supreme Courts in the vast majority of their cases," with a division of labor—or, in the economist's term, comparative advantage—having developed between the two levels. The Supreme Court concentrates on broader policy concerns; courts of appeals, on the other hand, "concentrate on statutory interpretation, administrative review, and error correction in masses of routine adjudication."[23]

Specialized Appeals Courts

In addition to the U.S. Courts of Appeals, there are some specialized appellate courts, just as there are specialized trial courts. Most notable has been the Court of Customs and Patent Appeals, which recently became part of the new Court of Appeals for the Federal Circuit. The CCPA, initially an Article I court, was created in 1910; its judges were given Article III (lifetime) status in 1948. The CCPA had appellate jurisdiction on matters of law over not only the Customs Court but also the Patent Office and Tariff Commission. That it was a specialized court may help us evaluate speculations and hypotheses that litigant interest groups, particularly if they are unified, have greater influence over such courts than over courts of general jurisdiction, so that specialist courts produce decisions different from those of generalist courts handling the same types of cases.

Until the mid-1950s, judges of the Court of Customs and Patent Appeals were nonspecialists not chosen from the patent bar, the lawyers who represent those seeking to obtain patents or defend patent holders against infringement of those patents. These nonspecialist judges tended to defer to Patent Office decisions denying patents because the Patent Office was an administrative agency. In the late 1950s, after the patent bar persuaded the president to appoint two patent attorneys to CCPA, the CCPA almost immediately changed direction. The court produced substantially more reversals of the Patent Office than earlier. After having had standards of patentability roughly comparable to those the district courts applied in cases involving issued patents, the CCPA became more lenient than the district courts. Although the CCPA's nonspecialist members reversed the Patent Office more than had their nonspecialist predecessors, they continued to be more deferential to the Patent Office than were the "specialist" judges. This history of the decisions of one specialized court does not allow us to say that specialized courts will invariably behave differently from general jurisdiction courts, but it does indicate that "specialization may create conditions," for example, success in getting certain people nominated, "that cause a court to take a distinctive path."[24]

Arguments for creating any specialized court were apparent in the recent move to centralize all patent appeals in one court. A principal argument—by attorneys and federal judges alike—for creating a specialized court for patent cases was that such cases are too technical for generalist judges. One response was that patent cases are no more complex than antitrust or environment cases. Another was that judges who hear only one type of case will lose perspective as they become divorced from developments in other fields of law and will become immune to subtleties in the cases before them. (When we discuss separate courts of criminal appeals—which some states have—we talk of judges becoming "case-hardened.")

The idea that patent appeals should be centralized bore fruit in 1981, when Congress created the Court of Appeals for the Federal Circuit from the Court of Claims and Court of Customs and Patent Appeals. The new court assumed the existing appellate jurisdiction of both the Court of Claims and the Court of Customs and

Patent Appeals, plus all appeals from the district courts in cases involving patents or monetary claims against the United States. In addition to hearing appeals in cases involving tort, contract, and eminent domain claims against the government and those involving claims for refunds of taxes, the court hears appeals from the Court of International Trade (formerly the Customs Court), the Patent and Trademark Office, and the Merit Systems Protection Board (created in the recent reorganization of the federal government's personnel system). Review from the court is on certiorari to the Supreme Court.

Perhaps the most significant part of the reorganization is that patent *appeals*, instead of being heard in several courts (the Court of Customs and Patent Appeals, the Court of Appeals for the District of Columbia—for certain types of cases, and other courts of appeals), are now centralized in one court. (Trials in patent cases still take place in the district courts.) By contrast, several paths remain for tax appeals: from the Claims Court to the Court of Appeals for the Federal Circuit, and from the Tax Court to the court of appeals to which a taxpayer would have taken an appeal from the district court; the result is several diverging bodies of tax law.

There have been other specialized appellate courts, but these have been staffed by Article III judges whose full-time positions are on other courts and who are appointed to the specialized courts by the Chief Justice. These include the Temporary National Emergency Court of Appeals for cases arising under the wage-price control and emergency petroleum allocation programs of the 1970s; the earlier Emergency Court of Appeals, established during World War II for wage-price cases, and a special court to handle problems under the Regional Rail Reorganization Act of 1973. (The Emergency Court of Appeals' exclusive appellate jurisdiction over decisions by the price administrator was upheld by the Supreme Court in *Yakus v. United States* in 1944.) An earlier experiment with a specialized court to hear cases from a single administrative agency—the Commerce Court, to hear cases from the Interstate Commerce Commission—was abandoned in 1913 after only a few years because the railroads preferred to deal with the ICC, shippers didn't like interference with the commission, and Congress saw a threat from the court to the commission, which it saw as more its own arm.[25]

There is also the three-judge Foreign Intelligence Surveillance Court of Review, to review applications for electronic surveillance denied by the Foreign Intelligence Surveillance Court (see page 41). Another such court, known as the Special Division of the United States Court of Appeals for the District of Columbia Circuit, has the task of designating special prosecutors called for under the Ethics in Government Act of 1978 in cases involving the president, vice-president, and other high government officials. One of its judges, who have two-year appointments, must be from the D.C. Circuit, with priority given to senior circuit judges and retired Supreme Court justices.

There is only one Article I specialized appeals court, the Court of Military Appeals, created in 1950 under congressional power to provide for the armed forces. Its three civilian judges, of whom no more than two may be of one party, serve for staggered fifteen-year terms. In applying the revised Uniform Code of Military Justice (UCMJ), they must review courts-martial decisions involving general or flag officers, capital punishment decisions affirmed by the Boards of Review in the military services, and cases the service judge advocate generals (JAG) certify for review. Its principal business, however, is discretionary review of courts-martial decisions involving bad-conduct discharges and prison sentences of more than one year. It considers such cases if a Board of Review approves a petition by the convicted person, granting approximately 10 percent of the petitions and denying the others without explanation. The Supreme Court may review the court's decisions only on habeas corpus as to the limited question of whether the military had jurisdiction over the court-martialed person, but in such rulings the Court has handed down important decisions concerning the military's authority to court-martial civilians or military personnel involved in nonservice-connected offenses.[26]

The National Court of Appeals

Problems generated by increased caseload in both the Supreme Court and courts of appeals, coupled with Chief Justice Burger's greater attention to administrative matters, led to the first serious structural examination of the national court system since the 1920s and to proposals to restructure that system. The basic change proposed would create a new federal appellate court located between the U.S. Courts of Appeals and the Supreme Court.

The first major proposal, recommended by a study group appointed by Chief Justice Burger and chaired by Harvard Law School Professor Paul Freund, called in 1973 for a National Court of Appeals, a "mini-Supreme Court," staffed by present appeals court judges on a rotating basis. The new court was to sort through the cases awaiting review by the Supreme Court and select roughly four hundred each year most worthy of the Supreme Court's attention. From these, the Supreme Court was to select 120 to 150 cases to which it would give full-dress treatment. The new court's denials of review and its determinations of legal conflicts between the courts of appeals would have been final. This hotly contested proposal was shelved, largely because it would have deprived the Supreme Court of considerable power through its finality of denials of review.

Then in 1975 the Commission on Revision of the Federal Court Appellate System, created by Congress, made recommendations based on its examination of the national court system's capacity for "declaring and defining the national law." If such capacity was to be increased without simultaneously increasing the diversity of legal interpretations, the commission thought such methods as appointment of additional judges, creation of new appeals court circuits, a changed basis of federal court jurisdiction, and new methods for disposing of caseload would be insufficient. Thus it proposed a National Court of Appeals of several judges to be appointed by the president. The new court would receive cases in two ways, as shown in the right-hand portion of Figure 2.2. (Movement of cases under the earlier proposal is shown on the left-hand side of the figure.) The Supreme Court could send cases before deciding them ("reference jurisdiction") and the courts of appeals would send them

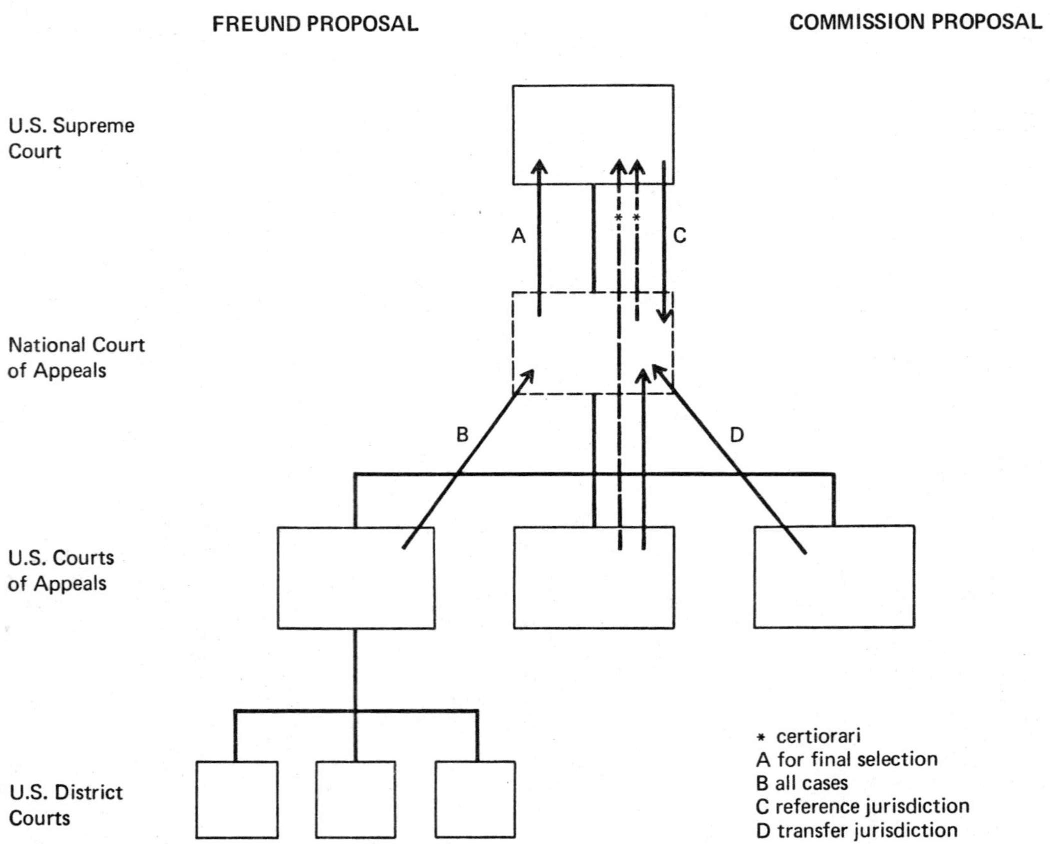

FIGURE 2.2 National Court of Appeal Proposals

when a rule of federal law was applicable to recurring factual situations or when federal courts had reached inconsistent decisions on a rule of federal law ("transfer jurisdiction"). The new court could refuse to accept cases, a decision which would not be reviewable, but its decisions of cases on the merits could be reviewed by the Supreme Court on certiorari.

This proposal received more substantial support than the Freund Study Group proposal had received, but it also was not enacted. Creation of the Court of Appeals for the Federal Circuit, discussed previously, did come as part of an effort to salvage some part of the proposal. The National Court of Appeals idea surfaced again in 1982 when Justice Stevens, asserting that the Supreme Court was not adequately handling its growing caseload, endorsed the idea of a National Court of Appeals that would screen cases on their way to the Supreme Court; this was the strongest support yet given the Freund group's proposal. Justice Brennan immediately attacked Justice Stevens' proposal sharply, as destroying the Supreme Court's role. For the first time, however, Brennan agreed that something had to be done about workload, such as Justice White's far more limited proposal for appellate courts with national jurisdiction over particular types of cases in order to avoid intercircuit conflicts on legal questions.[27] Then, in his early 1983 State of the Judiciary address to the American Bar Association, the Chief Justice renewed his call for a National Court of Appeals. In this most recent version of his proposal, he suggested that such a court—staffed by judges drawn from the existing courts of appeals—be established on an experimental basis for five years. The court would have the authority to decide cases in which the courts of appeals had reached conflicting positions, and review of their decisions (if necessary) could be sought in the Supreme Court. At the same time, a new commission would be appointed to study the need for additional national appellate capacity and would monitor the work of the new court.

Still another proposal for change, by Arizona Chief Justice James Duke Cameron, deals with conflicts between state high courts on important federal law questions and the delay in their resolution by the federal courts. A National Court of *State* Appeals, composed of nine Article III judges, would be established instead of, not in addition to, the National Court of Appeals. This court could have original but discretionary jurisdiction to review state court civil and criminal decisions in which federal questions were raised and in which state remedies had been exhausted; its rulings would be reviewable in the U.S. Supreme Court on certiorari. Perhaps most significant would be the court's exclusive original jurisdiction over federal court cases challenging state court decisions (see pages 141–142), thus "completely divest[ing] the federal district courts of jurisdiction to review decisions of state courts on federal constitutional questions."[28]

JUDICIAL ADMINISTRATION

Judicial administration is a low-visibility activity, yet neither any single court nor the judicial system as a whole could function without it. It encompasses activities related to processing cases, the judicial branch's personnel needs, budgeting for the judiciary, planning, and research. The federal courts' increasing caseload and Chief Justice Burger's efforts have focused more attention on judicial administration and have helped produce a greater desire to shift from haphazard, inefficient management to more organized and "professional" administration.

For many years, little attention was given even to the selection, retention, and supervision of personnel necessary to make the courts operate effectively, despite the number of people working in the federal judicial branch—in 1979 over 12,500 people, an increase of well over 100 percent since 1960. Hiring of administrative personnel was essentially a matter of judges' patronage and was unsystematic. This was certainly true with respect to the clerks of court, until recently fully responsible for administering court activities. Similarly, court reporters, who record and transcribe what is said in court, were not hired by the courts on a uniform basis until 1944; before then, most courts left it to the litigants to arrange for private reporters.

Before more attention was paid to such personnel who serve the court as an institution, some concern was shown about the law clerks, who serve not as administrators but as research assistants and opinion drafters for the judges. Usually recent top-ranked law school graduates, they serve for a year or at most two. There are now roughly 700 law clerks assisting federal judges. In addition, the courts of appeals are hiring staff attorneys who work for the court as a whole; there are now over 130 of them, whereas twenty years ago there were none. Despite their importance to the performance of judges' tasks, law clerks did not appear on a salaried basis until the mid-1940s in the district courts.

From the early years, the Chief Justice "received information on the state of judicial business in the far-flung districts."[29] Only in the twentieth century has serious and protracted attention been given to problems of judicial administration; two Chief Justices—William Howard Taft (1921–1929) and Warren Burger—have played particularly important roles. Burger is not only the first "Chief" since Taft to devote considerable effort to matters of judicial administration, particularly in the federal judiciary, but also, taking seriously his official title of Chief Justice *of the United States,* has been active in efforts to improve judicial administration in the states as well.

The range of Burger's activities is even greater than Taft's: he has made speeches to call attention to problems, such as those concerning the training of lawyers; has helped create institutions to assist in training court personnel for both federal and state courts; and is the first Chief Justice to appoint an administrative assistant to assist him with his administrative tasks for both the Court and the judicial system as a whole. Although he has had less direct contact with the executive branch and Congress than did Taft, his efforts have led to annual meetings among leaders of the judicial, legislative, and executive branches to discuss administration of justice issues.[30]

The basic units involved in administering the federal judicial system are the Judicial Conference of the United States, the Administrative Office of the United States

Courts, and the circuit councils. All were established relatively late in the national judicial system's history, largely as a result of judicial and administrative politics. Perhaps the primary reason was that federal judges wished to retain their independence both of each other and of any central authority. Their resistance, which includes lobbying of members of Congress by judges seeking support for their own policies, made it difficult to establish even something seemingly as simple as uniform personnel and salary systems for the federal courts. Pressure has nonetheless been substantial to make the courts' internal operations administratively efficient so that the courts might be more effective in performing their functions. Reformers have sought to improve court administration through "centralization, bureaucratization, and professionalization of judicial administration . . . at the expense of judicial informality and autonomy." Such trends, "accelerated by the law explosion," are "rooted in external demands for efficiency, fiscal accountability, and professional standards of personnel management."[31]

The difficulty in bringing about effective, rational management of the federal court system is demonstrated by the problems in developing methods for assignment of judges to handle cases where their help is needed. Until 1850, a federal judge could not sit outside his district. After 1850, he could be assigned only to a court within his own or a contiguous circuit—and only to help a sick or disabled judge. In the early twentieth century, the Chief Justice could ask that a judge serve elsewhere, but the chief judge of the judge's circuit could refuse the request—and did so. Judges, as a result of their primarily local or state orientation, did not see themselves as part of a national judicial system.

Problems surrounding intercircuit assignment of judges have changed—it is not as easy to block requested transfer—but have not disappeared. If all courts have crowded dockets, it is difficult to find anyone except senior judges to assist with particularly overloaded districts. Yet, despite Chief Justice Taft's support for the idea, a "pool" or "flying squadron" of federal judges available for assignment anywhere in the system has never been established on a *regular* basis, although, after elimination of the Commerce Court, its five judges were available for assignment to trial or appellate work throughout the country, and those senior judges who are willing can be assigned around the country, not just in their own circuit.[32]

Circuit Councils

The basic administrative unit of the federal judicial system is supposed to be the judicial *council* in each circuit. (Each circuit also has a judicial *conference*, which includes district judges and lawyer representatives, which meets once a year and may consider a wide range of matters.) Until 1981 the circuit judicial council was composed of all circuit judges on active-duty status, in effect, the *en banc* court of appeals wearing administrative rather than judicial hats. Legislation effective in 1981 affected the councils' responsibilities for judicial conduct (see pages 73–74) and also changed their structure by adding district judges. No longer are all the circuit judges automatically members of the council, although all active-duty circuit judges by majority vote determine council membership. They decide the number of circuit judges and, within a statutory formula, the number of district judges who would compose the council, which is chaired by the circuit's chief judge. (The chief judge of a circuit or district has been the most senior judge of the court under the age of 70. Under new legislation, a chief judge may serve for only seven years, and a judge cannot become a chief judge after age 64 unless no one else is eligible.) Nine of the twelve circuits chose to have all circuit judges serve on their new councils. The number of district judges ranges from two to six; specific arrangements for their choice vary among the circuits, with membership usually being rotated among a circuit's districts.

Among the councils' wide range of powers are approving judicial accommodations, directing where court records should be kept, and performing other "housekeeping" tasks; consenting to the assignment of judges to courts in other circuits and dividing judicial business in the districts if the district judges cannot agree among themselves; and the far more sensitive business of certifying to the president that because of disability a judge is unable to discharge his duties. The council also receives reports from the Administrative Office on the dockets in the circuit's courts and is supposed to take appropriate action on the basis of those reports.

The circuit councils are assisted in carrying out their tasks not only by clerks of courts, who generally focus on day-to-day processing of cases, but also by specially trained *circuit executives*, who assist the chief judge and the circuit council with general administration of the circuit and with special projects. Some circuits have made substantial use of their circuit executives, but experience over ten years shows clearly that more than appointing someone with such a title is necessary to solve administrative problems. Chief judges' inability to delegate responsibility to circuit executives, the executives' involvement in detail, and conflict between the executive and clerk of court—who increasingly is also likely to be well trained—are principal difficulties.[33]

One reason for establishing the circuit councils was to decrease the chance of an attack on the central judicial establishment in Washington. Yet diffusing responsibility among all the judges of the circuit often led to a lack of willingness to act on important matters or to exercise authority, perhaps because the councils "are required . . . to consider the behavior of judges with whom they interact on a judicial and sometimes even personal basis." For this reason and because the councils are more attached "to the ideal of local self-government and an independent judiciary,"[34] the circuit councils have played a less important role than the national Judicial Conference.

Judicial Conference

Establishment in 1922 of the Judicial Conference—originally the Conference of Senior Circuit Judges—was the first official manifestation that authority in the federal judicial system was being centralized. Chaired by the Chief Justice, the Judicial Conference consists of the chief judges of the courts of appeals and a district judge from each circuit; district judges were not part of the original membership. The new subsequently invalidated bankruptcy statute placed two bankruptcy judges on the Conference, but the House version of the bill—which gave the bankruptcy judges Article III status—would have placed one from each circuit on the Conference, adding an additional ten members. The Chief Justice has wielded significant authority in the Judicial Conference's work. That authority, initially enhanced because he had to speak for the Conference between meetings, was later strengthened because only he, and not the other justices, participated in the Conference.

The Conference was created to be the chief administrative policy maker for the federal judiciary but "constituted only a first step toward a more integrated administrative system."[35] At first it operated mainly by tying the senior circuit judges into a national communications network. However, it never developed the predominance for which it was intended. Its potential strength was reduced by its infrequent meetings and the later development of committees, which proliferated and became more important under Chief Justice Stone. (There are almost twenty standing committees plus assorted other groups.) Development of the committees left the Conference largely as a ratifying body for committee-recommended policies. Such policies covered a wide variety of matters, such as rules of evidence and procedure for the federal courts, the intercircuit transfer of judges, and the need for additional judges to deal with the ever-growing caseload of the federal courts. Although the growth of committees did serve to decrease the power of the Conference itself, its authority has remained substantial, and it has dealt with matters such as ethical standards for judges and other court personnel, qualifications for those personnel, bankruptcy administration, and most important, the budget for the federal judiciary. Because of the importance of the issues with which the Conference and its committees deal, pressure has recently been brought to bear to open up the process by which Conference policy is made. Sunshine legislation has been introduced in Congress to require the Conference and its committees and subcommittees, as well as circuit judicial councils, to hold public meetings to transact business.

Encompassed in the committees' work is the development of legislation to be submitted to Congress. The judges representing the Conference and its committees and the Director of the Administrative Office present legislative proposals to Congress. This allows the Chief Justice to stay away from a direct role in that area, which can cause trouble. When Director of the Administrative Office Rowland Kirks, in the company of an interest group lobbyist, visited Speaker of the House Carl Albert in late 1972 about a bill concerning product safety, Chief Justice Burger was accused of sending a lobbyist to argue against the bill. Denying the charge, the Chief Justice said his only concern was the bill's possible effect on the court system—part of his desire for "court impact statements." Another example of the difficulty into which the Chief Justice can get himself in acting for the Conference occurred in 1978 during final stages of consideration of the new bankruptcy statute. Before either House or Senate passed its version of the bill, Chief Justice Burger reportedly made telephone calls to several legislators asking that consideration of the bills be delayed until certain issues could be explored further and the Judicial Conference's opinion on compromise legislation heard. Although his position was based on Conference opposition to giving bankruptcy judges Article III status and having bankruptcy appeals go directly to the courts of appeals, Burger's reported anger—for example, in a call to the Senate subcommittee chairman in charge of the legislation—particularly irritated some members of Congress, who felt that the Chief Justice was going far beyond his proper role and exceeding the powers of the judicial branch.

The Administrative Office and the Department of Justice

From its creation in 1870, the Department of Justice performed day-to-day administrative tasks for the federal courts. The department's involvement was not ended by the formation of the Judicial Conference. Pervasive conflict over administration has taken place between the department and individual judges. Department field auditors visiting judicial districts to look over books, records, and accounts performed "a communication function as well as an investigative one."[36] However, clerks of court resisted department demands for the reporting of financial transactions. Despite such opposition, the department increased its control over district court clerks and their deputies in 1919, courts of appeals clerks in 1922, and the probation service in 1925. Yet obtaining statutory authority over particular functions did not lessen the need for the department to fight to obtain actual control, and its failure to submit recommendations of the Conference of Senior Circuit Judges to Congress or to support them when submitted did not win the judges' favor.

Considerable change in the administrative center of gravity for the federal judicial system occurred in 1939. In his "Court-packing" plan, President Roosevelt, proposing to reform judicial functioning, had suggested that a proctor (court administrator) be appointed for the Supreme Court. Although the plan to "pack" the Court was defeated, Congress did establish the Administrative Office of the Courts (A.O.). Its director is appointed by the Supreme Court. The provision that the director of the A.O. would perform duties assigned by the Supreme Court and the Judicial Conference acting together has, however, served to reduce the administrative role of the Supreme Court as a whole, although the Chief Justice has continued to be important after the director is named. This is true even when a Chief Justice like Earl Warren gives the director a relatively free hand, and is particularly true where there is a close working relationship, as there has been between Chief Justice Burger and the director.

When the A.O. was first established, members of the Judicial Conference acted to limit the authority of the office and its director. It was the Conference's intent that the A.O. be "an executive office with strictly limited power," dealing with judges and other court personnel only upon authorization of the Conference, circuit councils, or individual courts, and performing housekeeping functions for the courts without employing the courts' personnel. However, the A.O. has often initiated policies later considered by the Conference and its recommendations have carried great weight.[37]

The Administrative Office took over most functions the Justice Department had performed plus others that the department had not performed. The A.O. has the duty to compile suggested budgets and prepare vital statistics, examine dockets, determine personnel needs and procure supplies, and carry out additional tasks the Supreme Court or the Judicial Conference assigns, for example, establishing federal public defender systems to implement the Criminal Justice Act. The A.O. also serves as the secretariat for the Judicial Conference and its committees and as the liaison between the judiciary and Congress, individual judges, professional organizations, and other government agencies. As a result of the establishment (in 1976) of a Legislative Affairs Office, the A.O. has been able to focus its responsibilities for legislation better and to go beyond information-gathering to supplying of information and helping to resolve problems that develop during the process of enacting legislation affecting the judiciary.

The Federal Judicial Center is the most recently created (1967) element in federal judicial administration. It was set up to meet research and educational needs of the judiciary. Among the tasks that it has undertaken have been testing calendaring procedures and means of transmitting judicial documents. The Center has studied the basic elements of the court system and such matters as case screening, delays in the filing of transcripts, and case management. It has prepared a manual for complex and multidistrict litigation and a "bench book" for judges, and has conducted seminars and other training programs for newly appointed judges, magistrates, and probation officers.

THE SUPREME COURT

We are so accustomed to a United States Supreme Court of nine justices that altering that number would be extremely difficult. The Constitution provides for a Supreme Court but does not designate its size, which was six at first. The number of justices fluctuated until well after the Civil War as presidents left seats vacant (Lincoln did so with three seats) and Congress ordered positions not to be filled (during Reconstruction) or increased the number (to ten during the Civil War). In his "Court-packing" plan of 1937, President Franklin Roosevelt would have added a justice for each one over the age of seventy who did not retire. Chief Justice Hughes helped defeat the proposal with a statement to Congress that a Court of more than nine justices would be unwieldy and that the Court could not divide into panels or "divisions" to hear cases, as some state high courts do, because the Constitution speaks of "one Supreme Court."

Law Clerks

The nine justices are assisted by law clerks: all but two justices now have four, with Justice Rehnquist using only three and Justice Stevens only two. Because the usual clerkship is only one year—although Justice White has begun a practice of keeping one of his four clerks for a second year—the Court has now also hired some career law clerks to provide expertise and continuity. Like the selection process for the

Court's other staff members, regular government civil service procedures are not used to fill clerkships. Justices use several methods for selecting clerks. Some have depended on law school professors to make the selections; others enlist former clerks to screen candidates but make the final selection themselves.

The position of law clerk is highly prized, not only for the position itself and the contact with a justice it provides, but also for the opportunities it can open after the clerkship is completed. Those selected have, for the most part, been law review editors at the most prestigious law schools and have served as a clerk for a U.S. court of appeals (or less frequently, district court) judge immediately prior to the Supreme Court clerkship. There have been few black or female law clerks. Despite the Court's ruling in *Davis v. Passman* (1980) that the Constitution makes members of Congress subject to suit for racial and gender discrimination in hiring, the Court is not subject to employment discrimination rules, and its work force is disproportionately white and male.

Clerks perform a variety of tasks for the justices. They summarize petitions for review; they examine briefs and court records filed in cases; and, perhaps most important, they draft opinions. The extent of their input depends on the justice for and with whom they work; clerks in some chambers are able to offer ideas in addition to performing more basic writing tasks. Clerks also serve as a means of communication between justices' chambers, but have been expected to restrict their discussion of cases to their contacts with other clerks. Erosion of this expectation was quite evident in Woodward and Armstrong's *The Brethren*, based largely on revelations by present and former law clerks.

Whatever the relationship—and no matter how much substance the clerks contribute to opinions—the *justices*, not the clerks, are definitely in charge, as Justice Rehnquist (once Justice Robert Jackson's clerk) stated. He did assert, however, that the clerks' political orientations were more liberal than the justices' and affected the cases the clerks recommended the Court take for review.[38]

Original Jurisdiction

The Supreme Court's appellate jurisdiction is open-ended, subject to modification by Congress. Only the Court's original jurisdiction—cases brought to it directly—is detailed in the Constitution. (See Art. III, Sec. 2.) The Court's original jurisdiction accounts for only a very small proportion of its workload; there have been only approximately 150 such cases decided in the Court's history. The Court itself said in *Marbury v. Madison* that original jurisdiction was limited to the subjects designated in Article III. More important, the Court often changes its original jurisdiction into appellate jurisdiction by sending cases brought as original jurisdiction cases to the district court first. When the justices do accept an original jurisdiction case, and it cannot be resolved on the pleadings alone, they appoint a special master (often a senior federal judge) to hear testimony and to make findings and recommendations, which the justices decide to accept, modify, or reject after hearing from the lawyers.

In this way, the justices act, as usual, in an appellate capacity, with the master really serving as a trial judge.

> In all cases affecting ambassadors, other public ministers and consuls, and those in which a state shall be a party, the supreme court shall have original jurisdiction. In all the other cases before mentioned, the supreme court shall have appellate jurisdiction, both as to law and fact, with such exceptions and under such regulations as the Congress shall make. (Art. III, Sec. 2)

The Court's avoidance of original jurisdiction cases can be seen in some recent environmental litigation. When Ohio tried to invoke the Court's original jurisdiction for a case against companies for mercury pollution of Lake Erie, the justices ruled that Ohio state courts could decide the case under local law. Similarly when Illinois sued the city of Milwaukee for polluting Lake Michigan, the justices said the case could be tried on nuisance law in the lower federal courts, but subsequently the Court ruled that Congress' later passage of water pollution laws eliminated the need for such a federal court decision.[39]

Such rulings leave only cases between two states—for example, over boundaries or water allocation—or between a state and the national government for the Court's original jurisdiction. The suits by states to test the validity of the 1965 Voting Rights Act (*South Carolina v. Katzenbach*) and its 1970 successor (*Oregon v. Mitchell*) are examples of the latter. Yet even when two states are involved, the Court may try to send cases elsewhere, as it did when Arizona sued New Mexico over the latter's tax on electrical energy generation; all interests, said the Court, would be protected by a state court case filed by the affected utilities, and the Court has said that "the issue of appropriateness in an original action between the States must be determined on a case-by-case basis."[40]

Appellate Jurisdiction

The Constitution makes the Supreme Court's appellate jurisdiction, which accounts for the bulk of the Court's work, relatively open-ended and subject to modification by Congress (see pages 246–248). The Supreme Court long had to hear all cases appealed to it, at least if they fell within the Court's jurisdiction; the cases came to the Court on a *writ of error*. Now almost all cases come to the Court in one of two ways—*appeal* and *certiorari*. After the present courts of appeals were established, the Supreme Court was provided authority to pick and choose the cases it would hear, that is, its certiorari jurisdiction, which now accounts for the great majority of its cases. Litigants with cases in the Court's certiorari jurisdiction that they wish the Supreme Court to hear file a petition for a writ on certiorari, which is an order to a lower court to send up the records in a case; when the Court issues the writ, it has accepted the case.

Certiorari jurisdiction, initiated in 1914, was first restricted to state court decisions *favoring* rights claimed under federal law. Two years later, the Court's writ of error jurisdiction for appeals from state court decisions *denying* federal rights was curtailed. Cases in which a state court has decided against the validity of a federal law or federal authority, or in favor of the validity of a state law that had been challenged as inconsistent with federal law, remained in the Court's mandatory jurisdiction but other cases involving the denial of federal rights were shifted to the Court's certiorari jurisdiction. Because only state court decisions denying federal rights—not favoring them—were reviewable in the Supreme Court prior to 1914, the result was to increase the Supreme Court's jurisdiction but mostly on the discretionary (certiorari) rather than mandatory side. As noted earlier, the full growth of the Court's certiorari jurisdiction did not come until the Judges Bill of 1925. Among the categories of cases within that jurisdiction are state court "federal question" decisions favorable to the federal claim, for example, when a state law is invalidated under the Supremacy Clause, and decisions by the U.S. courts of appeals interpreting or applying the Constitution, treaties, and federal laws or holding that state laws or constitutional provisions are *not* contrary to federal law.

The other principal category of the Supreme Court's appellate jurisdiction, cases brought on *appeal,* is in theory mandatory, that is, the Court must hear all cases in this category. However, the justices have made this jurisdiction largely discretionary (see page 154). Cases eligible for appeal encompass decisions in which:

- the highest state court invalidates a federal law or treaty as unconstitutional or upholds a state law or state constitutional provision against a challenge that it violates a federal law, treaty, or the U.S. Constitution;
- a U.S. court of appeals declares a state law or constitutional provision unconstitutional or declares a federal law unconstitutional when the federal government is a party to a case;
- a federal district court declares a federal law unconstitutional, again when the United States is a party; or
- a three-judge district court (see page 35) has granted or denied an injunction in cases required to be brought before such a court.

Quite infrequently, the Court receives a case on *certification.* Here the lower court, faced with a new legal question, instead of resolving the case "certifies" the question for answer by the Supreme Court. If the Supreme Court accepts the certificate, the justices answer the question, and the court that certified the question then applies the answer to decide the case. (We might call this "upward" certification; for "downward" certification, a procedure for federal courts to send cases to state courts, see page 139.)

Supervisory Power

As the highest court in the federal court system, the Supreme Court affects rulings of the lower courts not only through its interpretations of statutes or the Constitution but also by exercising *supervisory power* over the lower federal courts. Some of the

Court's decisions on procedural matters are based on this power. A well-known example is *Mallory v. United States* (1957), holding that a suspect must be taken promptly before a magistrate for arraignment rather than being held by the police so they could obtain a confession. Because this ruling was based on the supervisory power rather than the Constitution, it was not applicable to the states through the Fourteenth Amendment.

Such exercises of the supervisory power illustrate another element of the Supreme Court's work: its role in the development of the procedural rules for the federal judiciary. Rules are developed only occasionally through cases. More complete sets of rules—the Federal Rules of Criminal Procedure, Civil Procedure, Evidence, Appellate Procedure, and Bankruptcy—are promulgated by the Court under a grant of authority from Congress. The Court does not itself develop the rules; an advisory committee, or more recently a committee of the Judicial Conference, prepares them, the Conference adopts them, and the Supreme Court then issues them. The statute granting the rule-making authority provides that the rules go into effect unless disapproved by Congress, with ninety days having been the period usually designed for congressional action.

Justices Black and Douglas often criticized the Supreme Court's involvement in the promulgation of the rules. They felt that the Court should restrict itself to deciding cases, and that because the Court could not give full consideration to the Conference-proposed rules, the Conference itself should have full power to promulgate them. There have also been occasional disagreements by some of the justices with the substance of the Rules transmitted to Congress. For example, when amendments to the Federal Rules of Civil Procedure affecting pretrial discovery were transmitted to Congress in 1980, Justices Powell, Stewart, and Rehnquist stated that the proposed changes were insufficient to bring about needed changes in civil lawsuits; they feared that acceptance of these rules would deter consideration of more thorough and more effective reforms.

For years, Congress accepted new Court-announced procedural rules without debate. However, when the Supreme Court announced new Federal Rules of Evidence in 1972, Congress, because of substantive disagreement over a number of the rules that embodied noticeable change from the past, delayed the effective date, subjected the rules to section-by-section reconsideration, and enacted them only in 1975. At the same time, Congress doubled the ninety-day "waiting period" for congressional consideration of the evidence rules and provided that each house of Congress could extend that period for a specified time or until the rules were specifically approved by legislation. Congress also postponed for a year the effective date for the Federal Rules of Criminal Procedure, a further indication that in the future the Court would have less freedom to make the rules for the federal judiciary.

Judicial Review

What makes the Supreme Court particularly important is the power of *judicial review*—the power to invalidate acts of Congress, the executive branch, and state and local governments. The Court itself developed this power, which is not mentioned in the Constitution. All courts in the United States may exercise judicial review, but the Supreme Court, because of its position, has the final judicial word on matters of judicial review concerning the United States Constitution.

Judicial review in the United States had several sources; the idea was not wholly original. Its establishment and development were affected by philosophical views on such matters as the distribution and separation of powers that influenced the Founding Fathers. Also relevant, although not determinative, was the practice concerning the review of decisions made in the American colonies. "Conformity clauses" in state charters required acts of the colonial legislatures to conform to the laws of England. They gave the king's Privy Council and its Committee on Appeals the power to disallow the legislation—power exercised in fact by the Board of Trade. Such action was, however, review without a written constitution, which England did not have, so that it did not lead those in the colonies to associate judicial review with a written constitution. Decisions of the courts in the colonies could also be appealed to the Privy Council when the royal governor granted a request to appeal. Here the Committee on Appeals often based its decisions on the colony's local law.

The Articles of Confederation did not establish judicial review, as the Articles contained no provision for a separate national judiciary. Congress became the court of last appeal, or the board of arbitration, for controversies between the states and for a limited number of cases involving individual rights. The Constitution's Supremacy Clause was anticipated, however, in the stipulation that the Articles and acts of Congress be accorded the status of law within the states:

> Every State shall abide by the determination of the United States in Congress assembled, on all questions which by this Confederation are submitted to them. And the Articles of this Confederation shall be inviolably observed by every State. (Art. XIII)

No plan submitted to the Constitutional Convention of 1787 conferred directly upon the judiciary any power of passing on the constitutionality of congressional acts. Under one major proposal—the Virginia Plan—there would have been a national court system whose judges would have been chosen by Congress. Congress would have had the right to disallow state legislation; a council of revision composed of the executive and a "convenient number" of the judiciary would have had a suspensive veto over national legislation. The major alternate plan made acts of Congress and treaties the "supreme law of the respective States." The state judiciary would be bound by congressional acts, notwithstanding state constitutional provisions. Because state courts would initially decide federal cases, the need for lower federal courts would be eliminated and the strength of the national government thus decreased. There would, however, be a supreme national tribunal, appointed by the executive. This court would have appellate jurisdiction in certain classes of cases coming from the state courts.

The Convention eliminated congressional disallowance of state legislation and judicial participation in the veto. Establishment of a Supreme Court was indicated, with Congress having the power to create lower federal courts. Although the jurisdiction of the courts generally and of the Supreme Court in particular was spelled out, and although supremacy of national law was established, not a word was said regarding the power of these federal courts to invalidate laws contrary to the Constitution. As with much of the rest of the document, the language was left general—perhaps a necessity if approval of the Constitution was to be obtained.

> This Constitution, and the Laws of the United States which shall be made in Pursuance thereof and all Treaties made, or which shall be made, under the Authority of the United States, shall be the supreme Law of the Land; and the Judges in every State shall be bound thereby, any Thing in the Constitution or Laws of any State to the Contrary notwithstanding. (Art. VI, cl. 2)

The leaders of the Constitutional Convention may not have foreseen that judges would engage in general expounding of the Constitution's meaning. However, they apparently did believe that the federal judiciary had the right to refuse to recognize unconstitutional federal law. Hamilton, Madison, and Jay, who wrote *The Federalist* papers to secure ratification of the Constitution in New York, argued strongly for judicial review. (They dealt summarily with the Supreme Court's right to overrule state legislation, thus indicating it was less of an issue, at least for them.) According to *The Federalist*, the Constitution as fundamental law was to be preferred when there was an irreconcilable variance between it and a legislative act, and the courts had a duty "to declare all acts contrary to the manifest tenor of the Constitution" void. There was, however, no direct empowerment to construe laws according to the Constitution's *spirit*. Judicial review was not an exercise of judicial power over the legislative branch. Instead, through judicial review the intention of the people—who ratified the Constitution—would be enforced against the intention of their agents, the legislators; the prior act of a superior authority would be preferred to the subsequent act of an inferior one.

The authors of *The Federalist* also noted that state judges were to be incorporated into the operation of the national government and would be bound by oath to support federal laws when those laws concerned legitimate and enumerated objects of federal jurisdiction. The Supremacy Clause was deemed imperative in helping produce needed uniform interpretation of federal law and treaties, as was national court jurisdiction and a supreme tribunal of last resort, because without appeal and review, state courts of final jurisdiction would produce an endless variety of decisions on the same point. So that all matters of national law would receive original or final determination in the national courts, appeal would run from state courts to either the federal district courts or the Supreme Court. However, in an appeal to states' rights interests, it was pointed out that the state courts—which would look beyond their own law in making decisions and would recognize relevant federal court rulings—would retain their former jurisdiction unless specifically limited by Congress, and that this system of initial state court determination with appeals from the state court to the federal courts would actually diminish the number of federal courts.

Judicial review of state decisions occurred before judicial review of national actions and, despite controversy, became firmly established earlier. In 1797, in *Ware v.*

Hylton, the Court held our treaty of peace with Great Britain superior to Virginia's statute sequestering property; the next year, in *Calder v. Bull,* the Court reviewed a state action challenged under the Ex Post Facto Clause, although it did not invalidate the statute in question. Twelve years later, in *Fletcher v. Peck,* stemming from the Yazoo land fraud case, the Court ruled a Georgia statute in violation of the Constitution.[41] The most severe early test of judicial review of state *court* decisions came when Virginia courts declared unconstitutional a provision of the federal Judiciary Act establishing appeal of state decisions affecting federal rights. Responding in *Martin v. Hunter's Lessee* (1816), Justice Joseph Story ruled that the U.S. Supreme Court had a right to review the decisions of state courts in order to produce uniform interpretation of the nation's "supreme law." Five years later, Virginia's claim that a criminal defendant's appeal from a state ruling violated state sovereignty—part of the early battle over "states' rights"—was rejected in *Cohens v. Virginia.* Chief Justice Marshall stated that the Supreme Court had the right to appellate jurisdiction over decisions of highest state courts in all questions of national power.

The need for uniform national interpretation of constitutional provisions has led to the feeling that the Supreme Court's power to review state decisions may be more important than its power over national government actions. As Justice Holmes put it, "I do not think the United States would come to an end if we lost our power to declare an act of Congress void. I do think the Union would be imperilled if we could not make that declaration as to the laws of the several states."[42] Throughout our history the Court has invalidated state laws more frequently than federal laws. Until the end of the Civil War, only two federal laws—but 60 state laws—were struck down. In the period from 1888 to 1937, over 400 state laws were invalidated, while only 70 national statutes were declared invalid. In the post-1937 period, well over 1,000 state laws were declared unconstitutional, but fewer than 75 federal laws (or portions of them) received such treatment.

The exercise of judicial review of state laws may be more readily accepted now than in the Court's earliest days, although particular rulings may be disputed. However, resistance to such judicial review *itself* still occurs at times. During the height of resistance to the Court's 1954 desegregation decision, Arkansas Governor Orval Faubus asserted that state governments were not bound by Supreme Court decisions because those decisions were not part of the "supreme law of the land." In the famous Little Rock case, *Cooper v. Aaron* (1958), the Supreme Court rejected this contention and stressed the supremacy of national law, *including* the Supreme Court's interpretation of it. More recently, when a federal judge's efforts to gain compliance with his orders concerning Native Americans' rights to their share of spawning fish (steelhead and salmon) encountered serious resistance from Washington State officials, the Supreme Court had to reiterate that a state's prohibition against compliance with a federal district court's decree could not survive under the Supremacy Clause.[43]

Judicial review of national government actions has been far more controversial. *Marbury v. Madison,* an 1803 case, was the first instance in which the Court invalidated a national statute, but the Court had earlier upheld a federal statute, an implicit recognition of judicial review. In 1796, in *Hylton v. U.S.*, the Court had reviewed an act of Congress imposing a carriage tax but, by ruling the tax not a direct one that would have had to be apportioned among the population, the Court did not have to rule on the statute's constitutionality. Four years earlier, in *Hayburn's Case* (1792) Chief Justice John Jay and four other justices had ruled that a statute subjecting Circuit Court decisions on individuals' eligibility for pension benefits to review by the Secretary of War and Congress was invalid because the courts' decisions were not final and thus were mere advisory opinions. However, this ruling came in Circuit Court decisions, not in a decision by justices sitting as the Supreme Court. Thus it was the *Marbury* decision that established judicial review. In the waning hours of the Federalist administration, Marbury had been appointed to a minor judicial position but had not received his commission. He sought a writ of mandamus from the Supreme Court to make the new Secretary of State, James Madison, hand over the commission. Chief Justice John Marshall, himself one of the last of the Federalist appointees, found that Marbury had a right to his commission and thus was entitled to a remedy. However, he ruled that the Court could not issue the requested writ because the Judiciary Act of 1789 unconstitutionally added to the Court's original jurisdiction:

> If congress remains at liberty to give this court appellate jurisdiction, where the Constitution has declared their jurisdiction shall be original; and original jurisdiction where the Constitution has declared it shall be appellate; the distribution of jurisdiction, made in the Constitution, is form without substance. . . .

Marshall thus gave himself an opportunity to lecture the Jeffersonians and established judicial review over acts of Congress, perhaps putting the administration on notice that future legislation might be declared unconstitutional.

Marshall's opinion is open to considerable criticism. Under today's standards, he would have withdrawn from the case because of his earlier involvement; as secretary of state, he had failed to deliver Marbury's commission. Had he followed usual procedure and looked first at whether the Court had jurisdiction, he could have invalidated the statute but could not have lectured the administration about not giving up the commission. More important, Marshall could have followed a rule of judicial self-restraint and construed the Act of 1789 to save its constitutionality by saying the items of original jurisdiction enumerated in the Constitution need not be exclusive but could be supplemented by Congress. Such criticisms, however, ignore the long-term implications of the case. The invalidation of the statute and what Marshall said about judicial review give the case its importance. Marshall insisted that the language of the Constitution be taken seriously. "It is a proposition too plain to be contested," he asserted, "that the constitution controls any legislative act repugnant to it; or that the legislature may alter the constitution by an ordinary act"; there were no other alternatives. The Constitution had to be either a "superior paramount law, unchangeable by ordinary means" or it was like any other law. But, Marshall said,

> Certainly, all those who have framed written constitutions contemplate them as forming the fundamental and paramount law of the nation, and consequently, the theory of every such government must be, that an act of the legislature repugnant to the constitution is void.

From this he concluded that the courts should invalidate the "repugnant" acts, giving the courts power over the other branches of government when constitutional questions were at issue.

This conclusion was not, however, the only one he could have reached. Judge Gibson of the Pennsylvania Supreme Court was later to say in *Eakin v. Raub* that the courts were limited to looking to see whether the legislature, in passing a law, had used the proper procedures because "the legislative organ is superior to every other, inasmuch as the power to will and command is essentially superior to the power to act and to obey." Judges implementing a law properly passed but in violation of the constitution were not, Gibson said, themselves committing an unconstitutional act but only doing what they were required to do.

It was, of course, Marshall's position, not Gibson's, that won the day. *Marbury* has come to stand for the Supreme Court's power—and by extension the power of other courts—to invalidate acts of Congress and the president. As Marshall asserted, in language the Court was again to use in *United States v. Nixon* in ruling that the president was not the sole judge of when he could invoke executive privilege:

> It is, emphatically, the province and duty of the judicial department, to say what the law is. Those who apply the rule to particular cases must of necessity expound and interpret that rule . . . . If a law be in opposition to the constitution; if both the law and the constitution apply to a particular case, so that the court must either decide that case, conformably to the law, disregarding the constitution, or conformably to the constitution, disregarding the law; the court must determine which of these conflicting rules governs the case; this is of the very essence of judicial duty.

Although judicial review was extended the year after *Marbury* to executive orders, in *Little v. Barreme*, the power was not used again until 1857, when the Court struck down congressional action concerning slavery in the territories in *Dred Scott v. Sandford*, only the first instance of national judicial review not dealing with strictly judicial matters. Perhaps in part because of the bad name given to judicial review of other branches of the national government by Chief Justice Taney's ruling in *Dred Scott* that slaves were not citizens and thus could not bring lawsuits, it became common only at the end of the nineteenth century. Because of this and the fact that it was not used frequently until the 1930s, we should remember Justice Cardozo's words: "The utility of an external power restraining the legislative judgment is not to be measured by counting the occasions of its exercise":[44] judicial review has become fully established. (For further discussion, see pages 219–224.)

NOTES

1. Julius Goebel, Jr., *History of the Supreme Court of the United States: Antecedents and Beginnings to 1801* (New York: Macmillan, 1971), p. 565.
2. See Joel Grossman and Austin Sarat, "Litigation in the Federal Courts: A Comparative Perspective," *Law & Society Review* 9 (1973):321–346.
3. *Thermtron Products v. Hermansdorfer*, 423 U.S. 336 (1976).
4. J. Woodford Howard, Jr., *Courts of Appeals in the Federal Judicial System: A Study of the Second, Fifth, and District of Columbia Circuits* (Princeton, N.J.: Princeton University Press, 1981), p. 34.
5. Ibid., p. 39.
6. Ibid., p. 34.
7. Ibid., p. 41.
8. See *Territory of Guam v. Olsen*, 431 U.S. 195 (1977).
9. This section, except for updating, draws extensively on Steven Puro, "United States Magistrates: A New Federal Judicial Officer," *Justice System Journal* 2 (Winter 1976):141–156. I wish to thank my former student Michael Wepsiec for assisting me in determining magistrates' present authority.
10. *Wingo v. Wedding*, 418 U.S. 461 (1974).
11. *United States v. Raddatz*, 447 U.S. 667 (1980).
12. *Mathews v. Weber*, 423 U.S. 261 at 272 (1976).
13. *Northern Pipeline Construction Co. v. Marathon Pipe Line Co.*, 102 S.Ct. 2858 (1982).
14. *Glidden v. Zdanok*, 370 U.S. 530 (1962).
15. Howard, pp. 20–21.
16. Ibid., p. 8.
17. See Stephen L. Wasby, "Communication Within the Ninth Circuit Court of Appeals: The View From the Bench," *Golden Gate University Law Review* 8 (1977):1–25; "Internal Communication in the Eighth Circuit Court of Appeals," *Washington University Law Quarterly* 58 (1980):583–605; and "Inconsistency in the United States Courts of Appeals: Dimensions and Mechanisms for Resolution," *Vanderbilt Law Review* 32 (November 1979):1343–1373.
18. Howard, p. 55.
19. Richard J. Richardson and Kenneth N. Vines, *The Politics of Federal Courts* (Boston: Little, Brown, 1970), pp. 118–119.
20. Ibid., pp. 127–129.
21. Howard, p. 42.
22. Ibid., pp. 3, 78.
23. Ibid., pp. 58, 76.
24. Lawrence Baum, "Judicial Specialization, Litigant Influence, and Substantive Policy: The Court of Customs and Patent Appeals," *Law & Society Review* 11 (Summer 1977): 845–846; see generally 833–846.
25. See Ellen R. Jordan, "Should Litigants Have a Choice Between Specialized Courts and Courts of General Jurisdiction," *Judicature* 66 (June–July 1982):14–27, for a discussion of this and other specialized courts.
26. See *Reid v. Covert*, 354 U.S. 1 (1957) (no courts-martial of wives of servicemen stationed overseas); *U.S.* ex rel. *Toth v. Quarles*, 350 U.S. 11 (1955) (ex-servicemen); *O'Callaghan v. Parker*, 395 U.S. 298 (1969) (non-service-connected offense). See also Norma G. Cooper

and John S. Cooke, "Military Justice: Marching to a Different Drumbeat," *American Bar Association Journal* 64 (September 1978):1363–1365.

27. John Paul Stevens, "Some Thoughts on Judicial Restraint," *Judicature* 66 (November 1982):177–183; William J. Brennan, Jr., "Some Thoughts on the Supreme Court's Caseload," *Judicature* 66 (December–January 1983):230–235.
28. James Duke Cameron, "Federal Review, Finality of State Court Decisions, and a Proposal for a National Court of Appeals—A State Judge's Solution to a Continuing Problem," *Brigham Young University Law Review* (1981):558.
29. Peter Graham Fish, *The Politics of Federal Judicial Administration* (Princeton, N.J.: Princeton University Press, 1973), p. 8. Fish's book is the source of much material for this section.
30. See Edward A. Tamm and Paul C. Reardon, "Warren E. Burger and the Administration of Justice," *Brigham Young University Law Review* (1981):447–521, particularly 452; and William F. Swindler, "The Chief Justice and Law Reform, 1921–1971," in *The Supreme Court Review*, ed. Phillip Kurland (Chicago: University of Chicago Press, 1971), pp. 241–264.
31. Howard, p. 275.
32. See Peter G. Fish, "Politics Rides the Circuits: State and National Itineracy," *Justice System Journal* 5 (Winter 1979):115–169.
33. See John T. McDermott and Steven Flanders, *The Impact of the Circuit Executive Act* (Washington, D.C.: Federal Judicial Center, 1979).
34. Fish, *The Politics of Federal Judicial Administration*, pp. 406, 308.
35. Ibid., p. 39.
36. Ibid., p. 93.
37. Ibid., p. 191.
38. William H. Rehnquist, "Who Writes Decisions of the Supreme Court?", *U.S. News & World Report* (December 13, 1957):74–75, reprinted in *The Courts: A Reader in the Judicial Process*, ed. Robert Scigliano (Boston: Little, Brown, 1962), pp. 166–169.
39. *Ohio v. Wyandotte Chemical*, 401 U.S. 493 (1971); *Illinois v. City of Milwaukee*, 406 U.S. 91 (1972); *City of Milwaukee v. Illinois and Michigan*, 451 U.S. 304 (1981).
40. *Maryland v. Louisiana*, 451 U.S. 725 at 744 (1981). See *Arizona v. New Mexico*, 425 U.S. 794 (1976) (parties' interests would be protected by state court lawsuit).
41. See C. Peter McGrath, *Yazoo: Law and Politics in the New Republic* (Providence, R.I.: Brown University Press, 1966).
42. Oliver Wendell Holmes, in *Collected Legal Papers* (New York: Harcourt, Brace, and Howe, 1920), p. 295.
43. *Washington v. Washington State Commercial Passenger Fishing Vessel Association*, 443 U.S. 658 (1979). Quoting the Ninth Circuit's opinion, the Court observed that, "except for some desegregation cases, . . . the district court has faced the most concerted official and private efforts to frustrate a decree of a federal court witnessed in this century." At 697.
44. Benjamin Cardozo, *The Nature of the Judicial Process* (New Haven: Yale University Press, 1921), p. 92.

Chapter 3

Judicial Selection

Federal judges—nominated by the president and confirmed by the Senate—are chosen by a political process involving both formal procedures and relatively well-defined patterns of participation by nongovernmental groups. Most nominees for federal judgeships are confirmed, but the process, particularly prior to nomination, can be far from routine, and rejections of nominations, even to the Supreme Court, indicate the importance of the process's nonformal aspects.

The Constitutional Convention debated several methods of selecting the justices. These included selection by the Senate alone, by the entire Congress, and by the executive alone. The method ultimately adopted was the one already in use in Massachusetts—nomination by the chief executive with the advice and consent of the Senate. However, the Constitution specifies no formal process by which the president is to choose those to be nominated. This leaves it to the executive, working with members of the Senate, to develop the process by which the name of a person reaches the stage at which it is to be sent to the Senate.

Usually a nominee to a federal judgeship does not assume office until after Senate confirmation of the nomination. However, the president may make a *recess appointment* to a vacant judgeship, allowing the person to take office immediately. Such appointments are valid, that is, the judge's salary may be paid, only under certain circumstances: if the vacancy occurred within the last thirty days of the Senate session or when the Senate was not in session; if the Senate rejected a nomination during the last thirty days of the session and the recess appointee is someone else; or if a nomination pending at the conclusion of a Senate session is not that of a previous recess appointee. Nominations of recess appointees must also be submitted to the Senate within forty days after the Senate's next session begins.

> The Judges, both of the Supreme and inferior Courts, shall hold their Offices during good Behaviour, and shall, at stated Times, receive for their Services, a Compensation, which shall not be diminished during their Continuance in Office. (Art. III, Sec. 1)

ATTRACTING, RETAINING, AND REMOVING JUDGES

In the Supreme Court's early years, presidents at times had difficulty obtaining men to serve as justices because of the job's lack of prestige. Some who did serve left the Court after brief service or simultaneously held other government jobs. Now, however, the position of justice of the Supreme Court is thought to be the highest to be attained in the legal profession and is likely to be accepted readily when offered—although apparently President Johnson's initial offer of a position was refused by Abe Fortas. Justices now only rarely leave the Court for other positions, and then only at the president's urging, for example, when James Byrnes became the president's special assistant during World War II and Arthur Goldberg became ambassador to the United Nations.

There are somewhat greater problems in attracting lower court judges and particularly in retaining them. The recent frequency of departure is certainly higher than it had been. Between 1970 and 1981, thirty federal judges (eight court of appeals judges and 22 district judges) resigned their positions. Three district judges were eligible for senior status but chose to resign instead; two were from the Canal Zone, where the district court was soon to be closed; and one was appointed senator. Most resigned to enter private law practice: of these, only one had more than ten years of service but seven had from five to ten years of service.

By comparison, only one of the eight resigning court of appeals judges had served for less then five years, and four had more than ten years' service each. Four of the appellate judges took major government positions. Judge Shirley Hufstedler of the Ninth Circuit, at the time the only woman federal appeals court judge, became Secretary of Education; Judge William Webster became Director of the FBI; Judge Wade McCree, then one of the few blacks on the federal appellate bench, became Solicitor

General; and Griffin Bell, with fifteen years' service on the Court of Appeals for the Fifth Circuit, became President Carter's Attorney General very shortly after resigning his judgeship. Of the remaining four, G. Harrold Carswell resigned after the rejection of his nomination to the Supreme Court, and Otto Kerner did so after conviction for bribery, mail fraud, and income tax evasion (for events prior to his becoming a judge).

What might be the reasons for the departures of district judges or the reluctance of others to become judges? Despite the high prestige of the job, some say its status has been diminished by the increased number of judgeships: there are now more U.S. court of appeals judges than U.S. senators and more district judges than members of the House of Representatives. For the politically active, a judgeship may mean too much isolation. Danger may also play at least a small part. The number of serious threats against federal judges has increased in the last few years. In 1979, a federal judge in west Texas, John H. Wood, Jr., was shot and killed, apparently as a result of the severity of his sentences in drug cases; in 1982 two men were charged with conspiring to murder a district judge in California (also in connection with a drug case); and someone seeking revenge against a Maryland federal judge abducted the judge's wife (she was quickly released).

The principal difficulty, however, is salary—cited as at least part of the reason for departure by many of those who left during the 1970s—because many judges could earn substantially more income in private practice. (Another element of compensation—limited annuities for survivors of judges who die early in their judicial careers—was the cause of the 1981 resignation of a court of appeals judge with ten years' service; the Judicial Conference has now recommended legislation to help resolve that problem.)

Salary

After having received no raises for more than six years until 1975, district judges in 1976 were receiving only $42,000, and the court of appeals judges, $44,600. As a result, 44 federal judges, later joined by 37 others, filed a suit asserting that the Compensation Clause, the constitutional provision that their pay shall not be reduced during their term in office (Art. III, Sec. 1), had been violated by the erosion of their pay by inflation since 1969—to the equivalent of $27,510 for a district judge and $29,230 for a court of appeals judge. Some judges proceeded with the lawsuit even after a pay increase of over $12,000 in early 1977, only to have the Court of Claims rule that the Constitution provided no protection against inflation-caused "indirect" reduction in judges' salaries.[1]

New litigation was initiated when Congress in four successive years (1976–1979) either stopped or reduced statutory automatic cost-of-living increases. (Congress also reduced salaries proposed for top executive branch personnel.) In two of the years, the stop or reduction became law before the start of the fiscal year, but in the other two years, because of congressional delay, the fiscal year had already begun, resulting in a temporary increase followed by a reduction. When the case (*United*

States v. Will, 1981) reached the Supreme Court, the justices first had to face the problem that with all judges affected by a ruling, no judge could decide it without being involved in a conflict of interest. On this point, the Court ruled that, when every judge has a conflict, some judge nonetheless has to hear a case (the Rule of Necessity) to assure that plaintiffs' complaints could be heard. Then, underscoring the Compensation Clause's importance for judicial independence, the Court ruled that Congress, which had the authority to set judges' salaries, could change an already-adopted salary formula *only* if the change were made before the beginning of the fiscal year. Thus judges were entitled to increases (of 4.8 percent and 12.9 percent) for two years, but not for the other two years when Congress acted in time. (Judges not under Article III, for example, magistrates and bankruptcy judges, were *not*, a lower court subsequently ruled, protected from Congress' reduction of proposed salary increases enacted ten days into the fiscal year.)

The Supreme Court's decision, further delays by Congress in 1980 and 1981 in reducing proposed salary increases, and an additional increase enacted by Congress in December 1982, brought salaries for district judges to $73,100 and for appeals court judges, to $77,300. Supreme Court justices, who received $63,000 in 1977 ($65,600 for the Chief Justice), now receive $96,700 ($100,700 for the Chief Justice). Some members of Congress object to further increases. They say the pool of those both competent and willing to serve is quite adequate, so that making judges' salaries so much higher than those of the "common person" to attract candidates is not necessary. However, inflation, increased costs of college education for judges' children, and availability of far higher compensation in private law practice (at least $200,000—and likely much more—in major corporate law firms) have led to recommendations for even higher salaries. Thus, before the late 1982 increase, the Commission on Executive, Legislative, and Judicial Salaries recommended levels roughly 20 percent above the existing ones: $85,000 for district judges, $90,000 for appeals judges, and $115,000 for Supreme Court justices. Some judges, frustrated about the Judicial Conference's apparent inability to convince Congress of their salary needs, have formed a group, the Federal Judges Association, to lobby Congress concerning pay and fringe benefits, although Chief Justice Burger strongly disapproves of such an organization.

Also relevant to judges' salary complaints is their outside income. The 1978 Ethics in Government Act requires high-level government officials, including judges, to file annual financial disclosure statements. When several judges argued that, as applied to judges, the law violated separation of powers and allowed intrusions on judicial independence, the Fifth Circuit upheld the law and the Supreme Court refused review.[2] Examination of lower court judges' statements for 1980 showed that only two had no outside income—including honoraria for speeches, book royalties, and pensions from previous positions—and only 16 had less than $5,000 such income, while more than twenty earned more than $100,000 from investments or the sale of property. Supreme Court Justice Thurgood Marshall had no outside income and no stocks or bonds worth more than $1,000 or savings accounts over $5,000 (the threshold figures for reporting, which is only within very broad categories); at the other extreme, Justice Lewis Powell had outside income of over $90,000 plus stock, bond, real estate, and trust holdings worth at least $1,600,000. In 1981, the Chief Justice had assets of at least $500,000. Justice Sandra O'Connor showed 1981 assets of at least $840,000; according to forms for 1978, Justice Stewart, whom she replaced, had been the wealthiest member of the Court until then.[3]

Discipline and Removal

A problem of potentially greater dimension than retaining judges is getting others—old, ill, or not functioning effectively —to leave the bench. Within the period of the Burger Court, there were problems with Black (loss of memory), Harlan (failing eyesight), and Douglas (a serious stroke), with Douglas being particularly reluctant to leave the Court even after he had formally resigned and a replacement (Stevens) had been named.

In earlier years, judges and justices died in office—some, it was said, long after they had become senile. The U.S. Constitution, unlike some state constitutions, makes no provision for judges' retirement at a certain age, and the entreaties of other colleagues have seldom proved successful in getting judges to retire on their then not-very-generous salary after ten years of service on reaching age 70. In 1937 Congress provided that those judges could opt for partial retirement, called senior status, with full pay *and* any subsequent salary increases. They could continue to hear cases if they wished—an incentive for older judges to reduce their workload without having to quit the bench completely—and are available to travel to courts that are temporarily in need of additional judges. (In 1954 Congress amended the law to provide senior judge status at 15 years of service on reaching age 65.) Because a judge taking senior status formally vacates a judgeship, a new judge is appointed and both the new judge and the senior judge can work on cases; senior judges' assistance to the federal courts is essential in dealing with the courts' substantial caseloads. A Supreme Court justice who wishes to retire—such as Potter Stewart in 1981 or Tom Clark, who retired so that his son, Ramsey Clark, could become attorney general without creating conflicts of interest for both—can sit on the lower federal courts, as Clark did and Stewart is now doing.

Another salary-related problem with an effect on retention of senior judges arose in 1983 as a result of amendments to the Social Security Act. As of January 1, 1984, federal judges were to become subject to having Social Security taxes deducted from their paychecks. More important, senior judges under the age of 70 would be subject to provisions of the Social Security law requiring reduction in Social Security benefits if they earned more than a certain amount; the actual time they devoted to cases would count for such purposes. The fear is that this provision will prompt judges to retire completely instead of continuing to hear cases as senior judges, thus causing the loss of valuable services to the judiciary.

Senior status, because it cannot be forced on a judge, is not a solution for the "difficult" judge who continues to serve, and further action is also necessary to terminate the judicial activity of "seniors" who wish to continue hearing cases. For example, Judge Julius Hoffman, the Chicago Seven trial judge, had finally taken senior status in 1972 at age 77. Although he was no longer hearing criminal cases or complicated litigation, in 1980 the Court of Appeals for the Seventh Circuit ordered that he not be given cases expected to take more than 35 hours of trial time; in 1982, amid complaints that his behavior was increasingly erratic, the court refused to allow any new cases to be assigned to him.

The controversy between the Tenth Circuit's Judicial Council and District Judge Stephen Chandler of the Western District of Oklahoma perhaps best illustrates the difficulties of dealing with a problem judge.[4] The council had removed Chandler—a defendant in civil and criminal lawsuits and the object of attempts to disqualify him from sitting in several cases—from deciding any pending or future cases. Chandler, not wanting to acknowledge the council's authority, did not appear at a council hearing on the matter. The council then left Chandler his pending cases, but distributed new cases to other judges in the district. Chandler's objection to the council's action was that because the Constitution provided nothing short of impeachment, impeachment was the only way to proceed against a judge. When he tried to obtain a writ of prohibition and mandamus against the council from the Supreme Court, the Court used jurisdictional grounds—his failure to seek relief from either the council or some other court—to rule against him, and thus did not deal with the substance of his claim. Chief Justice Burger, speaking for the Court, did, however, get in some strong language on the need for administration of court dockets:

> There can . . . be no disagreement among us as to the imperative need for total and absolute independence of judges in deciding cases or in any phase of the decisional function. But it is quite another matter to say that each judge in a complex system shall be the absolute ruler of his manner of conducting judicial affairs.

Justice Harlan, concurring in the Court's action, felt the Court should face the issues Chandler presented and said the council's orders were within its authority. Justices Douglas and Black, however, dissented strongly. Feeling that the Court was being unfair to Chandler in forcing him to recognize the council's authority if he wished relief, they agreed with him that impeachment was the only way to remove a judge, and argued against the circuit council control used against Chandler:

> It is time that an end be put to these efforts of federal judges to ride herd on other federal judges. This is a form of "hazing" having no place under the Constitution . . . If they break a law, they can be prosecuted. If they become corrupt or sit in cases in which they have a personal or family stake, they can be impeached by Congress. But I search the Constitution in vain for any power of surveillance which other federal judges have over those aberrations.

Some federal judges have been impeached, convicted, and removed from office, and others have resigned under certain threat of impeachment and conviction. Only one Supreme Court justice, ardent Federalist Samuel Chase, was impeached, and he was not convicted. An unresolved question concerning impeachment is whether indictment of a federal judge on criminal charges could precede or only follow impeachment. Because Judge Kerner did not raise the question at his trial but only on appeal, a court ruled he had waived his claim. When Judge Alcee Hastings, a district judge in Florida, was indicted in 1982 on bribery charges, he raised the issue prior to his trial, but lower courts ruled against him; when he was acquitted, the question was again left unanswered.

Impeachment has been thought too difficult to accomplish, inappropriate in instances of illness or senility, and too severe for most infractions of standards of judicial ethics. One effort aimed at dealing with questions of proper behavior by federal judges, intended to supplement earlier bar association Canons of Judicial Ethics, is the Code of Judicial Conduct for United States Judges, adopted by the Judicial Conference. The code indicates more clearly to judges what is expected of them, for example, when it is appropriate for them to disqualify themselves from hearing cases because of potential conflicts of interest; it serves as well to provide guidelines against which judges' conduct can be evaluated. The promulgation of the Code has not, however, served to still all concerns about judicial behavior.

The problem of dealing with noncriminal, recalcitrant, erratic, or possibly unbalanced judges within the confines of the Constitution without seriously eroding judicial independence, thus remains a real one. The Chandler case and another Tenth Circuit controversy involving Chief Judge Willis Ritter (D-Utah), embroiled in conflict with the Mormon Church, led to serious congressional attention to providing judicial discipline, including removal, short of impeachment. Proposals were based on the proposition that appointment during "good behavior" did not necessarily mean "for life" and permitted discipline for misbehavior. One proposal that passed the Senate covered all federal courts, including the Supreme Court, provided for filing complaints with a Judicial Conduct and Disability Commission, and allowed removal—except for Supreme Court justices, concerning whom recommendations would be made to the House of Representatives. The Judicial Conference's 1979 proposal and subsequent principal legislative proposals provided for filing of complaints with the circuit judicial councils; a Senate-passed 1979 version, which did *not* allow removal, provided for review of council actions by a separate Court of Judicial Conduct and Disability (five Article III judges appointed by the Chief Justice).

When, as one judge put it, Willis Ritter "joined the Great Judicial Conference in the sky," much of the urgency for these more stringent proposals was removed, and some circuit councils argued forcefully for a further chance to deal with the problem. The Judicial Conduct and Disability Act, enacted in 1980, deleted the provision for a separate conduct court and did not include removal among sanctions for Article III judges, nor did it cover Supreme Court justices. The central place of circuit councils in the disciplinary process was reaffirmed, and district judges were added to the councils (see pages 51–52) because of these newly reinforced council responsibilities.

Under the procedures established by the statute, any person may file complaints against a judge with the clerk of the court of appeals. Complaints then proceed through a three-tier arrangement, going first to the chief judge of the circuit, then to a panel of judges, and finally to the judicial council. The chief judge may dismiss a complaint if it simply concerns a ruling in a particular case (likely to be sour grapes), is frivolous, or does not allege "conduct prejudicial to the effective and expeditious administration of the business of the courts" or inability "to discharge all the duties of office by reason of mental or physical disability." The chief judge may also close a complaint upon finding that "appropriate corrective action" had been taken. If a complaint survives this review, the chief judge must appoint an investigating committee—the chief judge and an equal number of circuit and district judges— to report to the judicial council. The council may remove magistrates or bankruptcy judges; as to Article III judges, the council may issue a public or private reprimand, certify disability, request voluntary resignation, or prohibit further case assignments for a fixed period. If the council thinks the judge's conduct "might constitute" grounds for impeachment, the matter is to be transmitted to the Judicial Conference of the United States, which may in turn transmit the case to the House of Representatives. Any unsatisfied complainants and accused judges may petition the Judicial Conference or its appropriate standing committee to review judicial council actions on their complaints.

SELECTION: THE LOWER COURTS

Selection: President and Senate

The Constitution does not specify a formal process for the president's selection of judicial nominees and also fails to provide eligibility requirements or selection criteria. Different administrations have given varying weights to factors such as prior judicial experience, age, American Bar Association ratings, and, more recently, "affirmative action" to increase the number of women and minority group members in the judiciary. The Eisenhower administration explicitly stressed previous judicial experience, particularly for appeals court positions; age; and the ABA's ratings. The Kennedy administration said less about the age factor, and indeed had far less interest in judicial appointments than in social programs, despite judges' potentially great impact on those programs. The Carter administration gave substantial emphasis to nominees' "demonstrated commitment to equal justice" and to affirmative action, with the president promising to appoint at least one black federal judge in each state in the South. However, the administration also emphasized "stringent age and experience requirements," at least for the courts of appeals: only under unusual circumstances would those with less than fifteen years' experience or over 60 years of age be considered.[5]

Vacancies occur in judgeships as judges resign, die, or assume senior status, and as new judgeships are created to keep up with increasing caseload. Particularly significant is the creation of a large number of new judgeships at one time, a highly political issue because a president of one party thus is able to name many judges of similar ideology and party background. (At least informal allocation of appeals court judgeships within a circuit may also be necessary to obtain congressional approval of judgeships for the courts of appeals.) Omnibus judgeship bills were enacted in 1961 and 1966 by a Democratic Congress, with judgeships to be filled by a Democratic president. The 1970 judgeship act was somewhat unusual in that a Democratic-controlled Congress provided new judgeships to be filled by a Republican president. Despite repeated requests from the Judicial Conference for more judgeships, the Omnibus Judgeship Act of 1978, creating 35 court of appeals and 117 district court judgeships, came only after delay by a Democratic Congress unwilling to have a Republican president name a large number of judges, and it was not passed until there was a Democratic president. Such delays led Chief Justice Burger to propose in 1980 that the Judicial Conference be given the authority to establish federal judgeships as they are needed, subject to congressional veto.

The currently operative process of selecting nominees assumed its basic outlines during the Eisenhower administration, although important alterations in selection of names for the president's consideration occurred during the Carter administration (see below). Prior to formal nomination by the president, the Department of Justice, usually through the Deputy Attorney General, identifies and screens candidates for the president's consideration. For both district and appeals court positions, the Justice Department works as the president's surrogate with the appropriate senators. The president himself is seldom involved in the selection process except for Supreme Court vacancies or other matters his staff brings to his attention. The FBI conducts an intensive investigation of those being seriously considered, and other Department of Justice officials evaluate FBI reports. Prior to the Nixon administration, a background check was run only on the person already selected, but it is now usually performed earlier to assure sufficient information (and avoid embarrassment). (The FBI field check on Judge Sandra Day O'Connor was not performed until after the announcement of her nomination to the Supreme Court, in part because the announcement of the nomination was made earlier than the president had first planned to make it.)

The president has the formal constitutional power to make judicial nominations. However, under the practice of *senatorial courtesy*, judicial selection is shared with the senator(s) from the president's party in the state in which the appointment is to be made; if there are no senators from the president's party, the state party organization may be consulted. Under President Reagan, in states without Republican senators, Republican members of that state's House delegation submit recommendations as a group after consulting with the Democratic senators, part of a pattern in which minority party senators interact with the president and his representatives about appointments. (Members of the Cabinet may also serve as contact points for judicial appointments in states without senators from the president's party.) Senatorial courtesy operates most fully for district court vacancies. Because of the tradition that court of appeals seats are allocated among the states in a circuit, so that some seats "belong" to particular states, senatorial courtesy is also operative in the courts of appeals. For Supreme Court nominations, however, senatorial courtesy is virtually never operative, although the sponsorship or at least acquiescence of the senators from the nominee's state is helpful in achieving confirmation.

Most senators take senatorial courtesy seriously, feeling they should designate the nominee, and "some even take the proprietary view, that they own the job."[6] Others, however, play only a minor role in the selection process, perhaps to avoid owing the president a favor; they may do no more than submitting a list of acceptable nominees, leaving the final choice to the president's staff. Many senators also do not wish to trade a vote on an issue to obtain approval of a nomination. The executive regularly consults the appropriate senators and seldom challenges senatorial choices because either the nominations are noncontroversial or the president will later need senators' votes for his program. However, the president has available tools such as recess appointments and extended delay in filling a judgeship to pressure senators. The former has not been used recently for that purpose. Delay was used effectively by the Kennedy administration in one-fifth of judicial nominations and again in the Carter administration, when southern senators failed to nominate blacks, but it did not prove an effective tool.

Although the executive's consultation with senators over judicial nominees stems from senatorial courtesy, it does not operate formally until a nomination is submitted to the Senate and is not publicly invoked until the Judiciary Committee has sent the nomination to the floor. However, there is an equivalent of senatorial courtesy when a nomination is referred to the Judiciary Committee. Senators from the nominee's state are sent a *blue slip*; failure to return the slip is supposed to kill a nomination automatically. However, most senators seldom have used the blue slip except to comment or to sign off, or have delayed returning it to obtain more information or to negotiate over, rather than kill, nominations. When Senator Edward Kennedy (D-Mass.) became chairman of the Judiciary Committee, he decided that failure to return the blue slip would not automatically kill a nomination; instead the committee would vote on whether or not to proceed. Although a majority of senators would not necessarily defer to colleagues' use of the blue slip, a majority of senators supported continuing the mechanism, with greater support among Republicans, at that time the minority party.[7] Senator Strom Thurmond (R-S.C.), who replaced Senator Kennedy as committee chairman in 1981, retained the rule that the blue slip could not be used to delay committee consideration indefinitely.

Apart from the senators from the nominee's state, the members of the Judiciary Committee are the most important senators in the nomination process. In the late 1970s, because it was not satisfied with the FBI's investigations, the committee began to conduct its own, with committee investigators using FBI files and financial information about the nominees, and under Senator Kennedy the committee began to send its own questionnaire to all nominees to supplement information obtained by the administration. The committee's more independent examination of nominees resulted in rejection in 1980 of a nominee for a North Carolina district judgeship, the first time in 42 years the committee had taken such action.

The committee chairman's power can be substantial. A particularly stubborn chairman like Senator Eastland can force a hard bargain, delaying consideration of a much wanted nomination until the president submits others the chairman wants. The committee as a whole can test the president's will by delaying action on nominations. The committee holds hearings—although often by subcommittees of only a few senators—to take testimony from the nominee, supporters, and opponents. Through these hearings, at which the committee can decline to let someone testify, relegating objections to the less visible printed record, and can control the sequence in which witnesses appear and the hostile or friendly treatment they receive, the entire Senate, the media, and the general public can be attuned to objections against the nominee.

The Judiciary Committee also is able to affect selection criteria from time to time. Most recently, it became visible in controversies over the ABA's age guidelines (see pages 81–82) and judges' memberships in clubs with no minority group members. The latter issue was first exposed in the nomination of former judges to administrative positions—Griffin Bell to be Attorney General and William Webster to be FBI Director. With respect to judicial nominations, the matter came into the open when Judge Bailey Brown (W.D. Tenn.), nominated to the Sixth Circuit, felt that resigning from the all-white group to which he belonged would be to admit that his membership was improper, but he agreed to suspend his membership until he was "able to satisfy myself that the club does not discriminate against minorities with respect to membership." In the aftermath of this controversy, Senators Kennedy and Thurmond, then chairman and ranking minority member of the Judiciary Committee, agreed on a statement that "it is inadvisable for a nominee for a Federal judgeship to belong to a social club that engages in invidious discrimination." Roughly a dozen other nominees resigned from such clubs during 1979. A follow-up study showed, however, that many federal judges belong to all-white social clubs, and the Judicial Conference was to take up the issue as it applied to already-confirmed judges.

After the conclusion of hearings, the committee makes a recommendation to the full Senate, which then may conduct a debate before voting. The Judiciary Committee members lead the Senate debate, which provides senators with another opportunity to embarrass the president by questioning an appointment. Anticipating that such questions will be raised, a president may prefer to avoid a particular nomination or even, despite the resulting embarrassment, to withdraw it once made. It is at the floor stage that senatorial courtesy operates officially. Formerly a senator could invoke senatorial courtesy with little challenge simply by stating that, whatever the reason, an opposed nominee was "personally obnoxious," but expectations have developed that a senator has to substantiate rather than merely assert objections. Senatorial courtesy is used defensively to try to block a presidential nominee, not always successfully, but even its effective exercise does not assure acceptance of a senator's nominee. Senators have generally lost battles with the president over nominations, often because the successful appointee was sponsored by the state's other senator of the same party. Moreover, although not inclined to interfere regularly with district court nominations in other states, other senators may become involved—or may be pressured by interest groups to get involved—in nominations seen as affecting the federal judiciary's quality and image. Senators certainly do not accept either the president's or their colleagues' assessments totally at face value, and they also do look beyond the nominee's competence to the nominee's policy views as a basis for their vote.

Selection Commissions

Senators have always consulted informally with many people concerning judicial nominations. President Carter's belief that judges should be chosen through "merit selection" brought about a significant change in the way many senators selected those whose names were to be forwarded to the president, leading to more formal consultative and screening devices. The president had spoken of using merit selection for both district courts and courts of appeals, but Attorney General Griffin Bell and Senate Judiciary Committee Chairman Eastland "struck a deal" in which appeals court nominees would be produced by selection commissions established by executive order, with senators continuing to choose nominees for district judgeships.

The change in the selection process for vacancies on the courts of appeals, initiated by President Carter, significant both structurally and in the results produced, was terminated in May 1981 by President Reagan. President Carter first imposed the mandatory new process in February 1977 for any U.S. Court of Appeals vacancies (Executive Order #11972) and then extended it (E.O. #12059) to the 1978 Judgeship Act positions.[8] Thirteen selection panels were established—one for each circuit, with two each for the not-yet-divided Fifth Circuit and the Ninth Circuit. Originally each panel was to have equal numbers of members of the bar and laypersons and there was a mandate that women and minorities be represented. Roughly 55 percent of the initial commission members were male, over half were attorneys, and the predominant portion (approaching 90 percent) were white and Democrat. The panels had "a disproportionate number of Carter activists," with somewhat under half having participated in President Carter's campaign and almost two-thirds of those having favored Carter prior to the convention. However, the principal differences within panels in terms of attitudes were not between Carter activists and others but between lawyers and lay members, with the lawyers giving less weight to bar association recommendations than did nonlawyers.[9]

Under the original executive order, a commission—each one was convened for a specific vacancy—had 60 days from the president's request that they begin work to the submission of nominations. After passage of the 1978 Judgeship Act, panels had more flexible time periods in which to work, and they considered multiple vacancies, with separate sets of nominees under consideration because of allocation of appeals court judgeships to specific states. (Panelists' principal complaint was that they had inadequate time to screen and interview candidates and to debate their qualifications.[10])

Public notices of vacancies and inquiries to identify potential nominees were used to "open up" the selection process so that the panel did not restrict itself to those volunteering their candidacies. The panel was charged with ascertaining who of those under consideration were qualified; no less than three names nor more than five were to be submitted to the president for each position. Despite panel members' partisan involvement, they placed relatively little importance on a candidate's political activity or on partisan recommendations; panel members surveyed gave a candidate's mental health the highest ranking among the criteria considered, with the next six characteristics involving "character and personality traits."[11]

The 1978 Omnibus Judgeship Act (OJA) also gave a push to the use of the commission selection mechanisms for district judgeships. District judgeship vacancies under the Act were to be filled on the basis of merit selection guidelines to be enunciated in an executive order, and President Carter's order (E.O. #12097) encouraged use of selection commissions. Particularly when there was an OJA vacancy in a state, the idea of special selection panels for district judgeships took hold. As of 1979, senators in 29 states had established either ad hoc or permanent judicial nominating commissions—in 20 states where both senators were Democrats, six where both were Republican, three with divided representation, and one sponsored by an independent senator, Byrd of Virginia.[12] (After the change in party control of the Senate in 1980, there were commissions in only 15 states in 1983.)

Even with President Carter's encouragement, some senators refused to set up commissions. Senator Paul Sarbanes (D-Md.) said he would conduct his own investigations; Senator Lloyd Bentsen (D-Tex.) became known as "I am the Judicial Commission for Texas" Bentsen; and Senator Adlai Stevenson III (D-Ill.) attacked the new device. Stevenson said the commissions isolated senators from candidates and placed responsibility for recommending nominations "in the hands of a 'sanitized' committee" made up of various categories of persons (lawyers, nonlawyers, men, women, minorities) without regard to merit.[13]

Commission structure was not fixed, and they varied "considerably in duration, numbers of panels and commissioners, methods of appointment and terms of office of commissions, existence of written charters and rules of procedures, and the role of sponsors in designating preferred candidates for nomination."[14] Some senators sent the full commission-generated lists directly to the executive branch; others, giving themselves greater control over the nomination, reduced the lists first. Newer members of the Senate were more likely to accept a greater executive role in the process, undoubtedly a function of their use of the selection commissions; senior senators were more likely to assume a greater role in the selection process.[15]

The Judgeship Act included language *suggesting* that greater consideration be given to selecting minorities and women, and the Executive Order reminded selection panels to recruit qualified minority and women candidates actively, but this was not binding. The president could certify reasons for waiving the standards of the Executive Order, and no nomination could be considered defective for failure to comply. Indeed, a majority of senators felt that the selection process used by their Senate colleagues from other states was not a proper basis for voting against a nominee to a judgeship.[16]

Use of the selection commission device had some definite effects. Some were structural: the executive branch and the Judiciary Committee played larger and more independent roles than under the earlier, more traditional, selection mechanism. The number and variety of participants in the selection process—particularly persons from outside the government—increased. Scrutiny of applicants was greater and also more repetitive. Perhaps of particular significance is that commission-selected candidates thought the process was more open than it had been: half of those surveyed "believed they would not have sought or been considered for appointment under the traditional system," in large part because they did not know senators, were politically inactive, or were not "traditional" candidates (older, white males).[17] This view may have resulted because most senators defined their affirmative action obligations in terms of search and outreach, for example, expanding the candidate pool in terms of race and gender; the senators did not, however, view their responsibilities in terms of results, that is, nomination of a certain proportion of black, Hispanic, or female judges.[18] In any event, the district court selection process under President Carter, like that for the courts of appeals, did produce a rather different racial and gender mix than had earlier selection processes (see pages 85–86). However, senators who did not use selection commissions produced affirmative action outcomes not noticeably different from those in the commission states.

The ABA's Role

The American Bar Association (ABA), lawyers' principal national interest group, has assisted in selecting federal judges since 1946. Its Committee on the Federal Judiciary initially suggested names of candidates but sought to review nominations before they were made public—if not earlier. President Eisenhower's emphasis on "quality" in the federal judiciary led to increased ABA involvement. By 1953, instead of only making recommendations, the committee was evaluating the names of those under "active consideration." The ratings used by the ABA are Exceptionally Well Qualified, Well Qualified, Qualified, Not Qualified, or Not Qualified by Reason of Age. The Eisenhower administration's practice made it difficult for later administrations to avoid the ABA, despite objections to the ABA's special access and its alleged conservatism, masked by its claim to be interested only in judicial competence.

The weight given to ABA recommendations by subsequent administrations has, however, varied; ABA participation in judicial selection has been more significant in Republican administrations than in Democratic ones. In Eisenhower's last two years, for example, the ABA committee "had a virtual veto power" so that only those the committee rated Qualified or better were nominated.[19] The Kennedy administration tried to limit the ABA's role. Top Justice Department personnel were unwilling to give in to the ABA when they differed with its committee. Indeed, using "argument and cajolery,"[20] the administration was able to get the ABA to change some of its ratings. Almost one-third (29 percent) of the ABA's informal ratings differed from formal ratings finally announced. In 30 percent of the changes, the rating was *up*graded, perhaps as a result of the ABA's desire to appear successful when the administration was intent on a particular nomination. Although President Lyndon Johnson's initial relations with the ABA were strained, extremely negative reaction to some of his nominations made him more sensitive to the bar's reaction. The ABA committee ranked six of Johnson's first 56 appointments to the district and appeals court Not Qualified, but by 1966 the committee thought the administration's appointments quite good.

During the Nixon presidency, the ABA's position again strengthened. The president said he would not name someone considered Not Qualified, but late in his administration he broke his word over an appointment to the court of appeals. The ABA's importance in lower court nominations continued into the Ford administration, and the bar group seemed quite pleased, at least publicly, with its relations with the administration.

The ABA also seemed satisfied with the district judge selection commissions during the Carter administration. A higher proportion of commission-selected nominees than of nominees not chosen through the commission mechanism were rated better than Qualified. Friction between the Carter administration and the ABA did, however, occur. Most serious was conflict over the nomination of Donald O'Brien to be a district judge in Iowa. The ABA rated him Not Qualified not once but twice on the basis of his poor preparation for trials and some questionable conduct as a prosecutor—only the fourth instance in which the ABA had rated a candidate unqualified and had gone public with its opposition. Overall, however, ABA ratings of Carter district court nominees compared favorably with those in previous administrations. Despite previous Republican administrations' more favorable disposition toward the ABA, slightly *fewer* of President Reagan's first 33 district court nominees received Well Qualified or Exceptionally Well Qualified ratings than had Carter's district court nominees, with no difference at the appellate level.

Because many women have become lawyers at an older age than men and have been limited in the trial work available to them, the Carter administration's emphasis on appointing women conflicted with the ABA's preference that nominees have considerable trial experience. (Beginning in 1979, the Carter administration also allowed the Federation of Women Lawyers Judicial Screening Panel to review nominees for their "commitment to equal justice under law"—a practice terminated by the Reagan administration.) Not directly disagreeing with the ABA, Attorney General Civiletti said that certain standards, adopted years earlier, "ought not to be mandatory," although they would be given serious consideration. He felt there ought to be "room for an outstanding or qualified exception under certain conditions."[21] The friction between the ABA and the administration on this matter and the ABA's influence could be seen when a woman solicitor in the Labor Department was nominated to be a district judge in the District of Columbia: the ABA rejected her because of lack of trial experience, and the administration withdrew her nomination. Also noteworthy is that in 1977–1979, the only nominees to be rated Exceptionally Well Qualified (72 of 157) were white males, and, although 62.5 percent of all Carter judicial nominees were rated Well Qualified or Exceptionally Well Qualified, only 30 percent of the women were so rated, and only one was rated Exceptionally Well Qualified.[22]

Controversy over another appointment—to the Court of Appeals for the First Circuit—led to reevaluation of another ABA standard. Initially, Archibald Cox, Harvard Law School professor and former Watergate prosecutor, was proposed for nomination. He was rejected by the administration ostensibly for being over 65, although friction between President Carter and Senator Edward Kennedy may also have played a part. (The position eventually went to another, 40-year-old Harvard law professor who had been a Kennedy assistant.) Critics soon attacked the ABA's age policy, under which in no event would anyone not already a federal judge be considered for an appeals court judgeship if over 64, and those 60 and over had to be in excellent health and rated Well Qualified or better; a district judge could not be elevated to the court of appeals if over 68. In April 1980 the Senate voted unanimously in favor of a resolution calling for an end to the guidelines, and the House followed with a similar resolution in November 1980. Shortly thereafter, the ABA committee announced it was discontinuing its age guidelines and its Not Qualified by Reason of Age rating.

Judicial Backgrounds

Relations between federal judges' votes and their background characteristics, except for political party affiliation, have not been particularly clear. Nonetheless, considerable attention has been paid to the personal and social characteristics of federal judges—their race, gender, and religion; where they received their legal education; and their prior occupations. This attention stems basically from the feeling that in a democratic system judges should be roughly representative of the general population in a statistical sense. There is also an important symbolic element to this concern—that, in a government of all the people, an all white male judiciary is a slight to women and racial minorities. Few argue for appointment of women or black judges so those judges can serve as representatives of a point of view arguing "black" or "feminist" positions, although, as we will see, the possible relation between judges' background characteristics, such as race or religion, and certain types of cases has caused some litigants to raise questions about the judges' ability to be impartial in those cases. Yet some argue for broader representation on the judiciary because they feel that judges who are women or from minority backgrounds, because of their personal experiences, will be more sympathetic to concerns of those who share their characteristics—just as former business lawyers have been—or that, at a minimum, their very presence will serve to remind their white male colleagues of the concerns of such people.

More than nine of every ten times, the selection process for the lower federal courts produces judges of the president's political party. This was no less true of the Carter administration's "merit selection" mechanisms than of earlier methods of selection, although in states where senators from opposite parties jointly sponsored a selection commission, a portion of the available judgeships went to the party not in the White House. Some differences have been found between Democrats and Republicans on the courts of appeals, for example in the area of economic policy but not in other areas. Relationships between other factors and judges' voting disappeared when political party was taken into account, leaving it the single most helpful explanatory factor.[23] However, party affiliation does not have a uniform effect, having affected civil liberties decisions of district court judges more "in the wake of the transition from Warren to Burger" when the Supreme Court's cues were changing and more ambiguous than earlier.[24]

Federal judges' formal education and their parents' occupations have always been somewhat unrepresentative. During the nation's first century, both the nation's elite and particularly the "common man" were underrepresented in the lower federal courts: two of three judges were from middle-class homes.[25] Despite the small number of federal judges then, many appointees had other family members in the judiciary and even more had kinfolk in public service. Those appointed to the (Article III) district courts were usually of higher social status than territorial judges, who were "ambitious and generally successful middle-class lawyers" often not *from* the territories.[26]

Prior Occupation

The contemporary period has seen three basic paths to the federal judiciary: private legal practice and national party service or a local sponsor; in-service promotion from a position as U.S. attorney or from a district judgeship to the court of appeals; and lateral entry at an older age, such as from service as U.S. attorney after a career in private practice.[27] The Carter administration's new selection methods and affirmative action efforts meant additional paths to judgeships from public interest or civil rights law practice and from law schools. "Nontraditional" nominations were more likely when senators sent President Carter a list without designation of a preferred nomination than when senators exercised the nomination choice themselves. (A significant number of President Reagan's choices also have come from law schools.)

A president trying to increase the number of federal judges from groups not constituting a large proportion of the legal profession, such as women, blacks, or Hispanics, or who are disproportionately "junior" in legal experience, faces some problems. Because there is only a small initial "pool" of nontraditional candidates from which to select, finding appropriate candidates within that pool may not be easy. The pool becomes even smaller if ABA guidelines are used and nominees are submitted to usual evaluation processes. Moreover, there are relatively few alternative nominees available if questions are raised about any particular nontraditional nominee. This situation allowed the white southern establishment, which had refused to handle civil rights cases, opportunities to question the qualifications of black attorneys whose principal legal work was in the civil rights field, and to force withdrawal of some nominations.

Nominees to judgeships often have been judges or prosecutors. During the Johnson administration and Nixon's first term, only one-fifth of the appeals court nominees and a comparable proportion of district court nominees outside the South had neither type of experience.[28] Statements emphasizing the selection of people with prior judicial experience are not always matched in practice, however. Thus the Eisenhower administration, which stressed this factor, did not do as well in this regard as had the Truman administration. The Hoover administration had a particularly good record in rewarding prior judicial experience: eleven of sixteen appeals court appointees came from the district courts. Although President Reagan's appellate court appointees have been more likely than district court appointees to have had previous judicial experience, his early district court appointees were less likely than President Carter's to have judicial experience (roughly one-third compared to over one-half). Because a president is not likely to elevate district judges appointed by a president of the opposite party, efforts to promote district judges to the courts of appeals are limited when the presidency changes hands. Generally, district judges who move to the courts of appeals are likely to do so within a short time of their district court appointment or not at all.

Nomination of a member of Congress to a judgeship can present a special problem—possible violation of Article I, Section 6 of the Constitution, prohibiting appointment of members of Congress to any position "the Emoluments whereof shall have been increased" during their term in office. In 1937, when Hugo Black's appointment to the Supreme Court was challenged on this basis, the Supreme Court barred such a lawsuit on the grounds the plaintiff lacked standing to sue (*Ex Parte Levitt*, 1937). President Carter's choice of Representative Abner Mikva (D-Ill.) for the Court of Appeals for the District of Columbia led to strong opposition by conservatives and, after Senate confirmation, to a similar challenge. Very shortly after the nomination was confirmed, Congress passed a law granting standing to members of Congress specifically to challenge judicial appointments to the District of Columbia Circuit on eligibility grounds. Senator McClure(R-Idaho) then filed a suit, financed by the National Rifle Association, in which he claimed that Mikva's nomination violated the Constitution because an automatic pay raise went into effect during Representative Mikva's term (but after he had resigned his House seat). A three-judge district court ruled that notwithstanding the statute allowing the suit, the senator did *not* have standing to challenge an approved nomination. The Supreme Court affirmed without comment the lower court's ruling that Congress itself had to decide nominees' eligibility.[29]

Eisenhower's nominees were particularly likely to be from relatively large private law firms or from government practice; high-ranking Justice Department officials—likely candidates for federal judgeships—accounted for roughly 10 percent of his nominations. More of Kennedy's choices had been either in elective positions or some form of government administration; the private lawyers he nominated were more likely to have been in small firms or individual (solo) practice. The same differences occurred between the (Democratic) Johnson and (Republican) Nixon administrations; 40 percent of Nixon's district court appointees were partners in large law firms, with only 10 percent from small firm and solo practice, while roughly one-fifth of Johnson's appointees came from the latter sources. The higher socioeconomic status of Republicans was perhaps not, however, reflected in their differing educational backgrounds.

Religion

Differences in religion also existed between Republican- and Democratic-appointed judges. Over three-fourths of Eisenhower's appointees were Protestant, more than

Kennedy's district court (three-fifths) and appeals court (two-thirds) appointees. Similarly, proportionately more Nixon than Johnson appointees were Protestant; Johnson, like Kennedy, appointed proportionately more Catholics and Jews. Continued active participation as a church official recently caused a legal problem for the district judge assigned to hear a lawsuit challenging the extension of the Equal Rights Amendment ratification deadline and raising the question of whether states could rescind earlier ratification. Judge Marion Callister was a regional representative of the Church of Jesus Christ of Latter Day Saints (the Mormon Church), which opposed the ERA. On the basis of a statute providing that a judge "shall disqualify himself in any proceeding in which his impartiality might reasonably be questioned," the Justice Department asked that Judge Callister disqualify himself from the case because of his religion, which affected "the appearance of impartiality." The judge refused, noting that his legal judgment would not be affected even if he sat in high church councils. (Shortly thereafter, the church relieved him of his duties as regional representative.)

Race

Of greater current concern than religion are race and gender. President Eisenhower appointed no blacks to federal judgeships; Kennedy named five—four to the district court and one (Thurgood Marshall) to the court of appeals. Johnson, in addition to appointing Marshall to the Supreme Court, making him the first black to sit there, appointed five black district judges and two black court of appeals judges. (One Johnson district court nominee, not confirmed, was later appointed by President Ford and elevated to the appeals court by President Carter.) Nixon named only four black district judges.

Blacks and Hispanics accounted for a higher proportion of nominations in President Carter's administration—roughly one-fifth—than in previous administrations, and there was also an increase in the number of judges of Oriental background appointed in California. More important, President Carter appointed more blacks and Hispanics to the federal bench than the *total number* appointed by all previous presidents. Some black judges' right to preside over race relations cases has been challenged because of their prior civil rights involvement. Third Circuit Judge Leon Higginbotham, asked by litigants to excuse himself from a civil rights case, refused because to agree would mean that only white judges could hear such cases. Former NAACP lawyers Judges Constance Baker Motley (S.D.N.Y.) and Nathaniel Jones (Sixth Circuit) have taken the same position.

Gender

The first woman federal judge was Florence Allen, appointed to the Sixth Circuit in 1934. After her retirement in 1959, there was no new woman appeals court judge until Shirley Hufstedler was named to the Ninth Circuit nine years later. When she became President Carter's Secretary of Education, women were sitting on a majority of the courts of appeals; by mid-1980 there were ten women court of appeals judges. Presidents Johnson and Ford each appointed two women to the district court. When President Carter took office, there were only three women district judges, but by mid-1980, there were 31 plus three on the Tax Court and one on the Claims Court.

President Carter appointed twice as many women judges—roughly one-fifth of his appeals court nominations and 14 percent of his district court nominations—as had been appointed by all previous presidents. Of 23 women federal judges in late 1979, Carter appointed 19. The women appointed by President Carter were "far more likely to have been judges at the time of their appointment, far less likely to have been working for a large corporate law firm, and much less likely to have been party activists." In addition, nearly one-third of those appointed to the appellate bench came from academic positions—a figure well higher than for male appointees or for appointees from previous administrations.[30] Just as with his appointment of members of racial minorities, it was somewhat easier for President Carter to appoint as many women as he did because he often could nominate women and men simultaneously for multiple vacancies created by the Omnibus Judgeship Act. Similarly, it is easier to appoint women or racial minorities to multijudge courts than to one-judge district courts.

Older patterns of the backgrounds of judicial nominees returned with the Reagan administration, along with the reinstitution of traditional selection processes. President Reagan nominated the first woman Supreme Court justice, Sandra Day O'Connor. However, by mid-1983 he had named only six women district court judges out of more than seventy nominations, and none to the appellate courts out of more than twenty nominations; the only nomination of a black was of a district judge to the court of appeals.

THE SUPREME COURT

The Justices' Qualifications

The qualifications of Supreme Court justices can be categorized as representational, professional, and doctrinal.[31] One element of representation is geography. There have been more justices whose home states were in the East (the older part of the nation) than in the West, although some effort is made to avoid overrepresentation of any region. The principal representational qualification is political party. As with lower court judges, the great majority (90 percent) of the more than one hundred justices have been of the appointing president's party. Nonetheless, explicit partisanship is played down and could act as a disqualification. Party affiliation was a much better predictor of voting in the nineteenth century than it is now, because then the parties were more clearly divided on some issues, particularly regional/sectional ones like slavery.[32] A recent study has indicated that in cases involving presidential power where the decisions went one way or the other, the hypothesis that "a greater proportion of the judges from the president's party are likely to decide for him than are the judges for the opposition party" was confirmed in 64 percent of the cases.[33]

Representation of minorities has been apparent, although whether it has been purposeful is disputed. A "Jewish seat" seemed to exist once Louis Brandeis joined the Court (anti-Semitism infused much of the opposition to his nomination). In succession, Felix Frankfurter, Arthur Goldberg, and Abe Fortas served on the Court. Yet asserting existence of a "Jewish seat" is difficult because Benjamin Cardozo served with Brandeis, Frankfurter was appointed before Brandeis resigned, and Fortas was not replaced by another Jew.

Catholics have regularly served on the Court, but there has been less conscious attention to a "Catholic seat" than to a Jewish one. For example, Eisenhower's nomination of William Brennan resulted primarily from the president's need to find a highly qualified "sitting judge" to quiet criticism of the "political" appointment of Earl Warren, a former Republican vice-presidential candidate, and from the unavailability because of age of Arthur Vanderbilt, Chief Justice of the New Jersey Supreme Court of which Brennan was a member. No black reached the Supreme Court until Lyndon Johnson's appointment of Thurgood Marshall.

Most of the justices have come from upper-middle-class or upper-class surroundings; very few have been of "essentially humble origin." Into the nineteenth century, justices came from "socially prestigeful and politically influential" families of the gentry class; later, professional family backgrounds predominated, and economic rather than political prominence was likely.[34] The nation's more open political system resulting from Jacksonian democracy was not directly reflected in the Court's membership. Members of justices' families were often active in public life, and more than one member of the same family has served on the Court, for example, Stephen Field and his nephew David Brewer (some said this gave Field two votes) and the two John Marshall Harlans, one at the end of the nineteenth century and his grandson in the 1950s and 1960s.

Justices' ages increased as the nineteenth century progressed; this was a result of our political development and the concomitant growth of informal career lines. The likelihood that justices would be older was reinforced by formal law training and greater specialization in the legal profession, so that it took longer to become established in the profession and receive appropriate recognition. Although Justice Douglas was 40 and Justice Rehnquist in his forties when appointed, appointment to the Court in an individual's late fifties, as with John Paul Stevens, or sixties, true of three of the Nixon nominees, is more typical. Justice O'Connor was 51 at the time of her appointment.

Professional qualifications mean prior judicial and governmental service. The state courts provided most of the Supreme Court justices in the last century, although at the end of the century justices were more likely to have had national rather than local experience. A nominee's judicial experience has always been taken into account, although lack of it has not been a bar to appointment, as in the case of Hugo Black, who had served briefly as a police magistrate but whose primary activity had been as a U.S. senator. The American Bar Association focused more attention on this factor and criticized nominees who lacked judicial service, such as Earl Warren—criticism compounded by his being chosen to be Chief Justice. Warren's experience as a prosecutor and state attorney general as well as governor did, however, serve to diminish the criticism.

Most other recent appointees either had judicial experience, had held important government jobs, or were distinguished lawyers. Eisenhower appointees John Marshall Harlan, Potter Stewart, and Charles Evans Whittaker, Johnson appointee Thurgood Marshall (solicitor general at the time of his appointment), Nixon appointees Burger and Blackmun, and Ford appointee Stevens—a former Supreme Court law clerk—were federal appeals court judges, as were unsuccessful Nixon nominees Clement Haynsworth and G. Harrold Carswell, earlier a district judge; Sandra O'Connor was a member of the Arizona intermediate appellate court. William Rehnquist, also a former Supreme Court law clerk, was an assistant attorney general, and Kennedy appointee Byron White was deputy attorney general when appointed. Both Arthur Goldberg and Abe Fortas were distinguished attorneys, as was Lewis Powell, a former president of the ABA.

Counter to the bar's expectations, past judicial performance does not produce a greater reliance on precedent. Instead justices who had significant pre–Supreme Court judicial experience or who came from families containing judges were more likely to depart from precedent than were justices without such experience or without judges among their relatives.[35] Perhaps those familiar with the judicial role could understand that a judge has to depart from precedent in order to resolve disputes, but those without such experience would be more likely to follow the law-school-taught norm of following precedent. Those with prior judicial experience and those from "judicial families" have also been less likely to dissent, maybe because they have accepted the norm of minimal dissent, quite strong in the lower federal courts and state courts. Judges from the more liberal party, who were more likely to have prior judicial experience, were more prone to abandon precedent, but the liberals were also more likely to dissent than conservative judges. Those most likely to dissent were most often those adhering to an earlier status quo and unwilling to abandon it.

Presidential Expectations

Justices consistently support the policies of the presidents who select them. Such results stem from ideological affinity or "doctrinal qualifications," that the president attempts to ascertain through individuals' professional qualifications. Particularly when we consider presidents' lack of personal knowledge of most of those they nominate and the fact that many nominees are without (extensive) judicial records on which the president can draw, they have been quite successful in identifying their nominees' doctrinal proclivities. "About three-fourths of those justices for whom an evaluation could be made conformed to the expectations of the presidents who appointed them."[36]

With respect to the civil rights voting records of the justices appointed by Presidents Eisenhower through Nixon, we see only "limited support for [the] hypothesis that there would be a strong relationship between the civil rights support scores of presidents and those of the justices they appointed." There was divergence between presidents, with President Nixon's appointees more conservative than the justices appointed by the previous three presidents, but there was also divergence among appointees of each president except LBJ. Thus these presidents were "only moderately successful in appointing justices who would later take positions consistent with the appointing president's public statements on civil rights."[37]

Although some presidents appear to have few expectations of their nominees, others have expended much energy to ensure that those they have nominated will vote the "right" way on key questions. Yet even in such situations, the president's expectations are often disappointed. The best-known story involves President Theodore Roosevelt, who selected Oliver Wendell Holmes for the Supreme Court after assuring himself that Holmes would vote "correctly" on antitrust matters. Yet Holmes, in his first antitrust case, voted the "wrong" way, provoking Roosevelt to say he could make a judge with a stronger backbone out of a banana. And the Nixon nominees failed to reflect the president's position on abortion, aid to parochial schools, important aspects of desegregation, and electronic surveillance, and in the end handed down the rulings in the Watergate Tapes Case that led to his departure from office.

Prior Judicial Experience

Prior judicial service can help the president identify the nominee's ideological affinities, and presidents have been "much more likely to be successful in predicting the future voting behavior of a nominee when the nominee had a record of previous judicial experience that would provide a dependable clue to their probable future behavior on the Court."[38] A good example of prior judicial service facilitating a president's choice is Chief Justice Warren Burger. In the policy area in which Nixon was most interested, criminal procedure, Burger's decisions as a court of appeals judge showed a "judicial philosophy . . . generally described in terms of strict construction, conservatism, and judicial restraint." Burger had decided against the criminal appellant in twenty-five of twenty-six nonunanimous arrest and search and seizure cases during the 1956–1969 period, and his opinions on the question of "probable cause" to arrest or search reflected "a pro-prosecution orientation which reject[ed] legal technicalities in criminal procedures that restrict the police in conducting their business." Moreover, in fourteen *en banc* criminal procedural rulings between 1965 and 1969, Burger had not once voted in favor of the appellant.[39]

Even if judicial service can help the president make a choice, other factors argue against its use in selecting a Chief Justice from within the Court. Selection from inside the Court tends to expose animosities and has provoked threats of resignation, as when Justice Jackson was considered as a replacement for Chief Justice Stone. This may help explain why only three nominees to be Chief Justice—Edward White, Harlan Fiske Stone (neither from the president's party), and Abe Fortas (not confirmed)—have come from within the Court; Charles Evans Hughes had earlier been a member of the Court but was not a member when named Chief Justice.

A general risk in choosing someone with prior judicial service is that it provides an easy basis for criticism of disliked decisions. During consideration of his nomination to be Chief Justice, Fortas' presence on the Court facilitated criticism of the Court's civil liberties decisions, such as those on obscenity. The National Organization for Women (NOW) objected to John Paul Stevens' nomination because of some of his Seventh Circuit opinions, and labor and civil rights groups attacked the judicial actions of John Parker, Haynsworth, and Carswell, the Supreme Court nominees rejected in the twentieth century,[40] although Parker's defenders said his criticized labor ruling only properly implemented Supreme Court decisions, and Haynsworth's school desegregation decisions were said to reflect Supreme Court rulings accurately at the time he made them even though the Supreme Court later overturned some of those rulings.

Carswell's service as a district judge produced complaints that he had handled civil rights cases with hostility and had been rude to black lawyers and black defendants. Because the Court of Appeals for the Fifth Circuit had reversed Carswell more frequently than all but a few other district judges in the circuit, his professional competence was questioned. Indeed, former Yale Law School Dean Louis Pollak said that Carswell "presents more slender credentials than any nominee for the Supreme Court put forth in this century," the statement that provoked Senator Hruska (R-Neb.) to proclaim the need to have mediocrity represented on the Supreme Court.

Ethics

Prior judicial service may also reveal a judge's ethical sense, a matter that has received much attention in recent years. An indication of the closer attention now paid to matters of ethics was the close questioning of John Paul Stevens about the corporations in which he had held stock or been an officer. (He had resigned as officer when he joined the Seventh Circuit Court of Appeals and later sold most of the securities.) Attention came to be paid to the question of ethics after Justice Fortas resigned upon the disclosure that he had temporarily retained money from Louis Wolfson, a financier in trouble with the government, as part of a contract to be a foundation consultant to Wolfson. This action created the appearance that Fortas was practicing law for Wolfson while on the Court or perhaps—and worse—trying to influence the government's prosecution of Wolfson. The ABA's ethics committee found that Fortas had violated provisions that a judge should avoid "impropriety and the appearance of impropriety" and that a judge should not undertake work inconsistent with his judicial duties.[41]

Ethics was at the heart of the Senate's rejection of Judge Haynsworth's nomination. His not having recused (withdrawn) from a case in which he appeared to have a financial interest was said to be improper, as was his purchase of stock in a company that had been a litigant in a case before him; the purchase was made after the case was decided but before the decision was announced, something Haynsworth attributed to inadvertence. Haynsworth had been cleared of charges of unethical conduct relating to the first matter,[42] but the second matter hurt his cause, particularly in the aftermath of Fortas' conduct. Although ethics issues were also raised during consideration of Fortas' nomination to be Chief Justice and Carswell's subsequent nomination, "only in Haynsworth's case did ethics seem to have an important influence on the final vote."[43]

Political Activity

Doctrinal qualifications may be revealed not only by prior judicial service but also by previous political involvement, which is said to show "judicial temperament" or lack of it; the term is usually left undefined. Quite likely because he had advocated minimum wage and maximum hours legislation, Louis Brandeis was said to lack judicial temperament. Had Hugo Black's membership in the Ku Klux Klan been known before rather than after the confirmation of his nomination, it would have been used against him. However, he probably would have been confirmed in any event because of his overall liberalism and the norm of Senate approval of judicial nominations of its own members. (Moreover, his judicial defense of civil rights led to the comment that "Hugo Black used to go around in white sheets, scaring black people; now he goes around in black robes, scaring white people.") In the 1950s, John Marshall Harlan was questioned about his membership in the Atlantic Union, which supposedly indicated a diminished commitment to United States sovereignty, and about his attachment to the liberal faction of the Republican party. Carswell's alleged racism probably produced the defeat of his nomination; unlike Judge Parker's campaign statement that Negroes shouldn't vote, apparently an isolated incident that occurred in the political climate of 1920, a comparable campaign statement by Carswell came after World War II and was followed by his helping the Tallahassee, Florida, municipal golf course become a private club to avoid desegregation—action he took while U.S. Attorney.

Prior political activity also produced opposition to the Powell and Rehnquist nominations. Powell's membership on the Richmond, Virginia, School Board and the Virginia State Board of Education led Congress's Black Caucus to oppose him. Complaints about Rehnquist, whose nomination was opposed by the Leadership Conference on Civil Rights and the American Civil Liberties Union, centered on his 1964 opposition to a public accommodations ordinance in Phoenix, Arizona, his Justice Department work on policy concerning electronic surveillance and mass demonstrations, and his defense of Carswell's nomination as the administration's spokesman. The argument that he had only served as the government's lawyer was not accepted by many.

Opposition to Judge O'Connor came not on the basis of her past judicial record, and her position on federalism seemed quite compatible with contemporary Republican views. However, some religious and antiabortion groups did not feel her votes as a state senator indicated sufficient antiabortion sentiment. Her unwillingness to say how she would treat legal aspects of abortion as a judge further inflamed this opposition.

As these examples suggest, a nominee's past political participation is likely to produce opposition by a variety of interest groups—particularly labor and civil rights groups. Those groups have probably been more interested in protecting interests they thought the nominees would injure or in demonstrating their ability to block a nomination than in the particular individual involved, although opposition to Carswell as a person was quite severe.

American Bar Association

Largely as a result of actions by the executive, the American Bar Association's relationship to the executive concerning Supreme Court nominations has not been consistent over the last two decades. However, ABA actions have led to problems for itself. In 1962 it had decided to use only the ratings Qualified and Not Qualified for Supreme Court nominees, who, unlike nominees to lower court positions, were not cleared with the ABA before being announced. Prior to the Haynsworth nomination, the ratings Highly Acceptable, Acceptable, or Not Acceptable were adopted, but after Haynsworth's defeat and before Carswell's nomination the organization reverted to the Qualified/Not Qualified standards. Because people did not know of the change, Carswell's nomination was damaged when he was rated Qualified. (Had people known it was by a majority rather than a unanimous vote, it would have hurt more.) After Carswell's defeat, the ABA again changed its ratings. The new ones were that the nominee met "high standards of integrity, judicial temperament and professional competence," was "not opposed," or was "not qualified."

Probably because of embarrassing information about Haynsworth and Carswell not uncovered by its own investigations, the administration agreed to allow the ABA committee to evaluate not only the person already selected but all those being considered for a Supreme Court position. This arrangement lasted only a short time, however. After the committee rated one potential nominee Not Qualified and another Not Opposed, President Nixon (unfairly) accused the committee of having "leaked" the nominees' names to the press, and dropped the ABA's prior screening of nominees. The ABA thus knew no more than anyone else (nothing) about the Powell and Rehnquist nominations when they were announced.

The vacancy created by Justice Douglas's resignation provided the ABA its desired prior involvement in screening for the first time. Attorney General Edward Levi sent a list of potential nominees to the ABA, which could add to the list. Fifteen names were screened over a two-week period, and after interviewing lawyers and judges and reviewing over 200 of his opinions, the ABA gave John Paul Stevens, the ultimate choice, its highest rating. When Sandra O'Connor was nominated, the ABA—not consulted before the nomination —found that she had "the professional qualifications required of an Associate Justice of the Supreme Court of the United States" despite the absence of "extensive or challenging" judicial experience.

Judges' Involvement

Supreme Court justices themselves at times get involved in selection politics. Chief Justice William Howard Taft frequently exerted pressure on behalf of people he wanted nominated.[44] More recently, Chief Justice Warren attempted to exert some pressure on behalf of Arthur Goldberg and Byron White for the Frankfurter and Whittaker vacancies and also on behalf of Fortas to succeed him as Chief Justice, but he apparently also paid a visit to his old political enemy President Nixon to comment against Justice Stewart's effort to succeed him. Chief Justice Burger has apparently also not been silent concerning Supreme Court nominations, but appears to have been less active than Taft.

The most frequent method used in these efforts by the justices has been a letter of recommendation, followed in frequency by personal visits to either the president or the attorney general. Next most frequent has been a presidential request to the justices, in responding to which they are able to supply information and recommendations. Intense lobbying has been used only infrequently. Efforts in favor of a candidate appear to be less successful than those against, although judges' intervention is, of course, only one factor among many affecting the ultimate nomination.[45] Moreover, too much pressure from a Supreme Court justice can drive the president away from a potential nominee, not toward him, as appears to have been the case with Justice Frankfurter's efforts to obtain a Supreme Court appointment for Circuit Judge Learned Hand.[46]

Lower court judges may also try to play a role in the selection of Supreme Court justices. For example, the judges of the District of Columbia Circuit supported Burger's nomination to be Chief Justice, and all the judges of the Fourth Circuit supported Judge Haynsworth's nomination. Carswell's supporters in the lower federal judiciary also tried to gain additional support for his nomination, and after the press noted a lack of support for the nomination among Carswell's Fifth Circuit colleagues, 50 of 58 district judges and seven of 13 senior district judges in the Fifth Circuit sent the White House a statement endorsing the nominee.

President and Senate[47]

The president's position when he deals with the Senate is stronger for Supreme Court nominations than for those to the lower courts. That the president's position is not absolute is shown by the Senate's successive rejections of President Nixon's nominations of Judges Haynsworth and Carswell—the first formal rejections of a nominee since 1930 and the first "double rejection" since 1894. Despite these rejections and the Senate's failure to confirm the nomination of Justice Fortas to be Chief Justice and the nomination of Judge Homer Thornberry that accompanied it (both withdrawn), presidents have done far better in the twentieth century than earlier. Including those of 1894, seven nominations were rejected before 1900 and nineteen others have not been confirmed—for example, withdrawn after the Senate's extended delay in acting on them.

Most nominations sail smoothly through the confirmation process. Usually less than two months is necessary from submission of the nomination to the Senate to final Senate vote, and the time was less than three weeks each for Harry Blackmun and John Paul Stevens. Most of the time is consumed in the period between committee hearings and release of the committee's report; once it receives the nomination, the full Senate votes promptly. In Justice O'Connor's case, two months elapsed between the nomination and the hearings, with a Senate vote coming promptly thereafter. Judiciary Committee hearings are perfunctory in most instances, with one-day hearings the pattern in the past, although those for Brandeis occupied *19* days. A majority (10 of 18) of post-1950 hearings have occupied at least two days, but in only two instances were there more than four days: Haynsworth (8 days) and Abe Fortas to be Chief Justice (11 days). Negative votes have occurred in committee on only one-fourth of the nominations, and there have been close votes (margins of four or fewer votes) in only three of 52 cases in this century: Parker (6–10), Brandeis (10–8), and Haynsworth (10–7).

The nominee's actions during the confirmation process, particularly at these hearings, may have some effect on the outcome. When Harlan Fiske Stone was under fire from Senator Walsh of Montana, Stone offered to appear before the Judiciary Committee—not the custom at the time. Stone's offer was accepted and he handled himself quite successfully, indicating the importance of the nominee's candor with the committee. With Sandra O'Connor, what apparently proved important were her visits with individual senators shortly after her nomination and well before the hearing. On the negative side, although William Rehnquist provided affidavits to the committee chairman dealing with questions that arose after his hearing, his failure to reappear angered some senators. More damaging was Judge Haynsworth's failure to deal with ethical conduct charges, and Carswell's chances were hurt when he failed to indicate that former Fifth Circuit Chief Judge Tuttle, after saying he had confidence in Carswell and would testify in his behalf, had told Carswell he would no longer testify. Carswell's problem was compounded when the Justice Department failed to arrange a meeting between the nominee and three dubious senators.

The Senate takes no more than two days of debate on all except the most controversial nominations; it used five days each on Fortas (to be Chief Justice) and Rehnquist and seven days on Haynsworth. Until recently the Senate seldom even bothered with roll calls on the nominations, and Senate votes are often unanimous (Blackmun, Stevens, O'Connor) or nearly so (one negative vote on Powell, three on Burger). The rejections, however, have been relatively close: Parker, 41–39, Haynsworth, 55–45, and Carswell, 51–45. In only three twentieth-century confirmed nominations did the negative votes approach one-half the positive vote, and all occurred early in the century: Mahlon Pitney (50–26), Brandeis (47–22), and Charles Evans Hughes to be Chief Justice (52–26). Yet although few recent votes in favor of confirmation have been close (68–26 on Rehnquist was the closest), opposition has increased recently. Since 1949, seven nominees have received ten or more "no" votes. Opposition has even occurred when senators were nominated; Hugo Black and Sherman Minton (a Truman appointee) each received sixteen negative votes.

Other factors that may well affect the outcome of Senate consideration of a nominee include the Senate's partisan and ideological composition and the time during a president's term when the nomination occurs. Senators' liberalism is one element with a strong effect on their votes to confirm. Political considerations underlay the votes in fourteen instances from Brandeis through Rehnquist (including the cloture vote on Fortas' nomination to be Chief Justice) in which at least 10 percent of the Senate's votes were negative. In every one of these instances, senators favoring confirmation differed from their generally more cohesive Senate opposition on salient policy issues. In more than three-fourths of the confirmation votes, more than half of those opposing the nomination were clustered at either the most conservative or most liberal end of the political continuum with respect to the policy area at issue, although the ideology of the nominees' supporters was at the opposite extreme in only five cases. Thus "it is primarily dissatisfaction with the predicted policy behavior of the nominee which is the main motive force behind a vote against confirmation."[48]

With respect to timing, nominees have been confirmed roughly 90 percent of the time during the president's first three years in office, but less than two-thirds of later nominations have been successful. However, when there is a partisan difference between Senate and president (Nixon's situation), in the first three years of his term the president has had only a 64 percent success rate; this falls to a devastatingly low *27 percent* (4 of 15) in the last year. Independent of the time of nomination, the president's success rate is over 90 percent when the Senate majority is of his party, but only 42 percent when his party is in the minority.[49]

The president cannot control when a vacancy occurs. Jimmy Carter never had a vacancy to fill. He was the first president not to be able to make a nomination to the Supreme Court, but he was not the only one not to be able to do so during his first term. FDR had that problem, as rumors of Justice VanDevanter's impending retirement did not come until Roosevelt's Court-packing plan was under heavy fire. President Reagan was not able to control the timing of the vacancy caused by Justice Stewart's departure, which was a surprise because Stewart was one of only four justices under 70. However, because the vacancy came very early in his term, President Reagan benefitted from an early administration "honeymoon effect" and could make good on his campaign promise to name a woman to the Supreme Court.

Despite the problems just noted, the president may in the short run be able to affect the timing of a nomination. For example, immediately after the grueling fight over Haynsworth, the Senate, as suggested by one senator, was prepared to confirm anyone who had not raped a small child, in public, recently, so Nixon's delay in sending the Carswell nomination to the Senate misfired. The liberals regained their strength and discovered much negative evidence about Carswell. Rehnquist's nomination, on the other hand, was helped by timing, coming as it did at the end of a session when the necessity of completing normal end-of-session business meant less time for consideration of the nomination, when the Senate was tired from the fight over Earl Butz's nomination to be Secretary of Agriculture, and after substantial effort had been devoted to attacking some anticipated nominations. As this suggests, opposition to a nomination may have a carry-over effect. Hoover's nomination of

John Parker, which occurred late in Hoover's term, was affected by the earlier controversy over Hughes' nomination to be Chief Justice. Liberal opposition to Warren Burger's appointment as Chief Justice was still simmering when Haynsworth was nominated. That displeasure served to reinforce the deeper liberal and Democratic unhappiness both over the Republicans' having deprived them of the Chief Justiceship when they had blocked the Fortas nomination and over the Nixon administration's not-well-concealed role in helping drive Fortas from the Court. Similarly, when President Ford had to nominate a replacement for Justice Douglas, Ford's earlier unsuccessful attempt as House minority leader to impeach Douglas was in people's minds, and Ford might have had considerable difficulty had he named a conservative rather than the moderate Stevens.

Another element of the timing of nominations is the president's use of recess appointments to the Supreme Court, such as Eisenhower's appointments of Warren, Brennan, and Stewart. However, this device is likely to produce negative Senate reaction, such as delay in confirming the nomination, in which the Senate engaged with the Stewart nomination to show its displeasure. Yet there are pressures on the president to fill a vacancy on the Court that arises when the Senate is not in session. To wait to make the appointment until the Senate returns might mean injustice to those with pending cases, which might have to be delayed or reargued. Although the Court's senior justice could serve as de facto Chief Justice, a vacancy in the Chief Justice's position is particularly serious. Coupled with the fact that *Brown v. Board of Education* had been set for reargument when Chief Justice Vinson died, this probably explains the recess appointment of Earl Warren.

Despite the occasional need to make them, recess appointments cause problems for the president, the Senate, and the Court itself. If the Senate were to convene in special session to consider only the recess nomination, more attention would be focused on a single nomination than it deserved and the Senate's power would increase in relation to the president's. Yet the Senate finds it cannot get necessary information from an already sitting nominee because ethically he cannot respond to questions which touch on cases under consideration by the Court. There is also the possibility that an appointee concerned about Senate reaction to his or her votes might "pull punches" or cases in which the nominee is to write the Court's opinions might be "held" until after confirmation. (Two important opinions by Justice Brennan were not announced until nine weeks after his confirmation.)

Although often the president does no more—and need do no more—than announce the nomination, not only his timing but also his stance toward the nomination may affect the outcome, particularly if opposition arises. Both Woodrow Wilson's support for Brandeis and Eisenhower's support for Earl Warren (a public statement and a letter to the Judiciary Committee) had positive effects. President Hoover's calling in several Republican senators for discussions to gain support for the Parker nomination was, however, unsuccessful, and Lyndon Johnson's support of Abe Fortas's nomination to be Chief Justice backfired because Fortas was already under attack as a crony of Johnson. President Nixon failed to help the Haynsworth nomination with his initial heavy pressure, a special news conference repudiating anti-

Haynsworth charges in detail, and a statement that senators should not take a nominee's philosophy into account; Republican senators did not like Nixon's "arm twisting." His attempt at a "low profile" for the Carswell nomination was followed by overreaction when negative information was revealed. In a letter to Senator (later Attorney General) William Saxbe (R-Ohio), Nixon even claimed his right to appoint whom he wanted:

> What is centrally at issue in this nomination is the constitutional responsibility of the President to appoint members of the Court—and whether this responsibility can be frustrated by those who wish to substitute their own philosophy or their own subjective judgment for that of the one person entrusted by the Constitution with the power of appointment. The question arises whether I, as President of the United States, shall be accorded the same right of choice in naming Supreme Court Justices which has been freely accorded to my predecessors of both parties.[50]

Challenging the Senate, as the president did in this statement, is particularly unwise politically.

NOTES

1. *Atkins v. United States*, 556 F.2d 1028 (Ct.Cl. 1977), cert. denied, 434 U.S. 1009 (1978).
2. *Duplantier v. United States*, 606 F.2d 654 (5th Cir. 1979) and 608 F.2d 1373 (5th Cir. 1980), cert denied, 449 U.S. 1076 (1981).
3. Data from surveys by *National Law Journal*: May 28, 1979; June 2, 1980; July 6, 1981; also *New York Times:* May 18, 1982.
4. *Chandler v. Judicial Council of the Tenth Circuit*, 398 U.S. 74 at 130 (1970). For a thorough treatment of the entire Chandler matter, particularly the underlying conflict between Judge Chandler and his fellow judges, see Joseph C. Goulden, *The Benchwarmers: The Private World of the Powerful Federal Judges* (New York: Ballantine Books, 1974), pp. 234–284.
5. Elliot E. Slotnick, "What Panelists Are Saying About the Circuit Judge Nominating Commission," *Judicature* 62 (February 1979):322–323.
6. Harold W. Chase, *Federal Judges: The Appointing Process* (Minneapolis: University of Minnesota Press, 1972), pp. 36–37.
7. Elliot E. Slotnick, "Reforms in Judicial Selection: Will They Affect the Senate's Role?", *Judicature* 64 (August 1980):69–70.
8. For a description of procedure, see Elliot E. Slotnick, "The U.S. Circuit Judge Nominating Commission," *Law & Policy Quarterly* 1 (October 1979):465–496, on which I have drawn; Slotnick, "Federal Appellate Judge Selection During the Carter Administration: Recruitment Changes and Unanswered Questions," *Justice System Journal* 6 (Fall 1981):293–304; Larry Berkson, "The U.S. Circuit Judge Nominating Commission: The Candidates' Perspective," *Judicature* 62 (May 1979):466–482; and Larry C. Berkson and Susan B. Carbon, *The United States Circuit Judge Nominating Commission: Its Members, Procedures and Candidates* (Chicago: American Judicature Society, 1980).

9. Elliot E. Slotnick, "What Panelists are Saying," p. 321.
10. Ibid., p. 323.
11. Ibid., p. 322.
12. See Alan Neff, "Breaking with Tradition," *Judicature* 64 (December–January 1981): 256–278; and Neff, *The United States District Judge Nominating Commissions: Their Members, Procedures and Candidates* (Chicago: American Judicature Society, 1981); as well as Slotnick, "Reforms in Judicial Selection: Will They Affect the Senate's Role," *Judicature* 64 (August 1980):60–73 and (September 1980):114–131.
13. See Adlai E. Stevenson, "'Reform' and Judicial Selection," *American Bar Association Journal* 64 (November 1978):1683–1685.
14. Neff, "Breaking with Tradition," pp. 265–266.
15. Slotnick, "Reforms in Judicial Selection," p. 67.
16. Ibid., p. 119.
17. Neff. "Breaking with Tradition," p. 275.
18. Slotnick, "Reforms in Judicial Selection," p. 116. See also Sheldon Goldman, "Should There be Affirmative Action for the Judiciary?" *Judicature* 62 (May 1979):488–494.
19. Chase, pp. 130–131.
20. Ibid., p. 135.
21. "Q. and A. with the New Attorney General," *American Bar Association Journal* 65 (October 1979):1502. For a recent study, see Elliot E. Slotnick, "The ABA Standing Committee on Federal Judiciary: A Contemporary Assessment," *Judicature* 66 (March 1983):348–362 and (April 1983):385–393.
22. See Elaine Martin, "Women on the Federal Bench: A Comparative Profile," *Judicature* 65 (December–January 1982):309.
23. See three articles by Sheldon Goldman: "Voting Behavior on the United States Courts of Appeals, 1961–1964," *American Political Science Review* 60 (June 1966):374–383; "Conflict and Consensus in the United States Courts of Appeals," *Wisconsin Law Review* 1968:461–482; and "Conflict in the U.S. Courts of Appeals, 1965–1971: A Quantitative Analysis," *University of Cincinnati Law Review* 42 (1973):635–658.
24. C.K. Rowland and Robert A. Carp, "A Longitudinal Study of Party Effects on Federal District Court Policy Propensities," *American Journal of Political Science* 24 (May 1980): 300. See also Robert A. Carp and C. K. Rowland, *Policymaking and Politics in the Federal District Courts* (Knoxville: University of Tennessee Press, 1983).
25. Kermit L. Hall, "The Children of the Cabins: The Lower Federal Judiciary, Modernization, and the Political Culture, 1789–1899," *Northwestern University Law Review* 75 (October 1980):436. See also Hall,*The Politics of Justice: Lower Federal Judicial Selection and the Second Party System, 1829–1861* (Lincoln: University of Nebraska Press, 1979).
26. Kermit L. Hall, "Hacks and Derelicts Revisited: American Territorial Judiciary, 1789–1959," *Western Historical Quarterly* 12 (July 1981):279, 284.
27. J. Woodford Howard, Jr., *Courts of Appeals in the Federal Judicial System*, p. 113.
28. The data here and some that appear subsequently are drawn from Sheldon Goldman, "Characteristics of Eisenhower and Kennedy Appointees to the Lower Federal Courts," *Western Political Quarterly* 18 (1965):755–762; and Goldman, "Judicial Backgrounds, Recruitment and the Party Variable: The Case of the Johnson and Nixon Appointees to the United States District and Appeals Courts," *Arizona State Law Journal* 1974:211–222.
29. *McClure v. Carter*, 513 F.Supp. 265 (D. Idaho 1981), aff'd sub nom. *McClure v. Reagan*, 102 S.Ct. 559 (1981).
30. Martin, pp. 310, 312.

31. Robert Scigliano, *The Supreme Court and the Presidency* (New York: Free Press, 1971), p. 105.
32. John R. Schmidhauser, "Judicial Behavior and the Sectional Crisis of 1837–1860," *Journal of Politics* 4 (November 1971):615–640.
33. Stuart Nagel, "Comparing Elected and Appointed Judicial Systems," Sage Professional Papers #04-001 (Beverly Hills, Calif.: Sage, 1973), p. 25.
34. John R. Schmidhauser, *The Supreme Court: Its Politics, Personalities and Procedures* (New York: Holt, Rinehart and Winston, 1961), pp. 31–32.
35. John R. Schmidhauser, "*Stare Decisis*, Dissent and the Background of the Justices," *University of Toronto Law Review* 14 (May 1962):194–212.
36. Scigliano, p. 146. His full treatment of the subject is on pp. 125–128.
37. Edward V. Heck and Steven A. Shull, "Policy Preferences of Justices and Presidents: The Case of Civil Rights," *Law & Policy Quarterly* 4 (July 1982):333.
38. David W. Rohde and Harold J. Spaeth, *Supreme Court Decision-Making* (San Francisco: W.H. Freeman, 1975), pp. 107–108.
39. Charles M. Lamb, "The Making of a Chief Justice: Warren Burger on Criminal Procedure, 1957–1969," *Cornell Law Review* 60 (June 1975):756, 786; see also Lamb, "Exploring the Conservatism of Federal Appeals Court Judges," *Indiana Law Journal* 51 (Winter 1976):257–279.
40. This examination draws on Joel B. Grossman and Stephen L. Wasby, "Haynsworth and Parker: History Does Live Again," *South Carolina Law Review* 23 (1971):345–359; and Grossman and Wasby, "The Senate and Supreme Court Nominations: Some Reflections," *Duke Law Journal* (August 1972):557–591.
41. See Robert Shogan, *A Question of Judgment: The Fortas Case and the Struggle for the Supreme Court* (Indianapolis: Bobbs-Merrill, 1972).
42. For a correction and addition to the study by Grossman and Wasby based on correspondence with Judge Haynsworth, see Wasby, *Continuity and Change: From the Warren Court to the Burger Court* (Pacific Palisades, Calif.: Goodyear, 1976), pp. 27–28, note.
43. Donald R. Songer, "The Relevance of Policy Values for the Confirmation of Supreme Court Nominees," *Law & Society Review* 13 (Summer 1979):939.
44. See Walter F. Murphy, "In His Own Image: Mr. Chief Justice Taft and Supreme Court Appointments," *Supreme Court Review 1961*, ed. Philip Kurland (Chicago: University of Chicago Press, 1961), pp. 159–193.
45. Henry J. Abraham and Bruce Allen Murphy, "The Influence of Sitting and Retired Justices on Presidential Supreme Court Nominations," *Hastings Constitutional Law Quarterly* 3 (Winter 1976):37–63.
46. Bruce Allen Murphy, *The Brandeis/Frankfurter Connection* (New York: Oxford University Press, 1982), p. 320.
47. This is based on Grossman and Wasby, "The Senate and Supreme Court Nominations."
48. Songer, pp. 935–936.
49. See Scigliano, pp. 146–147.
50. Richard M. Nixon to William Saxbe, March 31, 1970, *Congressional Record* 116 (1970):10158.

Chapter 4

Lawyers, Interest Groups, and Appeals

Playing a crucial role in the judicial process are people who initiate cases and particularly their attorneys, who present the cases in court. In any examination of the Supreme Court, lawyers—individual attorneys in private practice, government lawyers, and interest group lawyers—are particularly important because of their role in deciding what cases to appeal. Not all types of cases are appealed in the same proportions, and during an appeal lawyers may shift the focus of a case from issues that were central in the trial to other issues. Although individuals *may* be able to present their own cases effectively in local courts, the assistance of lawyers is essential when cases are complex or when cases reach the higher levels of the judicial system. Because the Supreme Court accepts only cases involving issues of considerable public significance, the role of lawyers is especially important in helping shape those outcomes, which will affect many people in addition to the lawyers' clients. Moreover, although some corporations or wealthy individuals can afford the lengthy process of litigation and appeals, taking a case to the Supreme Court requires most litigants to obtain financial support, at times provided by interest groups.

Those interest groups participating in the judicial process and other well-organized actors are also involved in cases before the Supreme Court because of their stake in long-run outcomes extending beyond the particular facts of individual cases. The government is another party appearing regularly before the courts in general and the Supreme Court in particular. The government acts not only as a prosecutor and defender of its own policies, but also as another major actor trying to affect the Court's shaping of policies in cases in which the government itself is not a party. In this chapter, after some general comments about relations between lawyers and judges, we look first at federal government attorneys—the United States Attorneys, the Attorney General of the United States, and the Solicitor General—and then turn to a more extended examination of the role of private attorneys and interest groups in litigation.

LAWYERS, CASES, AND THE COURT

Relations between bench and bar take a variety of forms in and out of court. When lawyers become judges, they may withdraw somewhat from frequent contact with former lawyer colleagues, even when they continue to reside where they lived before becoming judges. Not all such ties are severed, however, and judges continue to participate in bar association activities, both nationally and at the state and local levels. Those activities include not only dinners and other social functions but also work on committees that make policy recommendations. Judges also have contacts with the lawyers who serve on advisory committees of both the Judicial Conference of the United States and the circuit judicial conferences. Lawyer representatives are regularly in attendance at the annual circuit judicial conferences, thus providing an opportunity for the attorneys to criticize federal courts' work. In short, lawyers and judges interact not only in formal ways in the courtroom—ways that, because of their frequency, may become regularized—but in a variety of ways that differ in their formality.

Lawyers' involvement in cases is, of course, crucial to the course of the judicial process and its outcomes. The importance of lawyers at all stages of litigation, from initiation to final appeal, cannot be underestimated, even though judges may have the final say in a case. Obviously lawyers help determine the cases that will be brought initially and that form the universe from which appeals may be drawn. Decisions to initiate cases are often the result of implicit interaction between lawyers and judges. On the basis of the precedents established by judges' rulings, lawyers may try to discourage clients from pursuing litigation they are sure to lose. Yet where the law is not clear or fully developed, a lawyer wishing to solve a client's problem may bring to the courts questions the judges have not previously considered. Judges may encourage lawyers to bring cases by making hints or suggestions that particular legal issues have not been raised. On the other hand, by showing firmness in disposing of a matter, they make clear that the court wishes to hear no more litigation on that subject.

Moreover, the general policy orientation of a court affects the cases lawyers bring to court and pursue on appeal. With the departure of Earl Warren and his replacement by Warren Burger, for example, one heard civil liberties lawyers talk about taking fewer cases to the Supreme Court; this view was strengthened after President Nixon made his other appointments and the full dimensions of the Burger Court's doctrines began to emerge. Yet despite their negative perceptions of Supreme Court rulings, liberal lawyers continue to bring cases—because clients press them to do so, because they believe they *may* achieve a victory even if they estimate their chances of doing so to be slim, and because they may fear that other lawyers will bring a case raising their issue before they have a chance to do so. On the other hand, conservative lawyers—both those representing public interest law firms and government lawyers who see the Court as now more open to their claims—would be more likely to appeal cases to the High Court.

In our supposedly adversary system of justice, courts are expected to make their decisions on the basis of material submitted by the parties. This serves to underscore the importance of lawyers' actions in presenting their cases. Reliance on party-submitted material is greatest with respect to factual matters at the trial, which are doubly important because the trial record serves as the basis for appeals. Thus lawyers' actions at one stage of litigation affect later actions and may even foreclose them. At the appellate level, the court's decision is also supposed to be based on material submitted by lawyers: the trial record, briefs, and arguments made in the appellate court. Thus to a greater or lesser degree lawyers' positions place constraints on the decisions judges can reach. If both lawyers in a case press the same position or at least focus directly on the same narrow issue, the judges' freedom of action may be decreased. At other times, however, those constraints are not tight, particularly when lawyers plead multiple claims, press procedural and substantive questions simultaneously, or argue broad grounds about which they are personally indifferent. The constraints are further lessened when interested individuals or (more likely) groups file briefs as an *amicus curiae* ("friend of the court") to urge legal positions related to the issues in the case but often somewhat different from those stressed by the direct litigants.

Judges can increase their freedom of action by expanding or contracting issues ("issue fluidity": see page 217), by relying more on material submitted by an *amicus* rather than by focusing exclusively on the parties' arguments, or by developing additional information through research they and their law clerks conduct. Judges' development of information has been criticized for not being consonant with a pure version of the adversary system and because the litigants don't have an opportunity to evaluate material serving as a partial basis for judges' decisions.[1] However, such use of additional material may be necessary if courts, and particularly the Supreme Court, are to issue decisions affecting more than the immediate parties to the case;

only in this way might a judge know, for example, of a case's broader implications and potential effects.

THE GOVERNMENT'S ATTORNEYS

United States Attorneys

Particularly crucial for the federal judicial process are United States Attorneys and the Attorney General and Solicitor General of the United States. There was no Department of Justice until 1870, but there have been United States Attorneys, one for each judicial district, and an Attorney General, serving as the lawyer to the president, since 1789. U.S. Attorneys are formally appointed by the president and confirmed by the Senate, although district judges have the authority to select "court appointees" to fill temporary vacancies. The realities of the appointment process, however, give substantial roles to senators, through senatorial courtesy, and to the Justice Department, which, in making its choices, takes into account the need to maintain good relations with the bench. The senators' role increases U.S. Attorneys' local orientations. On the other hand, the U.S. Attorneys' national orientation is evident in the fact that they generally submit their resignations when a new president takes office, although there have been some instances in which they have refused to do so, thus forcing their removal by the president.[2] U.S. Attorney offices vary greatly in size, roughly paralleling the relative size of a district's federal bench; they have ranged from an office that comprises the U.S. Attorney and one assistant to that for the Southern District of New York with well over 100 assistants. In the larger offices, the basic work is carried out by the assistant U.S. attorneys, hired by the U.S. Attorneys, with the latter generally acting as managers, although some seek to set policy and shape agency priorities.

U.S. Attorneys and their assistants are at the center of a set of relations—with the judges in their districts, other government agencies, and the Department of Justice. Relations between DOJ (Department of Justice) and the USAs (U.S. Attorneys) vary depending on the district and the incumbent; they also vary over time depending on DOJ efforts at control and the USAs' willingness to resist such control. U.S. Attorneys are under the formal supervision of the attorney general, who can control politically sensitive cases—for example, the bribery charges against then Vice President Spiro Agnew or those in certain categories such as civil rights—and can instruct the U.S. Attorneys as to whether or not to try a case. In areas of law that the Justice Department considers important, great effort is made to establish priorities for U.S. Attorneys. Overall policy direction is, or at least can be, established by the attorney general and the assistant attorneys general in charge of the department's various divisions—Land, Civil Rights, and Antitrust. In most instances, however, formal supervision is not matched by actual control of their work, so that the federal government has "not yet succeeded in establishing complete domination and control over U.S. attorneys' offices."[3]

U.S. Attorneys have traditionally exercised considerable independence of "headquarters." A few offices, most notably that for the Southern District of New York, have developed significant autonomy—especially symbolic autonomy—because of the high proportion of all federal cases, and particularly of the important federal cases, they handle. Indeed, U.S. Attorneys have considerable autonomy within the federal law enforcement establishment because of their resources, including their standing in the community, access to information that others do not possess, and others' dependence on their work. They have considerable discretion in determining what cases they will bring, resulting in considerable variation from one district to another in the way similar cases are handled.

U.S. Attorneys' activities are affected less by relations with DOJ than by relations with district judges and by interaction with the other federal agencies that initiate cases and on which they may need to rely for information. Because they can refuse to prosecute, U.S. Attorneys and their assistants may be in a superior position in dealing with investigative agencies. However, "many of the cases presented leave little room for the exercise of discretion": good cases cannot be turned down and trivial ones cannot be authorized.[4] Moreover, workload affects decisions as to what cases to accept: a heavy caseload may lead an office to decline prosecution of cases that an office with greater resources would have accepted. Judges have particularly significant effects on U.S. Attorneys' offices: they can affect not only case outcomes but also the way in which cases move through the court, and can supervise the assistant USAs, who spend much time in court. However, relations between judge and prosecutor are not unilateral: cases brought by the U.S. Attorney's office are the dominant portion of a district court's caseload and thus affect the conditions of the judge's conduct and the amount of work the judge has.

Attorney General

The Attorney General of the United States is often someone personally close to the president or someone closely involved in his political campaigns. An important question is whether a person chosen for this position on the basis of political party or friendship considerations— such as Robert Kennedy, with little previous legal experience, or William French Smith, a corporate attorney—has skills appropriate to being the nation's chief lawyer. However, the attorney general has special assistants available to provide supplementary skills, and specialists are chosen as assistant attorneys general. (Of recent attorneys general, former federal appellate judge Griffin Bell, President Carter's first attorney general, had perhaps the broadest prior exposure to federal legal problems.)

The attorney general has several roles to perform. One role is administrative head of the Department of Justice, including the Federal Bureau of Investigation, and of the decentralized collection of U.S. Attorneys and their assistants, although day-to-day administrative coordination is invariably performed by someone else. The attorney general's tasks as administrator may entail resolving friction not only between DOJ and USAs, but also between lawyers in the department's divisions and the political appointees heading those divisions. An example is the recent conflict between the department's top leadership, more conservative under President Reagan and Attorney General William French Smith, and the more liberal lawyers of the Civil Rights Division. Another role is chief prosecutor of those alleged to have violated the nation's laws, although the question of politicization of law enforcement arises when the lawyer who advises the president supervises government prosecutors.

Growth of the White House staff allows the president to obtain legal advice on his immediate responsibilities directly from counsel on his own staff. However, a crucial role for the attorney general remains being the "president's lawyer." Working with the president and the latter's assistants and at the president's direction, the attorney general is also chief maker of the nation's legal policy. This role includes making decisions to bring cases or to file briefs to establish particular legal points, such as the Reagan administration's participation in cases as part of its efforts to limit school busing or to restrict the breadth of the exclusionary rule in criminal cases. The government continues such efforts even after losing in one or more district or appellate courts. In trying to develop national policy, the government does not accept as authoritative a single court of appeals ruling adverse to the government on a particular point of law. Instead the government is willing to relitigate even within the same circuit if some basis can be found for distinguishing later cases from the initial ones. Only when three unanimous courts of appeals decisions have been decided against the government is the government willing to stop litigation on that point of law.[5] This continuous relitigaton is part of an effort to create an intercircuit conflict that it is hoped the Supreme Court will accept.

The attorney general's role as maker of national legal policy is also visible in changes in the government's litigation position, such as the shift, after the Reagan administration took office, on tax exempt status for private schools that discriminate against racial minorities (from opposition to the tax exemption to support for it) and on a state's obligation to provide education to children of illegal aliens (where the government terminated its support for nongovernmental litigants seeking such educational aid). (The administration lost both cases.) It is also seen in statements made by the attorney general on major policy issues, such as those by Attorney General Smith on limitations on federal court jurisdiction, proposed constitutional amendments, and on "judicial activism."

Solicitor General

The Solicitor General of the United States is the third-ranking official in the Justice Department. Perhaps best known from appearances before the Supreme Court, the solicitor general plays a crucial part in the executive branch's judicial activity, particularly in the appellate courts. Making up the bulk of the work of the solicitor general's office are decisions whether to appeal cases the government has lost in a district court and whether to seek Supreme Court review of adverse appellate rulings; these actions are closely related to the Justice Department's overall litigation concerns. Such decisions are crucial for federal agencies, as only a few regulatory commissions, including the Interstate Commerce Commission and Federal Maritime Commission, have statutory authority to appeal their cases without DOJ approval; even for them, absence of the solicitor general's approval is disadvantageous. (Government agency decisions *not* to appeal are seldom reviewed by the solicitor general, much less overturned.)

The solicitor general must also decide whether to defend the government against appeals from its lower court victories, whether to oppose opponents' certiorari petitions, and whether to support or oppose other parties through the filing of *amicus* briefs. In so doing, the solicitor general can be highly selective in choosing precisely the cases in which to press new legal arguments. Although usually defending the government, the solicitor general may decide that the government should have lost a case it has won, such as a case won because of improper actions like illegal wiretapping. In such instances the solicitor general makes a *confession of error,* that is, tells the justices that the government should lose. Decisions not to appeal government defeats to the Supreme Court may be related to the Court's caseload and the government's general legal policy position, including the desire to restrict the legal effect of the defeat to the district or circuit in which it occurred. In confession of error situations, other factors also come into play. Foremost is the need to protect the department's reputation and thus to increase the chance of winning later cases.

Despite the great weight the solicitor general's actions carry with the Supreme Court, at least some justices will not automatically accept a confession of error. When the majority had followed a suggestion by the solicitor general that a case involving promises made to a government witness be returned to the trial court, Justices Rehnquist and Powell and Chief Justice Burger, dissenting, complained that "this Court does not, or at least should not, respond in Pavlovian fashion to confessions of error."[6] Several justices have also criticized the solicitor general for trying to use the Court to remedy U.S. Attorneys' failures to follow Justice Department policy.[7]

Another of the solicitor general's principal functions is to decide when the government will appear as an *amicus curiae* to urge executive branch policies upon the courts in cases to which the government is not a party. The United States and its agencies (when the solicitor general approves), like state and local governments, do not need to seek approval in order to file *amicus curiae* briefs. Because, without the consent of both parties, *amicus* participation comes only upon a petition to the Supreme Court itself, the solicitor general must also decide, in cases in which the government *is* a party, when others will be allowed to appear as *amicus.*

The solicitor general's participation as *amicus* before the Supreme Court and the permission granted to others have varied over time, in part reflecting the Supreme Court's preferences. Thus after the Court seemed in 1949 to want fewer *amicus* participations before the Court, the solicitor general reduced the number of permissions to potential *amici.* Then as the justices seemed to relax their position on *amicus* participation, his consent was given more frequently.[8]

The solicitor general's responsiveness to the Court's wishes and policy positions may help explain the office's phenomenal success in getting the Court to accept its positions. There is little question that the Court pays close heed to the solicitor general's arguments. The solicitor general is far more successful than private litigants in getting the Court to accept the government's petitions for certiorari, doing so at a rate of roughly *70 percent;* as an *amicus* in support of others' certiorari petitions, the solicitor general is even *more* successful in getting the Court to take cases.[9] When the government is in the Court, either as a party or as an *amicus*, the solicitor general's "win-lose" record is also quite impressive.

One must be careful not to attribute too much influence to the solicitor general. Influence may instead run in the other direction, with the solicitor general "guided by the Court's ideological predilections in carrying litigation to the Court." For example, in the 1960s solicitors general authorized appeals in only a low percentage of cases when the government's position was conservative and a much higher percentage when the government's position—like the Court's at the time— was liberal. With changes in the Court's orientation and with the administration and the new Court majority sharing an ideological orientation, as the Reagan administration and the Burger Court do, we would expect comparable interaction.[10]

PRIVATE LAWYERS, INTEREST GROUPS, AND LITIGATION

Private Attorneys

Private attorneys, particularly those associated with interest groups, are also crucial to the federal judicial system's operation. Lawyers who bring cases to the Supreme Court have become associated with those cases in several ways. For example, lawyers in Warren Court reapportionment and loyalty-security cases got involved through friendship with potential litigants, while those in civil rights cases had group affiliations.[11] Lawyers also enter cases at various stages of litigation. Despite the importance for appeals of the way issues are raised and presented in the district court and the way the record is shaped there, not all lawyers are in a case "from the beginning." Over 85 percent of those who argued reapportionment and loyalty-security cases in the Supreme Court in the late 1950s and early 1960s were involved from the initial trial onward. By contrast, less than two-thirds of those who argued civil rights cases were involved in the initial trial; the remainder did not become involved until the Supreme Court stage. In criminal justice cases, where most attorneys became involved through court appointment, slightly over two-fifths were involved at the initial trial, another one-third-plus appeared in the case at the first appeal, and the remainder were first involved at the Supreme Court level. Lawyers handling federal criminal appeals are now quite likely to enter cases at the appellate level because the Criminal Justice Act of 1964 provides appointed appellate counsel for those who cannot afford to retain their own attorney. However, lawyers who set out to establish particular doctrinal positions— as by bringing a case in a purposeful challenge to a statute or regulation (a *test case*)—are more and more likely to be involved from the beginning of the case.

Certain lawyers appear much more frequently in the Supreme Court than do others. A "Supreme Court bar" of the Court's early days has dispersed but those from the solicitor general's office or representing some major civil rights groups appear regularly. However, improved transportation has made it easy for lawyers from the Midwest and Far West to "hop a plane" to Washington to appear before the Court to present arguments in their cases—a temptation few appear able to resist.

It is important to recognize that not all those who have achieved major Supreme Court victories establishing important precedent set out to do so. Attorneys in the major Warren Court criminal procedure cases were often simply trying to win cases for their clients. In that effort, they argued constitutional questions along with everything else they could find to present, thus giving the Court its opportunity to establish the broad rules it announced. By comparison, attorneys who argued sit-in, reapportionment, and loyalty oath cases were far more likely to have had more in mind than to win the case for their client; they were interested in broader goals.

Lawyers do not have identical orientations to the law; those orientations affect their choice of cases and appeals as well as the shape of those cases and appeals. Some lawyers act as the client's agent (or "hired gun") and use the law basically to resolve conflicts. Others, whose view of the social good or public interest may play a greater role in determining the course of litigation, see law and clients' cases more as means for bringing about social change. Lawyers in corporate practice are more likely to be in the former group; those in other types of practice—such as criminal, environmental, consumer, labor and civil rights law, and women attorneys more than men attorneys—are more likely to adhere to the latter view. [12]

The Supreme Court itself helped stimulate an increase in the number of lawyers with a "welfarist" orientation. The Court's ruling in *Gideon v. Wainwright* requiring appointment of counsel for indigents in serious criminal trials, followed and reinforced by establishment of the "War on Poverty" Legal Services Program with its emphasis on "law reform" instead of individual "band-aid" law, helped produce lawyers broadly interested in the problems of the poor. Such lawyers were more likely than others to initiate broad legal challenges, as in the area of welfare policy. Their action reinforced the Warren Court's reach toward broad rules, which in turn further encouraged the lawyers.

Lawyers' differing orientations affect not only the types of cases in which they become involved but also the factors they consider in deciding whether or not to appeal and the relative weights they give those factors. One set of federal appellate lawyers studied generally agreed that the chance of success is quite important, and the timing of a case, an organization's concern, and advice by other attorneys are unimportant factors, but "social welfarists" were more likely than "entrepreneurials" to give the chance of winning greatest weight in deciding whether or not to take a case to the court of appeals, and the "entrepreneurials" gave far less weight to "importance to society" than did the "social welfarists." A greater overall interest in obtaining a forum from which to make issues known led the latter to be more willing to file a petition for certiorari in the Supreme Court when the possibilities of its being granted were low. Women appellate attorneys appeared to want higher "odds" of winning than did the men before they would file a certiorari petition. They were also less likely than men to cite financial reasons, including a client's ability to pay, for appealing and placed more emphasis on strategic concerns than did men.

Interest Groups

Cases are usually brought in the name of individuals. However, in a large proportion of cases, particularly in "public law" cases involving challenges to government actions and in cases brought under new statutes protecting individuals' rights, *interest groups* are associated with the cases in some way. Although many interest groups become involved in the judicial process only infrequently and peripherally, some have become "repeat players," large-volume litigators able to obtain advantages in the choice of courts in which to bring cases, the choice of cases to pursue, and the pace at which they move cases.[13] Interest group participation in the judicial system, although occurring in forms specific to the legal system, serves to reinforce the political character of the judicial process.

The norm is that interest groups should not lobby judges the way they lobby members of Congress or administrative officials; thus direct contact with judges is generally avoided. However, there are occasional violations of the norm. The noted Washington lobbyist Thomas ("Tommy the Cork") Corcoran approached both Justice Black and Justice Brennan on behalf of oil interests in connection with the *El Paso Natural Gas Co.* case. His efforts to discuss the case were firmly and promptly rejected, but nonetheless caused a problem because of concerns that a justice who had been approached should withdraw from the case.[14] The norm also does not prevent many people from writing letters—often critical of particular cases—to the justices. Justice Blackmun, author of the Court's opinion in the 1973 abortion cases, is estimated to have received over 45,000 letters in the ten years after the decision, most of them unfavorable.

Beginning with the Warren Court era, many interest groups playing important roles in litigation had liberal ideologies. They sought to produce social change for less advantaged members of society such as racial minorities and women, or sought to advance new causes such as environmental protection.[15] Labor unions have also long used the courts in pursuit of their goals. However, such groups have no monopoly on interest group participation in the judicial process. A number of groups pursue conservative goals through legislation; for example, Citizens for Decency through Law seeks to limit obscenity; Americans for Effective Law Enforcement attempts to strengthen the hand of police and prosecutor; and the National Right to Work Legal Defense Fund is engaged in limit unions' authority. Dominant social interests favoring the status quo—such as business groups and trade associations—have long used the legal system to achieve their goals, not only to resolve disputes but also to create rules for their future advantage. In the late nineteenth and early twentieth centuries, they used the courts to attack laws they couldn't defeat in the legislatures, and they were behind the attacks on New Deal legislation during the 1930s. One has regularly been able to find not only the "aggressive litigant . . . seeking innovative interpretations of the Constitution," but also the "defensive litigant" whose strategy is to convince judges "that prevailing constitutional norms, already favorable to his interests, should be applied."[16]

Defensive litigants have often been at a disadvantage before the Supreme Court. Although effective in invoking precedent and custom before local judges who share their views, at times they have not been prepared to deal effectively with the different—and more nationally oriented—values invoked in the Supreme Court by aggressive litigants seeking social change. An example is provided by the effort to overturn racially restrictive covenants used to prevent the sale of housing to blacks. Defensive litigants were successful in enforcing the covenants in state courts; however, they failed in the Supreme Court (in *Shelley v. Kraemer*, 1948), in part because they were not prepared to defend their position in terms of nationally accepted values and lacked as well an appropriate organizational network for defending their position.[17]

There has been a noticeable increase in Supreme Court participation by better prepared conservative interest groups starting with the first term of the Burger Court. During the 1969–1980 Terms, either a liberal or a conservative interest group or both participated in half the cases decided by the Court. Liberal interest groups were participants, either as direct sponsors of litigation or as *amicus*, in two-fifths of the cases; conservative groups participated at one-half that rate. Thus, although participation by liberal groups predominated, participation by conservative groups was far from insignificant. Moreover, conservative participation increased during the period, although it was more likely to take the form of *amicus* participation than did that of liberal groups. The conservative groups were more likely to be found in cases involving economic regulation, while liberal groups were still more likely to be found in civil liberties cases.[18]

Types of Participation

Interest group participation is of several different types. Lawyers may be interest group "cooperating attorneys" receiving help in preparing briefs and assistance with expenses; a group may provide the total financing for a case; or a group may provide its own staff lawyers to try a case. Some groups have assisted with the expenses of a trial or an appeal. At times umbrella groups may be established to assist in raising funds, as was done with causes célèbres like the Chicago Seven, Harrisburg, and Wounded Knee trials of the 1960s and early 1970s. Other groups become involved only as *amicus curiae* at the appellate level—an effective way for a group to be involved in precedent-making cases while shepherding scarce resources. Such participation, particularly before the Supreme Court, increased substantially starting in the 1960s and is quite likely to be found in civil liberties and civil rights cases, although less so in criminal appeals.[19]

"Friends of the court" may at first have been thought to serve the court as neutral participants rather than to favor the parties. However, groups usually become involved in a case as *amicus* because they wish to present a position favorable to one side in a case. Over time there has been a shift in *amicus* participation from neutrality, actually being a friend of the *court*, to advocacy, being a friend of one of the *parties*.[20] They do not, however, necessarily repeat the principal parties' basic arguments and often either adopt a different perspective or argue positions the principal litigants do not wish to emphasize. Particularly when an *amicus curiae*'s approach to a case differs from the parties' approach, the *amicus*'s role can be quite significant, providing reinforcement for the justices' opinions or even alerting the justices to the importance of certain issues. This may result in a case being considerably transformed in the Supreme Court from what was presented in the lower courts. For example, in *Mapp v. Ohio* (1961) the argument by the parties to the case centered on the issue of convicting someone for "mere possession" of obscene material (that is, without intent to sell) and on the "shocking" nature of the search that led to discovery of the material, but the defendant's attorney had not urged a change in the rule that improperly seized evidence could be used in the trial. The *exclusionary* issue was raised in the *amicus* brief filed by the American Civil Liberties Union and the Ohio Civil Liberties Union, but it was not central even to their argument. The Supreme Court, clearly eager to reverse its position on the admissibility of improperly seized evidence, reached out to make the admissibility question the central one of the case, and, without reaching the obscenity issue raised by the parties, handed down a landmark ruling excluding illegally seized evidence from state trials.[21]

Despite the potential importance of *amicus* participation and particularly its symbolic significance for a group wishing to record its position in important litigation, interest groups increasingly have felt that more direct involvement in cases is necessary and that it is best to provide an attorney from the beginning of a case. Groups such as the American Civil Liberties Union, which tended to focus earlier efforts on appellate *amicus* work, now frequently participate in cases from the beginning and often will not become involved in a case unless they can do so. This gives the group a greater opportunity to control the case by shaping the trial record, instead of having to work on appeal with a record created by lawyers for whom the group's interests may not have been central. Control allows a group to concentrate on issues of particular concern and permits it to file multiple cases raising the same or closely related issues in different courts, in turn increasing the likelihood of having a "good" case available for appeal.

From time to time, groups bring lawsuits in their own name. They do so not only to protect their own members, as the NAACP did in protecting against demands for membership lists, but also to assert the group's basic interests. The latter type of involvement is quite likely to be found in environmental litigation, with cases being brought by groups such as the Sierra Club, the Wilderness Society, and the Natural Resources Defense Council. However, in other areas of litigation, interest groups, instead of waiting for potential litigants to come to the group seeking assistance, may seek out litigants who have a case raising issues important to the group and who have a "case or controversy," thus satisfying requirements for access to the courts (see Chapter 5). In such cases, despite the use of the names of individual plaintiffs, the group, not the individual, is bringing the case.

Resources[22]

Contemporary conservative interest groups are well financed. They could therefore afford to finance lawsuits directly. However, these same resources, coupled with favorable access to legislators, may lead them to devote more effort to legislative lobbying than to direct financing of court cases. Yet in order to have their views known by the judges, they will engage in *amicus curiae* participation in lawsuits. For most other groups, not so well financed, *amicus* participation may be necessary because they cannot afford to finance cases. However, they, too, seem to be moving toward direct sponsorship of cases.

Resources are indeed a major problem for many litigating interest groups. The set of cases constituting *Brown v. Board of Education*, the 1954 school desegregation ruling, cost at least $250,000 (in the preinflation dollars of that time) to bring, with much lawyer time donated. More recently, the Detroit school cases of the mid-1970s—long in the trial court, in the appeals court several times, and twice decided by the Supreme Court—cost the plaintiffs just under $4,000,000; the Dayton school cases, also involving two Supreme Court rulings, resulted in an application for fees and costs for the NAACP and retained counsel of $1.8 million.

On the basis of the frequency with which their names appear in the media, groups trying either to defend or advance the interests of minorities and the otherwise disadvantaged may seem to have adequate resources, but the actual situation is one of quite scarce resources, both absolutely and in relation to goals sought. If cases are long and complex—increasingly true for school desegregation and job discrimination suits and cases challenging conditions in mental institutions and prisons—resources must be stretched. For example, much time is needed to prove a constitutional violation in large northern school districts; additional resources are required to develop remedies; and because of the difficulty of overcoming school board and public resistance to achieve effective desegregation, litigation may have to be pursued for several years. Because there are too many lawsuits to be brought in too many different places, organizations may have to pass up cases because their attorneys are "pinned down in the trenches" somewhere else.

Resources can be stretched by enlisting the assistance of government agencies, at least when those agencies share group goals. Groups may shepherd scarce resources by transmitting individual complaints to those government agencies that have complaint-processing machinery. Indeed, agencies or factions within an agency may not object to being prodded by interest groups to use their resources in a particular way. Such actions serve to bring government pressure on those the interest group would otherwise pursue directly.

Interest groups' in-house legal staffs are not large—perhaps twenty lawyers in some of the most significant groups. Attorney resources are made considerably greater through use of *cooperating attorneys*. These are lawyers otherwise in private practice who handle cases for the interest group either *pro bono* (for free: *pro bono publico* means "for the public good") or for a fee or honorarium considerably less than their regular hourly rate; the interest group often also assists with expenses. Cooperating attorneys have their own law practices to attend to, and thus often cannot handle long and complex cases, leading to use of staff attorneys. Because cooperating attorneys' priorities may not be identical with the group's, delegating responsibility to them may cause problems and reliance on them leads to organizational decentralization. At times, local attorneys are used for cases in state courts, where they are more familiar with the rules, and national staff attorneys handle federal litigation and any Supreme Court cases. At other times, the relationship is sequential: local attorneys take matters through the lower courts and then "hand them off" to national staff attorneys for appeals. Such an arrangement may be necessary when a local lawyer does not seek an interest group's assistance until after the trial, requiring the group's staff attorney to begin the group's work with whatever the local attorney has accomplished—or failed to accomplish.

Interest group resources have been increased recently through court awards of attorneys' fees. When a group has supplied an attorney for a lawsuit, has prevailed, and has obtained an award of attorneys' fees, those fees can be plowed back into the organization to finance other litigation. The basic *American rule* has been that the winning party in a lawsuit is *not* entitled to attorneys' fees as part of the costs awarded at the end of the trial. However, the idea that individuals or groups serve as *private attorneys general* to enforce existing laws or constitutional rights—and thus are entitled to attorneys' fees—has been embodied in some statutes, such as the Civil Rights Act of 1964. In 1975, the Supreme Court ruled in the *Alyeska Pipeline* environmental litigation that, because Congress had not specifically provided for them in that type of case, attorneys' fees could not be awarded in cases where the public is said to benefit from pursuit of the lawsuit but where no single individual or small set of individuals may have suffered substantial economic injury. Congress then included attorneys' fees provisions in several substantive statutes and, more important, passed the Civil Rights Attorneys Fees Act allowing the prevailing party in civil rights cases to recover attorneys' fees and the Access to Justice Act allowing recovery of fees from the federal government.

Because resources are scarce, interest groups' decisions concerning allocation of whatever resources exist are difficult. These include not only decisions as to legal issues on which to concentrate but broader decisions about the relative weight to give to litigation, lobbying the legislature and administrative agencies, and developing public opinion. Such resource-allocation decisions are affected by the relative complexity and length of the contemplated lawsuits as well as by availability of cooperating attorneys to try them. Both attorney preferences for certain types of cases and membership concerns may lead to placing new topics on a group's litigation agenda. An example of the effect of membership concerns is civil rights groups' addition of criminal justice issues (police brutality, discrimination in jury selection, and application of the death penalty) to their earlier priorities of education, jobs, and housing.

Strategy

To talk of choices to be made in allocating resources may leave the impression that litigating interest groups have a well-developed litigation strategy. If we define strategy broadly as "overall plans, coordination and direction developed for a major area of litigation, general enough to allow for flexibility and adaptability to changing circumstances,"[23] that may be true in some situations. Some groups define in advance the policy positions to which they will give preference in bringing or defending lawsuits for individuals who seek their aid and may go further in orchestrating an attack on a policy, as the NAACP did with respect to racially restrictive covenants on housing. Yet one of two cases decided by the Supreme Court on this issue was not an "NAACP case" but had been filed by another lawyer. As this indicates, groups are often propelled into a case before a strategy is developed. This also occurred with the sit-in cases, where no strategy existed because lawyers for the "Inc. Fund" (the NAACP Legal Defense and Educational Fund) initially had no idea that so many cases would develop.

Groups can have substantial influence over some cases. Some cases are brought at the trial level with the intent to appeal them to the Supreme Court, but, on the other hand, some are initiated simply to obtain a trial court order and not as a part of a "grand plan." Groups that appear to have a strategy may simply be responding idiosyncratically to cases brought to them or engaging in "an ad hoc search for targets of opportunity."[24] Some groups conducting much litigation remain largely reactive. This was true of the American Civil Liberties Union until relatively recently, when it developed several special litigation projects, such as the rights of women, prisoners, and the mentally ill. Even when a group has a general blueprint, the often unpredictable course of litigation is as influential as any such blueprint. Much litigation, including some cases appealed to the Supreme Court, remains beyond the group's complete control.

Why is the existence of interest group strategy in the broad sense problematic? One reason is that groups have a variety of goals they wish to achieve. Some seek to achieve certain outcomes. These might be greater rights for women or minorities, the invalidation of restrictive economic regulations, district judges' detailed rulings on remedies to change public institutions like prisons, or Supreme Court rulings on constitutional principles. Others undertake litigation to achieve leverage for legislation and administrative regulations they want adopted or altered, as Common Cause did in its campaign for election finance laws.

Some interest group litigation goals are short-term because victories are necessary in the short run if the groups are to continue to obtain resources. Thus certain actions must be undertaken for publicity purposes, to show supporters that the organization is alive and well, and to reinforce the group's ideological position. (*Amicus* participation may help in this respect, particularly if the group is short of resources for other types of litigation participation.[25]) Yet attention to short-term concerns may tie up precious resources needed for the longer term and may interfere with development of strategy aimed at achieving long-run goals, which perhaps can be achieved only by a series of cases, each building incrementally on the next but none of them particularly glamorous.

Control of cases is central to group strategy. A resultant question is whether client or group controls a case, particularly when an interest group supplies counsel and when it seeks out litigants. Because resources are scarce, a group is not likely to get involved in a case unless its own interests can be advanced. However, the ethics of the legal profession require that an attorney act in the interest of the client. If the client shares the group's interests, there is no problem, but when interests are not identical, the lawyer may define the client's interests in terms of group interests rather than vice versa. For example, when the client is offered a settlement in a case that might "make new law" if the case were to proceed to trial, the lawyer might be tempted to recommend against acceptance of the settlement instead of "sacrificing" the group's investment in seeking new legal principle. Most groups say that the case is indeed the client's, not the group's, but instances can be found that indicate that the group has settled for a symbolic victory rather than more concrete rewards for the client or that the group has emphasized precedent-setting cases at the expense of actions to enforce the rights won in such cases.[26]

Indeed, groups like the NAACP and ACLU have been accused of *barratry*, more commonly known as ambulance-chasing. This is the stirring up of litigation in which the instigator has no direct interest, usually for a share of the proceeds. The Supreme Court has made clear that a group, as part of its members' right of association, may help protect their constitutional rights through litigation. That groups such as the NAACP and ACLU have not profited financially from the litigation has undoubtedly been a factor in such rulings.[27]

Certain elements of interest group litigation *are* likely to increase separation of client interest from group concerns. Attorneys serving on the staffs of national organizations often have backgrounds and political ideologies different from those of the membership of the groups for which they are working. In addition, professionals such as lawyers often dominate laypersons such as clients. In interest groups such lawyer dominance, which tends to extend beyond the details of litigation to the general setting of policy, is quite likely if the group has a successful litigation record. There is often considerable geographical distance between an organization's staff attorneys (working at headquarters, usually New York City or Washington, D.C.) and the communities in which the group's members/clients are found, and there is often little if any personal contact between the staff attorneys and the clients, with local counsel handling the face-to-face interaction with the client. Contact between lawyer and client is further diminished by use of lawsuits on behalf of large classes of people. Although an organization has to use such *class action suits*—brought in the name of one or more specific plaintiffs on behalf of all those "similarly situated" legally—to stretch scarce resources, those within the plaintiff class who disagree with the dominant class view are quite likely to be submerged.

Environment

Strategy to achieve groups' multiple goals is affected by the environment in which groups must act. In the early 1970s and the 1980s, changes in public opinion, coupled with corollary changes in congressional mood and particularly in the executive branch's posture, produced an atmosphere far less favorable to civil rights interest groups and more favorable to conservative groups than had existed in the 1960s.

Included in a group's environment are not only legislative or administrative receptivity to the group but also existing statutes and regulations. Because, until the mid-1960s, groups representing the politically disfavored were unable to achieve legislation necessary to protect their rights, they regularly turned to the courts; thus, for many years national civil liberties and civil rights policy was made almost entirely in the courts. The passage of the Civil Rights Act of 1964 and the Voting Rights Act of 1965 altered the political environment by requiring group attention not only to maintainance of existing judicial precedent but also to implementation of the statutes through regulations and follow-up litigation.

Supreme Court decisions on both procedural and substantive issues have definitely affected the course of interest group litigation. An example of the effect of procedural rulings is the obstacle that a decision on who may bring lawsuits asserting the rights of disadvantaged individuals (see pages 126–129) posed for attacks on exclusionary zoning by suburbs. However, that ruling did nudge groups toward greater use of state courts, where they received favorable rulings in some states.[28] The Court's decisions on substantive issues also have affected interest groups' litigation strategy, as when NAACP lawyers' efforts received a substantial boost from a ruling that facilitated a new attack on whites-only primary elections.[29] Similarly, the NAACP's shift toward a more direct attack on "separate but equal" facilities came after the Supreme Court ordered desegregation of law schools on the basis of intangible factors, in *Sweatt v. Painter* (1950).

Interest groups turn to the courts not only because they are unable to achieve their goals elsewhere but also because of the *myth of rights*, the idea that litigation can produce statements of rights as well as their implementation.[30] Their belief in this myth is one reason why lawyers return again and again to court even when rights "won" there are not implemented and even when courts like the Supreme Court seem to be less receptive to lawyers' claims.

At least since the Warren Court's favorable consideration of civil rights and civil liberties claims, interest groups seeking protection for civil rights have gravitated particularly to the federal courts. One reason why a national interest group might prefer federal over state courts—apart from the question of which provided more favorable rulings—is that federal court litigation is "the surest and fastest route to the Supreme Court" for those seeking constitutional precedent.[31] An organizational factor is that litigating in federal court provides a single legal framework (the federal rules of procedure) that allows staff attorneys to bring cases anywhere in the nation and to coordinate local attorneys' work more effectively. The complexities of the multiplicity of state procedural and substantive legal provisions, which would force staff attorneys to devote scarce time to their mastery, are thus avoided.

Organizational Factors

Other important intra- and interorganizational factors affect litigation strategy and make the existence and course of planned litigation problematic. One factor is a group's *organizational structure*, such as whether it is membership based, with official policy established by representatives at an annual convention, or is limited to a collection of attorneys and an advisory board and is funded by contributions and foundation grants. There has been an increasing number of the latter, generally referred to as *public interest law firms*, which exist to serve not only liberal causes, such as the National Resources Defense Council or the Mexican-American Legal Defense Fund (MALDEF), but also conservative ones, such as the Mountain States Legal Defense Fund, with which Secretary of the Interior James Watt was associated before joining the government.

A group's *longevity* and continuity allow it more strategic flexibility because a group that has been around for some time and is in no danger of collapse can wait out bad times more easily, adjusting the pace of its litigation to changing judicial doctrine. Thus longevity affects a group's ability to control litigation. Longevity can, however, lead to inertia, in which a group continues down tried-and-true paths, unable to adapt to changes in judicial doctrine or political environment. Group inertia or momentum can be reinforced by opponents' resistance to earlier judicial victories and is particularly likely to result from success in the courts: lawyers may feel that "after all, if we've been successful there, we will continue to be." Victorious litigants certainly do not wish to give up, or to be seen as giving up, what they had pressed hard to achieve. Moreover, a group that has developed expertise in presenting cases in court will want to continue to utilize, rather than dissipate, that expertise.

The existence of and *relations with other organizations*, an important part of an interest group's political environment, also affect a group's litigation activities. The number of groups litigating in a particular area of the law—thus competing for resources—is part of the interorganizational situation. For example, for a long time the NAACP Legal Defense and Educational Fund (LDF), closely allied with the NAACP, was the dominant if not the sole civil rights litigator, thus having substantial control over litigation when it engaged in planned strategy. Now the NAACP and LDF are separate (indeed, feuding) and there are many, many civil rights litigating units: public interest law firms; private law firms that provide regular fee-for-service lawyering to private clients and also engage in public interest law practice; other private law firms closely affiliated with particular interest groups; individual private attorneys who bring cases, such as employment discrimination cases under Title VII of the 1964 Civil Rights Act, from which they can receive attorneys' fees if they win; and "back-up centers," created through the Legal Services Program, that assist with litigation. A growing "rights consciousness" has also produced more causes—including women, the poor, and the handicapped—for which litigating capacity has developed. The large number of groups in any one of these areas, such as the large number of women's groups, has caused problems of coordinating litigation.

Proliferation of litigating units had led to a loss of control by any single litigator and decreased ability to pursue a concerted strategy. Also important is the presence of groups that, as an ideological matter, do not use litigation and may disdain it. In the 1960s, for example, new civil rights groups, whose style was far more activist and confrontational, felt that the NAACP had not accomplished enough through the courts. The activities of groups such as the Congress of Racial Equality (CORE) and the Southern Christian Leadership Conference (SCLC, the Rev. Martin Luther King, Jr.'s group), caused older groups to shift priorities and resources as well as to pay more attention to membership concerns.

In addition to competition and conflict between groups seeking goals in any policy area, there is considerable cooperation. At times lawyers whose organizations are formally "at war" work together toward common goals—true in the small and cohesive "civil rights bar," in which a convergence of perspectives has developed. At times groups work together explicitly, primarily through exchange of information, which is quite important for control of cases as well as for efficient allocation of resources. Representatives of litigating groups also meet to exchange ideas or even to work out strategy; the three primary plaintiffs' interest group litigants in the church-state area (the American Jewish Congress, American Civil Liberties Union, and Americans United [for Separation of Church and State]) have worked together in this way.[32] On the conservative side, the Heritage Foundation has held monthly luncheons attended by representatives of most conservative litigators. Some groups go even further, perhaps providing auxiliary legal services for other interest groups.[33] Much cooperation is, however, implicit rather than overt. Through awareness of what other groups are doing, groups maintain at least somewhat differentiated central thrusts in which some concentrate on some types of cases while others focus their efforts on other areas. At times, such "comparative advantage" leads to the explicit cross-referral of cases from one organization to another better fitted for the particular task.

NOTES

1. See Arthur Selwyn Miller and Jerome A. Barron, "The Supreme Court, The Adversary System, and the Flow of Information to the Justices: A Preliminary Inquiry," *Virginia Law Review* 61 (1975):1187–1243; Charles M. Lamb, "Judicial Policy-Making and Information Flow to the Supreme Court," *Vanderbilt Law Review* 29 (January 1976):46–124.
2. On selection of U.S. Attorneys, see James Eisenstein, *Counsel for the United States: U.S. Attorneys in the Political and Legal Systems* (Baltimore: Johns Hopkins University Press, 1978), pp. 35–47. The following paragraphs also draw on Eisenstein's study.
3. Ibid., p. 16.
4. Ibid., p. 156. See also Robert L. Rabin, "Agency Criminal Referrals in the Federal System: An Empirical Study of Prosecutorial Discretion," *Stanford Law Review* 24 (June 1972): 1036–1091.
5. Paul Carrington, "United States Appeals in Civil Cases: A Field and Statistical Study," *Houston Law Review* 11 (1974):1101.
6. *DeMarco v. United States,* 415 U.S. 449 (1974).
7. See *Watts v. United States,* 422 U.S. 1032 at 1035–1036 (1975) (Chief Justice Burger and Justices White and Rehnquist, dissenting); and *Rinaldi v. United States,* 434 U.S. 22 (1977) (Rehnquist and White).
8. See Robert Scigliano, *The Supreme Court and the Presidency,* pp. 167–168. See also Samuel Krislov, "The Role of the Attorney General as Amicus Curiae," in Luther Huston et al., *Roles of the Attorney General of the United States* (Washington, D.C.: American Enterprise Institute, 1968), pp. 71–104.
9. Scigliano, p. 176.
10. Ibid., pp. 191–193, for the earlier period; for a comparison of the actions of three solicitors general, see Karen O'Connor, "The Amicus Curiae Role of the United States

Solicitor General in Supreme Court Litigation," *Judicature* 66 (December–January 1983):256–264.

11. Jonathan Casper, *Lawyers Before the Warren Court: Civil Liberties and Civil Rights, 1957–1966* (Urbana: University of Illinois Press, 1972), tables 4 and 5, pp. 88–89.
12. Gregory J. Rathjen, "Lawyers and the Appeals Process: An Analysis of the Appellate Lawyer's Beliefs, Attitudes and Values," paper presented to the Midwest Political Science Association, 1975; Rathjen, "Lawyers and the Appeals Process: A Profile," *Federal Bar Journal* 34 (Winter 1975):21–41; Susan Ann Kay, "Sex Differences in the Attitudes of a Future Elite," *Women & Politics* 1 (Fall 1980):35–48.
13. See Marc Galanter, "Why the 'Haves' Come Out Ahead: Speculations on the Limits of Legal Change," *Law & Society Review* 9 (Fall 1974):95–160.
14. See Robert Woodward and Scott Armstrong, *The Brethren*, pp. 79–84.
15. For stories and studies of the work of these groups, see Richard Kluger, *Simple Justice: The History of Brown v. Board of Education and Black America's Struggle for Equality* (New York: Alfred Knopf, 1976); Michael Meltsner, *Cruel and Unusual: The Supreme Court and Capital Punishment* (New York: Oxford University Press, 1973); and Robert Belton, "A Comparative Review of Public and Private Enforcement of Title VII of the Civil Rights Act of 1964," *Vanderbilt Law Review* 31 (May 1978):905–961, all on the work of the NAACP Legal Defense and Educational Fund; Robert Rabin, "Lawyers for Social Change: Perspectives on Public Interest Law," *Stanford Law Review* 28 (January 1976): 207– 261, on the Legal Defense Fund and the American Civil Liberties Union; Frank J. Sorauf, *The Wall of Separation: The Constitutional Politics of Church and State* (Princeton, N.J.: Princeton University Press, 1976); and Karen O'Connor, *Women's Organizations' Use of Courts* (Lexington, Mass.: Lexington Books, 1980).
16. Richard C. Cortner, "Strategies and Tactics of Litigants in Constitutional Cases," *Journal of Public Law* 17 (1968):288.
17. See Clement Vose, *Caucasians Only* (Berkeley: University of California Press, 1959).
18. Karen O'Connor and Lee Epstein, "The Rise of Conservative Interest Group Litigation," *Journal of Politics* 45 (May 1983):479–489.
19. Karen O'Connor and Lee Epstein, "Amicus Curiae Participation in U.S. Supreme Court Litigation," *Law & Society Review* 16 (1981–1982):701–710.
20. Samuel Krislov, "The Amicus Curiae Brief: From Friendship to Advocacy," *Yale Law Journal* 72 (March 1963):694–721.
21. Lynn Mather and Barbara Yngvesson, "Language, Audience, and the Transformation of Disputes," *Law & Society Review* 15 (1980–1981):802–805.
22. This material and the remainder of this section draw heavily on the author's article, "Interest Groups in Court: Race Relations Litigation," in *Interest Group Politics*, ed. Allan Cigler and Burdett Loomis (Washington, D.C.: CQ Press, 1983), pp. 251–274.
23. Jeanne Hahn, "The NAACP Legal Defense and Educational Fund: Its Judicial Strategy and Tactics," in Stephen L. Wasby, *American Government and Politics* (New York: Scribner's, 1973), p. 396.
24. Stuart Scheingold, *The Politics of Rights: Lawyers, Public Policy, and Political Change* (New Haven: Yale University Press, 1974), p. 5.
25. O'Connor, *Women's Organizations . . .* , p. 117.
26. See Stephen C. Halpern, "Assessing the Litigative Role of ACLU Chapters," in *Civil Liberties: Policy and Policy Making*, ed. Stephen L. Wasby (Lexington, Mass.: Lexington Books, 1976), pp. 159–168, for a criticism of group strategy.

27. See *NAACP v. Button*, 371 U.S. 415 (1963); and *In Re Primus*, 436 U.S. 412 (1978).
28. *Warth v. Seldin*, 422 U.S. 490 (1975). See Michael N. Danielson, *The Politics of Exclusion* (New York: Columbia University Press, 1976), p. 318, and Geoffrey Shields and Sanford Spector, "Opening Up the Suburbs: Notes on a Movement for Social Change," *Yale Review of Law and Social Action* 2 (Summer 1972):310.
29. Clement E. Vose, *Constitutional Change: Amendment Politics and Supreme Court Litigation Since 1900* (Lexington, Mass.: Lexington Books, 1972), p. 321.
30. Scheingold, p. 5.
31. Sorauf, *The Wall of Separation*, p. 111.
32. Ibid., p. 82. See also Vose, *Caucasians Only*, pp. 58, 151; Meltsner, *Cruel and Unusual*, pp. 114, 238–239.
33. Edward V. Heck and Joseph Stewart, Jr., "Ensuring Access to Justice: The Role of Interest Group Lawyers in the 60's Campaign for Civil Rights," *Judicature* 66 (August 1982): 84–95.

Chapter 5

Getting Into Court

Very few cases filed in federal or state trial courts ever get to the United States Supreme Court, even in the form of a request for review. Most cases that are filed do not proceed to trial. Many are not pursued; a great many civil cases are settled before trial; and most criminal cases, as much as 85 to 90 percent in some jurisdictions, are resolved with a guilty plea. Of those cases that reach the trial stage, most never proceed further. Of the relatively small proportion taken to the first appellate level, few are pursued beyond that point. State cases that do move further are first appealed through the state court system. The great majority of state cases that the Supreme Court can hear are within its certiorari jurisdiction, allowing the Court to reject the great majority, the same disposition it gives most federal appeals.

In this chapter, we examine both the rules the Supreme Court has developed concerning access to the courts and its doctrines concerning relations between federal and state courts. The Court's requirements on access mean that not everyone can get into court to pursue certain issues; some people with complaints that they wish judges to decide may not be able to satisfy necessary procedural requirements. Others must take care to assure that the rules are satisfied; this may require that issues be shaped in a certain way or that particular plaintiffs be chosen for cases.

ACCESS TO THE COURTS

The formal paths along which cases move are clearly delineated (see Figures 2.1 and 5.1). However, before cases may be moved along those paths, requirements concerning who can have access to the courts and which cases can be brought to court must be satisfied. Congress creates some of these rules in statutes providing *causes of action*, the substantive legal claims that are the basis of lawsuits. Congress also spells out the courts' jurisdiction, their legal authority to hear cases, and provides certain procedural rules, such as those on how appeals should be processed. Beyond those statutory rules, the Supreme Court, through its decisions, sets many rules on access to the federal courts. If the Court is restrictive in those rulings in granting access, major claims may never reach the lower federal courts, much less the Supreme Court itself. Although the Supreme Court cannot tell state courts which cases to hear, it is not bound to accept appeals from state cases when its own access requirements have not been met. The Court has also affected access to the federal courts by developing rules intended to keep cases in the state systems. This is done in an effort to ensure that cases are given complete treatment there before being brought to the federal courts and that once the claims are in the federal court system, review of state court decisions is limited. These include decisions on which set of courts should decide issues that seem subject to decision by both federal and state judges. Among these are rules covering use of habeas corpus petitions in federal courts to challenge state convictions, federal courts' authority to issue declaratory judgments (see below) and injunctions against state laws, and removal (transfer) of cases from state to federal court—rules that affect litigants' ability to challenge the actions of state and local legislators and administrators.

Many rules concerning access to the courts revolve around the stipulation in Article III that courts deal with "cases" or "controversies," a corollary of the idea that courts are legal institutions operating with a specific set of procedures. Although at times rules on access to the courts are dismissed as "narrow technicalities," they are of broad importance and central to the courts' powers in our political system.

> The judicial power shall extend to all cases, in law and equity, arising under the Constitution, the laws of the United States, and treaties made, or which shall be made, under their authority; to all cases affecting ambassadors, other public ministers and consuls; to all cases of admiralty and maritime jurisdiction; to controversies to which the United States shall be a party; to controversies between two or more states; between a state and citizens of another state; between citizens of different states; between citizens of the same state claiming lands under grants of different states; and between a state, or the citizens thereof, and foreign states, citizens or subjects. (Art. III, Sec. 2)

Before deciding a case "on the merits," that is, before turning to substantive issues such as "Did John Jones discriminate against Sally Smith in considering her employment application?", "Did the Giant Corporation attempt to monopolize the business in its field?", or "Did the government prove that the Porn Corporation transported obscene materials in interstate commerce?", a judge must be satisfied that a number of procedural prerequisites have been met. Indeed, the outcomes of cases may be determined by procedural considerations, without the merits being reached.

The procedural prerequisites fall essentially into three interrelated categories: *jurisdiction,* a court's *authority* to hear a case; *standing,* whether the right *person* is bringing a case; and *justiciability,* whether a *case* is appropriate for judges to hear. Justiciability includes the requirements that the parties be adverse to each other and not have manufactured a case to get into court; that the court not be asked for an *advisory opinion*; that the case be both *ripe* and not *moot*; and that it not entail a *political question.* Once the government has imposed restrictions on an individual, it is relatively easy to challenge them. For example, as a defense to a criminal charge, one may question the validity of the law under which the charge has been brought. Thus an individual who has been arrested or indicted by that fact often satisfies requirements to challenge laws on which that action has been based, although the Supreme Court has recently imposed restrictions on who may challenge an allegedly improper search (see page 129). As a result, controversies over access to the courts are most likely to arise when someone wishes to challenge a law and to obtain a *declaratory judgment,* a declaration of legal rights prior to the law's enforcement against that person. The large number of declaratory judgment and injunction actions filed against government officials for violations of civil rights, for improperly institutionalizing the mentally retarded, "double-celling" prisoners, or engaging in police brutality, has produced a substantial increase in cases dealing with questions of access to the courts. During the past two decades, such "1983 actions" (named for 42 U.S.C. §1983 [Section 1983 of Title 42 of the United States Code], the law under which the cases are brought) thus have been at the heart of much Supreme Court activity concerning access to the courts.

> Every person who, under color of any statute, ordinance, regulation, custom, or usage, of any State or Territory, subjects, or causes to be subjected, any citizen of the United States or other person within the jurisdiction thereof to the deprivation of any rights, privileges, or immunities secured by the Constitution and laws shall be liable to the party injured in an action at law, suit in equity, or other proper proceeding for redress. (42 U.S.C. §1983)

The Burger Court, while increasing claimants' access to federal court to proceed against local governments and local officials, restricted access in other ways; state courts' authority was strengthened through restrictions on state prisoners' access to federal courts for review of their convictions and by limits on use of the federal courts to decide issues pending in the state courts. In becoming considerably more restrictive concerning a number of important aspects of access, the justices forced the judicial process toward a more traditional model of our adversary legal system—as part of which access rules were initially developed.

Particularly as civil rights claims brought in federal court increased, not surprisingly parallels developed between the differences in the Warren Court's and Burger Court's access doctrines and the differences in their respective support for civil liberties/civil rights claims. The Burger Court tightened access rules (and is said to have done so intentionally), excluding the poor and disadvantaged from the benefits of certain constitutional provisions. Dissenting justices complained that the majority, explicitly deciding a case in terms of access considerations, had really implicitly reached the underlying substantive claim instead of treating the access claim first.

At times, the justices seem to have treated access rules flexibly to allow the Court to accept important questions presented to the justices for resolution or so that they could reach particular conservative or liberal results. For example, in *Sosna v. Iowa* (1975), a woman—the only named plaintiff in a case—had challenged durational residency requirements for a divorce in class action suits (see page 115). The district judge certified the suit as a class action involving all those precluded from seeking divorces by the residency rule. By the time the case reached the Supreme Court, the woman had obtained a divorce elsewhere, eliminating her particular "case or controversy" by making it moot. The Court's majority said that, despite the absence of other named plaintiffs, the case was still alive because the district judge had certified the case as a class action; the justices then went on, over the dissenters' objection that the case *was* moot, to uphold the residency requirement, definitely the conservative outcome in that situation.

Are the Court's rulings on access, which we are about to discuss in some detail, really a cover for justices' ideology? Several elements might underlie their access rulings. Judges might want to limit access to facilitate the handling of increasing caseload, an administrative concern; they might limit access because of legal or jurisprudential concerns, a belief in courts' limited role, an aspect of judicial self-restraint; or they might do so for reasons more directly "political"—to "evade certain policy choices and [to] indirectly legitimize preferred policy choices made elsewhere."[1]

For the 1969–1975 Terms, none of these possible reasons served to explain access rulings for the Court as a whole, but in varying ways they influenced individual justices, few of whom have been consistent in the direction of their access voting over longer periods. The Court's rulings were, on the one hand, partly "a function of an underlying attitude toward access *per se*," a combination of administrative and legal concerns about proper party and proper forum (court) for cases, and, on the other hand, a function of attitudes about substantive issues ("political" considerations).[2] The access votes of four justices, including Nixon appointees Powell and Rehnquist (the other two were Stewart and White), were predominantly affected by administrative and legal concerns; two, Brennan and Douglas, were affected predominantly by political concerns; and three (Marshall, Blackmun, and Chief Justice Burger) showed no dominance of either set of concerns. Putting together the various factors affecting the justices' votes, we find that three of the four Nixon appointees (the Chief Justice, Rehnquist, and Powell), although with differing motivations, were "willing (and ostensibly anxious) to close access," three (Stewart, Blackmun, and White) "leaning generally toward access closure," and three (Brennan, Douglas, and Marshall, all liberal holdovers from the Warren Court) "generally willing . . . to open access."[3]

Jurisdiction

Jurisdiction is the power of courts to hear a case, that is, their legal authority to do so. Rules of jurisdiction are found either in the Constitution—for example, the Supreme Court's original jurisdiction is stated in Article III—or in statutes, with most detailed matters of jurisdiction being spelled out in the latter. Jurisdiction has components concerning geography, level of court, subject matter, individual parties to a case, and federalism. The first, or horizontal, aspect concerns the question, Which district court has jurisdiction to hear a particular case? For example, should a Voting Rights Act case be brought in the Western District of North Carolina (W.D.N.C.) or in the District Court for the District of Columbia (D.D.C.)? The second component is the vertical element of jurisdiction. For example, felonies must be tried in district court, and only certain lesser offenses can be tried before magistrates.

Courts must have jurisdiction over the subject matter of a lawsuit as specified by Article III and, within Article III's limits, congressional statutes. For example, appeals in all patent cases must now go to the Court of Appeals for the Federal Circuit. Courts must also have personal jurisdiction over the individuals who bring the lawsuit and especially those against whom it is brought; jurisdiction over the latter, as the Court has pointed out, is a matter of due process. The federalism aspect of jurisdiction concerns whether a case is properly brought initially in a state or federal court. For example, cases involving citizens of different states (diversity of citizenship cases) can be brought in either state or federal court, but can be brought in the latter only if at least $10,000 is at issue, a statutory requirement.

A recent controversial issue concerning jurisdiction is whether federal courts may hear lawsuits against states and local governments and against their officials, or whether such suits are prevented by the Eleventh Amendment. That amendment, ratified in 1798 to overturn an early Supreme Court ruling, prevents suits against a state by citizens of another state, but the Court has said the amendment also embodies the rule of *sovereign immunity*, which prevents suits against a government without its consent, so that a state could not be sued by its own citizens without the state's consent.[4] However, the justices have ruled that congressional action enforcing the Fourteenth Amendment may remove a state's immunity, and the Court has also stripped many state and local officials of legal immunity for actions violating people's rights.

> The judicial power of the United States shall not be construed to extend to any suit in law or equity, commenced or prosecuted against one of the United States by citizens of another state, or by citizens or subjects of any foreign state. (Eleventh Amendment)

In *Scheuer v. Rhodes* (1974), one of the cases stemming from the 1970 killings at Kent State University, the Supreme Court ruled that state officials' immunity from suit was removed—so that they became personally liable for damages—if they violate the U.S. Constitution. However, the higher the official's position, the more discretion the official is to be allowed; thus high-level state officials are given what amounts to executive immunity. Reinforcing officials' liability, the Court ruled in *Wood v. Strickland* (1975) that school board members, superintendents, and school principals would be personally liable if they violated the rights of students either maliciously or knowingly or in a situation where they should have known they were doing so. The justices nonetheless closed off damage suits against those connected with law enforcement and courts. In 1976, in *Imbler v. Pachtman,* the Court ruled that a state prosecutor acting within the scope of his duties was absolutely immune from suit under the civil rights statutes, even when it was claimed that he had knowingly used false evidence and suppressed material evidence at a trial that resulted in reversal of a defendant's conviction. Without absolute immunity, the prosecutor would have to spend much of his time defending against lawsuits instead of carrying out his assigned duties. Then, as noted earlier (see pages 3–4), judges were ruled absolutely immune from damage suits for actions taken in a judicial capacity.

The Court has also ruled that federal suits (under 42 U.S.C. §1983) seeking declaratory judgments and injunctions against the state are permissible because they are considered aimed at officials rather than the state itself. In 1975 the Court significantly expanded the basis for such lawsuits by saying they could be brought not only when it was claimed that personal *constitutional* rights, such as freedom of speech or the right to associate or property rights, had been violated but also when states were said to violate federal statutes such as the Social Security Act (*Maine v. Thiboutot,* 1981).

Perhaps even more significant was the Court's reversal of its position in *Monroe v. Pape* (1961) that, although suits against local government *officials* (in their "private person") were proper, local *governments* could not be sued for damages under §1983. In 1978 and 1980, the Court first ruled in the *Monell* case that local governments may be sued for actions implementing official policy statements. This was followed by a decision that local government officers' "good faith" was not a defense to lawsuits against the government itself. The Court was, however, unwilling to allow plaintiffs to collect punitive damages for municipalities' violations of people's rights—so ruling in a case stemming from a city's cancellation of a concert by Blood, Sweat, and Tears.[5]

Standing

To bring a case, a person must have *standing,* that is, must be a proper party. If no one has standing, the court lacks jurisdiction to hear a case, leaving the possibility that unconstitutional laws will remain on the books because no one can "get at them." Although some rules on standing are found in statutes (see below), most are judge-made, which allows flexibility. As with any judge-made rules on access to the courts, it also allows justices' ideologies to affect those procedural rules.

The basic rule on standing is that the litigant must show real or potential injury to himself or herself or have a personal stake in the outcome; thus a doctor could not challenge anticontraceptive statutes solely on the basis that they would injure his patients.[6] At times, however, the rights of others may be asserted to reinforce one's own claim, particularly where there are obstacles to others' asserting their own rights and where the party in court would assert those rights effectively. Thus a white woman, sued for damages for selling her house to blacks in violation of restrictive covenants, was granted standing to assert blacks' rights to purchase housing; a married man charged with violating a law that prohibited supplying contraceptives to single people but that did not punish the recipients was able to assert their rights; and doctors were allowed to assert the rights of Medicaid patients who might seek abortions in the doctors' suit to recover payment.[7] Standing has also been granted to whites to challenge the exclusion of blacks from juries and to men to challenge the exclusion of women on the basis that all have a right to a jury that is a properly drawn cross-section of the community.[8]

During the late 1960s the Court relaxed the rules on standing. The class of people said to be injured was expanded and federal taxpayers were granted standing to sue in some instances. In expanding the scope of those "injured," the Court also recognized in *Sierra Club v. Morton* that injury to "aesthetic and environmental well-being" was among the interests that could provide a basis for standing. However, the majority made clear that to obtain standing a group would have to do more than state a general interest in the environment; its members would have to be among those injured. Justice Blackmun, who would have allowed standing without the personal injury requirements, asked in dissent, in what was hardly a position of judicial self-restraint: "Must our law be so rigid and our procedural concepts so inflexible that we render ourselves helpless when the existing methods and the traditional concepts do not quite fit and do not prove to be entirely adequate for new issues?" Later, when a personal injury claim was added to claims of injury to the environment, the Court was willing to grant standing (*United States v. S.C.R.A.P.*, 1973). The Court also sustained the standing of an environmental group, labor union, and individuals living near the site of a planned nuclear power plant to challenge the Price-Anderson Act, which limits recovery of damages for injury in the event of accidents at privately owned nuclear plants. Without the statute, the plant might not be built, and, if built, it might produce adverse effects including production of nonnatural radiation, increases in lake temperature, interference with normal use of river water, and a threat of nuclear accident. (Having found standing, the majority sustained the act.)[9]

Prior to 1968, federal taxpayers alleging that money was being used for an unconstitutional project could not use their taxpayer status to establish standing to sue the government. In 1968 the court ruled in *Flast v. Cohen*, a case brought to test the 1965 Elementary and Secondary Education Act (ESEA) provisions for assistance to parochial schools, that a federal taxpayer could have standing to sue the government if the challenged program were alleged to violate a specific constitutional prohibition, such as the First Amendment's "establishment of religion" clause. However, when an organization dedicated to church-state separation challenged a transfer of government property to a religious organization with no payment required—under the clause allowing the government to dispose of property (Art. IV, Sec. 3, cl. 2)—the Court found no personal injury, only a general grievance, and refused to grant standing.[10]

Taxpayer attacks on governmental action on the basis of constitutional provisions more general than the First Amendment's prohibition of establishment of religion have also still not been permitted, because there was little to distinguish taxpayer complaints from general citizen grievances, which are not considered an adequate basis for standing. The Burger Court reinforced this position by saying there was insufficient connection (or "nexus") between a taxpayer and Congress's failure to require the CIA to produce detailed reports of its expenditures to allow the taxpayer standing, even though the plaintiff asserted agency failure to comply with the Statements and Accounts Clause (Art. I, Sec. 9, cl. 7). Justice Powell emphasized that under our system of government, such claims should be brought to Congress rather than to the courts, and Chief Justice Burger stressed that taxpayers could not use federal courts to assert general citizen or voter grievances. Burger's position was promptly applied to deny standing to armed service reserve officers trying to prevent congressmen from holding reserve commissions as a violation of the Incompatability Clause (no executive official should be a member of Congress).[11]

Civil Rights Claims

The Burger Court's restrained view of standing has perhaps been clearest in civil rights claims. When both whites and blacks in Cairo, Illinois, the site of serious racial conflict, sued to obtain relief from racially discriminatory judicial bonding and sentencing practices in *O'Shea v. Littleton* (1973), the Court denied standing because the plaintiffs had not shown either that they had already been injured or that they could suffer continuing injury from the practices. (Showing that multiple aspects of access doctrine may appear in the same case, the Court's nonintervention was also based on a desire to avoid having the federal judiciary regularly supervise state judges.) Similarly, in a suit against Philadelphia Mayor Joseph Rizzo and the police commissioner over improper police practices against minorities and mishandling of complaints (*Rizzo v. Goode,* 1976), the Court said the complainants lacked standing to bring about an overhauling of police disciplinary procedures because their claims rested on what a small, unnamed minority of officers might do in the future and on incidents that *might* happen to others *if* the police procedures were not changed.

Similarly, when an attack was made on restrictive and exclusionary suburban zoning ordinances by low- and moderate-income minority residents of a city, a nonprofit corporation trying to alleviate their housing shortage, central city taxpayers, and a homebuilders' association, the Supreme Court turned them all aside. The justices said in *Warth v. Seldin* (1975) that those bringing the case would have to indicate specifically both how the challenged ordinances would harm them (for example, without the zoning rules, they would have been able to lease or purchase suburban homes) and how judges could protect their rights. (That the ruling was based at least in part on the majority's view of the ordinances' validity can be seen in Justice Powell's comment that "the economics of the housing market," not the ordinances, prevented plaintiffs' move to the suburbs.) The dissenters' view that the Court was making it virtually impossible for anyone to challenge the suburb's action was somewhat undercut by the ruling in the following term that a developer challenging denial of a requested rezoning for low- and moderate-income housing had standing, although the Court then found no intentional racial discrimination.[12]

Questions of standing also appeared in criminal procedure cases. This has allowed the Burger Court to demonstrate its law enforcement conservatism in a procedural context. The cases involved challenges to searches and thus implicated the controversy over the exclusionary rule (see pages 306–308): if fewer people had standing to challenge searches, the exclusionary rule would be applied less often. In limiting standing to challenge searches, the Burger Court, starting in 1978, built on the Warren Court's *Alderman* decision that only those whose rights were violated by the search itself, not those against whom evidence is used, could urge suppression of the evidence. The Burger Court, in a case involving the search of a car thought to have been used in a robbery and in which a rifle and ammunition had been found, said that the question of a violation of Fourth Amendment search and seizure standards could not be raised by those who did not own either the car or its contents or who did not have an expectation of privacy in those parts of the car that were searched (*Rakas v. Illinois*, 1978). After extending this basic approach to noncar searches in the *Salvucci* case (1980), the majority overturned the Warren Court's 1960 ruling in *Jones v. United States* that standing to challenge a search was automatically available to those charged with possession offenses (e.g., possession of stolen mail or drugs). Now someone charged with possession offenses would have standing to assert Fourth Amendment rights only if that person's expectation of privacy in home or possessions had been violated.

Statutory Rulings

At times Congress has specified who may or may not bring certain types of cases in the federal courts. For example, in passing the law establishing the National Railroad Passenger Corporation (Amtrak), Congress provided that the attorney general should enforce its provisions; this meant, said the Court, that a railroad passenger group was barred from protesting passenger train discontinuances. The Court similarly ruled that trade associations and political action committees (PACs) cannot invoke certain Federal Election Campaign Act procedures because they were not among the three specified categories of plaintiffs entitled to use of specially expedited lawsuits to challenge the act's constitutionality. An example of expansive interpretation of statutory grants of standing was the Court's ruling that under Congress' open housing legislation, white tenants of an apartment complex have standing to complain about discrimination against blacks.[13]

Closely related are questions of whether, in the absence of explicit language, Congress intended to allow private citizens to sue to enforce certain statutes that provided other remedies, such as a government cut-off of funds to an agency discriminating against individuals (Title VI, Civil Rights Act of 1964). A number of such cases in the last few years, a result of Congress' failure to be clear, have seriously divided the Court. The justices ruled, for example, that customers could sue brokers under the Commodity Exchange Act to recover for alleged fraud and deceptive practices, but divided 5–4 in so doing. More typical of the "private cause of action" cases are claims under civil rights statutes, such as whether a woman who claimed discrimination in medical school admissions practices could bring a federal court suit under Title IX of the Education Amendments of 1972 (barring sex discrimination in government-funded programs); the justices voted 6–3 that she could sue.[14]

The justices have also been called upon to resolve "cause of action" questions involving the Constitution—whether the Constitution by itself is an adequate basis for a claim. The Court has now established such direct constitutional causes of action against federal agents for violations of the Fourth Amendment in improper searches; against prison officials for inadequate medical treatment under the Eighth Amendment (cruel and unusual punishment); and against members of Congress for sex discrimination under the Fifth Amendment (into which the Court some years ago read an "equal protection" element).[15]

The Supreme Court decisions on procedures for class action suits (see page 115) require interpretation of federal court rules. Although class actions save time for the courts by avoiding repetitious litigation, the Court has limited their use. The justices have ruled, for example, that a consumer suing a utility could not satisfy the $10,000 jurisdictional requirement for federal diversity-of-citizenship cases by joining his small claim with others' in a class action, and then later ruled in an antipollution case against a paper company that each and every member of the class had to satisfy that $10,000 figure or there could be no class action suit.[16]

Justiciability

Rules on justiciability—the question of cases appropriate for judges to hear—are, like rules on standing, judge-made; they are even more flexible than the rules on standing. The concept of justiciability includes norms against issuing advisory opinions or deciding feigned controversies, moot or unripe cases, or "political questions." All but the last are based on a fundamental rule, settled early in the Court's history, that the Supreme Court will not issue opinions on abstract legal questions, but will decide questions of law only when presented in the fact context of a particular lawsuit.

This basic principle was stated in the course of deciding that the Court would not issue advisory opinions, but it extends far beyond that—to other situations where the question would be abstract and the result would be the equivalent of an advisory opinion, such as cases without adverse parties, cases that are not ripe, and cases that are moot. In none of those situations would adequate information be given to the judge: in our adversary system of justice, judges are expected to be passive in the sense of receiving information and legal arguments rather than developing them for the parties. Nor in those situations would the law be given its operative meaning through facts about the law's application. A law might appear to be constitutional "on its face" but be applied in an improper manner, or a law of dubious validity may have been applied—or interpreted by the lower courts—so as to preserve its constitutionality. Judges are likewise reluctant to grant declaratory judgments because prosecution after a violation will bring out fuller sets of facts on the operation of the statute. However, increased use of summary judgments—cases decided on the pleadings—and on motions to dismiss (also on the pleadings) somewhat undercut this idea.

Advisory Opinions

Narrowly defined, an *advisory opinion* is an opinion given by judges to the legislature or executive about a proposed bill or action. Some state high courts do issue such opinions. However, the justices of the U.S. Supreme Court firmly established a rule against the justices giving advisory opinions when President Washington asked the Court for advice on some treaty questions; the justices responded through Chief Justice Jay that they would not do so. Early in the present century, the Court amplified the rule. Congress had passed a law allowing the Cherokee Indians to file suit to test a statute, but in *Muskrat v. United States* the Court said that Congress was seeking a ruling on the law's constitutionality without the presence of a live controversy, therefore in effect asking for an advisory opinion, and the justices would not allow the case to be heard.

Some informal exceptions to the ban on advisory opinions have, however, occurred. In 1822 President Monroe asked several members of the Court about the legality of federal "internal improvements." Justice William Johnson made a general if oblique reply for himself and several other justices, indicating their position that governmental construction of military roads and postroads was constitutional. Certainly Chief Justice Hughes's comment on behalf of the Court as to Roosevelt's Court-packing proposal—that the "one Supreme Court" called for by the Constitution could not sit in divisions—could be called an advisory opinion. At other times, individual justices have provided the president with legal advice and have helped draw up legislation, as Justice Frankfurter did for President Roosevelt and Justice Fortas did for President Lyndon Johnson.

In the course of deciding cases, justices also comment on matters on which the Court is not ruling or give suggestions to the other branches as to how to deal with problems, making their statements informal advisory opinions. Thus, in striking down a statute regulating a part of the economy, justices have suggested how Congress could deal with the problem by relying on another constitutional clause, and recently, in a case on the constitutionality of at-large municipal elections, Justice Stevens suggested that a statute amending the Voting Rights Act to outlaw such elections would be constitutional.[17] Justices are more likely to make statements of this sort when they write concurring or dissenting opinions than when they write the "opinion of the Court." When the author of the Court's majority opinion does make comments not necessary for the Court's ruling, the statements are called *obiter dictum*, that is, language beyond the *holding* or basic rule of the case. (Sometimes it is difficult to tell what is *obiter* and what is not, although speculation about hypothetical situations not before the court is clearly *obiter*.) In a sense, whenever the Court goes beyond the specific facts of a case to anticipate general questions of policy not yet directly presented to it, it is issuing an advisory opinion. However, as the nation's highest tribunal, the Court accepts for review cases intended to be representative of large issues. It thus decides more than the particulars of the dispute between the immediate parties; in so doing, the Court is expected to issue opinions with a reach broader than the specific case being decided.

Feigned Controversies

As part of its effort to have the federal courts avoid handing down advisory opinions, the Court insists that litigation not be "made up" simply to obtain a ruling on some matter that the parties would like to see settled, particularly to the detriment of a third party not involved in a case. Thus the parties in a case must be adverse to each other. This rule against feigned controversies is aimed at collusive litigation. It does not mean that the litigants have to be "at each other's throats" but only that their interests be opposed. One of the Court's earliest statements of the rule was in a case, *Lord v. Veazie*, in which a stockholder, claiming ownership of river navigational rights also claimed by someone else, sold some stock based on his own presumed control of the rights. By prearrangement, the stock purchaser, a relative of the seller, sued the seller to determine ownership of the river rights. Both parties obviously wanted the same result, which they were trying to ensure without the third party's involvement. The Supreme Court ruled that no court should hear such a lawsuit. Nonetheless, there have been efforts to get into court with collusive cases from time to time.

An example of the courts *not* throwing out a case as a "feigned controversy" is *Carter v. Carter Coal Co.* (1936), in which the president of a company sued his own company to prevent compliance with the Guffey Bituminous Coal Act. Although both sides had lawyers who made strong arguments in the Supreme Court, the common interest of both parties in getting the law invalidated should have been clear. Moreover, under the then existing rules, the United States—whose statute was at issue—was not a party to the case and was thus at a disadvantage in trying to argue the statute's validity. Because of that situation—in which the Court *did* invalidate the statute, Congress promptly passed legislation that made the United States a party whenever the constitutionality of a federal statute is brought in issue in a case in which the United States is not initially a party.

Mootness and Ripeness

Another aspect of the "case or controversy" requirement is that a case not be moot, that is, that a dispute not be completed or that it not be too late for judges to apply a remedy. However, there have always been exceptions to this basic rule. For example, the courts will hear issues where the government has made it difficult to challenge its actions by voluntarily eliminating the questioned rule in the face of a lawsuit while retaining the option of later reinstating the rule or by issuing one order after another, each of brief duration so all would expire before they could be effectively challenged.

The Supreme Court in the 1960s changed its basic direction on mootness, making it easier for courts to decide issues likely to arise again. Under traditional interpretations of mootness, challenges to election rules, particularly those excluding candidates, were usually moot before they reached the appellate courts because the election had already taken place. However, because the issue involved in the challenge would recur in a subsequent election, when it might again become moot on appeal, the Supreme Court began to rule on some election cases even after the election had passed.[18] The application of mootness rules to prisoners' challenges to their convictions was also relaxed. The Court said a prisoner's habeas corpus challenge to his conviction was not moot upon his release from prison because disabilities resulting from the conviction remained. However, if prisoners were only attacking *sentences*, not convictions, and those sentences expired before a court decided the case, the matter would be moot.[19]

One of the most significant uses of the more flexible approach to mootness occurred in the Court's 1973 abortion cases, *Roe v. Wade* and *Doe v. Bolton*. Justice Blackmun stated that if traditional mootness rules were applied, questions related to pregnancy could never be reviewed on appeal because the pregnancy would be completed. He said, however, that the issues should be decided because pregnancy was likely to recur, both for the woman challenging antiabortion laws and for other women as well, and he ruled that such matters, "capable of repetition yet evading review," should be dealt with.

A case also cannot be *premature* or *unripe* if judges are to decide it. Ripeness, like mootness, is related to standing. Someone bringing a case that is not ripe lacks standing. Similarly, someone without a definite injury lacks standing because the matter is speculative and thus unripe. For example, because only a subjective "chill" to First Amendment rights, not actual injury, resulted from Army surveillance of civilian political activity, the Court—in *Laird v. Tatum* (1972)—ruled a challenge to that activity not ripe. There are few clear rules concerning ripeness, the contours of which are established on a case-by-case basis. For example, the Court held a challenge to anticontraceptive laws not ripe because, although a prosecutor said he would prosecute those violating the law, contraceptives were widely available and there had been no such prosecution for twenty years; thus a declaration of people's rights was not necessary, said the majority. (However, when a doctor opened a birth control clinic, he was arrested, and the Court then invalidated the law.)[20]

An important element of the rules on ripeness is that a litigant have previously exhausted available administrative and judicial remedies. The administrative ones should be exhausted before one comes to court, so that the administrative agencies' views on the dispute will be known and so that the dispute might be resolved before ever reaching court; available judicial remedies should be exhausted before one proceeds to a higher court, to allow the lower courts to play their proper role in the judicial system, leaving appellate courts free to review lower court decisions. One must also make full use of state court remedies before using federal courts to challenge convictions and must avail oneself of appeals within an administrative body before taking matters to court. For example, the Court had ruled that challenges to courts-martial cannot be heard by civilian courts until military courts have completed their review, even where the military's jurisdiction to hold the court-martial is the subject of the challenge.[21] The exhaustion doctrine in areas such as welfare may exhaust the individual rather than the remedies and has had a particularly harsh effect on those denied Conscientious Objector status by their draft boards, where, as a result of statutes sustained by the Court, review is available only through a challenge to a criminal indictment for refusing induction.

"Political Questions"

The most ambiguous part of justiciability is the *political question* doctrine. Under this doctrine, courts will not decide questions that the judges think "belong" to the other branches of government under the terms of the Constitution or would be more appropriately handled by the legislative or executive branches. For example, when Kent State University student government officers challenged Ohio National Guard riot control rules, the Court in *Gilligan v. Morgan* (1973) said that judges could not rule on the case because the requested remedy would engage federal judges in constant review of the executive branch, charged with supervision of the National Guard.

Over the course of its history, the Court has considered a variety of issues to be "political questions." These include whether a state may rescind its ratification of a constitutional amendment, recently at issue with respect to the ERA, and which of two "regimes" in a particular state was the legitimate one—matters that could be dealt with by Congress (in determining the ratification of an amendment or the credentials of members of Congress); whether state constitutions may provide for recall of judges; and whether or not a president should enforce certain laws—something the justices felt should be left to the executive's discretion.[22]

Until the 1960s, the "political question" doctrine had substantial content. However, the Warren Court drastically reduced that content. First, although for many years reapportionment had been thought to be a "political question," in 1962 the Court said in *Baker v. Carr* that complaints about malapportioned legislative districts could be heard by the courts. Then, although legislatures had been allowed to judge the qualifications of their own members without judicial interference, in *Bond v. Floyd* the Court overturned the Georgia legislature's refusal to seat Julian Bond because of his antiwar statements and in 1968 ruled that Congress should seat Congressman Adam Clayton Powell (D-N.Y.). The ruling in *Powell v. MacCormack* came close to rejecting the "political question" doctrine entirely. When President Nixon claimed that the request for the Watergate tapes was nonjusticiable because it was an "in-house" controversy between president and special prosecutor, the Court in *United States v. Nixon* rejected the claim that there was a "political question" and went on to decide the case.

The political question doctrine is still applied in some situations, almost exclusively involving our relations with foreign nations. The validity of treaties under international law and our recognition of foreign governments are still considered to be "political questions"; thus the courts will not interfere with the executive branch's decisions. The federal courts often used the political question doctrine as the basis for refusing to decide the validity of the Vietnam War under either our own Constitution or international law.[23]

Related to the political question issue in the foreign affairs area is application of the "act of state" doctrine, under which our courts will not question another nation's acts such as expropriation of property done within that nation's territory. Here the question is not whether the decision about the validity of another nation's acts should be made by another branch of our government, making it a "political question," but whether any American court can appropriately decide the issue, that is, whether it is justiciable. When the executive branch has indicated in specific instances that the "act of state" doctrine need not be applied, the Court has proceeded to hear and decide cases that challenge actions of other nations. However, several justices have objected, because they feel it inappropriate to accept the executive's word on whether or not the courts can proceed.[24]

RELATIONS BETWEEN FEDERAL AND STATE COURTS

Relations between federal and state courts can be smooth or awkward, with much friction. The friction has abated substantially since the early years of the Republic, when there was considerable resistance to judicial review of state court rulings (see page 62). Although relations are now less difficult, problems still abound, such as conflicts over federal court interpretation of state law and over review of state criminal convictions. The Warren Court's rulings allowing federal court review of state convictions, coupled with its liberal constitutional interpretations, particularly ruffled conservative states' feathers; the Burger Court's rulings limiting such intervention have reduced states' displeasure.

If judicial rulings are the source of much friction between federal and state courts, there are also day-to-day problems of relations between federal and state courts. In a number of states, these are handled through relatively new bodies for exchanging views, *federal-state judicial councils*, composed of federal and state judges who meet to discuss and try to resolve judicial problems. More than thirty councils were set up after the Chief Justice called for them in his 1970 State of the Judiciary message; however, two-thirds of those had become inactive after ten years had passed.

Composition of the councils varies, but the chief judge of the federal district court, a court of appeals judge (if one resides in the area), and the state's chief justice are usually among the members. The councils have dealt with a broad range of questions, including the handling of habeas corpus petitions, diversity of citizenship litigation, and other jurisdictional matters affecting both state and federal judicial systems, as well as administrative matters such as overlapping federal and state jury service and the scheduling of conflicting trial schedules for lawyers. Some councils have worked out joint judicial hearings—with both a federal and a state judge present—for certain special cases.[25]

If we return our attention to the Supreme Court's rulings, we find that friction between state courts and the Supreme Court has resulted when the high court's interpretations of the U.S. Constitution's protection of civil liberties have been at variance with state court interpretations. When the Supreme Court rules that the Constitution *permits* but does not require a certain state practice, such as non-unanimous jury verdicts, the states are at liberty to adopt more rigorous standards (by retaining the requirement of a unanimous jury). However, the justices have recently ruled that state courts cannot interpret the U.S. Constitution to provide greater civil liberties protections, such as greater restrictions on law enforcement, than the Supreme Court itself has established when the justices have decided that the Constitution requires no more than a certain practice in order to preserve constitutional rights.

Overruling the Oregon Supreme Court's determination that, under the U.S. Constitution, a confession obtained after a defendant was inadequately warned of his rights under the *Miranda* decision could not be used to impeach his testimony, after a U.S. Supreme Court ruling to the contrary, the justices stated, "A State is free *as a matter of its own law* to impose greater restrictions on police activity than those this Court holds to be necessary under federal constitutional standards. . . . But . . . a State may not impose such greater restrictions as a matter of *federal constitutional law* when this Court specifically refrains from imposing them."[26] Such a statement stems from the Supreme Court's views, enunciated in the Little Rock case (see page 62), that not only the Constitution but also the *Supreme Court's interpretation* is the "supreme law of the land."

Because the Supreme Court seldom interferes with state decisions thought to rest on adequate state law grounds, if state courts carefully base their rulings solely on their own constitutions (and statutes) they can both avoid Supreme Court review and establish rules different from those the Supreme Court requires under the U.S. Constitution. In 1980, the Supreme Court made good on its promise that state courts could establish greater protection for civil liberties under their state constitutions. Although the Supreme Court had said only a few years earlier that leafletting in a privately owned shopping center was not protected by the First Amendment, the California Supreme Court had ruled that it had to be allowed under the California Constitution. Writing for a unanimous court, Justice Rehnquist said that the state court was not prevented from "adopt[ing] in its own Constitution individual liberties more expansive than those conferred by the Federal Constitution."[27]

Formal relations between federal and state courts, which the Supreme Court interprets, are depicted in Figure 5.1. The Supreme Court has issued a set of decisions delineating relations between federal and state courts: those concerning habeas corpus and civil rights claims are based on interpretation of federal statutes; others are based on basic conceptions of national court deference to the state judiciary.

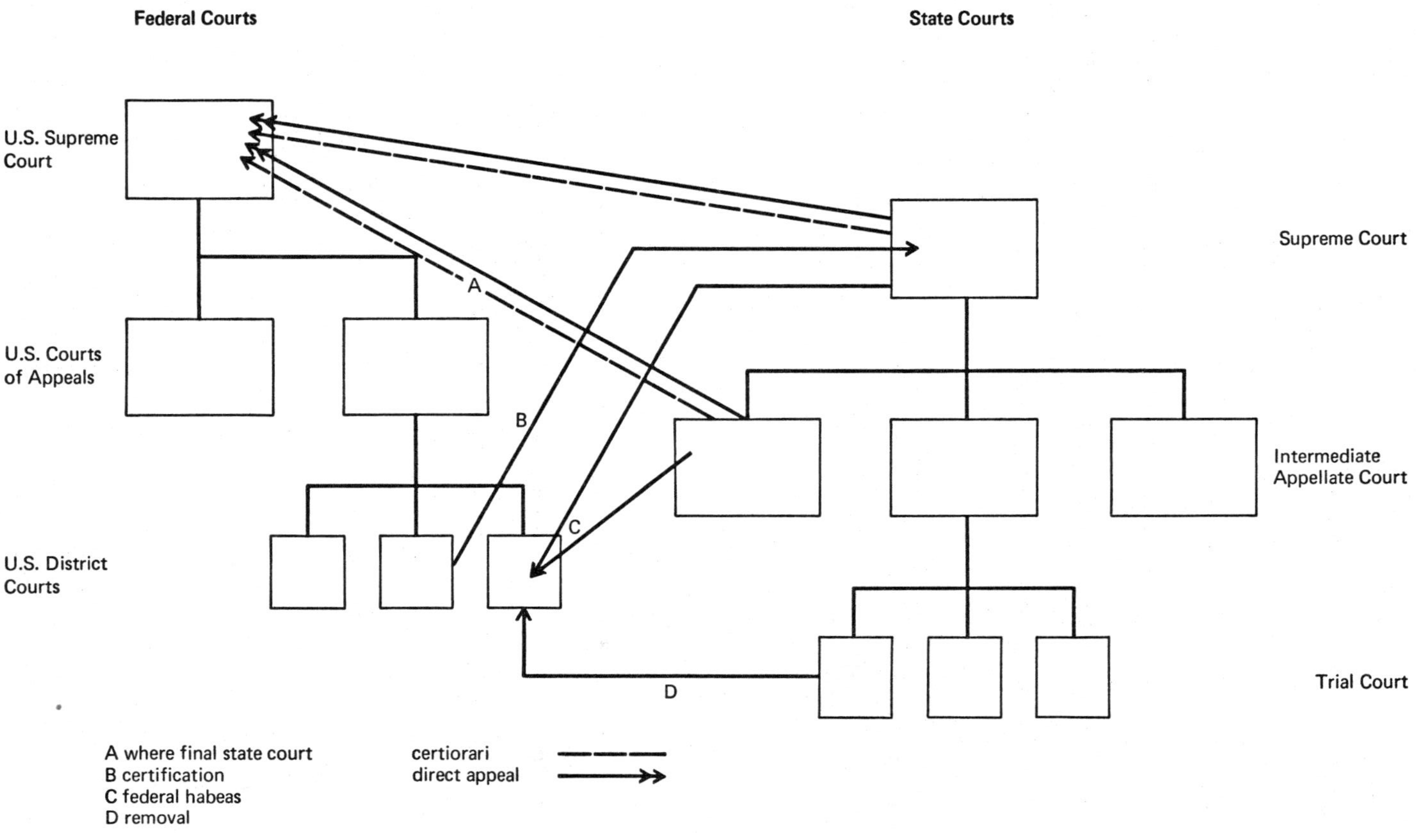

FIGURE 5.1 Relations Between Federal and State Courts

Diversity and Removal

Among Supreme Court rulings on federal court–state court relations are those dealing with diversity of citizenship cases and removal, the basic provisions for which are established by statute. *Diversity of citizenship suits* are those between citizens of one state (including corporations) and those of another; they may be brought in federal court if more than $10,000 is involved. Federal courts' application of federal rather than state law in such cases has caused substantial friction within the federal system. In 1842 in *Swift v. Tyson* the Supreme Court ruled that the federal courts could establish their own common law in diversity cases. The Supreme Court did not reverse itself until 1938. In *Erie Railroad Co. v. Tompkins*, the Court declared that its earlier decision was unconstitutional, that there was no federal common law, and that the federal courts should apply the laws of the states in diversity litigation. Despite *Erie*, there is still the equivalent of a federal common law of procedure because the federal courts have to have a set of rules as to which state's law to apply when different results would occur, but state law now has much greater authority in such suits. (There is, however, still some use of federal common law in other types of cases, such as labor-management disputes.)

Controversy over diversity of citizenship jurisdiction continues, with the Court trying to impose some limits[28] and Congress not yet having eliminated it. Federal courts' diversity caseload increased by roughly 50 percent from 1960 to 1976. However, it *decreased* from less than one-third to less than one-fourth of federal civil filings. Chief Justice Burger, who has suggested eliminating it altogether to reduce federal court caseload, argues that state judges are no longer less fair to out-of-state litigants than are federal judges, thus eliminating an earlier rationale for such jurisdiction. Nor have federal judges helped to develop the state law they must apply in such cases, but instead have had to take considerable time to ascertain (or guess) that state law. However, diversity cases, because they present general legal issues like those often heard in state court, have kept federal judges (and attorneys who concentrate on federal practice) from becoming narrow federal law specialists and have provided them with a broader perspective.[29]

A recent survey, although indicating considerable variation among lawyers from one location to another, shows that lawyers remain concerned about local favoritism in state courts but not necessarily about a separate bias against corporations. In their varying relative use of federal and state courts for cases eligible for federal diversity jurisdiction, lawyers pick the court, state *or* federal, that will most expeditiously process their cases. That factor, a preference for the federal rules of procedure, and a concern for judges of high quality (federal courts are given higher ratings) play the largest roles in lawyers' choice of court.[30]

Diversity jurisdiction and *removal* of cases from state to federal court are related because many diversity cases are started in state courts—where they also can be brought—only to be shifted (removed) to federal court by out-of-state defendants. During the 1960s, removal was attempted in another category of cases—those of civil rights workers in the South who argued that they were being arrested and tried in order to harass them. Their efforts to transfer their cases to federal court failed when the Supreme Court, sensitive to the problem of taking cases away from the state courts, took a narrow view of the federal removal statute. Removal could occur, the Supreme Court said, only when there was a statutorily protected federal right involving racial equality, such as the right to service in a place of public accommodation after passage of the 1964 Civil Rights Act, and a state law or rule prevented the protection of rights in a state trial; an allegation of an unfair trial was an insufficient basis for removal, as errors at trial could be corrected on appeal.[31] The Court has continued to stand by this limited interpretation.

Abstention

Another linkage between federal and state courts derives from federal court interpretation of state law in the course of applying it. Federal judges do not have to decide what state law means when the state law is clear "on its face" or when state courts have provided a clarifying interpretation (or "gloss"). It is considered inappropriate for federal judges to decide what the state law means when it is ambiguous and state courts have not clarified it. *Abstention* is a doctrine that judges have developed to avoid federal court–state court conflict over interpretation of state law. Under this doctrine, federal courts "stay their hand" until state courts have an opportunity to rule on state law questions, because such state court action might allow federal courts to avoid federal questions or might modify those questions so that federal court action would be affected. When the doctrine of abstention was not applicable, "wise judicial administration"—such as avoidance of piecemeal litigation of legal questions—might make it best for a federal court to leave matters to the state courts, particularly when the federal court was several hundred miles from the dispute and state court proceedings had been initiated first. However, federal courts do not invariably abstain from deciding cases when state courts may also be involved in an issue. Justice Brennan has said that abstention was "the exception, not the rule" because federal courts could not abdicate their duty to decide cases unless some important countervailing interest was present.[32]

A specific mechanism for prompt state court interpretation of unanswered state law questions in pending federal cases is for the federal court to *certify* the questions to the state courts, which then provide an answer the federal court applies to the case before it. An increasing number of states have provided for such "downward certification" (different from lower federal courts asking higher federal courts to answer novel legal questions: see page 58). The Supreme Court itself has made use of such a mechanism, for example, remanding a death penalty case to the Georgia Supreme Court for interpretation of that court's opinion.[33] Similarly, the Supreme Court returns cases to state courts for rulings on unanswered questions that might provide an "adequate and independent state ground" to support the state ruling. It also does so when it is unclear whether a state court has used federal law, state law, or both as the basis for a decision, to ascertain whether there were separate state law grounds for the ruling.

A state litigant wishing to pursue a federal law claim must clearly and explicitly present that claim in the state courts so that they can "be afforded the opportunity to perform their duty, which includes responding to attacks on state authority based on the federal law or, if the litigation is wholly private, construing and applying the applicable federal requirements."[34] This is an example of the notion of *comity*—of respect for state courts' ability to decide issues—that the Supreme Court tries to implement. Questions of comity and federal statutory law (the Tax Injunction Act) were combined in recent rulings reinforcing limits on federal court action against county and state tax officials. The Court, although it has generally not applied comity to civil rights claims because of their federal basis, has used comity to bar §1983 civil rights challenges to administration of a state tax system and has shown similar deference to county tax authorities in holding state tax remedies were sufficiently "plain, speedy, and efficient" to require operation of the federal statutory bar on injunctions in tax suits.[35]

A closely related matter is the question of whether state court action is "final" so that appeal to the Supreme Court is proper. The Supreme Court does not wish to accept an appeal from a state court in a case in which only some questions have been answered when other proceedings are still pending, because a Supreme Court ruling at that stage may mean interference in state proceedings. On the other hand, not accepting the appeal may mean needless continuation of the trial and thus injury to the appellants if resolution of an issue would terminate the proceedings. On this question of "finality," the Court takes a pragmatic approach despite complaints that the number of exceptions to the finality rule has become larger.

Competing with the preference that state courts decide state law questions is a preference that all claims in a case be heard by either state or federal courts. At times, the preference for having all claims decided in one court may lead to all claims being decided in federal rather than state courts, the reverse of the result produced by abstention. When state matters are raised in federal court along with an adequate federal claim, they may be heard by the federal judge under the doctrine of "pendent jurisdiction." If the federal court then follows normal rules of self-restraint and avoids federal constitutional questions, it may decide the state claim first, thus ironically not resolving the federal questions.[36] Despite the preference for "all claims in one court," the idea is not followed consistently. Eliminating those without $10,000 claims from diversity of citizenship class actions means that the same legal questions may be argued by some plaintiffs in federal court, and by others in state court, with potentially conflicting results. A similar problem can result with prisoners' claims, depending on whether they are embodied in a habeas corpus petition or a civil rights suit. There is no requirement that state remedies be exhausted in civil rights cases, which can thus move directly to federal court, but the exhaustion rule does apply to habeas claims, taking them back to state courts. The same facts may thus be heard simultaneously in federal and state courts, producing duplicative litigation with potentially inconsistent results.[37]

Injunctions Against State Laws

An important issue touching on abstention and comity is whether federal courts should enjoin enforcement of state laws or other action by state officials, or should insist that an individual against whom the state has acted use federal claims as a defense in state court, thus assuring that state courts had the first opportunity to rule on such matters and to apply the Constitution. The Warren Court facilitated obtaining injunctions against improper state action. When illegal raids had been made on a civil rights organization and the prosecutor had made public use of seized documents, the Court, in *Dombrowski v. Pfister* (1965), saying that First Amendment rights could not be sufficiently protected during a state criminal trial, allowed an injunction against state prosecution under a broad statute that infringed freedom of speech. When lower federal courts interpreted this ruling broadly, there was a considerable increase in federal court challenges to state laws; these occurred even where state courts, given a chance, might have enforced federal constitutional rights.

Chief Justice Burger felt this practice overused federal courts and denigrated state court authority, and he was clearly determined to put an end to it. The Court's change of position came in 1971 in *Younger v. Harris.* The majority ruled in that case that federal courts were no longer to issue injunctions against already instituted state criminal prosecutions; state court proceedings were to be allowed to continue, except where great and immediate irreparable damage was threatened and that harm could not be prevented by raising the constitutional claims in a later state trial. This rule was to apply, said the Court, even when the challenged statute was clearly unconstitutional. After this ruling, the Court at first increased rather than further decreased access to federal court injunctions, for example, in *Steffel v. Thompson* (1974), allowing plaintiffs *threatened* with prosecution for handing out antiwar leaflets to obtain a declaration of their rights even when they could not show the irreparable injury necessary for obtaining an injunction.

The Court then returned forcefully to the *Younger v. Harris* doctrine and extended it. In *Hicks v. Miranda* (1975), the Court ruled that a federal injunction could not be obtained against a prosecution initiated in a state court *after* the federal challenge had been started—prompting the dissenters' complaint that whether you could get an injunction depended on an improper "race to the courthouse" in which the state could start later and get there first. The *Younger* doctrine was also extended to *civil* proceedings closely related to criminal matters, for example, a state civil nuisance proceeding against a theater showing allegedly obscene movies, and to other civil matters as well.[38]

If federal court actions against many types of state court actions are barred, state courts also may not prevent the filing of appropriate federal court suits. In 1977 and 1978, the Supreme Court twice had to order a New Mexico judge not to interfere with a litigant's rights to file certain federal cases related to on-going state litigation concerning obligations under a contract for delivery of uranium in the face of a five-fold price increase.[39]

Federal Habeas Corpus

Filing of habeas corpus petitions in federal court by those challenging state convictions, often many years after state appeals have concluded, is the most controversial present issue concerning relations between federal courts and state courts. A substantial increase in such federal habeas corpus petitions resulted from Warren Court rulings that, first, existence of an "adequate and independent" basis in state law for affirming a conviction would not bar such petitions and, second, a prisoner need not have first exhausted state remedies for challenging a conviction before coming to federal court if those remedies were no longer available.[40]

The Burger Court reduced use of federal habeas challenges to state convictions. The Chief Justice, saying that the lack of finality in criminal cases results in considerable extra work for all the courts, has complained about state prisoners' ability to challenge their convictions for years after the event. (A law review article by Justice O'Connor, expressing her views on this matter, helped indicate the compatibility of her views with those of President Reagan and the Nixon appointees to the Court.) The Court first reinforced the basic exhaustion-of-remedies requirement by ruling that a federal habeas petition could not be filed until the specific claim it contained had been brought before the state courts. The justices then decided that a defendant could not use a federal habeas corpus petition to challenge a grand jury's composition if that issue had not been raised prior to trial, *unless* the petitioner showed "cause" for such an omission *and* actual prejudice to rights from the challenged unconstitutional action.[41] The justices continued to extend this "cause and prejudice" rule concerning state court procedural defaults. They did so, first, when a defendant failed to make timely objection at trial to admission of his prior statements, and then, with Justice O'Connor writing for the Court, when a defense lawyer failed to object to the judge's self-defense instructions to the jury.[42]

Particularly significant in the Supreme Court's efforts to limit state prisoners' access to federal courts was the rule (*Stone v. Powell*, 1976) that search and seizure claims already reviewed by a state court could not be raised again in federal court. The Supreme Court demanded the same deference be given to state court judges by all federal courts when it ruled that, in federal habeas proceedings, state courts' factual determinations must be given a "presumption of correctness"; furthermore, a federal court overruling such determinations must indicate in writing its basis for doing so.[43]

NOTES

1. Gregory J. Rathjen and Harold J. Spaeth, "Access to the Federal Courts: An Analysis of Burger Court Policy Making," *American Journal of Political Science* 23 (May 1979):366.
2. Ibid., p. 374.
3. Ibid., p. 380. However, another study shows Burger and Blackmun increasing their support for access claims. Burton Atkins and William Taggart, "Substantive Access Doctrines and Conflict Management in the U.S. Supreme Court: Reflections on Activism and Restraint," in *Supreme Court Activism and Restraint*, eds. Stephen C. Halpern and Charles Lamb (Lexington, Mass.: Lexington Books, 1982), p. 373.
4. For a discussion of the application of the Eleventh Amendment to suits against the state, see *Florida Department of State v. Treasure Salvors, Inc.*, 102 S.Ct. 3304 (1982), which produced a badly divided Court.

5. *Owen v. City of Independence*, 445 U.S. 622 (1980); *City of Newport v. Fact Concerts*, 453 U.S. 247 (1981).
6. *Tileston v. Ullman*, 318 U.S. 44 (1943).
7. *Barrows v. Jackson*, 346 U.S. 259 (1953); *Eisenstadt v. Baird*, 405 U.S. 438 (1972); *Singleton v. Wulff*, 428 U.S. 106 (1976).
8. *Peters v. Kiff*, 407 U.S. 493 (1972); *Taylor v. Louisiana*, 419 U.S. 522 (1975).
9. *Duke Power Co. v. Carolina Environmental Study Group*, 438 U.S. 59 (1978).
10. *Valley Forge Christian College v. Americans United For Separation of Church and State*, 102 S.Ct. 752 (1982).
11. *United States v. Richardson*, 418 U.S. 166 (1974); *Schlesinger v. Reservists Committee to End the War*, 418 U.S. 208 (1974).
12. *Village of Arlington Heights v. Metropolitan Housing Development Corp.*, 429 U.S. 252 (1977). However, on remand, the court of appeals decided in plaintiff's favor on a statutory basis and the Supreme Court denied review.
13. *National Railroad Passenger Corp. v. National Association of Railroad Passengers*, 414 U.S. 453 (1974); *Bread Political Action Committee v. Federal Election Commission*, 102 S.Ct. 1235 (1982); *Trafficante v. Metropolitan Life Insurance Co.*, 409 U.S. 205 (1972).
14. *Merrill Lynch, Pierce, Fenner & Smith v. Curran*, 102 S.Ct. 1825 (1982); *Cannon v. University of Chicago*, 441 U.S. 667 (1979).
15. *Bivens v. Six Unknown Federal Narcotics Agents*, 403 U.S. 388 (1971); *Carlson v. Green*, 446 U.S. 14 (1980); *Davis v. Passman*, 442 U.S. 228 (1979).
16. *Snyder v. Harris*, 394 U.S. 334 (1969); *Zahn v. International Paper Co.*, 414 U.S. 211 (1973).
17. *Rogers v. Lodge*, 102 S.Ct. 3272 at 3283 (1982).
18. See *Moore v. Ogilvie*, 394 U.S. 814 (1969).
19. *Carafas v. LaVallee*, 391 U.S. 234 (1968) (challenge to conviction); *Lane v. Williams*, 102 S.Ct. 1322 (1982) (sentences).
20. *Poe v. Ullman*, 367 U.S. 497 (1961); *Griswold v. Connecticut*, 381 U.S. 479 (1965).
21. See *Noyd v. Bond*, 395 U.S. 683 (1969); and *Schlesinger v. Councilman*, 420 U.S. 738 (1975).
22. *Coleman v. Miller*, 307 U.S. 433 (1939); *Luther v. Borden*, 7 How. 1 (1849); *Pacific States Telephone and Telegraph Co. v. Oregon*, 223 U.S. 118 (1912); and *Mississippi v. Johnson*, 4 Wall. 475 (1867).
23. See Anthony D'Amato and Robert O'Neil, *The Judiciary and Vietnam* (New York: St. Martin's Press, 1972).
24. *First National City Bank v. Banco National De Cuba*, 406 U.S. 759 (1972); *Alfred Dunhill of London v. Republic of Cuba*, 425 U.S. 682 (1976).
25. See John W. Winkle, "Toward Intersystem Harmony: State-Federal Judicial Councils," *Justice System Journal* 6 (Summer 1981):240–253.
26. *Oregon v. Hass*, 420 U.S. 714 at 719 (1975) (Justice Blackmun). The earlier case is *Harris v. New York*, 401 U.S. 222 (1971).
27. *PruneYard Shopping Center v. Robins*, 447 U.S. 74 at 82 (1980). The earlier case was *Lloyd Corp. v. Tanner*, 407 U.S. 551 (1972).
28. For example, a federal court may not hear a diversity case unless all defendants are citizens of states different from those of all plaintiffs; where there are several defendants, a plaintiff may not obtain federal court jurisdiction by suing the only one with diverse citizenship, who would then "join" the other, nondiverse defendants. *Owen Equipment and Erection Co. v. Kroger*, 437 U.S. 365 (1978).

29. See David L. Shapiro, "Federal Diversity Jurisdiction: A Survey and a Proposal," *Harvard Law Review* 91 (December 1977):317–355.
30. See Kristin Bumiller, "Choice of Forum in Diversity Cases: Analysis of a Survey and Implications for Reform," *Law & Society Review* 15 (1980–1981):749–774; and Jolanta Perlstein, "Lawyers' Strategies and Diversity Jurisdiction," *Law & Policy Quarterly* 3 (July 1981):321–340.
31. *Georgia v. Rachel*, 383 U.S. 780 (1966); *City of Greenwood v. Peacock*, 383 U.S. 808 (1966).
32. See *Colorado River Water Conservation District v. United States*, 424 U.S. 800 at 815–817 (1976).
33. *Zant v. Stephens*, 102 S.Ct. 1856 (1982).
34. *Webb v. Webb*, 451 U.S. 493 at 499 (1981).
35. *Fair Assessment in Real Estate Association v. McNary*, 102 S.Ct. 177 (1981); *Rosewell v. LaSalle National Bank*, 450 U.S. 503 (1981).
36. *Hagans v. Lavine*, 415 U.S. 528 (1974); see also *Moor v. Alameda County*, 411 U.S. 693 (1973).
37. *Preiser v. Rodriguez*, 411 U.S. 475 (1973).
38. *Huffman v. Pursue*, 420 U.S. 592 (1975) (nuisance provision); *Trainor v. Hernandez*, 431 U.S. 434 (1977) (action for return of welfare payments).
39. *General Atomic Co. v. Felter*, 434 U.S. 12 (1977) and 436 U.S. 493 (1978).
40. *Townsend v. Sain*, 372 U.S. 294 (1963); *Fay v. Noia*, 372 U.S. 391 (1963). A district judge's order denying a habeas corpus petition may be reviewed only if that judge or an appellate judge issues a certificate of probable cause, which requires a substantial showing that a federal right has been denied.
41. *Picard v. Connor*, 404 U.S. 270 (1971); *Francis v. Henderson*, 425 U.S. 536 (1976). The Court did rule that claims of racial discrimination in state grand jury selection *could* be challenged through federal habeas even if the subsequent trial jury had not been improperly constituted. *Rose v. Mitchell*, 443 U.S. 545 (1979).
42. *Wainwright v. Sykes*, 433 U.S. 72 (1977) (admission of defendant's statements); *Engle v. Isaac*, 102 S.Ct. 1558 (1982) (failure to object to judge's instruction). The Court also applied the "cause and prejudice" standard to postconviction proceedings involving *federal* defendants. *United States v. Frady*, 102 S.Ct. 1584 (1982). For a recent attack by the Chief Justice on excessive use of federal habeas corpus by state prisoners, see *Spalding v. Aiken*, 103 S.Ct. 1795 (1983).
43. *Sumner v. Mata*, 449 U.S. 539 (1981) and 102 S.Ct. 1303 (1982).

Chapter 6

The Supreme Court: Its Docket and Screening Decisions

Lawyers' and groups' decisions to take cases to the Supreme Court, decisions made within the confines of rules on access to the courts, provide the basic pool from which the Supreme Court, using certain regular procedures, takes its cases. By "skimming off" most cases at early stages and disposing of some others through brief orders (summary dispositions), the Court can concentrate on those it considers worthy of full treatment.

All this is part of *docket management*, which provides the Court with opportunities to engage in strategic actions. Selectivity is crucial to the Court's work—not only administratively but also politically: "It helps to keep the Court abreast of new trends in litigation, and it helps to maintain the Court's flexibility in responding to change."[1] Deciding which cases to accept and which to reject is crucial if the justices are to have cases with the best factual settings for rulings they may be predisposed to make and if they are not to have to hand down the wrong decision at the wrong time.

In this chapter, we look first at the cases brought to the Court, that is, the size and content of its docket, and then at the ways in which the justices skim off most of the cases. We turn in the next chapter to the Court's "full dress treatment" of the remaining cases.

THE COURT'S BUSINESS

Docket Size and Growth

The size of the Supreme Court's docket is affected by a variety of external factors, which, in combination, create pressures leading to increased case filings. Some of these factors are external. They include the existence of social problems that have been transformed into legal issues; people's propensity to litigate and to appeal, which is itself affected by perceptions of the Court's caseload; and increases in the number of federal judges, such as those added by the 1978 Omnibus Judgeship Act. The Court's own actions also affect its caseload. The Court's willingness to rule on a topic increases the number of cases filed, just as consistent refusal to review cases on a particular subject results in review being sought in fewer such cases. Similarly, adoption of certain doctrinal rules serves to make clear to potential litigants that it will not be fruitful to bring certain types of cases. If, while deciding cases, the justices make statements indicating the Court would welcome cases raising questions not presently before the Court, lawyers are likely to try to bring those questions to the Court for resolution. If, as critics suggest, the justices feel compelled to take more cases instead of allowing lower courts to resolve them, if they operate from an apparent presumption that only *they* can decide certain cases, they will produce a serious continuing caseload problem.

References to the Supreme Court's *docket* are really references to its dockets. Until 1970, there were three: the Original Docket, for the few original jurisdiction cases; the Appellate Docket, containing certiorari petitions or jurisdictional statements (for appeals) in *paid* cases, that is, where the petitions or statements have been printed; and the Miscellaneous Docket, containing the unpaid or *in forma pauperis* (i.f.p.) cases where the requirement of a printed submission and filing fee has been waived because of indigency. The Appellate and Miscellaneous Dockets are now combined in the Appellate Docket, but paid and i.f.p. cases can still be distinguished because different numbering systems are used for each. (There are also separate dockets for special motions, for applications for stays of lower court proceedings, and for disbarment of lawyers who are members of the Supreme Court bar.)

The Supreme Court's present docket—over 4,000 filings a year—makes us forget the Court's small early caseload. From 1790 to 1801, the Court's appellate jurisdiction was invoked in only 87 cases, of which 80 were federal cases (36 diversity-of-citizenship cases, 35 admiralty cases, and 9 civil cases brought by the government).[2] In the earliest years, workload was largely a matter of circuit duty, not the Court's own small docket. As late as the Civil War years (1862–1866), the Court still was not handing down many decisions: 240 cases were decided in that period. However, paralleling an increase in federal district court caseload, the Court's output grew to 1,125 for the 1886–1890 period.

The Supreme Court's docket—cases filed and not disposed of—contained only 63 cases in 1870, but there were 1,212 cases on the docket eight years later. By 1891, the figure was up to 1,816, another 50 percent increase. The passage of the Court of Appeals Act that year produced an immediate drop in Supreme Court filings—from over 600 in 1890 to 275 in 1892—and the number of petitions for review continued to decline at the rate of 2 percent during the last decade of the century.[3] The post-Civil War docket growth resulted largely from statutory changes, including provision for removal of cases to the federal courts and addition of federal question jurisdiction. The Court, although finding ways to restrict jurisdiction, interpreted federal question jurisdiction in a way that added to the docket. Despite justices' complaints that they were overworked, "a few important cases decided differently would have had the effect of discouraging much litigation."[4] The Court's later adoption of more flexible rules on standing and mootness produced a similar increase in cases. As Casper and Posner observe, "A frequently overlooked point is the extent to which the Supreme Court itself controls the demand for its services through its power to recognize a new, or extinguish a recognized, federal statutory or constitutional right by interpreting or reinterpreting a federal statute or constitutional provision."[5]

Despite a rate of docket growth of roughly 2 to 3 percent for the first half of the twentieth century, as recently as the early 1940s fewer than 1,000 cases were filed annually. The number of filings fluctuated between 1,000 and 1,500 from 1944–1954, and then began rather steady increased growth, reflecting an increased annual rate of filings 5 percent plus starting at about midcentury. The result was that the 1971 docket contained three-and-a-half times as many cases as the 1951 docket and roughly seven to eight times the number in 1925, when the Court received full certiorari authority. Despite a slight, uneven decline after 1973, filings again increased, reaching over 4,400 in the 1981 Term, but dropping slightly the following year. The *rate* of increase had decreased somewhat since 1968, but the larger base meant that absolute increases in filings were substantial.[6] So was the size of the docket—over 5,300 cases in the 1981 Term. Roughly half of the recent increase in filings is in unpaid cases, primarily prisoner petitions, which increased in part because of the 1964 Criminal Justice Act provision for appointed counsel for indigent federal criminal defendants. New federal statutes containing new causes of action also contributed to the "pool" of cases among those from which lawyers brought appeals to the Supreme Court.

A further indication of the increased size of the Court's docket is the fact that on the first day of the 1981 Term (October 5, 1981), the Court disposed of:

- 839 certiorari petitions (815 denied, 24 granted)
- 39 appeals (35 dismissed, probable jurisdiction noted in 4)
- One motion for leave to file a bill of complaint (an original jurisdiction case)(granted)
- 8 habeas corpus petitions and 17 requests for writs of mandamus or prohibition (denied).

plus a variety of miscellaneous orders, including summary affirmance of a lower court ruling and the adoption of a report and recommendations of a special master.

TABLE 6.1. Supreme Court Filings (rounded)

1955	1,600	1969	3,400
1956	1,800	1971	3,600
1960	1,900	1973	3,900
1961	2,200	1980	4,200
1965	2,800	1981	4,400
1967	3,100		

Source: Casper and Posner, *The Workload of the Supreme Court,* p. 3; updated.

Has the Supreme Court been able to keep pace with docket growth? One indication is the number of cases carried over from one term to the next. The Court is current with its work in the sense that, except for a few cases set for reargument the next term, all cases argued within a term are disposed of during that same term; in this sense, the Court has no backlog. The Court now hands down 140 decisions with full opinion each year (up from 120 a few years ago), plus another 40 summary rulings (see below), but increases in the Court's docket have not generally led to comparable increases in the number of cases decided. We would thus expect at the end of each term to see an increase in the number of petitions for review not yet accepted or denied as well as an increase in the number of cases accepted for review but not yet heard and decided, producing a backlog of cases not decided. Indeed, the time from granting of review to disposition—much longer than one year—has increased.

The total carryover at the end of the Court's term, after declining to 453 cases in 1966, reached almost 900 cases in the 1972 Term. The carryover reached over 1,200 the following year before falling to over 800, where it has remained since. The number of cases not acted upon during the term (carryover + cases docketed − dispositions), after being below 500 at the end of the 1975 Term, reached almost 800 by the 1978 Term.[7]

By the late 1970s, at the end of each term the Court carried over roughly the same number of cases previously accepted for argument as had been on the argument calendar at term's beginning. The Court continued to accept more cases for argument without similarly increasing the number of cases argued—the usual number being in the vicinity of 150 per term. Thus the argument calendar filled up earlier each year—in the 1981 Term, by Christmas recess, and the Court began the 1982 Term with 126 cases already accepted for argument, despite a record number of cases having been argued in the 1981 Term. However, in the 1982 Term, the Court significantly reduced the number of cases accepted for hearing.

Do these statistics mean the Court is "overloaded"? Overload complaints were heard even when dockets were much smaller, for example, before the courts of appeals were established and again before certiorari jurisdiction was provided. Particularly if the justices were not already overworked, an increase in caseload would not necessarily mean "overload," and increases in supporting staff, such as law clerks after 1914, can enable the Court to cope with higher caseload. In the 1970s, the "overload" argument was renewed with particular force. The Commission on Revision of the Federal Court Appellate System, which extensively examined the matter, said that "overload" could not be evaluated only in terms of cases filed. There was also a *hidden docket*—cases in which people were deterred from seeking review by the size of the Court's docket because the probability of obtaining a decision on the merits was not worth the expense and delay. The Commission stressed the need for adequate capacity for the declaration of national law. Absence of such capacity led to lack of Supreme Court review for cases that twenty years earlier would certainly have been accepted for review. This in turn led to unresolved conflict on points of law between the circuits and to delay as well as to uncertainty for both lawyers and lower court judges, who needed precedents on which to base decisions. Unresolved intercircuit conflict would also produce repetitive litigation, further increasing cases filed in the Supreme Court. Making the matter worse was that the Supreme Court would be forced to take cases "otherwise not worthy of its resources," because it was the only court capable of resolving conflict between the circuits.[8]

The justices themselves, especially the Court's new members, then joined in the "overload" discussion. The more senior justices were less likely to complain. In 1972 Justice Douglas, who said the courts of appeals were the overloaded courts whose judges had a much heavier opinion-writing load, called Supreme Court overwork a "myth" and stated that the Court was "if anything, underworked, not overworked."[9] He pointed out that the Court had no backlog and was accepting roughly the same number of cases for argument as in the 1939 Term. Justice Douglas was perhaps a "workhorse," saying that "no Justice of this court need work more than four days a week to carry his burden," which he claimed was "comfortable" even when he was hospitalized,[10] but other judges agreed with him. Justice Stewart, for example, joined Douglas in needling their colleagues for complaining about overwork when they insisted on taking cases of little importance. As Justice Stevens remarked more recently, the Court's "expressions of concern about the overburdened Federal Judiciary will ring with a hollow echo" when the Court "creates unnecessary work for itself" by "granting certiorari without adequate justification" and by not showing sufficient respect for decisions of the U.S. courts of appeals (from which he had come to the Supreme Court).[11]

Cases that seem unimportant to some may, however, seem quite important to others, requiring judicial capacity to decide them. The feeling that there are too many such cases has led several justices to call for creation of a court to assist the Supreme Court with its caseload, and concern has now been expressed even by some, such as Justice Brennan, who did not feel there was a problem earlier (see pages 47, 49). In 1978 Justice White, who found numerous cases that met the Court's criteria for granting review (see page 161) but to which the Court had denied review, observed, "We are performing at our full capacity, *i.e.*, we are now extending plenary review to as many cases as we can adequately consider, decide and explain by full opinion."[12] Justice White's comment, the gist of which he repeated to an ABA audience in 1982, suggests that it is not docket size per se that is the issue but the need for time for adequate deliberation to resolve certain types of cases. Justice Rehnquist has argued that for the Court to be current in its docket is insufficient: "It is essential that it have the necessary time for careful deliberation and reasoned decision of the very important types of cases which are the staple of its business today."[13] And Justice Blackmun has declared that "the heavier the burden, the less is the possibility of adequate performance and the greater is the probability of less-than-well considered adjudication," with the possibility of a "breaking point" beyond which a judge's work might become second-rate.[14] Adequate time is necessary for the Court to pay attention to those cases in which it wants to develop policy positions, so that "the contours of the change desired can be adopted and implemented in such a way that social stability rather than social upheaval is promoted."[15] Chief Justice Burger has also made several proposals to deal with the Court's docket. In addition to the proposal for a National Court of Appeals and the already-enacted elimination of most three-judge district courts so that cases would not come directly to the Supreme Court from the district courts, Burger has also suggested that prospective appellants get approval from the courts before they appeal their cases.

Docket Content

The content of the Court's docket is at least as significant as its size. Over time that content has shifted toward cases raising constitutional questions. In the nineteenth century and extending into the twentieth century, the Supreme Court was primarily a private-law court. Cases with constitutional questions began to increase in the 1930s, when matters of due process constituted the greatest portion; other constitutional cases then involved the Commerce Clause, impairment of contract, and full faith and credit. Cases based on the Bill of Rights were only 5 percent of the constitutional cases in this earlier period, but by the late 1950s they made up over one-third of the cases filed, and *half* in the late 1960s.

During the Vinson Court and Warren Court's first two terms, economic and civil liberties cases averaged 58 percent of all cases decided on the merits, but before the Burger Court produced changes, the figure rose to 80 percent in the remaining Warren Court years, most of that increase coming from civil liberties cases.[16] Prior to 1960, nonconstitutional holdings made up two-thirds to three-fourths of the Court's rulings. However, as a result of the Warren Court, constitutional cases constituted one-half to two-thirds of the Court's full-opinion decisions. Much of this change can be explained by the increase in the number of state criminal cases, almost 100 percent of which entailed constitutional questions.

The Burger Court was expected to give less attention to constitutional problems and more attention to matters of statutory interpretation, in part by shifting from civil liberties cases to commercial or regulatory litigation. At first, there was a shift, with full opinion cases on economic issues constituting over half the output in the 1972 Term, while the proportion of criminal and habeas corpus cases decreased to under one-third, falling further—to just over one-fourth—in the 1973 and 1974 Terms. Private civil actions increased from one-third (1968) to one-half (1973–1974) of the cases accepted.[17]

Nonetheless, instead of "deconstitutionalizing" its working docket, the Burger Court has remained largely a constitutional court. This is clear from examination of the cases to which the Burger Court gave full treatment (its plenary docket) through 1976. Examination of Supreme Court output also shows it to be a *civil rights court*. Cases with constitutional individual rights issues, just over one-fourth of the plenary docket in the 1959 Term, by the 1970s became the plenary docket's largest single component—over two-fifths, and even higher if one adds cases with procedural issues affecting individual rights and those with individual rights as secondary issues. Civil rights cases *displaced* other types of cases on the docket during the 1960s. That displacement did not, however, continue in the 1970s both because the Court expanded its output somewhat and because there was no further increase in review granted in civil rights cases. Nor is such continuous expansion necessary: "There comes a point where the new rights have been incorporated into the fabric of the law, and the Court can move on to new issues, except perhaps for an occasional decision made necessary by a novel context or the imaginative use of precedents by lawyers or lower courts."[18]

Roughly two-fifths of the individual rights cases involved criminal procedure questions; another two-fifths involved other due process and equal protection questions under the Fifth and Fourteenth Amendments; the remainder were cases on the First and Seventh (jury trial) Amendments and other noncriminal protections. Cases with criminal procedure issues and freedom of expression issues, the latter composing a smaller proportion of the plenary docket, followed comparable patterns of growth. These two areas combined, along with equal protection and access cases, accounted for most of the growth in the civil rights component of its plenary docket. There was a *three-fold* increase in equal protection cases involving school desegregation and other racial discrimination issues from 1959–1976; reapportionment, which received less attention in the 1970s; and the new areas in the 1970s: illegitimacy, aliens' rights, and gender discrimination.[19]

Increases in cases involving criminal procedure questions are of particular interest because of the public's increased concern about crime and political candidates' "law and order" campaigns. However, over a forty-year period, changes in the number of the Court's full opinion criminal procedure cases appear not to have reflected changes in the incidence of crime, media coverage of crime, or public concern about crime or changes in that concern. Differences in the ideologies of the justices controlling the Court and changes in chief justices *have* made a difference, with the Court significantly more likely to increase the number of criminal justice decisions when liberals control the Court than when conservatives do.[20] In the Burger Court, criminal procedure cases provided a stable level of business for the Court in the 1970s, although there was growth in double jeopardy, cruel and unusual punishment (death penalty), and right to counsel cases. There were also changes in the *sources* of the

Court's cases, with a 1967–1973 increase in federal habeas corpus cases and a decrease in criminal cases from the courts of appeals; the number of federal and state direct criminal appeals cases remained roughly the same.

Dominance of the plenary docket by constitutional individual rights cases did not mean other types of cases were absent. However, by comparison with 383 individual rights cases from 1971–1976, there were only 107 cases in which the Court performed its role of umpire in the federal system, with primary attention to questions of federal preemption of state powers and cases raising questions whether states had exceeded their powers. There had been a sharp drop in cases involving interpretation of federal statutes and federal common law at the end of the Warren Court, from at least 40 percent of the Court's plenary docket until the 1967 Term, below 30 percent thereafter.

The subject matter of cases decided also shifted considerably. New statutes, on environmental protection, securities regulation, and employment discrimination, along with Freedom of Information Act (FOIA) cases, came to the fore, while taxation and labor law received less attention. Antitrust provided the largest segment of business-regulation cases, regulation of power and patent/copyright litigation retained stable proportions of the docket, and there was an obvious decline in Interstate Commerce Commission cases.[21] Among "federal specialties," immigration and citizenship cases constituted a decreasing portion of the plenary docket from 1959–1976, while Federal Employer Liability Act (FELA) and admiralty cases were almost totally gone from the docket. Such changes indicate the Court's ability to respond to the need for interpretation of new statutes but raise the question of whether sufficient attention is being paid to reexamination of earlier rulings in other statutory areas. Infrequent attention to a subject area may deprive the justices of the appreciation of the context in which such cases arise that they gain when the cases are frequently before the Court.[22]

This broad picture of docket content and trends should not obscure the wide variety of particular issues explored by the Court in any single term. Rarely are there more than one or two cases per term on any single topic, a result of the Court's usually deciding fewer than 150 cases with full opinion and its attempt to develop law on the many topics on which people have sought its guidance and direction. However, there were five antitrust, three FOIA, and four welfare rights decisions in 1974, and in 1976 there were *ten* cases on double jeopardy.

A partial listing of issues decided during the October 1981 Term includes:

- Railway Labor Act coverage for state-owned railroads
- where Howard Hughes' will is to be resolved
- application of a state tax to a Department of Energy contractor
- employer withdrawal from a multiemployer bargaining unit
- municipalities' antitrust liability
- preemption of state utility regulation by federal statute

The list also includes a wide range of civil rights/civil liberties matters:

- rights of involuntarily committed persons
- exclusion of press and public from a trial
- exhaustion of remedies under §1983
- presidential immunity
- admission of a male to an all-women's university
- contractor's liability for union racial discrimination at the hiring hall and in apprenticeship programs
- state regulation of "kiddieporn"
- death penalty for those who aid and abet a murder
- economic boycott aimed at racial discrimination
- standard of proof for terminating parental rights
- use of college facilities by a religious group
- limitations on political contributions to a referendum
- employment of aliens by the state
- advertising by lawyers
- whether an Amish employer must pay Social Security taxes
- municipal regulation of an entertainment center and a "headshop"
- school board authority to remove books from a library
- whether housing discrimination "testers" have standing
- application of the speedy trial requirement
- education for children of illegal aliens
- searches of cars and their contents

"SKIMMING OFF": DENYING REVIEW

The Court's decisions denying review and its other summary actions are of generally low visibility. Moreover, the reasons underlying them are often intentionally well hidden. The sheer numbers of such decisions and the variety of factors potentially playing a part in any particular Court action further mask their meaning but do not decrease their extreme importance, which stems from the fact that such decisions account for the bulk of the Court's actions, far exceeding in number the Court's formal statements of policy. For the Court to make a decision not to hear a case may be as important—not only for the litigants but also for the (unaware) public—as for it to decide particular controversial questions explicitly. The patterns of the Court's actions, reinforced by statements by some of the justices, provide strong evidence that the Court's actions denying review have clear policy implications.

The Court's means for managing its docket have varied. At times the Court has sought additional statutory authority to reduce the proportion of cases it must decide, as when it obtained its discretionary jurisdiction in the 1925 Judges Bill. The Court has also taken its appeals jurisdiction, theoretically mandatory, and made it discretionary in fact. Also, many appeals have been disposed of summarily, a recognition of the Court's flexibility. As early as a hundred years ago, the Court allowed appeals (formerly writs of error) to be affirmed on motion without argument when the appeal appeared to be frivolous or to have been undertaken for purposes of delay.

The important shift toward de facto discretionary treatment of appeals came in 1928, when the Court requested submission of a *jurisdictional statement* stating why the Court should take the case, later extended to indicating why the question was "substantial." For the Court to take an appeal from a state court, the case must contain a "substantial" *federal* question; appeals from federal courts must also raise "substantial" questions. A large proportion of appeals do not meet these standards as the Court has applied them. In the 1972–1973 Terms, for example, over one-fourth of the appeals presented to the Court were dismissed "for want of a substantial federal question," slightly under one-fifth were dismissed for want of jurisdiction, and under 5 percent were dismissed for miscellaneous reasons.

Although dismissal for lack of jurisdiction is not a ruling on the merits, dismissal for want of a substantial federal question is more than a rejection of review. Such a dismissal is formally considered to be a decision on the merits because of the requirement that appeals be decided. As the Court recently reminded lawyers and judges about such cases:

> A federal constitutional issue was properly presented, it was within our appellate jurisdiction . . . and we had no discretion to refuse adjudication of the case on its merits . . . . We were not obligated to grant the case plenary consideration; and we did not; but we were required to deal with its merits.[23]

The Supreme Court expects lower courts to be bound by such rulings, just as it expects them to be bound by full opinion decisions. This causes several problems. Because the Supreme Court has not described the facts and issues covered by lower court rulings in such cases, or explained the basis for its dismissals beyond the "want of a substantial federal question" language, lower court judges are faced with a tedious task in comparing cases they have under consideration with previous Supreme Court summary actions, and then often have a difficult time deciding what the justices intended, for example, *why* they felt no "substantial federal question" was presented. According to Justice Brennan, making such dismissals rulings on the merits also deprives the Supreme Court of lower courts' thinking on complex legal problems: being bound by the dismissals, those courts are expected only to *apply* them, not to explore further the issues in them.

Brennan has also pointed out another confusing aspect of the Court's practice in disposing of appeals: federal appeals are affirmed while state appeals are dismissed for want of a substantial federal question. He suggested that the latter action could mean either that there was no substantial federal question or that one had been decided correctly below so that further consideration by the Supreme Court would not be fruitful.[24]

In picking and choosing from among the cases that people wish the Court to consider, the justices select for further action about half of those that fall in the appeals category and a small and decreasing percent of those brought on certiorari. The latter proportion decreased significantly from 1941 through 1971 and has continued a slow decrease to below 5 percent since 1971:

1941	17.5%	1961	7.4%
1951	11.1%	1971	5.8%

The Supreme Court granted certiorari petitions in 6.3 percent of cases coming from the U.S. Courts of Appeals in 1974. This compared to 15.1 percent thirty years earlier (3.1 percent of courts of appeals' terminations) and 11.8 percent twenty years earlier. The 1974 figure was only one percent of appeals court terminations, making the courts of appeals the courts of last resort, or "mini-Supreme Courts," for *over 98 percent* of federal appeals—actually closer to 99 percent if we include cases in which the Supreme Court grants review and then affirms the appeals courts. Moreover, because the Supreme Court reviews selectively, it seldom supervises areas of litigation in which individual circuits specialize. The two levels of courts thus perform "fully differentiated functions": the Supreme Court is a "policy Court" primarily pursuing constitutional issues; the courts of appeals, without discretionary jurisdiction, are engaged far more in "statutory interpretation, administrative review, and error correction in masses of routine adjudication."[25]

The Supreme Court's choice of cases is not random. This leads one to question whether the Court is a passive body waiting until someone brings a "case or controversy" for decision. A discretionary jurisdiction court like the Supreme Court *is* active. The ability to pick and choose cases makes it like a fisherman of cases: the Court can't place fish in the stream, that is, it cannot create a lawsuit where none exists, but it may stimulate others to stock the stream when the Court's pattern of granting review or the justices' statements prompt litigation to resolve previously undecided or currently unsettled issues. Particularly when those fishing (the justices) change, there may also be changes in those who stock the streams; for example, the change in membership from the Warren Court to the Burger Court led to a partial shift from defendants seeking to suppress evidence or to reverse convictions to prosecutors seeking to have judges' suppression of evidence reversed. In short, the Court's activity may increase the level of nutrients for certain types of fish more than for others, while for other types of cases the Court may provide "acid rain," killing off—or at least reducing—certain types of fish, although it may take considerable time before the Court's actions have an effect.

In managing its docket, the Court must reduce the number of cases to a reasonable amount, but in doing so it does not pick cases at random or through some previously adopted formula. For one thing, there are some cases that the justices find quite difficult to ignore. Included are challenges to major new federal statutes such as the public accommodations section of the 1964 Civil Rights Act and the 1965 Voting Rights Act and instances of extreme resistance to the Court's rulings, such as the Little Rock school desegregation situation, when the Court not only departed from its pattern of not reviewing cases in that area but also held a special session to hear the case. These cases also show that other units of government—Congress, the president, and state officials—have definite effects on the Court's agenda. While there are some cases the Court cannot avoid, the justices must take care not to concentrate their efforts disproportionately in one or only a few areas of case law. Thus when it takes up one or more major cases on a particular subject, it is imposing limits on its ability to take more in the near future. The Court must also be concerned with the timing of its decisions in relation to external events such as Congress' consideration of legislation and to its own major rulings, which the justices do not wish to undercut. When the court enters a policy area but then hesitates to follow through—true with school desegregation after *Brown*—disobedience to its will may be encouraged.

Despite such limits, the Court does have considerable flexibility in case selection. The wide variety of issues that people want the justices to hear does allow the Court to avoid certain fields completely, at least in the short run, and its pattern of accepting cases for review varies from one policy area to another. In some areas the Court accepts virtually all cases, as it did with sit-in cases in the early 1960s, but in others it may take very few, as it did in school desegregation after *Brown v. Board of Education.* Accepting cases allows the Court to prevent departure from its policy or to indicate that aspects of certain issues have not been settled; rejecting cases allows the Court to show that certain questions are settled, that it does not wish to comment further on the issues.

Docket management also involves selecting cases of desired breadth or narrowness, weeding out cases with peripheral issues and altering issues presented by the parties. When lawyers seeking review present several questions of varying breadth, the Court can limit its grant of review to one or more of the questions presented. The more issues raised in the request, the more likely the Court is to limit those for which review is granted. The Court may instead choose cases that focus directly on a broad issue "to establish a broad precedent applicable to cases percolating in the lower courts or being readied for the 'launching pad'" and thus to "head off large numbers of cases" coming to Court.[26] The Court can reach the same goal by adding issues to cases—by asking lawyers to address questions not raised in their petitions for review. If offered only a small number of cases in a particular issue area, the Court can use this ability to increase the number of issues to provide complexity otherwise provided by a larger number (and wider range) of cases. Such issue modification is more likely to occur in cases brought to the Court on certiorari than on appeal, because it fits better with the discretionary character of certiorari.

Summary Dispositions

The decision to grant review is linked to the decision on how to process a case. Most cases accepted for review proceed to plenary consideration—full briefing, oral argument, and a full opinion signed by the author. However, some—roughly 40 cases per year during the last few terms—are given summary treatment, being decided solely on the basis of the certiorari or appeals papers, with only a one- or two-line statement issued to explain how the case is being decided. Summary treatment may, however, result in a full but usually unsigned *per curiam* ("by the Court") opinion. First used only to indicate cases with "indisputably clear" substantive law, *per curiam* rulings were later also used for orders in original jurisdiction cases, dismissals of appeals for want of a substantial federal question, and obviously moot cases. Although once placed with the Court's full opinions in the Reports, most cases in which new law is not announced are now placed is such categories as "affirmed on appeal" and "vacated and remanded on appeal" with the Court's other orders, such as those granting and denying review.

Some *per curiam* dispositions—those announcing new substantive law—are almost indistinguishable from full signed opinions. When the Court issues a major *per curiam* opinion in a case involving novel legal issues or significantly changing or extending the law after giving a case only summary treatment, some justices are likely to complain strongly.

In recent years, such complaints have been made when the Court, without full briefing and argument, upheld a search when a police officer ordered a man from his car; stated the standard of proof for obscenity in a public nuisance abatement action directed at a theater; and sustained a 40-year prison term for possession of marijuana against a cruel and unusual punishment claim.[27] Perhaps the most significant recent use of summary treatment has been the *Snepp* case, in which a former Central Intelligence Agency employee was required to disgorge the profits from his book because he was held to have breached his duty to submit material for prepublication review.

Those justices who complain about such action by the Court feel it creates a "great risk of rendering erroneous or ill-advised decisions" because it is taken without full briefing or oral argument and the justices may have had only limited opportunity to review the record. Justice Marshall has now suggested that the Court should request briefs on the merits before summary disposition of a case.[28] Justice Blackmun recently commented on the Court's "disturbing tendency of late to dispose of difficult cases by summary *per curiam* reversals," a tendency "prompted, at least in part, by the growing pressures of the Court's calendar and an ill-conceived conviction that we must stay abreast of the increasing workload whatever the costs may be." Blackmun thought the results not worth the costs because it "demeans the Court and its work" and served "to lessen the quality of its legal product."[29]

Despite these protests, summary dispositions do provide the justices an additional option for cases for which the Court does not have time for full-dress treatment but on which they wish to act. Use of a *per curiam* ruling rather than a signed opinion may indicate that a case is considered routine or may be used to signal that the outcome is obvious and should receive prompt compliance—as in the 1969 ruling in *Alexander v. Holmes County* ending "all deliberate speed" in school desegregation. The Court also sometimes uses *per curiam* opinions when it is very badly divided; the opinion is limited to policy on which the justices can agree, while each justice spells out his or her own reasoning separately. Examples are provided by *Furman v. Georgia*, the 1972 death penalty cases where each majority justice appended a separate opinion to the brief *per curiam*, and *Buckley v. Valeo*, the 1976 ruling on campaign finances where five justices dissented from various parts of the ruling, making it difficult to identify an opinion of the Court.

Those summary decisions issued without opinion have been criticized for providing little guidance to lower court judges and lawyers, who must attempt to figure out what the Court meant in its brief order with its citation of one or two cases. One cannot tell whether the Court has merely affirmed the lower court's result or adopted its reasoning, a problem even when the Court cites one of its own earlier rulings for support. For example, Justice Brennan argued that the Court's approach to obscenity cases prior to 1973 hopelessly confused the lower courts because the justices reversed convictions while writing no opinion and citing only *Redrup v. New York*, a case in which the Court conceded its internal disagreement about obscenity. Such action by the Court settled particular cases "but offer[ed] only the most obscure guidance to legislation, adjudication by other courts, and primary conduct," with the Court "deliberately and effectively obscur[ing] the rationale underlying the decision."[30] As the Hruska Commission noted, summary affirmances or dismissals of appeals "cannot be considered the equivalent of plenary disposition for purposes of providing an adequate body of precedents on recurring issues of national law."[31]

By indicating that summary rulings are not to be given the same precedential weight as the Court's full opinions, the Court has now compounded the difficulties summary rulings produce. According to Chief Justice Burger, a summary affirmance does not necessarily mean that the Supreme Court is adopting the lower court's ruling, but the Court also need not adhere to a position appearing to result from several summary actions. Thus "the Court has not hesitated to discard a rule which a line of summary affirmances may appear to have established" when the justices later give fuller attention to another case raising the same issue.[32]

Despite this criticism, summary dispositions allow the Court to "clean up" a large number of cases in a particular policy area. They may also be used to make clear to lower court judges that their rulings need to be reexamined and cases disposed of more completely in the lower courts. Summary actions may also preserve freedom of action for the justices by providing a result, and thus perhaps an implicit message, without the constraints that full development of doctrinal reasons would impose. However, a summary action's visibility may be too low for the ruling to have its intended effect, particularly when resistance to the Court's policy exists. Thus the Court's mid-1960s attempt to communicate through *per curiam* rulings that desegregation should take place more rapidly was generally ignored, requiring more explicit rulings in 1968 and 1969.

Certiorari

The power to grant or deny certiorari is fully discretionary. The justices can also change their minds once the writ has been granted; they then dispose of the writ by dismissing it as "improvidently granted" (DIG). They do so when developments affecting the legal posture of a case occur after certiorari is granted, or when briefs or oral argument make the case look quite different from the way it appeared in the more limited certiorari petition. However, frequent use of the DIG "escape" provokes criticism. Specific instances are also criticized: when the Court, immediately after *Brown v. Board of Education*, after hearing oral argument in a case involving discrimination by a cemetery association, dividing evenly, and receiving a request for rehearing, dismissed certiorari to avoid deciding the case.[33]

By *custom*, certiorari is granted by a vote of at least four justices, the "rule of four" that is also applicable to decisions to "note probable jurisdiction" in an appeal. An important norm is that once the "rule of four" has been satisfied, the justices who opposed review, if they comprise a five-judge majority, should *not* turn around and vote to dismiss the case, and *all* should participate in deciding it on the merits. Yet Justice Frankfurter at times violated this norm. When he thought certiorari should not have been granted—as in Federal Employer Liability Act (FELA) cases—he refused to participate in deciding them. Had all the justices followed his practice, the "rule of four" would be a "rule of five." Despite Frankfurter, adherence to the rule is generally routine, but controversy can still develop over it. For example, when in 1976 the Court dismissed a writ of certiorari as improvidently granted, Justice Brennan complained that a justice who had voted *not* to grant review should not vote to DIG the case until and unless all four justices who had favored review agreed in that disposition. Justice Stevens, then the Court's newest member, thought the "rule of four" was satisfied as long as *one* originally favoring certiorari was in the majority voting to dismiss.[34]

The "rule of four" problem can arise because the decision to grant review is seldom unanimous or nearly so. According to Justice Brennan, only 9 percent of the Court's 1972 Term decisions to grant review were unanimous, with only five votes or the minimum four votes for review in roughly three-fifths of the cases.[35] Some of these four-vote decisions to review result from justices' deference to their colleagues. At times when there are only three votes for review, some justices will cast the fourth vote so the case can be heard. At other times, when four judges favor review, they do not necessarily insist that the Court hear the case. For example, the four justices who voted to grant certiorari in some obscenity cases, an area where the Burger Court's majority was firm, said they would not insist the cases be heard because they knew that the other five justices would be in the majority on the merits. Justice Stevens has now suggested that such an alignment is a sufficient reason for the four to vote to deny certiorari.[36] He has also suggested that, because cases granted review with only four votes were not significant, the "rule of four" should become a "rule of five."

In the process by which the Court decides whether or not to grant certiorari, the Chief Justice plays a particularly important role because, assisted by his law clerks, he carries out the initial sifting of the certiorari petitions and also makes the conference presentation of most cases. (For the purpose of screening certiorari petitions, in a change initiated by Justice Powell, at least five or six justices now have "pooled" their clerks instead of having each justice's clerk go through the entire batch of petitions.) The Chief Justice formerly prepared a *dead list* of cases that were not discussed at conference unless such consideration was requested by another justice. The Chief Justice's function was particularly significant for *in forma pauperis* petitions (often from prisoners)—so-called *unpaid* petitions—of which there might be only one handwritten copy rather than one for each justice. After the Chief Justice had sorted out and "special listed" cases, review was granted to as many as one-third of the cases remaining.[37] Now all members of the Court get copies of the papers on all the petitions, and the Chief Justice prepares a *discuss list*. Cases not on that list are not discussed unless another justice specifically requests it; if such a case is an "unpaid" one, the requesting justice makes the conference presentation about it; few cases are added. Cases not on the "discuss list" and not added to it are automatically denied review. Although the factors accounting for a case's being special-listed are not "easily identifiable," cases on the special list during the tenure of Justice Harold Burton (1947–1958) seemed to be those where the certiorari petitions (and law clerks' summaries) contained one or more characteristics that served as "demerits" but "no countervailing considerations in favor of review."[38]

What Does Certiorari Denial Mean?

The granting of certiorari is discretionary but not random. The Court need not give any reasons in granting, denying, or dismissing review, and seldom does so. Chief Justice Warren claimed that "the standards by which the justices decide to grant or deny review are highly personalized and necessarily discretionary . . . . Those standards cannot be captured in any rule or guidelines that would be meaningful."[39] However, there has also been talk of "*informed* discretion" or "*informed* arbitrariness." References to justices' ability to determine *certworthiness* (a case's significance for review) suggest that even if a large degree of "feel" or educated intuition remains in the process, there are regular criteria on which there is concensus. However, because litigants or potential litigants "differ in their capacity to deduce probable review criteria from the pattern of grants and denials and the Court's meager guidelines on review criteria," those with considerable experience and expertise in the process of seeking review ("repeat players") "tend to benefit from the obscurity of standards for review," while those who are inexperienced lack that advantage.[40]

Individual justices, in off-the-court statements, have indicated what the Court looks for in considering petitions for review. Chief Justice Vinson once said that the Court does not grant certiorari merely to correct errors of the lower courts, but instead uses the writ to deal with cases with broader effects, "questions whose resolution will have immediate importance far beyond the particular facts and parties involved." And Justice Harlan stated from the bench that "the certiorari jurisdiction was not conferred upon this Court 'merely to give the defeated party in the . . . Court of Appeals another hearing,' . . . or 'for the benefit of the particular litigants,' . . . but to decide issues, 'the settlement of which is of importance to the public as distinguished from . . . the parties.'"[41] More recently, Justice Stevens said he did not "believe that error is a sufficient justification for the exercise of this Court's discretionary jurisdiction," because the Court was "much too busy to correct every error that is called to our attention in the thousands of certiorari petitions that are filed each year."[42] That political—and strategic—considerations in the broadest sense are behind the Court's review-granting choices is also clear from Chief Justice Warren's statement that certiorari jurisdiction was "designed by Congress for a very special purpose . . . not only to achieve control of its docket but also to establish our national priorities in constitutional and legal matters."[43]

The Court has also set forth an official statement, in its Rule 17 (formerly Rule 19) of some factors it will *consider* in deciding whether to grant certiorari. This statement stresses legal considerations. Changes in the rule in 1980, when the Supreme Court adopted a new set of rules, were minor. One item not appearing in former Rule 19 (Rule 17.1(b)) had long been taken into account in practice. Deleted from the previous listing were those situations in which the U.S. Courts of Appeals had "decided an important state or territorial question in a way in conflict with applicable state or territorial law," a situation that would arise only in diversity-of-citizenship cases, so the change perhaps reflects the Court's lessened interest in such jurisdiction (see page 138).

CONSIDERATIONS GOVERNING REVIEW ON CERTIORARI

1. A review on writ of certiorari is not a matter of right, but of judicial discretion, and will be granted only when there are special and important reasons therefor. The following, while neither controlling nor fully measuring the Court's discretion, indicate the character of reasons that will be considered.

(a) When a federal court of appeals has rendered a decision in conflict with the decision of another federal court of appeals on the same matter; or has decided a federal question in a way in conflict with a state court of last resort; or has so far departed from the accepted and usual course of judicial proceedings, or so far sanctioned such a departure by a lower court, as to call for an exercise of this Court's power of supervision.

(b) When a state court of last resort has decided a federal question in a way in conflict with the decision of another state court of last resort or of a federal court of appeals.

(c) When a state court or a federal court of appeals has decided an important question of federal law which has not been, but should be, settled by this Court, or has decided a federal question in a way in conflict with applicable decisions of this Court.

(Rule 17, adopted June 30, 1980)

The presence of an "adequate and independent" state ground has always been understood to bar Supreme Court review or, if it were discovered after review had been granted, to serve as a basis for dismissing certiorari. Where it is unclear whether a state court has based its ruling on state or federal law, the Court can defer acting on a certiorari petition until a certificate is obtained from the state court explaining its action (see page 139) or the Court can grant the petition and vacate the lower court ruling and remand it for such clarification.

Although recently it has been doing so more frequently, the Court only occasionally says much about why specific cases have been accepted for review. Seldom is the Court's statement more than "We accepted this case in order to [answer the question presented]." At times the importance of the case is noted, but without elaboration as to *why* it is important. In the 1956–1958 Terms, reasons for granting certiorari were given in about two-thirds of the Court's full opinion cases, but in 20 percent of the cases the reason was only "to decide the issues presented." Eliminating those, the reason was given in only 46.7 percent of the cases; the only often-mentioned reasons were a conflict between the circuits, the importance of the issue (mentioned more frequently), or both; why the case was important was not indicated.[44] In 200 cases from the 1970 and 1972 Terms, 88 contained clear reasons why the Court had granted review; most of the rest, particularly the Court's summary rulings, contained no reasons at all. In thirty cases, the Court said only that it was taking the cases to examine "important" or "substantial" or "novel" nonconstitutional federal questions.

Only infrequently does the Court offer a more complete explanation. One such recent statement was made in a case involving prompt access under the Freedom of Information Act to the Federal Reserve System's monetary policy directives; the Court granted review "on the strength of the Committee's representations that this ruling could seriously interfere with the implementation of national monetary policy." Another statement came in cases on Indians' treaty fishing rights, which were accepted to allow the Court to "interpret [an] important treaty provision and thereby to resolve . . . conflict between the state and federal courts . . . and to remove any doubts about the federal court's power to enforce its orders."[45]

Some cases are taken to eliminate lower courts' misreading of earlier Supreme Court decisions. In probably its most extended recent statement explaining a grant of review, the justices said that they had taken a major regulatory case because of concern that the appeals court "had seriously misread or misapplied . . . statutory and decisional law cautioning reviewing courts against engrafting their own notions of proper procedures upon agencies entrusted with substantive functions by Congress."[46]

Even if the justices seldom provide explicit reasons for granting review, certain *cues*—characteristics of cases—may help explain the Court's actions. Two cues are the source of the case and the party seeking review. As to the former, one study of cases from the 1953–1956 Terms indicated that federal appeals were much more likely to be accepted than were state appeals, although state and federal certiorari petitions received roughly the same disposition.[47] Another study, of 1947–1958, showed certiorari granted in 49.1 percent of cases in which the only cue was that the federal government favored review, while the Court accepted only 5.8 percent of cases in which all other parties sought review—the same rate as when no cue appeared.[48] When the U.S. government sought review, at least one justice was likely to vote for review in most cases—impressive in view of the fact that more than 80 percent of other denials were unanimous.[49]

With respect to subject matter cues, one study showed that presence of an economic issue alone did little to improve chances of review being granted. However, a civil rights or civil liberties issue had significant, positive effects when it was the only cue present, and later analysis showed a high correlation between presence of a civil liberties or civil rights petitioner and granting of review. However, cases with civil liberties issues were certainly not immune from being "dead-listed," although they met this fate less frequently than cases without cues.[50] Cue analysis has also shown that certiorari was granted in 12.8 percent of cases where the sole cues were disagreement between *judges* in a single court, that is, nonunanimous decisions, or disagreement between *courts*, such as where an appeals court had reversed the trial court. Disagreement *within* a court of appeals may provide a stronger signal to the justices than disagreement *between* levels. However, an indication of conflicting findings from cue analysis is the conclusion of another study that, overall, "the Supreme Court . . . is not primarily guided by lower court agreement—either intercourt or intracourt—in deciding the cases it will hear or reverse."[51]

If cues in certiorari petitions help us understand the nonrandom nature of the Court's exercise of discretion in granting review, arguments about the meaning of the Court's denial of review may also help. Although individual justices may comment in dissent, the *Court* gives reasons here even less frequently than when it grants review. A sample of more than 3,000 denied petitions over twenty years produced less than forty explanations, of which the most common was dismissal on motion of the parties or failure to file timely.[52] In the 1972 and 1973 Terms, 60 percent of the dissenting opinions in certiorari denials stated the need for a national decision to resolve conflicts between lower courts or between the lower courts and the Supreme Court, the presence of statutory questions that needed to be resolved, or "the existence of important questions for decision."[53]

In a way, the Court is better off *not* explaining its denials, at least if it wishes to avoid open disagreement from its own members, as occurred twice in 1978. When the Court indicated in denying review that it appears "that the judgment of the Illinois Supreme Court rests on an adequate state ground," Justice Stevens complained that such statements were "inconsistent with the rule that such denials have no precedential value."[54] And when the Court denied a petition "for failure to file the petition within the time provided" by the relevant statute, Stevens, along with Justices Brennan and Stewart, objected both because the lack of precedential value of a certiorari denial meant the notation "serves no useful purpose," but also because "the question of timeliness [in filing] is not always easy to answer . . . and may produce different answers from different Members of the Court." Thus important time would be wasted and confusion caused because such explanations are offered only "spasmodic[ally]" and without consistency.[55]

A certiorari denial means formally only that the Court has not accepted the case to decide it, thus leaving the ruling of the lower court undisturbed. As Justice Frankfurter reminded us some years ago, the justices "do not have to, and frequently do not, reach the merits of a case to decide that it is not of sufficient importance to warrant review here." Thus certiorari denial "imports no expression of opinion upon the merits of the case." Such denial "means only that, for one reason or another, which is seldom disclosed, and not infrequently for conflicting reasons, which may have nothing to do with the merits and certainly may have nothing to do with any view of the merits taken by a majority of the Court, there were not four members of the Court who thought the case should be heard." Or, as Justice Jackson observed in the same case, "denial of certiorari . . . creates no precedent and approves no statement of principle entitled to weight in any other case."[56]

These statements about the nonmeaning of certiorari denials are not accepted by many observers of the Court. Some infer consideration of the merits of a case from denials of review. Thus, "when the Court consistently leaves undisturbed decisions at variance with principle, or when it denies certiorari in a notorious case . . . the public may well believe that the Court is implementing an unspoken constitutional judgment."[57] Despite Justice Frankfurter's 1953 admonition that "the Bar [was] not to draw strength for lower court opinions from the fact that they were left unreviewed here,"[58] lawyers continue to cite certiorari denials. This further stimulates guesses about the meaning of the denials, although such action by lawyers may be no more than their way of indicating that a legal issue is not settled and should therefore be decided.

Recognizing the effect of certiorari denials, Chief Justice Warren wrote after his retirement, "Denials can and do have a significant impact on the ordering of constitutional and legal priorities. Many potential and important developments in the law have been frustrated, at least temporarily, by a denial of certiorari."[59] He did, however, stop short of saying such action was purposeful. More fuel is added to the fire when the justices themselves cite the Court's certiorari denials in concurring or dissenting opinions, at times doing so as more than a matter of form. Justice Blackmun speculated in 1973 that dissents from an earlier certiorari denial were "not without some significance as to [the justices'] and the Court's attitude." This provoked an extended response from Justice Marshall, who said justices may simultaneously agree about an issue's importance and feel the case was not the "appropriate vehicle for determination of that issue." Perhaps too defensively, Marshall even attacked speculation about reasons why certiorari is denied. He said that "the point of our use of a discretionary writ is precisely to prohibit that kind of speculation" and asserted, "Reliance on denial of certiorari for *any* proposition impairs the vitality of the discretion we exercise in controlling the cases we hear."[60] This is particularly true if there are different reasons leading individual justices to vote to deny review, as is often the case. As Justice Rehnquist recently observed, "Some Members of the Court may feel that a case is wrongly decided, but lacking in general importance; others may feel that it is of general importance, but rightly decided; for either reason, a vote to deny certiorari is logically dictate[d]."[61]

Justice Jackson, in a significant contribution to the debate, has raised questions about certiorari denial's formal meaning. Conceding that "the Court is not quite of one mind of the subject," he continued, "Some say denial means nothing, others say it means nothing much." However, he asserted, "Realistically, the first position is untenable and the second is unintelligible." Jackson felt lawyers could no longer believe denial of review to be meaningless when justices began to file statements dissenting from such denial. Lawyers, said Jackson, "will not readily believe that

Justices of this Court are taking the trouble to signal a meaningless division of opinion about a meaningless act." Moreover, he added, "every lower court does attach importance to denials and to presence or absence of dissents from denials."[62]

Justice Stevens has recently questioned the validity of dissents from certiorari denials because the strong, perhaps emotional, case the dissenters make can create the impression that the Court has acted improperly in denying review, particularly with the Court providing no response. Stevens, without himself going to the merits of the case as the dissenters have often done, has suggested some possible reasons for denial of review, such as procedural defects, not mentioned in the dissenters' complaints.[63] He also noted that the dissenters' written statements have at times been more persuasive than statements made at the Court's conference and have led other justices to change their votes so that review was granted. However, argued Stevens, such results only justified writing and circulating these memoranda, not publishing them when the dissenters failed to persuade their colleagues.[64] Going further than Stevens, in separate cases Justices Blackmun and Brennan have written statements *in support of* certiorari denials—Blackmun disagreeing with dissenters from the denial and Brennan suggesting alternative procedural resolutions of the problem presented by a case.[65]

A substantial increase in the number of dissents from certiorari denials has occurred despite the norms against their use and the absence of time for writing separate opinions. Some justices, such as Justice Douglas, have accounted for much of the increase. Douglas, like Black, was a "review prone" justice, while others, like Burton and Frankfurter, were "review conservative."[66] Dissents from denials of review can also be explained by justices' ideologies; thus, during the Burger Court's early years, the liberals Douglas, Brennan, and Marshall were frequently dissenters from denials of review. This indicates that dissents from denials of review may be related to the justices' likely position on the merits, although justices exhibit varying degrees of "merits-consciousness," the degree to which they take the merits of a case into account in decisions to grant or deny review.[67] Where the government has won a criminal case in the lower courts, a justice generally favoring criminal defendants (as shown by his votes in full opinion cases) would vote to grant review, while justices who would support the government once the case was accepted would vote not to grant certiorari; when the government was appealing from a ruling excluding evidence in a case, the reverse pattern would occur.

A judge's certiorari votes helped predict the judge's votes on the merits in cases accepted in the 1947–1956 Terms. Liberal and conservative voting blocs among the justices could be identified not only from votes on the merits but also at the certiorari stage: a justice who voted with one set of justices in full opinion cases was *un*likely to vote with his remaining colleagues at the review-granting stage.[68] Indeed, on the basis of "paid" cases from selected terms from 1954 through 1975, decisions to grant review can be explained on the basis of whether petitioners are "Upperdogs" or "Underdogs." Although Upperdogs do better than Underdogs in getting their cases accepted, Underdogs' success rate was much higher during the Warren Court (55%) than in the Burger Court (39%), when the justices most clearly differentiated between the two in accepting and rejecting cases.[69] However, judges' attitudes cannot explain the fact that cases most often unanimously denied review have tapped dissimilar ideological matters, such as prisoner petitions and commercial suits by business interests, or the high proportion of unanimous decisions on granting or denying review. Such unanimity is likely the result of shared views as to the types of cases to which the Court should devote its attention.

Evidence of judges' strategy in their certiorari votes has also been used to explain certiorari denial in political terms rather than formal-legal ones, for example, to suggest that judges may try to disguise their attitudes from their colleagues or that certiorari votes on particular issues can be explained in terms of the strategies of game theory. Schubert suggested that during 1942–1948 in Federal Employers Liability Act cases, a bloc of four justices (Murphy, Rutledge, Black, and Douglas) voted together on certiorari so as to achieve victory on the merits. He thought their voting paralleled a strategy of never voting for the railroad (the employer) but always voting for the worker on certiorari when the court of appeals had reversed a proworker district court decision, then always voting for the worker on the merits. He reported that the four had a 92 percent success rate (twelve of thirteen) when they followed that pattern, but when they voted for certiorari when workers had lost in both the trial and appeals courts, they had only a 73 percent success rate (eight of thirteen). In the 1956–1957 Terms, when the four-judge bloc grew to five, they "won" thirteen of fourteen cases, with the "lost" case one in which no justice voted for certiorari because the appeal was so frivolous.[70]

Whatever may have appeared to be the case when Schubert looked at justices' final votes, Justice Burton's docket book shows that the members of Schubert's "certiorari bloc" went "off the reservation" on some votes, voted for some railroad petitioners, and showed a lack of consistency; at times only nonbloc members' votes for review favoring workers led to review being granted. That justices favoring workers on the merits did cast a high proportion of their certiorari votes on the question of review so as to favor workers does indicate the effect of ideology, but the other evidence shows limited use of strategy and the absence of "a tightknit power bloc" during that period.[71] Justice Burton's records also provide evidence as well that some justices vote to grant review with little apparent regard for whether the cases they want the Court to review will produce the policies they wish from the Court.

The Court's disposition of cases to which it does grant review further suggests that whatever the justices' intent, certiorari decisions have policy implications. A pattern "too definite to have arisen by sheer happenstance"[72] appears in the Court's reversal of the lower courts in roughly two out of three certiorari cases over the last thirty years. This seems to indicate a better-than-even chance that the Court approved of lower court decisions to which it did not grant review. Further confirmation comes from Burton's docket book, which indicates that, despite differences between them, justices were more likely to vote to reverse the lower court in cases in which they had voted to grant review than in those in which they did not cast a vote favoring review, and that the Supreme Court reversed the lower court more frequently when five justices (a majority of the full Court) voted to grant review.[73]

There is further confirmation that certiorari is granted primarily so that lower court decisions can be reversed and so the Supreme Court can state its own values and develop its own policy. In the last half-dozen years, with one exception the proportion of reversals in full opinion cases has hovered around 70 percent; the proportion is even higher if we add *per curiam* rulings and summary affirmances. For example, in the 1967–1972 period, the Supreme Court reversed the lower federal courts in more than four cases out of five (82.7%) and the state courts more than nine times out of ten (91.1%). For *per curiam* rulings alone, the reversals were closer to 100 percent for lower federal courts and 90 percent for state courts. In *per curiam* rulings not announcing substantive law and in the Court's other summary orders, virtually *all* lower court rulings were reversed: in 96.1 percent of the federal cases and 98.8 percent of the state cases.

Reversals of lower court rulings are also quite likely in appeals, particularly those disposed of summarily. In 1953–1956, appeals from state courts were more likely to be reversed than were those from federal courts, which were affirmed more frequently than they were reversed. However, federal court appeals were particularly likely to be reversed in formal opinions—so that the Court could explain the law to the lower federal courts. In the 1967–1972 Terms, somewhat over three-fifths of federal appeals were affirmed, while over three-fourths of state appeals were reversed. In appeals decided with formal opinions, both federal and state appeals were reversed more than three times out of four. *Per curiam* appeals decisions announcing substantive law, although few in number, produced more reversals than affirmances. In nonsubstantive *per curiam* rulings and orders, federal appeals were affirmed at a high rate (77.1 percent, but over 85 percent for 1967–1968), while there was an extremely high rate of reversals (92.3 percent) in state cases.

NOTES

1. Doris M. Provine, *Case Selection in the United States Supreme Court* (Chicago: University of Chicago Press, 1980), pp. 62–63.
2. Gerhard Casper and Richard A. Posner, *The Workload of the Supreme Court* (Chicago: American Bar Foundation, 1976), pp. 11–12.
3. Ibid., p. 6.
4. Mary Cornelia Porter, "Politics, Ideology and the Workload of the Supreme Court: Some Historical Perspectives," paper presented to Midwest Political Science Association, 1975, pp. 8, 10.
5. Casper and Posner, p. 31.
6. See Gerhard Casper and Richard A. Posner, "The Caseload of the Supreme Court: 1975 and 1976 Terms," *The Supreme Court Review 1977*, ed. Philip B. Kurland and Gerhard Casper (Chicago: University of Chicago Press, 1978), pp. 87–98, updating their earlier study.
7. For additional data, see the Statistical Tables in the *Harvard Law Review's* annual (November) issue on the Supreme Court's previous term. See particularly Five Year Tables I and II:82 (November 1968):310; 87 (November 1973):310–311; 92 (November 1978): 336–337.

8. Commission on Revision of Federal Court Appellate System, *Structure and Internal Procedures* (Washington, D.C., 1975), pp. 29, 31.
9. *Tidewater Oil Co. v. United States*, 409 U.S. 151 at 174–176 (1972).
10. *Warth v. Seldin*, 422 U.S. 490 at 519 (1975).
11. *Watt v. Alaska*, 451 U.S. 259 at 273–274 (1981) (concurring).
12. *Brown Transport Corp. v. Atcon*, 439 U.S. 1014 at 1024 (1978).
13. William H. Rehnquist, "The Supreme Court: Past and Present," *American Bar Association Journal* 59 (April 1973):363.
14. Justice Blackmun to Senator Hruska, in Commission on Revision of Federal Court Appellate System, *Structure and Internal Procedures*, pp. A-237–A-238.
15. S. Sidney Ulmer and John Alan Stookey, "How Is the Ox Being Gored: Toward a Theory of Docket Size and Innovation in the U.S. Supreme Court," *University of Toledo Law Review* 7 (Fall 1975):7, 9–10.
16. Glendon Schubert, *The Constitutional Polity* (Boston: Boston University Press, 1970), p. 10.
17. J. Woodford Howard, Jr., "Is the Burger Court a Nixon Court?", *Emory Law Journal* 23 (Summer 1974):757.
18. Arthur D. Hellman, "The Business of the Supreme Court Under the Judiciary Act of 1925: The Plenary Docket in the 1970's" *Harvard Law Review* 91 (June 1978):1754.
19. Arthur D. Hellman, "The Supreme Court and Civil Rights: The Plenary Docket in the 1970's," *Oregon Law Review* 58 (1979):3–60.
20. Gregory A. Caldeira, "The United States Supreme Court and Criminal Cases, 1935–1976: Alternative Models of Agenda Building," *British Journal of Political Science* 2 (1981): 457–461, 463.
21. For this material, see Arthur D. Hellman, "The Supreme Court and Statutory Law: The Plenary Docket in the 1970's," *University of Pittsburgh Law Review* 40 (Fall 1978): 1–45.
22. Ibid., p. 39; and Hellman, "The Business of the Supreme Court," p. 1796, n. 305.
23. *Hicks v. Miranda*, 422 U.S. 332 at 344 (1975), also quoting Justice Brennan, *Ohio ex rel. Eaton v. Price*, 360 U.S. 246 at 247 (1959), to the same effect.
24. *Colorado Springs Amusements v. Rizzo*, 429 U.S. 913 (1976).
25. Howard, *Courts of Appeals in the Federal Judicial System*, p. 76.
26. S. Sidney Ulmer, "Issue Fluidity in the U.S. Supreme Court: A Conceptual Analysis," in *Supreme Court Activism and Restraint*, eds. Stephen C. Halpern and Charles Lamb, p. 339.
27. *Pennsylvania v. Mimms*, 434 U.S. 106 at 115–116 (1977) (Justice Marshall), 117 (Justice Stevens); *Cooper v. Mitchell Brothers' Santa Ana Theater*, 102 S.Ct. 172 at 174 (1981) (Justice Stevens); *Hutto v. Davis*, 102 S.Ct. 703 at 712 (1982) (Justice Brennan).
28. *Harris v. Rivera*, 102 S.Ct. 460 at 466 (1981).
29. *United States v. Hollywood Motor Car Co.*, 102 S.Ct. 3081 at 3086 (1982).
30. *Paris Adult Theater I v. Slaton*, 413 U.S. 49 at 83 (1973).
31. Commission on Revision, p. 14.
32. *Fusari v. Steinberg*, 419 U.S. 379 at 391–393 (1975).
33. *Rice v. Sioux City Memorial Park Cemetery*, 349 U.S. 70 (1955).
34. *Burrell v. McCray*, 426 U.S. 471(1976); for an account, see Robert Woodward and Scott Armstrong, *The Brethren* (New York: Simon and Schuster, 1981), pp. 424–425.
35. William Brennan, "The National Court of Appeals: Another Dissent," *University of Chicago Law Review* 40 (1973):479.
36. *Dyke v. Georgia*, 421 U.S. 952 (1975) (obscenity); *Liles v. Oregon*, 425 U.S. 963 (1976) (Justice Stevens).

37. S. Sidney Ulmer, William Hintze, and Louise Kirklosky, "The Decision to Grant or Deny Certiorari: Further Consideration of Cue Theory." *Law & Society Review* 6 (May 1972): 640.
38. Provine, p. 82.
39. "Retired Chief Justice Warren Attacks . . . Freund Study Group's Composition and Proposal," *American Bar Association Journal* 59 (July 1973):728.
40. Provine, p. 4.
41. Fred M. Vinson, "The Work of the Federal Courts," *Courts, Judges, and Politics,* eds. Walter F. Murphy and C. Herman Pritchett (New York: Random House, 1961), pp. 55–56; *Jones v. Mayer,* 392 U.S. 409 at 478–479 (1968) (Justice Harlan).
42. *Idaho Department of Employment v. Smith,* 434 U.S. 100 at 105–106 (1977).
43. "Retired Chief Justice Warren Attacks . . . ," p. 728.
44. Joseph Tanenhaus, Marvin Schick, Matthew Muraskin, and Daniel Rosen, "The Supreme Court's Jurisdiction: Cue Theory," *Judicial Decision-Making,* ed. Glendon Schubert (New York: Free Press, 1963), p.114.
45. *Federal Open Market Committee v. Merrill,* 443 U.S. 340 at 344 (1979); *Washington v. Washington State Commercial Passenger Fishing Vessel Association,* 443 U.S. 658 at 675 (1979).
46. *Vermont Yankee Nuclear Power v. Natural Resources Defense Fund,* 435 U.S. 519 at 526, 536–537, n. 14 (1978).
47. Glendon Schubert, *Quantitative Analysis of Judicial Behavior* (Glencoe, Ill.: Free Press, 1959), pp. 53–55.
48. Tanenhaus et al., p. 123.
49. Provine, p. 32, Table 1.4 and p. 82.
50. Tanenhaus et al., p. 123; Provine, p. 82.
51. Howard, p. 67; Richard J. Richardson and Kenneth N. Vines, *The Politics of Federal Courts* (Boston: Little, Brown, 1970), p. 153.
52. Tanenhaus et al., p. 114.
53. Commission on Revision, pp. 48–49.
54. *Illinois v. Gray,* 435 U.S. 1013 (1978).
55. *County of Sonoma v. Isbell,* 439 U.S. 996 (1978).
56. *Brown v. Allen,* 344 U.S. 443 at 491–492 (Frankfurter), 543 (Jackson) (1953).
57. David Adamany, "Legitimacy, Realigning Elections, and the Supreme Court," *Wisconsin Law Review* 1973:801, drawing on Jan Deutsch, "Neutrality, Legitimacy, and the Supreme Court," *Stanford Law Review* 20 (1968): 207.
58. *Brown v. Allen,* at 491.
59. "Retired Chief Justice Warren Attacks . . . ," p. 728.
60. *United States v. Kras,* 409 U.S. 434 at 443 Blackmun), 461 (Marshall) (1973).
61. *Huch v. United States,* 439 U.S. 1007 at 1008 (1978).
62. *Brown v. Allen,* at 542–543.
63. See *Huffman v. Florida,* 435 U.S. 1014 at 1018–1019 (1978); *Vasquez v. United States,* 102 S.Ct. 528 at 528–529 (1981).
64. *Singleton v. Commissioner of Internal Revenue,* 439 U.S. 940 at 943–947 (1978).
65. *Kerr-McGee Chemical Corp. v. Illinois,* 103 S.Ct. 468 (1982) (Blackmun); *James v. United States,* 103 S.Ct. 465 (1982) (Brennan).
66. Provine, p. 114.
67. Ibid., pp. 110–113.
68. See S. Sidney Ulmer, "Supreme Court Justices as Strict and Not-so-Strict Constructionists: Some Implications," *Law & Society Review* 8 (Fall 1973):27–28; and Ulmer, "Voting

Blocs and 'Access' to the Supreme Court: 1947–1956 Terms," *Jurimetrics Journal* 16 (Fall 1965):8, 12.

69. S. Sidney Ulmer, "Selecting Cases for Supreme Court Review: Litigant Status in the Warren and Burger Courts," paper presented to American Political Science Association, 1979; see also Ulmer, "Selecting Cases for Supreme Court Review: An Underdog Model," *American Political Science Review* 72 (September 1978):902–910.
70. Schubert, "The Certiorari Game," in *Quantitative Analysis,* pp. 210–254.
71. Provine, pp. 166–170.
72. Schubert, *Quantitative Analysis,* p. 66; for his data, see pp. 55–67.
73. Provine, p. 127.

Chapter 7

The Supreme Court: Full-Dress Treatment

In this chapter we examine the "full-dress" treatment given cases accepted for review. In describing the Court's basic procedures for reaching decisions, particular attention is given to oral argument, the Chief Justice's practices in opinion-assignment, and the release of opinions. Then we analyze disagreement within the Court and the alignments of the justices as they decide cases. The Court's power of judicial review and the considerations the justices take into account in reaching their decisions and writing their opinions—matters of precedent, strategy, and activism and self-restraint—are examined in the next chapter.

PROCEDURE IN THE COURT

The Supreme Court's annual term begins in October and receives the designation of the year in which it starts. Although public sessions of the Court and the announcement of decisions usually continue only until the end of June or the first few days of July, the term now formally extends until the beginning of the next term. (The justices use the summer to prepare for the Court's new term.) The justices hear oral argument from the beginning of the term through late March or early April, although in special situations such as the Nixon Tapes case of 1974 argument can be heard as late as June. The Court has also held special sessions—in 1958 for the Little Rock school desegregation case and in 1972 for the Democratic National Convention delegate challenges. Cases to which the Court grants review early in the term are argued in the same term and are decided within the term; those accepted later in the term are not argued until the following term.

Six justices constitute a quorum for doing business. The Court can thus operate during vacancies, illness, and a justice's withdrawal from a case (recusance). However, a Court evenly divided 4–4 or 3–3 does not write an opinion, and the lower court's ruling is affirmed. In order to avoid such tie votes, the Court has generally tried to wait until vacancies are filled and there is a full complement of nine justices before deciding controversial cases that might produce such division.

A justice's participation in a case solely to create a full Court is not necessarily proper, as a particular problem involving Justice Rehnquist illustrates. Shortly before he became a justice, as Assistant Attorney General Rehnquist had testified before Congress on military surveillance of civilian political activity and had commented that a pending case challenging such surveillance was nonjusticiable—the central issue in the case. The lower court had ruled that the case could be heard, and the Supreme Court granted review before Rehnquist began his service on the Court, but did not hear argument until later. The vote would have been 4–4 without his participation, sustaining the lower court. However, Rehnquist participated, casting the crucial fifth vote to reverse the lower court, thus eliminating the challenge to the government activity. This caused the American Civil Liberties Union (ACLU) to petition for a rehearing of the case in which Rehnquist's disqualification was specifically requested. The Court denied the hearing petition without comment—its usual procedure. Rehnquist, however, wrote a memorandum supporting his participation. He said he had only been the government's attorney, expressing the administration's position, not necessarily his own. He added that someone in government service prior to joining the Court was quite likely to have made statements of opinions on subjects that would arise later in litigation. To have a blank mind on such subjects would, he said, "be evidence of lack of qualification, not lack of bias." The American Bar Association code of judicial ethics showed a clear preference for avoiding even the appearance of impropriety, but Rehnquist stressed a duty to participate, particularly where his vote was necessary to resolve the case.[1]

Justices usually recuse without explanation or comment because of acquaintance with the parties or their lawyers; financial interest, however small or indirect, usually from ownership of stock; or involvement with a case before the justice began Supreme Court service. For example, Justice White, who had been Deputy Attorney General before becoming a justice, recused himself from a number of cases involving the U.S. government, as did Justice Thurgood Marshall, who had been Solicitor

General. (Marshall also recused from some NAACP-supported cases because of his long connection with that organization.) Justices Brennan, Stewart, and Stevens, all former appellate judges, removed themselves from cases coming from the courts on which they had sat. Financial holdings apparently accounted for the disqualification of Justice Powell, Justice Stewart, and Stewart's successor, Justice O'Connor, in a number of cases in recent years. In 1980 the Court amended its rules to require that when corporations file papers with the Court, the papers "include a listing naming all parent companies, subsidiaries (except wholly owned subsidiaries) and affiliates of each such corporation" (Rule 28.1). This was apparently done to facilitate identification of cases in which a justice, a justice's spouse, or other close relatives might have a financial interest, after some apparent embarrassments when justices participated without knowledge of such matters.

Although they no longer ride circuit (see pages 30, 32), each Supreme Court justice still has responsibility for one or more circuits for emergencies and other matters that must be dealt with when the Court is not in session or before the full Court can meet to consider them, such as requests to stay executions, often at the last moment. Most requests to a circuit justice are passed along to the full Court. However, a circuit justice can stay lower court orders until the full Court has a chance to act on petitions for review and can order someone released on bail. In addition to death penalty cases, circuit justices often have to contend with school desegregation controversies and particularly with school board efforts to block busing orders shortly before the school year begins.[2]

Because the action of "the lower court, which has considered the matter at length and close at hand," is presumed to be correct,[3] a circuit justice acting alone does not decide a case on the merits but grants a stay only when the applicant shows that the lower court's decision is erroneous and that irreparable injury would occur without the stay; the circuit justice also decides (really predicts) that the other justices would consider the matter sufficiently serious to grant review. Although formal action on a stay request is the circuit justice's alone, occasionally other available justices are consulted, and when the circuit justice considers the matter, such as denial of a death penalty stay, too important for a single justice's decision, colleagues definitely are consulted, at times by telephone. One instance of this procedure took place during the controversy over the bombing of Cambodia. A district judge had enjoined the bombing and the court of appeals had stayed the injunction. Those seeking to stop the bombing sought to have Justice Thurgood Marshall, the Circuit Justice, set aside the appellate court order, but Marshall said that as a single justice he would exceed his authority if he were to do so because he thought the appellate court had not acted improperly. Then, as sometimes happens when petitioners are unsuccessful with the first justice they contact, the plaintiffs went to Justice Douglas, who did set aside the appeals court stay on the grounds that the case was like any capital punishment case in which one tries to avoid having someone die unnecessarily. Douglas was, however, overruled *the very same day.* Justice Marshall, indicating he had communicated with all other members of the Court, directly stayed the district court injunction.[4]

Oral Argument

Oral argument, the next major step after briefs are filed, was used long before written briefs but is now used to supplement the briefs and other records submitted in a case. The Court's rule that submission of a case solely on the briefs is disfavored, with the Court able to order argument nonetheless (Rule 38.1), shows the importance the Court attaches to oral argument. At one time, argument went on without limits. Now, unless a case is exceptional, only thirty minutes is allowed each side. Additional time is, however, usually allowed when the government appears as *amicus*, and consolidation of several cases for argument may mean more time on basic issues common to the cases.

Lawyers wishing to argue before the Court are supposed to be members of the bar of the Supreme Court. If a lawyer who wishes to argue a case is not yet admitted to the Supreme Court bar, that lawyer's admission *pro hac vice* (p.h.v.) for that particular case can be moved by another lawyer or the agency employing the lawyer, and such requests are usually granted. Joining the Supreme Court bar—often largely symbolic, as few lawyers really intend to argue cases there—is usually a routine matter. The lawyer must have been a member of the bar in good standing in his or her home state for at least three years, must pay a small fee, and must be recommended by two present members of the Supreme Court bar. The Court used to swear in lawyers in an admissions ceremony at the beginning of its public sessions, but as the number of lawyers seeking admission increased—it is now roughly 7,000 per year—that was discontinued as too time-consuming.

Only a few applications to become a member of the Supreme Court bar are rejected each year, and those rejections are generally not made public. However, starting in 1979, Chief Justice Burger filed written dissents to the admission of several lawyers who had received disciplinary sanctions or were under investigation for disciplinary violations in their home states. He felt those lawyers failed to meet the Supreme Court's standard that the "applicant appears . . . to be of good moral and professional character" (Rule 5.1) and were using their admission to the Supreme Court bar to "launder" their professional records. (When a state disbars a lawyer who is a member of the Supreme Court bar, the Court issues an order leading to the prompt removal of the lawyer from the Supreme Court bar.)

Oral argument, although it may not determine the result in a case, is often quite important in the decision.[5] Justice Harlan stated that there was "no substitute" for this "Socratic method of procedure in getting at the heart of an issue and in finding out where the truth lies," and Justice Brennan said he would be "terribly concerned" were he to be denied the opportunity to participate in oral argument because there had been "many occasions when my judgment of a decision has turned on what happened" there.[6]

The justices' questions at oral argument are particularly important. Lawyers appearing before the Court seldom get to make uninterrupted speeches, and the justices often engage in exchanges with them. Although a lawyer may use notes, the Court has made clear that it does not wish to have a lawyer read from a prepared text (see Rule 38.1). Other aids are generally prohibited, but the Court recently allowed a deaf lawyer—arguing the *Rowley* case concerning the amount of assistance a school district had to supply a deaf child—to use a video display screen from which he could read the justices' questions typed into the system by a stenotypist.

Some justices are more frequent questioners than others, and the Court as a whole usually asks more questions of one side than of the other. For example, in the *Briggs* school desegregation case argued along with *Brown*, John Davis, defending segregation, was interrupted only 11 times, but Thurgood Marshall was interrupted 127 times.[7] The justices not only ask questions; they make statements and suggest positions not raised by the lawyers. In so doing, they often disagree with the lawyers, at times forcing them to back down. When the government's lawyer in the Pentagon Papers case complained that his client had been forced to prepare its case too hastily, Justice Stewart responded, "The reason is, of course, as you know, . . . that unless the constitutional law as it now exists is changed, a prior restraint of publication by a newspaper is presumptively unconstitutional."[8] And in the Little Rock case, when the state's lawyer tried to gain sympathy for Governor Faubus's position by recalling Chief Justice Warren's service as governor of California, Warren forcefully pointed out that he had as governor abided by rulings of the courts, adding, "I never heard a lawyer say that the statement of a governor as to what was legal or illegal should control the action of any court."[9]

Oral argument performs a variety of functions. Because there is no assurance that the justices have actually read the briefs although it is quite likely that they have done so, it serves to assure the lawyers—and through them their clients—that the Court has actually heard the case. It also helps both lawyers and judges by forcing the lawyers to focus on the arguments they consider most important. Judges' questions quickly lead to a separation of central from collateral issues, a distinction often not discernible from the lawyers' briefs, which are organized point after point in correspondence to the facts and statutes involved in the case, and which often intentionally lack emphasis as the lawyer, never knowing which argument(s) might be persuasive, tries to convince the Court in as many ways as possible.

For the judges, for whom it is probably more important, oral argument not only legitimizes their judicial function but can also be used to obtain support for their positions or to assure them about an outcome toward which they are already inclined. Judges also use oral argument to communicate with their colleagues, asking questions of counsel that are of greater concern to their associates than to themselves and debating each other through those questions. A justice hammering on a particularly difficult point may be trying to persuade his colleagues that they will have to resolve that point to decide the case in a certain direction.

Oral argument is basically intended to provide the judges with information. Sometimes they simply want to clarify the lawyers' positions; for example, the differences in rates at which Marshall and Davis were asked questions in the *Briggs* argument can be explained in large part by that need for clarification. "Davis was usually so unmistakably clear that the justices did not need to ask him to restate an idea," while "Marshall was questioned because his occasional oral 'shorthand' (as Chief Justice

Vinson once called it) puzzled someone on the bench." This difference was reinforced by "Marshall's attitude toward the Court's questions and his mode of answer [which] provided a vivid contrast, . . . invit[ing] questioning," while Davis's responses to questions "discouraged questioning."[10] However, the particular frequency with which Marshall's 1953 argument attacking the "separate but equal" doctrine was interrupted—fifty-three times in roughly three-quarters of an hour—also resulted from the fact that it was the central part of his case and from his position as the person wishing the Court to adopt a major new position.

Oral argument also can provide judges with information to assist them in determining the Court's strategies, that is, how the Court should exercise its broader political role. Questions as to how many people might be affected by a decision and where the Court might be heading if it decided a case a certain way help elicit this type of information. "The Justices' purpose in oral argument is to force the lawyers to think out the political, social, and constitutional implications of their arguments." In so doing, "the Justices constantly seek to relate the immediate problem to analogous situations . . . and try to cut through the rhetoric of the lawyers to see the concrete result of any argument advanced."[11]

Conference and After

With the exception of Christmas and Easter recesses and recesses for opinion writing, the justices meet in conference throughout the term. When the Court is hearing oral argument, the conference meets twice a week, on Wednesday and either Thursday or Friday. In the conference, the Chief Justice makes the initial presentation concerning a case, including his own comments about it. Each justice, the most senior justice first and the most junior last, then comments. Tradition had been to take a formal vote in order of reverse seniority so that the most junior justice would not be influenced by the senior justices' votes, but in most cases a separate vote is not necessary because the justices' votes are clear from their initial statements. The initial conference vote is considered only tentative, allowing justices to change positions before the final vote is taken later. Thus at times what began as the majority becomes the minority, and vice versa.

After the vote, the Chief Justice, if in the majority, assigns the task of writing the Court's opinion. If the Chief Justice is not in the majority, the assignment is made by the most senior justice in the majority. Chief Justice Burger is reported to have tried to control opinion assignment even when not in the majority. Apparently blocked from making this change, Burger is also thought to "pass" his vote at conference until the other justices' alignment is evident so that he could vote with the majority (even when this did not appear consonant with his conference comments) and thus assign the opinion.[12]

The justice assigned the opinion circulates drafts to all the other justices for comments, doing so each time changes are made in the opinion. To provide other justices the opportunity to express additional views in a concurring opinion or in a dissent from the majority's views, each justice must see all that every other justice has written. No one assigns the writing of a minority opinion, although dissenters may decide informally among themselves who will write.

Although some justices may engage in joint action in advance of initial conference consideration of a case as they attempt to put together a majority, there is considerable exchange, even caucusing, among the justices between opinion-assignment and completion of the opinion. Negotiation may take place, with a justice "holding out" his vote until the author of the opinion adds, deletes, or modifies language. Thus an opinion issued under one justice's name, for example, Chief Justice Burger's opinion in the Nixon Tapes case, may really be an amalgam of several justices' contributions.[13] The justice writing the Court's opinion may even add a separate opinion stating his or her individual views,[14] but this is rare. There may be threats to file a dissenting opinion or a separate concurring opinion. A well-stated draft of such opinions may prompt changes in the language of the opinion of the Court, leading the writer of the draft to withdraw the draft.[15] A persuasive draft dissent may even attract votes and lead to reversal of the Court's original position, with the dissent becoming the opinion of the Court. The justice assigned to write the Court's opinion, upon reexamining the case materials, may also completely change position, perhaps taking the majority along.

In the give-and-take leading to the final result in a case, personal friendships between justices may affect voting, and in particular cases the opinion author may find cross-pressures developing, with pulls in different directions coming from different friends on the Court. Justices also look to the longer run as well, and *may* vote against conscience in a particular case to attract a colleague's support in later cases. More common have been instances when justices, to obtain eventual support on other matters, have ingratiated themselves to colleagues—by writing positive responses in the margins of circulated draft opinions ("returns"). All such exchanges are not surprising in a multimember "collegial" body that is expected to work together cohesively. If a justice, for example Justice Douglas, desires isolation from colleagues, refuses to seek others' votes, and objects to their "prosletyzing," obtaining necessary agreement might be quite difficult.

From initial conference and vote to the ultimate outcome in a case, actual shifts are not insignificant. For selected terms during Justice Harold Burton's tenure, there was no change from 88 percent of the justices' original conference votes to their final votes; in 3 percent of the votes, changes were made from not casting a vote to voting either to affirm or reverse the lower court or from such votes to nonparticipation, while in 9 percent of the votes there was *strong fluidity*, a change from a vote to affirm to a vote to reverse or vice versa. No justices changed their votes in 39 percent of the *cases*, but in the remaining 61 percent, at least some shift occurred. In four-fifths of those cases, only one or two justices changed their votes. The original minority actually became the ultimate majority in 14 percent of the cases in which there were vote changes. The majority remained intact in the other cases, increasing its size five times as often as it lost size. The picture was much the same during Justice Clark's tenure. If individual votes are examined, strong fluidity took place 10 percent of the time and weak fluidity 3 percent. In one-sixth of the cases with vote changes, a minority became a majority, but most majorities remained majorities and increased in size—68 percent compared to the 24 percent that lost votes.[16]

On the whole, exchanges among the justices in the postconference period produce increased agreement concerning the way the justices view the cases. As changes are more likely to be in the direction of the initial majority, "the movement suggests that postconference activity led to increased similarity of perceptions, which in turn led to greater agreement." The studying and discussing of issues after the conference is what produces the increased similarity of perception. During this period the justices do not change their basic values or their role conceptions—neither of which changes easily—but they can change perceptions.[17]

Opinion Release

The Court's decisions and the justices' opinions are not final or binding until announced by the Court. After that, there are to be no further changes (except in grammar, punctuation, or case-citation) in the opinions because that would deprive other justices of the opportunity to comment on *all* the language in all opinions. Such instances have, however, occurred. Before present-day uniform methods of release of the Court's opinions, Chief Justice Roger Brooke Taney, in the *Dred Scott* case, held back his opinion and added "a considerable amount of material that few if any of the other justices heard or read before its publication,"[18] adding to the friction the case produced. Quite recently, when the Court struck down limitations on pharmacists' advertising of prescription drug prices, Chief Justice Burger changed his concurring opinion between the advance sheets (the initial official released opinion) and the final, bound Court reports. Initially he described pharmacists as "no more render[ing] a true professional service than does a clerk who sells lawbooks." After criticism of this description, the opinion was changed to delete all reference to "true professional service" and to read: "the pharmacist performs largely a packaging rather than a compounding function of former times."[19]

The Court has been particularly careful to assure that its opinions do not become public until they are officially announced, even maintaining its own print shop for the printing of opinions, including drafts. This and the more recent computerized word processing capability installed at the Court are part of the Court's more general pattern of "maintain[ing] its own administrative and research capabilities rather than rely[ing] on the more generally available administrative support office."[20]

When ABC News reported, two days before the Court announced *Herbert v. Lando* (1979), a major libel case, that Justice White had written an opinion for the Court in which the media would suffer a defeat, the Chief Justice fired a typesetter from his job in the Court's print shop. Another leak, concerning the Chief Justice's authorship of a Nebraska prisoners' rights–parole case, also occurred during the same term. The Court's attention to secrecy stems partly from the public embarrassment suffered by the Court when President Buchanan referred to the soon-to-be-announced *Dred Scott* case in his inaugural address, and partly from fear that people who were able to learn about the Court's intended decisions, particularly those with financial implications, could benefit unfairly from such information.

Justices once read extended portions of their opinions in open court. This practice has been eliminated; justices now read short statements of the facts and issues in a case and what the Court has decided. Until 1965, Monday was the only Decision Day, the day when decisions are announced. In 1965, under Chief Justice Warren, the Court began to use other days as well, to allow greater media coverage of its opinions, and also moved its public sessions from 12:00N–4:30PM to a 10:00AM start, to help the media meet deadlines.The Court has an information officer, but that person's basic task is only to see that the news media get the opinions, not to explain them nor to respond to questions about what the Court or individual justices may have intended. Thus the opinions are released without additional comment—by the justices or other Court personnel. The Burger Court has, however, assisted the press in its task of digesting rulings unassisted by having the Reporter of Decisions prepare a case *syllabus* or headnote, a concise summary of facts, issues, and the Court's holding, prepared for every full opinion case and released when the decision is issued, a change from the earlier practice of not having it prepared until months later for the official reports. (The headnote, not officially part of the opinion of the Court, does not digest any concurring or dissenting opinions.)

The Court's former practice of using only Monday for Decision Day meant that large numbers of important full opinion cases—not to speak of certiorari denials and other orders—were handed down on the same day. This was a particular problem at the end of the term, with the media being deluged with cases. After the Court shifted in 1965 to using non-Mondays as Decision Days, one-fourth of the Court's full opinion cases were issued on days other than Mondays in the first full term with the new practice.[21] However, in the remaining three Warren Court terms, the Court made only minimal use of non-Mondays, with no more than 15 percent of the Court's opinions being released on those days. Moreover, toward the end of each term, when spreading out cases might have helped most because most decisions are handed down then, Monday remained the only Decision Day. Thus there were such unusually high outputs as twelve (June 10, 1968), thirteen (June 12, 1967), and fourteen (May 20, 1968), many of which announced significant constitutional doctrine.

Chief Justice Burger definitely changed output patterns in this respect. The Court developed a pattern of handing down cases on several days each week at the end of the term, even overcoming Monday's late-in-the-term predominance. The Court thus succeeded in spreading out the cases more when the flow was heaviest. For example, a total of twenty signed opinions and one substantive *per curiam* ruling were handed down during the week of June 23, 1975, but no more than six opinions were issued on any one day during that week. In fact, except for the end of the 1972 Term, with one day of twelve opinions and two each of fourteen opinions, generally no single day produced a glut of cases; eight or nine seemed to be the new upper limit for a single day's output.

In Burger's first term, non-Mondays were used for 24 percent of the Court's full opinion decisions. This rose to 39 percent for the 1970 Term and then again to just under half before rising to two-thirds of all signed full opinion cases in the 1975 Term. The Court's subsequent use of non-Monday Decision Days for full opinion

TABLE 7.1. Decision Day—Full Opinions

	1975	*1976*	*1977*	*1978*	*1979*	*1980*	*1981*
Monday	32.6%	46.8%	34.1%	48.5%	37.4%	50.4%	39.7%
Non-Monday	67.4	53.2	65.9	51.5	62.6	49.6	60.3

cases fluctuated, but in the next six terms (1976–1981) only once fell below half (and then barely), as Table 7.1 shows. Almost all *per curiam* rulings are handed down on Mondays along with the Court's list of orders, which includes grants and denials of review. If we combine release of signed opinions and *per curiam* opinions, we find that over half the Court's rulings in decided cases were released on Monday in three of those six terms; after 1975, no more than 60 percent were released on non-Mondays in any year. During the term, the most consistent use of non-Mondays appears in the January–March period. For 1975–1981, never less than two-thirds (and usually closer to three-fourths) of the full opinion cases appear on non-Mondays during January–March. Monday is the predominant Decision Day in the last third of the term, with more than half the full opinion cases being released on Monday in the 1976–1981 Terms, perhaps because the Court no longer sits to hear argument after April and thus is inclined to release cases on the Monday following the Friday conference and on the Thursday following the Wednesday conference.

Changes in Decision Day practices have not been accompanied by changes in the flow of cases through the term. Few opinions can be expected in October, November, and December when oral argument has just begun, but disparities in output between the second three months (January–March) and the last three (April–June) have been considerable. As Table 7.2 indicates, only a very small portion of the Court's output appears by the end of December. Less than half the Court's full opinions have been announced by the end of March.

Not only does the Court release most of its output in the last third of the term, but as much as one-third of the Court's entire output for the term is announced in the last six weeks. In the 1967 Term, for example, over two-fifths (43.6%) of the output appeared in that period. That was nothing, however, compared to the end of the 1981 Term, when over two-fifths of the term's output (42%) was released in the last *three* weeks of the term and almost one-fifth (18.4%) was released in the last week of the term alone. (*Per curiam* rulings are released quite evenly across the term's trimesters, because, although a brief opinion must be written in such cases, the decision process for them is much less extended than for full opinion cases.)

CONSENSUS AND DISSENSUS IN THE COURT

Unanimity and Dissent

Lack of unanimity among judges of a multijudge court results from a variety of causes, including intellectual processes of reasoning about past doctrine, differences

TABLE 7.2. Opinion Flow—Signed Cases

	Term													
	1975		*1976*		*1977*		*1978*		*1979*		*1980*		*1981*	
October, November, December	6	4.3%	10	7.9%	9	7.0%	11	8.5%	9	6.9%	11	8.9%	11	7.8%
January, February, March	41	29.7	36	28.6	33	25.6	34	26.2	40	30.5	36	29.2	39	27.7
April, May, June	91	65.9	80	63.5	87	67.4	85	65.4	82	62.6	76	61.8	91	64.5
TOTAL	138		126		129		130		131		123		141	

in judges' values, attitudes about judicial role, personal animosity, such as that between Justice Frankfurter and several other members of the Court, including Chief Justice Warren,[22] and leadership (or lack of it). The desire to have judges put aside personal values and engage in deliberate, logical consideration of cases, so that the result is determined only by the facts of the case and relevant precedents, makes all these reasons except the first somewhat suspect, and helps explain the sharp criticism of a justice whose decisions seem fully controlled by personal attitudes.

Justice Douglas was the target of such criticism, not only for his civil liberties decisions—as predictable in the liberal direction as Justice Rehnquist's have been in the conservative direction—but for his tax rulings as well. Although Douglas prior to 1942 supported the taxpayer less than did the Court as a whole, his support of the taxpayer then became very much higher than the Court's average. In 1943–1959 the taxpayer won one-fourth of the time, but Douglas' votes favored the taxpayer in 47 percent of the cases, increasing to 73 percent in the next five years, while the taxpayer was winning only 17 percent of the cases. In 1964–1973, Douglas supported the taxpayer in 59 percent of his decisions, well over the taxpayer's 26 percent "win rate."[23]

Even if not in such an extreme fashion, justices' attitudes are important in Supreme Court decision making. Were this not so, shifts in the Court's direction would not stem, as they do in fact, directly from changes in personnel, although other factors soften or reinforce the effects of these changes. It should also be no surprise that justices, not newcomers to major political issues prior to judicial service, do not decide all cases unanimously and that they disagree about the opinions explaining the Court's results. Such disagreement is not necessarily destructive. Conflict within the Supreme Court "makes for alertness, clarifies issues, raises alternative approaches, and tests the intensity of justices' commitments to given positions." It can, however, be destructive if it "becomes highly emotional and antagonistic."[24] One would expect division on controversial cases. From that perspective, the alignment in a case like *Bakke*, with Justice Powell casting the deciding vote for two different four-vote groups of his colleagues (in a 4–1–4 alignment) should not cause concern, nor should 5–4 rulings on other major issues. What does cause concern, however, is the perceived lack of stability in the Court's decisions and in the fracturing of majority voting groups so that either several concurring opinions appear in addition to the opinion of the Court or, more serious, there is only a plurality opinion rather than an opinion of the Court.

A *plurality* or prevailing opinion is one in which some majority justices join the Court's judgment (its decision or result) but not what would otherwise be the "opinion of the Court," thus leaving fewer than five justices supporting the basic opinion. An example would be a case in which the justices divided 5–4, with three of the majority justices favoring one opinion and the other two concurring only in the result—but not the opinion.

Plurality opinions officially have no binding effect, although they have persuasive value and, as time passes, people may come to treat them as precedent—long true of Justice Frankfurter's plurality opinion in *Colegrove v. Green* that reapportionment was a "political question." Nonetheless, plurality opinions frustrate the lower courts—trying to apply the Supreme Court's doctrine—as well as the other justices. For example, the Court's long-time inability to produce an opinion of the Court in obscenity cases during the 1960s led Justice Tom Clark to say, with some irritation, that his colleagues were "like ancient Gaul . . . split into three parts."[25] The absence of leadership is likely to increase such outcomes, even when a justice writing the separate opinion sounds apologetic about it. As Justice Rehnquist said in adding a dissent in a case already lacking an opinion of the Court:

> It is a genuine misfortune to have the Court's treatment of the subject be a virtual Tower of Babel, from which no definitive principles can be clearly drawn. . . . I regret even more keenly my contribution to this judicial clangor, but find that none of the views expressed in the other opinions written in the case come close enough to mine to warrant the necessary compromise to obtain a Court opinion.[26]

Disagreement among the justices does not mean that they *express* that disagreement through dissenting opinions or separate opinions concurring with the majority, whether or not the justice joins the majority opinion and simply writes additional thoughts or instead agrees only with the majority *result* but on the basis of different reasoning. Because they must be written in addition to the opinions of the Court a justice is assigned to write, they add to a justice's workload. There are additional constraints as well, [27] some of which are strategic. For example, dissents are said to encourage noncompliance, particularly with controversial rulings like school desegregation. The Court may also be criticized for being divided frequently, just as justices are criticized for writing concurring opinions if doing so results in plurality opinions rather than opinions of the Court. A justice contemplating a dissent must also remember that, apart from the fact that open disagreement may be interpreted as an attack on the Court's integrity, a strong dissenting opinion may make the majority opinion more visible and thus more damaging than would silence. On the other hand, dissents may give the losing side the feeling that someone has listened to their position. Dissents, which also make the majority justices sharpen their reasoning, may allow them to write more forcefully because they do not have to compromise with the dissenting justices.[28]

Individual justices, or groups of justices, nonetheless dissent in order to state their principled opposition to the majority's doctrine, although they are less likely to write concurring opinions, which are less useful to later justices and thus less frequently cited by them. Dissents may be written to appeal not only to the dissenter's colleagues and to the Court's immediate audience, but also to lawyers and judges in the future. Dissents are indeed potential majority opinions of the future, and certain "Great Dissenters" such as Holmes and Brandeis are certainly well remembered, although many dissenters are defending an outdated status quo (see page 88). Although other factors contribute to the Court's overruling of past decisions, in three-fourths of the Court's overruling actions from 1958 through 1980, justices gave dissents in earlier cases as the basis for overruling those decisions or based overruling opinions on ideas from the prior dissents.[29]

If such considerations as the encouragement of noncompliance and the appearance of attacking the Court's integrity do not prevent justices from dissenting, they also do not prevent dissenters from directly attacking not only the majority's policy positions but also its intelligence and ability. At times, the justices' language in their opinions becomes rather testy, raising questions about the "respect" in "I respectfully dissent." For example, in 1978, Justice Brennan accused Justice Rehnquist of straining to bring a case on federal court jurisdiction within certain jurisdictional categories, adding: "In so straining, the opinion reaches a result supported by neither policy nor precedent, ignores difficult legal issues, misapprehends the significance of the proceeding below, and casts doubts upon a decision that has stood unquestioned for nearly 70 years." As if that were not enough, he accused Rehnquist of "ignoring wholesale the analytical framework" of a recent important case, of committing "case-reading errors," and of avoiding discussion of certain important issues.[30] Rehnquist showed himself able to hand out comparable criticism in his dissent in the 1979 school desegregation cases, where he said, in discussing the Court's "lick and a promise" opinions, that "perhaps the adjective 'analytical' is out of place, since the Court's opinions furnish only the most superficial methodology."[31] More recently, in a particularly sharp attack in a case involving federal preemption of state regulatory action, Justice Blackmun criticized Justice Sandra O'Connor, the Court's newest member, for a "rhetorical assertion" about federalism that was "demonstrably incorrect" if it were to be taken literally. He then added that "while Justice O'Connor articulates a view of state sovereignty that is almost mystical, she entirely fails to address our central points."[32]

The extent of disagreement within the Court has varied over the years. In the Court's earliest years, each justice wrote an opinion in each case and there was no "opinion of the Court." Chief Justice John Marshall brought an end to these seriatim opinions; indeed, he wrote most of the Court's opinions, even when he did not agree with the result: from 1801 to 1804, the Court handed down twenty-six decisions containing opinions, and Marshall wrote for the Court in twenty-four. The "first dissenter"—in the context of unified opinions—was a Jefferson appointee, Justice William Johnson. His dissents not only served to break Marshall's monopoly but led to present practices of opinion-assignment by the Chief Justice, although pressures remained strong to limit the statement of separate views.

Despite year-to-year variation, the level of disagreement within the Court has generally increased over the years; there has been a marked shift from justices acquiescing in all except very major cases to more routine expression of dissent, as expectations of what is appropriate changed, reinforced by a failure of leadership by Chief Justice Stone (1941–1946). Because most of the Court's cases in the late nineteenth century were not highly controversial, all but a few were decided unanimously. The development of the Court's certiorari jurisdiction led to a substantial increase in dissents. In 1930 only 11 percent of the Court's cases were split decisions. However, that percentage more than doubled in each of the next two decades, to 28 percent in 1940 and 61 percent in 1950. After Earl Warren became Chief Justice, the figure rose to over three-fourths of the cases in 1957.

Only about two-fifths of the Court's full opinion cases in the early 1960s were unanimous. That figure dropped to one-third in the Warren Court's last term, but relatively few of the cases then were decided by close votes. Moreover, although Justice Harlan was a particularly frequent dissenter during the Warren Court's more liberal years, most justices' dissent rates were low. Toward the end of the Warren Court, Warren himself, Brennan, and Marshall seldom dissented. In the last Warren Court term (1968), four justices had fewer than ten dissenting votes each and four justices cast no "solo" dissents.

The transition to the Burger Court produced an obvious drop in consensus. In Burger's first three terms, the Court achieved unanimity in only roughly one-third of its full opinion cases. The proportion of unanimous cases then fell to one-fourth in the 1972 Term before rising above one-third (to 36%) in the 1975 Term. In the 1976–1981 Terms, the proportion of unanimous cases never fell below one-fourth, but in only one of those years did it rise above one-third. (See Table 7.3.)

Chief Justice Burger, exhibiting dissent behavior quite different from his predecessor's, was one of the Court's two most frequent dissenters in his first term—a clear indication that he found ideology more important than solidarity. As the Nixon bloc came to control the Court, Burger's rate of dissent decreased. Although Nixon appointee Rehnquist established himself as a frequent dissenter, the liberal justices became the most frequent dissenters. Yet the level of dissent within the Burger Court cannot be explained solely by their votes or by Justice Douglas' prodigious dissent frequency (57 dissenting votes in the 1971 Term, 15 solo, and 60 the following term).

An important part of the reason for the Court's high level of explicit disagreement was that newer members of the Court knew their own minds and did not wait to assert their positions. The suggestions that justices "bide their time" before assuming a position at either the liberal or conservative side of the Court, perhaps staying "in the middle" for several terms before "making their move," and that each waits cautiously to cast his first dissent in a case of substantial importance have not applied to the recent justices. Perhaps as a result of their past judicial and legal experience, they have spoken out in dissenting and concurring opinions within a short time of reaching the bench. Thus Justice Stevens, despite his nonparticipation in roughly one-third of the cases in his first term, dissented in nineteen cases.

The size of majorities may reflect disagreement even more clearly than the proportion of cases that are unanimous. During the 1969 Term, Burger's first, there were wide margins (at least four votes) in 62 percent of the signed cases. The proportion fell to under half the next year, with one-vote margins in over one-fourth of the cases. A full one-fifth of the 1972–1974 cases were decided by only one vote. However, after 1972 the proportion of cases decided by wide margins returned to over one-half (over 70 percent in the 1975 Term).

In the 1976–1981 Terms (see Table 7.3), between 50 and 60 percent of the cases were decided by unanimous votes or votes of 8–1 and 7–2. In five of those six years, the proportion of cases decided by either 6–3 or 5–4 votes was one-third or slightly higher, but was over two-fifths (43.3%) in 1981. The proportion of 5–4 votes ranged from 13.2% (1977) to over one-fifth (22.7% in 1981).

TABLE 7.3. Distribution of Votes—Full Opinion Cases

	1976			*1977*			*1978*			*1979*			*1980*			*1981*		
Unanimous	40	31.7%		36	27.9%		47	36.2%		34	26.0%		39	31.7%		47	33.3%	
8–1	10	7.9		7	5.4		10	7.7		14	10.7		15	12.2		12	8.5	
7–2	25	19.8		25	19.4		16	12.3		18	13.7		19	15.4		15	10.6	
"Wide Margins"			59.4%			52.7%			56.2%			50.4%			59.3%			52.4%
6–3	20	15.9%		26	20.2%		23	17.7%		33	25.2%		29	23.6%		29	20.6%	
5–4	22	17.5		17	13.2		26	20.0		25	19.0		18	14.6		32	22.7	
"Close Votes"			33.4%			33.4%			37.7%			34.2%			38.0%			43.3%
Other	9	7.1		18	14.0		8	6.2		7	5.3		3	2.4		6	4.3	
TOTAL	126			129			130			131			123			141		

TABLE 7.4. Concurring and Dissenting Opinions and Votes—Full Opinion Cases

	Opinions		*Votes*	
	Concurring	*Dissenting*	*Concurring*	*Dissenting*
1976	95	130	117	226
1977	88	122	116	251
1978	79	113	123	231
1979	78	137	100	266
1980	89	101	116	221
1981	91	121	129	264
	Ave = 87	Ave = 121	Ave = 117	Ave = 243

Also part of patterns of disagreement is the number of concurring and dissenting opinions. The number of concurring opinions, 40 in the 1962 Term and 67 ten years later, reached a new high of 85 in the 1975 Term, only to have that number topped in four of the next six terms (see Table 7.4). That period produced an average of just under 90 concurring opinions and roughly 120 dissenting opinions per term. Justices were, however, more likely to write dissenting than concurring opinions. As the relationship between the number of dissenting *votes* and the number of dissenting opinions shows, the justices were also far more likely to join in other justices' dissents than in their colleagues' concurring opinions.

The variation in the frequency of dissent is an indication of the Court's overall alignment. Thus it should be no surprise that in the 1976–1981 Terms, those at the ideological extremities of the Court cast the most dissenting votes. Justices Brennan and Marshall did so in three years, Justice Rehnquist in the other three years, with the Chief Justice not far behind him in 1981. The high rate of dissent for the Chief Justice was perhaps more surprising—and certainly more remarked upon—than Justice Rehnquist's behavior, because of our expectation that a Chief Justice will try to "mass" the Court and will cast fewer dissents as part of that effort.

The size of the Court's majorities may be affected by a tendency, noted by students of small group decision making, for decisions to be made by *minimum-winning coalitions*, that is, the smallest majority necessary. A body threatened from the outside is, however, thought to increase the size of the decision-making coalition. During the period of Justice Burton's Court service, when coalitions at the initial conference vote were smaller than minimum-winning, they were likely to become minimum-winning by the conclusion of the case, probably because the justices wished an "opinion of the Court." However, when original coalitions were larger than minimum-winning, they were unlikely to shrink to minimum-winning size. When justices changed position, size of majority increased far more often than it decreased (see pages 177–178).[33]

In the Warren Court, in nonthreat situations, 31 percent of the *decision coalitions*—justices joining in the vote for the result in a case—and 40 percent of the *opinion coalitions*—justices joining in support of the Court's principal opinion—were minimum-winning and 17 percent were unanimous. However, under conditions of threat, for example, legislative proposals to limit the Court's jurisdiction, only 13 percent of decision coalitions and 23 percent of opinion coalitions were minimum-winning, 44 percent unanimous. If six-justice coalitions are added to combinations of five justices, 56 percent of decision coalitions were minimum-winning in nonthreat situations, while only 31 percent were minimum-winning under conditions of threat (opinion coalitions: 63 percent minimum-winning nonthreat, 45 percent threat). Furthermore, large coalitions formed under threat conditions were more likely than otherwise to include justices with divergent policy positions, but opinion coalitions smaller than the decision coalitions were more likely than other coalitions to contain ideologically "connected" justices.[34]

Chief Justice: Leadership and Opinion Assignment

In addition to the Chief Justice's role in screening certiorari petitions and directing meetings of the conference, the Chief Justice can play a particularly important role in opinion-assignment and in the subsequent process by which the Court reaches its conclusions. There are three leadership roles to be performed within the Court: task or intellectual leadership; social leadership, through which solidarity is produced among the justices and their "emotional needs . . . as individuals" are attended to; and policy leadership, moving the Court toward a particular position over the long term. The Chief Justice may be the Court's social leader (like Taft) or the task leader, and it is possible the Chief will perform both roles (like Hughes). When the Chief Justice performs neither role (like Stone), an extremely uncohesive Court results. If the Chief Justice does not perform one of the necessary roles, someone else will; for example, Justice Willis Van Devanter was task leader when Taft was social leader.

Even if the Chief Justice does not perform either role for the Court as a whole, he can perform both roles or neither for a bloc of justices. Chief Justice Burger may have done this for the Nixon appointees during the early years of his tenure, although he has not done so subsequently, and the criticisms of Burger as a weak Chief are legion. One must, however, take into account his attention to judicial administration (see page 50); a Chief Justice devoting much attention to matters outside the Court, such as judicial administration, is less likely to be an in-court leader than one who invests most of his energies in the Court itself. If the Chief does not lead, others will fill the vacuum, even in (or particularly in) the Court's most crucial cases, as appears to have occurred in development of the opinion in the Nixon Tapes case.

The Chief Justice's leadership is affected by the degree to which he dissents: a dissenter may exercise *policy* leadership, but exercising leadership over colleagues in the short term is difficult if one is often in dissent. Thus Chief Justice Stone's lack of leadership is reflected in the fact that he dissented in a larger proportion of nonunanimous cases than did any other Chief Justice, and Chief Justice Burger's dissent rate of more than 14 percent from 1969–1981 helps explain claims that he does not provide strong leadership. For all chief justices prior to Burger, the dissent rate was "a function of the complexity of the cases, internal feuding among sitting justices, and turnover in justices and appointing presidents."[35]

The Chief Justice's leadership skills are also reflected in the absence of "conflict cases," those revealing disagreement within the Court. From this perspective, Chief Justice John Marshall (1801–1835) has the highest place as a leader: 97.7 percent of the cases during his tenure did not reveal conflict. In the second rank (88–90 percent nonconflict cases) are Chief Justices Salmon P. Chase (1864–1873), Edward White (1910–1920), and William Howard Taft (1921–1929). At the next level (84–85 percent nonconflict cases) are Chief Justices Taney (1836–1863), Melville Fuller (1888–1909), and Hughes (1930–1941). Far behind are Chief Justice Stone (1941–1946) (almost half the cases during his tenure involved conflict) and Chief Justices Vinson (1946–1953) and Warren (1953–1969) (only 20–26 percent not entailing conflict). A problem with this indicator is that the cases facing the Court have varied over time in complexity and controversiality, as have justices' attitudes toward dissent and the level of interpersonal friction in the Court.

Opinion Assignment

The assignment of opinions by the Chief Justice is one of the ways in which he can attempt to exercise his and his colleagues' influence outside the Court—on the Court's multiple audiences, particularly lawyers. There are, however, numerous constraints on the Chief Justice's choice of an opinion writer for the Court. These include his efforts to influence his colleagues through the assignment of opinions and the necessity of distributing the writing workload evenly among all the justices, something not easy to do if some colleagues are frequently in dissent. Justices are expected to be "generalists," that is, to write opinions in all fields of law, but informal specialization appears from time to time—for example, Justice Stephen Field in land law and, apparently, Justice Powell in business cases. The Chief Justice must participate in writing opinions, and he thus retains some cases. It is expected that the Chief Justice will write in some of the Court's "big" cases, but the Court's internal social relations prevent him from keeping all the most important ones.

Danelski has suggested two strategies that the Chief Justice might use in assigning opinions to accomodate some of these pressures:

> RULE 1: Assign the case to the Justice whose views are the closest to the dissenters on the ground that his opinion would take a middle approach upon which both majority and minority could agree.
>
> RULE 2: Where there are blocs on the Court and a bloc splits, assign the case to a majority member of the dissenters' bloc on the ground that he would take a middle approach upon which both majority and minority could agree and that the minority justices would be more likely to agree with him because of general mutuality of agreement.[36]

Those justices never "closest" to the assigners are usually given unanimous cases or cases in less controversial areas of the law.

In close political cases through 1962, Chief Justice Warren, seeming to follow the strategies suggested by Danelski, "overassigned" cases to justices who joined the majority through votes inconsistent with their usual positions. In the 1962 Term, he also assigned Justice Goldberg, closest to the Court's center of the five reliable liberal votes, six of his twelve opinions in 5–4 rulings. In economic cases, however, Warren assigned opinions to maximize the liberal policy position.[37] When majorities were large, he tended to overassign to those in the midmajority position. Although assigning justices have generally favored justices "closest to them in various issue areas,"[38] Warren used those large majorities to help create an opinion of the Court considerably different from his own particular position. The rule of assigning cases to moderate justices was evident in Justice Clark's opinions in cases with liberal results, such as *Mapp v. Ohio* on the exclusionary rule for improperly seized evidence, where his background as attorney general was probably thought to produce a better reception in the law enforcement community than if a justice with a predictably liberal record had written for the Court. As had Chief Justice Vinson before him, Warren underassigned to himself, although toward the end of his tenure, he seemed to keep more of the Court's important cases than he had earlier.

At first, Chief Justice Burger did not allocate workload evenly. After Justices Powell and Rehnquist joined the Court, he could more evenly divide opinion-writing chores. Nonetheless, discrepancies remained in the rates at which the justices were assigned cases when they were available to the Chief Justice, that is, when participating and not in dissent. Starting with the 1976 Term (Justice Stevens' first), with limited exceptions, some of which can be explained by a justice's illness, the writing of the Court's signed opinions was divided evenly among the justices. However, the proportion of times the Chief Justice assigned a case to each justice when that justice was available did vary, with much of the variation resulting from some justices' high dissent rates. Thus in the 1976 Term, frequent dissenter Justice Marshall was assigned cases 18.3 percent of the time he was available. The Chief Justice assigned cases to Justice Brennan, another frequent dissenter, at a disproportionately *low* rate, for example, only 7 percent of the times he was available in 1977; however, as senior justice, Brennan had the duty to assign opinions when the Chief was in the minority, and in such situations Brennan often assigned cases to himself. In fact, for the six-year period, those self-assigned cases accounted for *half* of Brennan's signed opinions and in the 1981 Term, for 12 of the 15 opinions he wrote.

At times certain justices have written for the Court more frequently in particular situations. The Chief Justice assigned less important or unanimous cases to Justice Brennan (the 1973 Denver school desegregation case is an exception), Marshall, and Douglas. Justice White, closer to the center of the Court, wrote in criminal procedure cases for a divided Court, and some other justices have been more likely to write in cases with closely divided votes; examples are Powell and Rehnquist in 6–3 and 5–4 rulings in 1974. As this suggests, Burger definitely used his assignment of opinions to reward White and Stewart and particularly the other Nixon appointees, even though assignment of Rehnquist in criminal procedure cases ran counter to the strategy of using mid-Court members. Assignments to Rehnquist may have resulted either from the majority coalition's single-mindedness in this policy area or from a feeling that the coalition was sufficiently solid that Rehnquist's positions would not

TABLE 7.5. Assignments, 1976–1980 (combined)—Full Opinion Cases*

	Unanimous	8–1 + 7–1	7–2 + 6–2	6–3	5–4	*Other*	
Burger	30 (42%)†	7	13 (18%)	13 (18%)	6	3	(72)
Blackmun	19 (31%)	2	11/1‡ (20%)	10/1	8/6 (23%)	3	(61)
Powell	20 (27%)	9	12/1 (18%)	10/6 (22%)	10/3 (18%)	2	(73)
Rehnquist	16 (22%)	7	13/1 (19%)	17 (23%)	16/1 (23%)	3	(74)
White	14/1 (20%)	12/1 (18%)	6/2	13/3 (22%)	12/4 (22%)	5/1	(74)
Stewart	16 (22%)	7	7/4	14/6 (28%)	10/5 (21%)	1/2	(72)
Brennan	20/1 (32%)	4/1	3/12 (23%)	3/9 (18%)	3/8 (17%)	0/2	(66)
Marshall	34 (52%)	9	11 (17%)	6/1 (11%)	3/2 (8%)	0/1	(66)
Stevens	24 (35%)	6/1	10/1 (16%)	12/6 (26%)	5/3 (12%)	—	(68)

*These are inferred assignments, calculated from final vote, not initial vote (data not available). Fluidity might mean assignments have shifted from the original assignment. Data is accurate as to the number and proportion of opinions for the Court. When the Chief Justice concurred, it is assumed that he assigned and then wrote separately.

†The percentages indicate the proportion of cases of that vote type of the total cases written by that justice, that is, the percentages should be read horizontally.

‡When two numbers appear separated by a slash (5/3), the first indicates the number of opinions assigned by the Chief Justice, the second those assigned by others when the Chief Justice was in the minority.

lose votes. (Despite the supposed tradition that a new justice's first opinion comes in a noncontroversial, unanimous case, both Justices Powell and Rehnquist wrote for divided courts in their first opinions; the "tradition" was, however, true for Justices Stevens and O'Connor.)

In the 1976–1980 period, some justices wrote more frequently when the Court was unanimous, others when the Court was divided. (See Table 7.5.) More than half of Justice Marshall's opinions were in unanimous cases, less than 20 percent in 6–3 and 5–4 rulings. Roughly one-third of opinions by Justices Blackmun, Brennan, and Stevens were unanimous. Justices who wrote a high proportion of their opinions in divided cases were either Blackmun, Powell, and Rehnquist from the "Nixon Four" or White and Stewart, the Court's centrist judges. However, Justice Stewart received many assignments in close-vote cases from Justice Brennan—and in a couple of instances, from self-assignment when the assignment duty passed to him. Justice Blackmun likewise received almost half his assignments in 5–4 rulings from Justice Brennan, who was perhaps trying to woo him from the other Nixon appointees. Not surprisingly, most of Brennan's opinions in cases with votes closer than 8–1 came from himself (for example, three of his eleven opinions in 5–4 rulings). Despite the frequency with which he and Marshall voted together, Brennan did not assign a significant number of cases to Marshall until the 1981 Term.

As Table 7.5 indicates, the Chief Justice assigned himself primarily unanimous cases, which had been his pattern in his first two terms. After those terms, he assigned himself more major cases than had Chief Justice Warren. He again took major cases in 1975 and particularly 1981. Among those major cases were the *Swann* and Detroit busing cases, rulings on access to the media, school attendance by the Amish, plea bargaining, and the major obscenity case of *Miller v. California.*

Except for 1975 and 1981, Burger also did not hesitate to write in close cases, for example, in nine 5–4 rulings in the 1975 Term; Warren, by comparison, wrote most often in cases with wide vote margins or unanimous votes.

Over a longer span of Court history, Chief Justices have assigned majority opinions to themselves relatively more often than they have to their colleagues, but they have done so *less* in the post–World War II period. However, in important cases, all Chief Justices have engaged in higher self-assignment. Here, too, there have been differences between justices, with Stone and Warren using their self-assignment prerogative least and Chief Justice Taft and Chief Justice Hughes "pursu[ing] the relatively most advantageous self-assignment policy in important cases."[39] The Chief Justices have also been likely to assign themselves unanimous opinions and to write less frequently for highly divided courts. This is true even in important cases: they are more likely than their colleagues to write for a unanimous Court in important cases and less frequently for a moderately or highly divided Court. This means that, on the whole, the Chief Justice is not put in the position of writing frequently for badly divided courts in a large proportion of major cases.

Judicial Values and Alignments

A number of factors help account for the fact that the votes of Supreme Court justices are as patterned as they are. Attitudes and values are among the central elements. The justices' ideologies or broad preferences as to the proper scope of government and the content of government policy are another. That two justices vote the same way does not, however, mean that they share an ideology. Perhaps the best example of this phenomenon is Brandeis and Holmes. Both "believed that the executive and legislature should be given wide latitude in the formulation of social and economic policy," but Brandeis' basic premise was that scientific expertise in government could resolve the problems brought to the government for solution. On the other hand, Holmes was a skeptic and Social Darwinist: the best-fitted would win in the end, so he should not interfere.[40]

Personality is another major factor that helps explain the pattern of Supreme Court votes, particularly because of its effect on a justice's role conceptions and on interpersonal relations within the Court. For example, Felix Frankfurter, "intense, nervous, arrogant, [and] domineering, . . . could not accept serious, sustained opposition in fields he considered his domain of expertise." Thus when he reached the Court, where he could no longer operate as a behind-the-scenes adviser, but was "formally committed to sharing power with strong-willed individuals who had ideas of their own," he "reacted to his opponents with vindictive hostility."[41] His suppressed self-doubts made it difficult for him to work out contradictions in his belief system "between his endorsement of judicial self-restraint," for which he is perhaps best known, "and his belief in the existence of a hierarchy of constitutional values."[42] Not only did he "harden his stands," but he became "preoccupied with the motives of his judicial opponents," attributing impropriety to them; colleagues differing on how to decide cases were not simply fellow professionals with whom one had reasonable disagreements but opponents to be battled as if one were under seige.[43] When he was not trying to ingratiate himself to his colleagues (before he gave them up as lost causes), he was deluging them with suggestions both about cases and about court procedures—something that drove them further away instead of attracting them to his position.[44] To be sure, with Frankfurter or any other justice, personality is not a sufficient explanation, but it is important: "a simple, 'rational' explanation cannot account for [a justice's] personal style on the Court."[45]

Closely related to personality may be processes of aging and senescence, which, along with personal learning over time, seem particularly relevant in explaining the increasingly conservative voting behavior of Justice Black, who, like Justice Douglas, was most liberal in midcareer. The shift in Black's judicial behavior in civil liberties cases, like that of some other twentieth-century justices, may also have reflected new types of civil liberties cases facing the Court as well as responses to changes in the Court's action. In Black's case, the new types of cases involved not "pure" free speech (speech not connected with action), but "free speech plus," particularly civil rights demonstrations to which he had a strong negative reaction.[46]

Most studies of the relationship of justices' values or attitudes and their voting have been based only on the justices' recorded votes, supplemented by their papers and, recently, by their docket books, which provide initial conference votes. Materials from a justice's experience prior to Court service have, however, been used to shed light on their values such as morality, tradition, or religion—for such experience could affect the justice's perceptions concerning those values. There was a congruence between the values evident in justices' speeches prior to Supreme Court appointment and the justices' judicial positions reflected in solo dissents but the justices' pre-Court values sometimes caused them internal conflict. For Justice Pierce Butler, these noncongruent values were patriotism and individual freedom. Butler resolved the conflict between them by deciding in favor of patriotism in free speech cases but in favor of individual freedom in criminal procedure cases.[47]

The voting studies of the Court have been based primarily on the justices' voting interagreement (bloc analysis) and on Guttman scaling. The latter technique, based on the idea that the case is a stimulus and the judge's vote a response, is used for testing the consistency of attitudes underlying a set of decisions. Scales are sets of cases in which the justices were aligned so that a consistent underlying attitude accounted for their votes. If attitudes do underlie justices' votes in a set of cases, the Guttman scale will indicate a "breakpoint," the case or cases where a justice's votes shift from support for a value to opposition, and a justice whose value or attitude influences his or her voting will vote consistently on either side of the "breakpoint." (However, when two justices vote the same way, it is not clear whether they are treating the same stimulus or perceiving different ones.)[48]

Most bloc analysis studies have been based on the voting interagreement of pairs of justices. The pairs are arranged in a matrix, with blocs identified from sets of high interagreement scores. However, if a bloc is defined as a cohesive group whose members vote together regularly, so that a "bloc" really exists only if Justices Jones, Green, and Brown vote together frequently, and if the three are frequently found alone, bloc behavior may not be very frequent. If they vote together primarily when they are also voting with others, they do not constitute a bloc. Similarly, the members of several pairs of justices do not constitute a bloc unless all the members of the pairs in the set are in high interagreement. For the 1963–1965 Terms, for example, it was difficult to determine the identity of blocs that persisted over time, and identifiable blocs "voted together alone less than half the number of times [they] voted together." Moreover, three- and four-judge dissenting blocs seldom joined in the same *opinion* even when they voted together, making tenuous the idea of "stable, persistent and exclusive . . . blocs, whose members interact substantially as a bloc."[49]

Whatever their methods, researchers have regularly discovered blocs in the Supreme Court. For example, for the 1931–1935 Terms, there was a "Left bloc" of Stone, Cardozo, and Brandeis, and a "Right bloc" of Van Devanter, Butler, Sutherland, and McReynolds. Justice Roberts and Chief Justice Hughes were members of the Right bloc in terms of overall interagreement, although in dissent Roberts was independent and Hughes was marginally affiliated with the Left bloc. Extending this analysis, Schubert calculated what Hughes and Roberts ("Hughberts") would have to have done in the 1936 Term to increase their power, that is, their ability to determine the outcome of the Court's decisions.[50] A "pure" strategy for them would have been to have formed a minimum-winning coalition of five with the Left bloc when possible, and to join with the Right bloc when the first strategy was not possible, and to join the rest of the Court (Right and Left together) when all agreed, so as not to be isolated. The Hughes/Roberts behavior indeed closely approximated the specified strategy: the two were affiliated with the Left in total interagreement, voting with the Right only when they could not form a majority with the Left.

Part of the "conventional wisdom" concerning the Court's response to FDR's attack was that only Roberts had shifted his position to produce the "switch in time that saved nine." Roberts' own explanation was that he had earlier indicated his change in positions on the validity of minimum wage legislation. However, when a case containing the appropriate challenge did arise, Justice Stone's illness produced a delay in decision of the case, which as a result was not decided until after the Court-packing plan.[51] Schubert's analysis, which led him to conclude that both Roberts *and* Hughes had shifted, contradicts both explanations but is reinforced by a radical shift in bloc dissenting rates from the five previous terms to the 1936 Term. Furthermore, the study covers an entire term of Court, not just a few cases, and reveals patterned rather than idiosyncratic behavior.

Another bloc that has been identified is a "Truman bloc" in the late 1940s consisting of Truman appointees Vinson, Clark, Burton, and Minton and Roosevelt appointee Reed. During the 1946–1948 Terms, in terms of overall interagreement, Reed, Burton, and Chief Justice Vinson formed a bloc in the center of the Court, while Justices Jackson and Frankfurter formed a bloc on the right of the Court. There was a five-judge conservative majority on the Court except when the Reed-Vinson-Burton trio split, which made liberal majorities possible. In the 1949–1952 Terms, Black and Douglas were isolated on the left of the Court and Jackson and

Frankfurter were between them and the five-member Truman bloc. Some voting in this period can be explained by justices wishing to avoid isolation (Burton in the 1950 Term, Reed in the 1951 Term, and Jackson in the 1951 and 1952 Terms), while other justices voted their basic ideological positions (Frankfurter, Douglas, and Black for all three terms, Jackson in the 1950 Term).[52]

Justices' interagreement in the Warren Court and afterwards indicates the presence of blocs as well as variance in the patterns of interaction among and within those groupings. From the 1961 through 1963 Terms, in the Court's nonunanimous full opinion cases, Chief Justice Warren voted at least three-fourths of the time with each of Justices Brennan, Black, and Douglas, and in the 1962 and 1963 Terms with new Court member Goldberg. In the 1961 Term, Warren joined the Brennan-Black-Douglas trio in over half the nonunanimous cases, voted with two of the three in the majority in another one-fifth of the cases, and was in dissent with Black and Douglas in another one-sixth of the cases. In the 1962 Term, the Warren-Brennan-Black-Douglas quartet was together in two-thirds of 48 nonunanimous full opinion cases, always in the majority; Goldberg joined them in 40. That Justice Stewart held a central position in the Court is shown by his pairing with liberal bloc member Goldberg as often as with the more conservative Harlan, but more than half his votes with Harlan were in dissent. The 1964 Term revealed change: Warren's interagreement with Justice Brennan—to be over 90 percent throughout the remainder of the Warren Court—remained high, but his interagreement with Black, Douglas, and Goldberg decreased.

For the 1962–1964 Terms, the middle period of the Warren Court, the justices' alignment was a liberal bloc of Justice Douglas, the Court's most liberal member, Black, Warren, Brennan, and Goldberg, with a conservative bloc of Clark, White, Stewart, and Harlan, the most conservative justice.[53] The conservative bloc "utterly shattered" as Justice Harlan became separated from its other members. Justices Clark and Stewart agreed as often with the liberal bloc's centrist members as they did with each other, and Justice White voted over 80 percent of the time with liberals Brennan and the Chief Justice. When Justice Fortas replaced Justice Goldberg, fundamental changes in bloc alignments did not occur, although there was greater fluidity, resulting in interlocking blocs of three justices each rather than one cohesive liberal bloc.[54] In the 1965 Term, the Chief Justice voted with Justices Clark, White, and Fortas more than with Douglas and Black. Black, who had earlier begun his movement away from the liberal bloc while remaining affiliated with it, now moved to a point midway between the liberal and conservative blocs, and Douglas moved to isolation left of the liberal bloc, which now included Thurgood Marshall.

The departure of Warren and Fortas and the arrival of Chief Justice Burger immediately affected voting alignments. One did not, however, have a Burger Court in the new Chief Justice's first term, with Burger "most out-of-step with the majority" in nonunanimous civil liberties cases. The majority participation of Justice Brennan, who had been in Warren Court majorities in *over 95 percent* of its post-1962 cases, dropped to below 90 percent in the 1969 Term, but Brennan, along with Marshall and White, were the justices most often in the majority.[55] An indication of change is that Justice Black voted with Burger more than with former voting companion Douglas.

In the 1970 Term, Burger acquired Justice Blackmun, the other half of the Minnesota Twins. They voted together in 90 percent of the term's nonunanimous cases and in all but one criminal procedure case. The Chief Justice's rate of dissent dropped sharply from the previous term, and his support for civil liberties claims dropped further. In the next term, Burger-Blackmun agreement decreased somewhat, to only 80 percent and—an indication of things to come—Burger's highest interagreement was with Rehnquist (95 percent). At the same time the Chief Justice voted with Douglas in only 4.2 percent of the cases, Brennan in only 10.9 percent, and Marshall in only 21 percent. Change was also evident in two facts: (1) Although the Marshall-Brennan-Douglas liberal core of the Court needed only two other justices to form a majority, they were not able to attract other votes very often.[56] (2) In the 1971 Term, White and Stewart voted together in 70 percent of the cases, were never in dissent together, and helped the Nixon appointees control the Court: the term's most frequent majority voting combinations were the Nixon Four plus Stewart and White or White alone. (In 1973, Stewart, along with White and Nixon appointee Powell, formed a "midbloc" on the Court.)[57] In the 1972 Term, typical of what was to follow, Burger, Blackmun, Powell, and Rehnquist were together in almost three-fifths of the nonunanimous cases, only once in dissent, and three of the four Nixon appointees were together in 85 percent of those cases.

In the 1975 Term, the most common pattern in nonunanimous cases remained the four Nixon appointees plus White and Stewart. However, as might be expected of centrist judges, White and Stewart voted together less frequently than the conservative pairs or the Marshall-Brennan liberal pairing. The six justices were often joined by Justice Stevens, the Court's newest member, although, showing his initial mid-Court position, Stevens paired at roughly the same rates with Burger, Stewart, White, *and* Brennan. The Nixon Four were together in 50 of 90 nonunanimous cases, never in dissent. With Douglas gone, the most frequent dissenters were liberals Brennan and Marshall.

In the 1974 Term, Justice Blackmun was the member of "the Four" most likely to defect and the Nixon appointee most likely to be in the majority in civil liberties cases, although he still voted against 60 percent of civil liberties claims. (Rehnquist and Burger voted against close to 70 percent of the civil liberties claims.) The 1975 Term produced seven cases in which a defection by Powell or Blackmun produced a loss of control of the Court by the Nixon Four. Despite such occasional division, over several terms when the Court opposed defendants' criminal procedure claims, the Nixon bloc was in the majority in all but two cases (97 percent); however, when the Court supported defendants' claims, the Nixon bloc was in the majority only slightly more than half the time.[58]

The 1975–1978 Burger Court showed fluid blocs: only Brennan and Marshall had an interagreement score over 90 percent. Although Burger and Rehnquist voted together almost 90 percent of the time, Rehnquist disagreed with Powell and Blackmun in more than one-fifth of the cases. Powell, Blackmun, the Chief Justice, and Justice White formed a marginally cohesive bloc (interagreement just over 80 percent). Powell, now occupying the place occupied by Justice Brennan during the Warren Court, was in the majority more than any other justice in the 1971–1977 period, casting only 75 dissents in 852 cases. Stevens joined Powell in providing the largest number of decisive votes in the 1977 Term, but he also added to the fluidity of the Court's alignments, "dissenting regularly in the company of both libertarian and conservative justices," although he inclined more to the liberals than the conservatives.[59]

In the 1975–1978 period, the center of gravity in civil liberties decisions was Justice Powell, not Chief Justice Burger. Powell voted with the majority in 93.1 percent of such cases. Other mainstream justices were Blackmun, White, and Stewart; the Chief Justice ranked fifth in terms of voting with the majority. Holdover liberals Marshall and Brennan were farthest from the mainstream; they registered well over *one hundred* dissents each.[60] Comparison of justices' votes on *all* civil liberties cases with their votes on *close* civil liberties cases for the 1976 and 1977 Terms (see Table 7.6) indicates that the more conservative and more liberal justices

TABLE 7.6. Civil Liberties—Full Opinion Cases

	1976 All Cases	*1976 Close Cases**	*1977 All Cases*	*1977 Close Cases†*
Burger	19–76 (20%)	0–21 (-0-)	24–93 (21%)	1–23 (4%)
Blackmun	36–61 (37%)	6–15 (29%)	47–72 (39%)	7–16 (30%)
Powell	31–64 (33%)	7–14 (33%)	42–75 (45%)	8–15 (35%)
Rehnquist	11–71 (13%)	1–19 (5%)	17–91 (16%)	0–21 (-0-)
Stewart	38–59 (40%)	9–11 (45%)	52–66 (44%)	11–13 (46%)
White	38–58 (40%)	9–13 (41%)	48–71 (40%)	10–12 (45%)
Brennan	71–22 (76%)	21–0 (100%)	90–27 (77%)	23–0 (100%)
Marshall	71–22 (76%)	21–0 (100%)	88–28 (75%)	23–0 (100%)
Stevens	54–39 (58%)	18–1 (95%)	67–49 (58%)	20–3 (87%)

*5–4 + 5–3
†5–4
NOTE: The figures indicate votes in favor of the civil liberties claim and those against; the percentage is the proportion of votes favoring the civil liberties claim.

had more extreme voting patterns in the close cases than for all cases. Thus in close cases Burger and Rehnquist almost never supported civil liberties claims, and Marshall and Brennan almost never opposed the claims. Centrist justices, such as White and Stewart, showed relatively little difference between their support for civil liberties claims in all cases and those in close cases.

For a slightly different time period, the 1976–1981 Terms, the four Nixon appointees were not found together as frequently as expected. However, either three or all four did vote together in roughly 80 percent of the cases, giving them an opportunity to control the Court on a regular basis. However, the liberal pair of Brennan and Marshall, not Chief Justice Burger and Justice Blackmun or Justice Rehnquist and the Chief Justice, had the highest level of interagreement of any pair of justices. Stewart and White, at the Court's center, voted together regularly but far less frequently than either the most conservative or most liberal pairs.

The 63 cases in the 1979 Term in which the Chief Justice and Justice Brennan were on opposite sides provide another clear indication of Burger Court patterns. Burger and Rehnquist voted together 61 times in these cases, but Rehnquist voted with Brennan only *twice.* Powell voted with the Chief 46 times, only 15 times with Brennan. Although Justice Blackmun did vote 36 times with the Chief Justice, he was increasingly independent of the other Nixon appointees, voting 27 times with Brennan. Similarly, in the 1980 Term, Chief Justice Burger and Justice Rehnquist were together 109 times, apart in only 12 cases, while Brennan and Marshall were together 111 times and apart only 12 times.[61]

In the 1981 Term, Justice O'Connor's first, she joined the Nixon Four 17 times and voted with three of the four another 44 times. Perhaps indicating the formation of the "Arizona Twins" (or "Phoenix Pair"), Justice O'Connor and Justice Rehnquist voted together in 123 cases, a rate of interagreement exceeding that of Rehnquist and Burger (118 cases), but below that for Brennan and Marshall (132 cases of 141). In 70 cases in which Rehnquist and Brennan were on opposite sides, Justice O'Connor was with Rehnquist in 51 of the 66 in which she participated, with Brennan only 15. A clear manifestation of Justice Blackmun's movement away from the Chief Justice is that he voted with Brennan more than twice as often as he did with Rehnquist.[62]

Studies of the Court's alignments based on Guttman scaling have produced findings comparable to those derived from bloc analysis. The basic scales which regularly appeared were the "C" and "E" scales.[63] The C scale covers civil liberties cases, matters of personal rights and freedoms such as the First Amendment, fair trial, and racial equality. In some terms of the Court, the C scale was a general civil liberties scale; at other times it had subcomponents. The E scale includes economic regulation matters: government regulation of business, antitrust, and labor-management cases. In some years, other scales, including one encompassing questions of federalism and another for judicial activism in reviewing decisions of the other branches of government, have also been identified.

By combining justices' positions on the political (C) and economic (E) scales, Schubert identified four categories of justices: the Individualist, conservative in economics

TABLE 7.7. Voting Patterns, 1976–1981—Nonunanimous Cases

	1976 (n = 86)				*1977 (n = 93)*				*1978 (n = 83)*			
	Majority	Dissent	Total		Majority	Dissent	Total		Majority	Dissent	Total	
Nixon Four	46	0	46		24	0	24		35	0	35	
Three/Four	15	10	25		31	6	37		25	6	31	
TOTAL	61	10	71	(82.6%)	55	6	61	(65.6%)	60	6	66	(79.5%)
Minn. Twins	57	7	64	(74.4)	42	4	46	(49.5)	55	2	57	(68.7)
WEB + WR	53	14	67	(77.9)	45	19	64	(68.8)	45	12	57	(68.7)
BW + PS	46	1	47	(54.7)	47	3	50	(53.8)	39	1	40	(48.2)
WBr + TM	33	41	75	(86.0)	48	24	72	(77.4)	32	38	70	(84.3)
	1979 (n = 97)				*1980 (n = 84)*				*1981 (n = 94)*			
Nixon Four	28	2	30		34	0	34		19	1	20	
Three/Four	40	7	47		29	7	36		36	14	50	
TOTAL	68	9	77	(79.3%)	63	7	70	(83.3%)	55	15	70	(74.5%)
Minn. Twins	59	7	63	(64.9)	47	1	48	(57.1)	33	3	36	(38.3)
WEB + WR	50	15	65	(67.0)	59	14	68	(81.0)	43	26	69	(73.4)
BW + PS	51	2	53	(54.6)	49	1	50	(59.5)	—	—	—	
WBr + TM	46	33	79	(81.4)	39	34	73	(86.9)	55	31	86	(91.4)
WBr + TM + JPS	37	13	50	(51.5)	22	12	34	(40.5)	41	8	49	(52.1)

Nixon Four: How often the four Nixon appointees (Burger, Blackmun, Powell, Rehnquist) vote together
Three/Four: How often three of the Nixon Four vote together
Minn. Twins: Burger and Blackmun
WEB + WR: Burger and Rehnquist
BW + PS: White and Stewart
WBr + TM: Brennan and Marshall
WBr + TM + JPS: Brennan, Marshall, and Stevens

but politically liberal; the Liberal, liberal on both scales; the Conservative, conservative on both; and the Collectivist—an economic liberal but a political conservative. Further classification produced three ideological dimensions. One was Equalitarianism/Traditionalism; someone liberal on both C and E scales would hold the Equalitarian ideology, a belief in greater equality of opportunity for all. The Authoritarian/Libertarian dimension dealt with the scope of freedom as opposed to the scope of authority; those holding the Authoritarian ideology were political conservatives and economic liberals. The third policy dimension was Collectivism/Individualism, involving emphasis on the individual human being as against emphasis on society as such, with a political liberal and economic conservative an Individualist. A fourth dimension cut across the others: Dogmatists, those who believed highly in the authority of precedent, and Pragmatists, those less concerned about precedent and more concerned about decisions' effects.

In the period from 1946 through 1962, Traditionalism was dominant in 1946–1948, Collectivism in 1949 and 1954 (both transitional periods), Authoritarianism in 1950–1953, and Equalitarianism in 1955–1962. In that same overall period, conservatives were divided into Pragmatists and Dogmatists, but liberals were not. Seven justices—Frank Murphy and Wiley Rutledge from the early Vinson Court, Black, Douglas, Brennan, Goldberg, and Warren—scored positive on the dimension of political liberalism; six were neutral; and five, including Chief Justice Vinson and Justice Clark, were negative. On the E scale, six justices, the same as on the C scale except for Goldberg, were positive, eight neutral, and four negative: Jackson, Frankfurter, Harlan, and Whittaker. Thus six justices who "sponsored change in the Court's policymaking in the direction of support for both civil liberties and greater economic egalitarianism" were positive on both scales, and four, the "economic conservatives," were neutral as to political liberalism but negative as to economic liberalism. Their "support of civil liberties was sufficiently unzealous that, when the Court itself came under political attack in 1956 and 1957 because of its emerging zeal for political liberalism, they readily supported the third cluster justices in checking the liberals." That third cluster was composed of the five (the "political conservatives") who were neutral as to economic matters but negative on political liberalism.[64] Only three justices—Warren, who became more liberal after his first few terms, Black, and Frankfurter—changed ideological positions once they joined the Court. Because so few justices changed positions, shifts in domination of the Court had to come through changes in personnel that in turn altered the three clusters of judges.

Using some different categories to examine a period including the Warren Court and extending into the Burger Court, other scholars found that more than 85 percent of the Court's rulings could be explained in terms of two major dimensions related to civil liberties and one dimension, New Dealism, based on economic activity. The first civil liberties dimension, freedom, covered cases involving criminal defendants and those in political "crimes," such as the loyalty oath cases; the other, equality, covered political, economic, or racial discrimination. Two other relatively minor dimensions—privacy (libel and obscenity) and taxation—also helped explain Warren

Court rulings.[65] Six justices—Warren, Douglas, Brennan, Goldberg, Fortas, and Marshall—were liberal, that is, positive on the three major dimensions. Seven, the four Nixon appointees, Frankfurter, Whittaker, and Harlan, were conservatives, negative on all three. Justices Stewart and White were considered Moderates, Black was a Populist—negative as to equality but positive as to freedom and New Dealism—and Clark was a New Dealer, positive only on economic matters, negative on the other two dimensions.

Guttman scaling studies have also suggested whether the Court's decisions have been based on the justices' attitudes toward a situation (AS) or toward an object (AO), that is, whether they would vote in terms of their attitude toward that type of person regardless of the situation. In the Warren Court's last eleven terms, AS was found to be more determinative in cases involving labor unions and persons exercising freedom of communication, while AO was more important in security risk cases and physically injured employees.[66] For the 1971–1973 Terms, the attitude toward object—support for the individual or for the government—dominated situational variables for eight of the nine justices in both criminal and noncriminal cases. Only Justice Powell differed between criminal and noncriminal cases, supporting the government to a statistically significant degree in the former but not the latter. That the other Nixon appointees favored the government over the individual in both criminal and noncriminal situations indicated clearly that their voting resulted from broader ideology, not a narrower and isolated "law and order" stance.[67]

All these studies are helpful in understanding the Court and its members, but they are also limited. They show only justices' positions relative to each other, not in absolute terms. Thus we cannot tell from scale positions either where the judges on the extremes are going to fall or exactly where the division between majority and minority will occur. Because they are based only on nonunanimous cases, the scales also cannot explain why the Court achieves unanimous decisions not only on noncontroversial legal questions but on important matters of law such as school desegregation and the Nixon tapes. They show overwhelmingly that attitude and ideology affect justices' votes but not the other factors that also influence the result and that help to explain why not all justices can be located easily on all scales.

A related problem is that, although scaling may indicate a relatively clear alignment of the justices in a broad subject matter, such patterns do not always hold for more specific issue-areas. For example, during the 1972–1980 period in cases involving freedom of the press, the more liberal and more conservative justices demonstrate consistent attitude-based voting patterns; however, mid-Court justices cast some antipress and some propress votes without an apparently coherent pattern. Such a picture does not mean that random choices are at work, but only "that the Justices differ markedly in their approach to the cases," stressing different elements of "models" of press-government relations, with "detailed examination of [their] votes and opinions" necessary if we are "to isolate the factors which influence each Justice's votes."[68]

Perhaps most significant is that these studies are based only on votes rather than on the justices' opinions and generally do not take into account the fact that justices who vote together do not necessarily write together. Because they capture only the Court's final product, its decision, these studies miss such important matters as interaction among the justices and the changes in written opinions and even results that may occur between the initial conference vote and final announcement of a decision. The result in a case as determined by the vote is perhaps the most important to the litigants, but the doctrine of an opinion is generally thought to be more important for the Court's role as a policymaker. It is to these considerations that enter into writing an opinion that we now turn.

NOTES

1. The case was *Laird v. Tatum*, 408 U.S. 1 (1972). Rehnquist's statement is at 409 U.S. 824 (1972). See John MacKenzie, *The Appearance of Justice* (New York: Scribner's, 1974).
2. See *Board of Education of City of Los Angeles v. Superior Court of California*, 448 U.S. 1343 at 1346-1347 (1980) (Justice Rehnquist).
3. *Whalen v. Roe*, 423 U.S. 1313 at 1317 (1975).
4. *Holtzman v. Schlesinger*, 414 U.S. 1304 and 414 U.S. 1316; *Schlesinger v. Holtzman*, 414 U.S. 1321 (1973). The early lower court's rulings were *Holtzman v. Richardson*, 361 F.Supp. 544, 553 (E.D.N.Y. 1973). After the activity in the Supreme Court, the court of appeals reversed the district court order and remanded with instructions to dismiss. 484 F.2d 1307 (2nd Cir. 1973).
5. This section draws on Stephen L. Wasby, Anthony A. D'Amato, and Rosemary Metrailer, "The Functions of Oral Argument in the U.S. Supreme Court," *Quarterly Journal of Speech* 62 (December 1976):410–422.
6. Quoted in Commission on Revision of the Federal Court Appellate System, *Structure and Internal Procedures*, pp. 104–105.
7. Milton Dickens and Ruth E. Schwartz, "Oral Argument Before the Supreme Court: Marshall v. Davis in the School Segregation Cases," *Quarterly Journal of Speech* 57 (February 1971):39.
8. James F. Simon, *In His Own Image: The Supreme Court in Richard Nixon's America* (New York: David McKay, 1973), pp. 208–209.
9. Anthony Lewis, "Supreme Law of the Land Still Rests in High Court," *Portland Oregonian* July 14 1974:F3.
10. Dickens and Schwartz, pp. 36–37.
11. Leon Friedman, "Introduction," in *Argument: The Oral Argument Before the Supreme Court in Brown v. Board of Education of Topeka, 1952–1955*, ed. Leon Friedman (New York: Chelsea House, 1969), p. vii.
12. Woodward and Armstrong, *The Brethren*, pp. 170–172, 179–181, 187–189, 417–422.
13. Ibid., pp. 63, 288–347.
14. See *Logan v. Zimmerman Brush Co.*, 102 S.Ct. 1148 (1982). Justice Blackmun, who wrote for the Court, added his own opinion, saying, "It cannot be suggested that in cases where the author is the mere instrument of the Court he must forego expression of his own conviction" (at 1159).
15. For examples see Alexander Bickel, ed., *The Unpublished Opinions of Mr. Justice Brandeis* (Cambridge, Mass.: Harvard University Press, 1957).

16. Saul Brenner, "Fluidity on the United States Supreme Court: A Reexamination," *American Journal of Political Science* 24 (August 1980):526–535, and "Fluidity on the Supreme Court, 1956–1967," *American Journal of Political Science* 26 (May 1982):388–390.
17. David Danelski, "Explorations of Some Causes and Consequences of Conflict and Its Resolution in the Supreme Court," paper presented to American Political Science Association, 1982, pp. 21–22.
18. Fehrenbacher, *The Dred Scott Case*, p. 321.
19. The original text reads as follows: "In dispensing these items, the pharmacist performs three tasks: he finds the correct bottle; he counts out the correct number of tablets or measures the right amount of liquid; and he accurately transfers the doctor's dosage instructions to the container. Without minimizing the potential consequences of error in performing these tasks or the importance of the other tasks a professional pharmacist performs, it is clear that in this regard he no more renders a true professional service than does a clerk who sells lawbooks." The ultimate opinion covered the same ground in one sentence: "In dispensing these prepackaged items, the pharmacist performs largely a packaging rather than a compounding function of former times." *Virginia State Board of Pharmacy v. Virginia Citizens Consumers Council*, 425 U.S. 748 at 774–775 (1976).
20. Charles W. Nihan and Russell R. Wheeler, "Using Technology to Improve the Administration of Justice in the Federal Courts," *Brigham Young University Law Review* (1981): 667n.
21. Data through the first Burger Court term from Donald D. Gregory and Stephen L. Wasby, "How to Get an Idea from Here to There: The Court and Communication Overload," *Public Affairs Bulletin* 3, no. 5 (November–December 1976); later data developed by the present author.
22. See Bernard Schwartz, "Felix Frankfurter and Earl Warren: A Study of a Deteriorating Relationship," *Supreme Court Review 1980*, ed. Phillip Kurland and Gerhard Casper (Chicago: University of Chicago Press, 1981), pp. 115–142.
23. Bernard Wolfman, Jonathan L. F. Silver, and Marjorie A. Silver, *Dissent Without Opinions: The Behavior of Justice William O. Douglas in Tax Cases* (Philadelphia: University of Pennsylvania Press, 1975).
24. Danelski, p. 34.
25. *Manual Enterprises v. Day*, 370 U.S. 478 at 519 (1962).
26. *Metromedia v. City of San Diego*, 453 U.S. 490 at 569–570 (1981). Justice White wrote for himself and Justices Stewart, Marshall, and Powell; Justice Brennan (with Justice Blackmun) concurred in the judgment; Justices Stevens, Rehnquist, and Chief Justice Burger *each* wrote dissents—a total of five opinions.
27. See Steven A. Peterson, "Dissent in American Courts," *Journal of Politics* 43 (1981): 412–434.
28. An important examination of the Court's efforts to remain unanimous is Dennis J. Hutchinson, "Unanimity and Desegregation: Decisionmaking in the Supreme Court, 1948–1958," *Georgetown Law Journal* 68 (October 1979):1–96.
29. Danelski, p. 42.
30. *Will v. Calvert Fire Insurance Co.*, 437 U.S. 655 at 670 (1978).
31. *Columbus Board of Education v. Penick*, 443 U.S. 449 at 493 (1979).
32. *Federal Energy Regulatory Commission v. Mississippi*, 102 S.Ct. 2126 at 2138, n. 25, and 2141, n. 30 (1982).
33. Saul Brenner, "Minimum Winning Coalitions on the U.S. Supreme Court," *American Poli-*

34. David W. Rohde, "Policy Goals and Opinion Coalitions in the Supreme Court," *Midwest Journal of Political Science* 16 (May 1972):218–219; Micheal W. Giles, "Equivalent Versus Minimum Winning Opinion Coalition Size: A Test of Two Hypotheses," *American Journal of Political Science* 21 (May 1977):405–408.
35. S. Sidney Ulmer, "Exploring the Dissent Patterns of Eleven Chief Justices: John Marshall to Warren Burger," paper presented to American Political Science Association, 1982; this paragraph and the next are based on this paper.
36. David Danelski, "The Influence of the Chief Justice in the Decisional Process of the Supreme Court," in *Courts, Judges, and Politics*, eds. Walter F. Murphy and C. Herman Pritchett, p. 503.
37. William P. McLauchlan, "Ideology and Conflict in Supreme Court Opinion Assignment, 1946–1962," *Western Political Quarterly* 25 (March 1972):16–27.
38. David W. Rohde, "Policy Goals, Strategic Choice and Majority Opinion Assignments in U.S. Supreme Court," *Midwest Journal of Political Science* 16 (November 1972):667; see also S. Sidney Ulmer, "The Use of Power in the Supreme Court: The Opinion Assignments of Earl Warren, 1953–1960," *Journal of Public Law* 19 (1970):49–67.
39. Elliot E. Slotnick, "The Chief Justices and Self-Assignment of Majority Opinions: A Research Note," *Western Political Quarterly* 31 (June 1978):224. See also Slotnick, "Who Speaks for the Court?: Majority Opinion Assignment from Taft to Burger," *American Journal of Political Science* 23 (February 1979), particularly pp. 68–72, and Slotnick, "Judicial Career Patterns and Majority Opinion Assignment on the Supreme Court," *Journal of Politics* 41 (May 1979):640–648.
40. H. N. Hirsch, *The Enigma of Felix Frankfurter* (New York: Basic Books, 1981), pp. 129–130.
41. Ibid., pp. 5–6.
42. Ibid., pp. 136–137.
43. Ibid., pp. 9, 153, 176.
44. Ibid., p. 188. See Dennis J. Hutchinson, "Felix Frankfurter and the Business of the Supreme Court, O.T. 1946–O.T. 1961," *Supreme Court Review 1980*, pp. 143–209.
45. Hirsch, p. 211.
46. S. Sidney Ulmer, "The Longitudinal Behavior of Hugo Lafayette Black: Parabolic Support for Civil Liberties, 1937–1971," *Florida State University Law Review* 1 (Winter 1974): 131–153. See also Ulmer, "Parabolic Support of Civil Liberty Claims: The Case of William O. Douglas," *Journal of Politics* 41 (May 1979):634–639; and H. Frank Way, "The Study of Judicial Attitudes: The Case of Mr. Justice Douglas," *Western Political Quarterly* 24 (March 1971):12–23.
47. David Danelski, "Values as Variables in Judicial Decision-Making: Notes Toward a Theory," *Vanderbilt Law Review* 19 (1966):721–740; and Danelski, *A Supreme Court Justice is Appointed* (New York: Random House, 1964).
48. Still more sophisticated methods are used by some scholars. See Glendon Schubert, *The Judicial Mind* (Evanston, Ill.: Northwestern University Press, 1965), for use of "smallest space analysis"; and S. Sidney Ulmer, "The Discriminant Function and the Theoretical Context for Its Use in Estimating the Votes of Judges," in *Frontiers of Judicial Research*, eds. Joel B. Grossman and Joseph Tanenhaus (New York: John Wiley, 1969), pp. 335–369.
49. Joel B. Grossman, "Dissenting Blocs on the Warren Court: A Study in Judicial Role Behavior," *Journal of Politics* 30 (November 1968):1083, 1089.
50. Schubert, *Quantitative Analysis of Judicial Behavior*, pp. 192–210.

51. For Roberts's explanation, see Glendon Schubert, *Constitutional Politics* (New York: Holt, Rinehart and Winston, 1960), pp. 168–171.
52. David N. Atkinson and Dale A. Neuman, "Toward a Cost Theory of Judicial Alignments: The Case of the Truman Bloc," *Midwest Journal of Political Science* 13 (May 1969): 271–283.
53. Glendon Schubert, *The Constitutional Polity* (Boston: Boston University Press, 1970), pp. 124–125. See also S. Sidney Ulmer, "Toward a Theory of Sub-Group Formation in the United States Supreme Court," *Journal of Politics* 27 (1965):133–152.
54. Edward V. Heck, "Justice Brennan and the Heyday of Warren Court Liberalism," *Santa Clara Law Review* 20 (Fall 1980):845–846, 858–859.
55. Edward V. Heck, "Changing Voting Patterns in the Burger Court: The Impact of Personnel Change," *San Diego Law Review* 17 (1980):1030.
56. Ibid., p. 1033.
57. Sheldon Goldman and Thomas Jahnige, *The Federal Courts as a Political System*, 2nd ed. (New York: Harper and Row, 1976), pp. 162–163.
58. David W. Rohde and Harold J. Spaeth, *Supreme Court Decision-Making* (San Francisco: W. H. Freeman, 1975), p. 109.
59. Edward V. Heck, "Civil Liberties Voting Patterns in the Burger Court, 1975–1978," *Western Political Quarterly* 34 (June 1981):199.
60. Ibid., pp. 195–202.
61. Linda Greenhouse, "High Court Kept Commitments to Civil Rights and Enforcement," *New York Times*, July 12, 1980: pp. 1, 22; Greenhouse, "Affirmation of Federal Power Marked Court Term," *New York Times*, July 9, 1981:pp. 1, A16.
62. Linda Greenhouse, "High Court: Divisions on Rights in Last Term," *New York Times*, July 9, 1982:pp. 1, D14.
63. What follows is drawn primarily from Schubert, *The Judicial Mind.*
64. Glendon Schubert, *The Judicial Mind Revisited: Psychometric Analysis of Supreme Court Ideology* (New York: Oxford University Press, 1974), summarized in "The Judicial Mind Reappraised," *Jurimetrics Journal* 15 (Summer 1975):279.
65. Rohde and Spaeth, pp. 137–138.
66. Harold J. Spaeth et al., "Is Justice Blind?: An Empirical Investigation of a Normative Ideal," *Law & Society Review* 7 (Fall 1972):119–137.
67. S. Sidney Ulmer and John A. Stookey, "Nixon's Legacy to the Supreme Court: A Statistical Analysis of Judicial Behavior," *Florida State University Law Review* 3 (Summer 1975): 331–347.
68. Paula C. Arledge and Edward V. Heck, "Freedom of the Press: Decisionmaking Models in the Burger Court," *Whittier Law Review* 4 (1981):10–11.

Chapter 8

The Court's Opinions: Basic Considerations

In the previous chapter, we examined the justices' voting patterns and dissensus within the Court, emphasizing the part played by justices' *values.* Those values are but one consideration entering into the writing of an "opinion of the Court" through which the Court's policy is most explicitly developed. The justices' views of their roles as justices and of the Supreme Court's place in the American political system also play a significant part in opinion-writing, just as they do in decisions to accept or reject cases. Even if a justice starts constructing an opinion from a personal value position, its ultimate content is also affected by an understanding of what the Court's audiences or attentive publics expect to be treated in a Supreme Court opinion. This is not suprising when we realize that the Court's basic impact on other government units comes through those opinions. The breadth of an opinion, its doctrinal bases, and the other content it contains—including precedent and history to establish continuity with the past as well as social science materials, generally used sparingly—affect not only an opinion's immediate policy effects but also its value as precedent. Whether an opinion is framed narrowly, staying within the grounds urged by the parties or seemingly applicable only to the facts of the particular case, or departs from those facts to embrace other situations, and whether it is confined to a statute rather than reaching a constitutional question, are thus quite important.

There are some problems in examining the Court's opinions. One is that there have been important changes over time in the Court's decision-making style—the way the justices have made decisions as well as the overall matrix in which the potential elements of an opinion, or factors influencing it, are taken into account. Giving the Court the power to decide which cases to accept had an important effect on such decision making. When the Court had to decide all cases brought to it but its caseload was still small, the justices could decide each case carefully and deliberately—that is, they could engage in rational decision making. With time to consider each case, the likelihood that they would depart from precedent would be greater than otherwise.[1] When the Court had an increased caseload but was still operating under the pre-1925 requirement of hearing all cases, decision making was incremental. Changes from past cases were limited, with precedent serving as a cue to allow prompt disposition. Instead of making law, the Court was more likely to be engaged in interpretation of existing doctrine.

Once it obtained the power to turn away cases, the Court could return to rational decision making, at least for those cases it accepted, thus allowing more policy innovation. With the caseload again growing, "mixed-scanning" decision making is produced. A quick glance is given to most cases before they are rejected, while those accepted get more extended and careful treatment. Here the justices' basic doctrinal attitudes affect not only the Court's full decisions but its decisions to grant review as well. The Court's ability to innovate may, however, be hindered if docket size gets too large and approaches "overload chaos," an unmanageable situation that some justices suggest now exists.

The shift from mandatory to discretionary review, by eliminating the less controversial cases, also produced more disagreement, with which the Court has had to learn to cope. After 1925, an increase in dissent first appeared in the appeals jurisdiction, from which less important cases had been removed and shifted to the certiorari category. This left the more controversial appeals cases, which would naturally produce more dissent. As winnowing progressed in the certiorari cases as well, dissent later increased there, as did the number of concurring opinions.[2]

Another matter to be kept in mind is that what justices write is not necessarily a "true" reflection of their reasons and motives in voting for a particular result. A justice's solo dissent may accurately reflect his or her motivations, but the author of an opinion of the Court must accommodate colleagues' views. However, not even the solo dissenter may provide a fully accurate account of his or her views. Judges' opinions are not "stream of consciousness" writing leading from premises through rethinking to the ultimate product; they thus seldom indicate the process by which that judge has reached the conclusions presented, the serial iterations in the judge's writing process, or changes resulting from interaction with colleagues.[3] Instead they are likely to state conclusions along with explanations for those conclusions. Opinions thus are "the reconstituted logic by which the justices justify themselves."[4]

Does this mean, to paraphrase one cynic, that a judge shoots an arrow at a target and then draws the bullseye around the place where the arrow struck, or that opinions are only an elaborate display of erudition serving as window dressing to mask initial gut reactions? Certainly what Justice Oliver Wendell Holmes, Jr., called a judge's "inarticulate major premises" affect the judge's written opinions. Thus the justice writing for the majority and justices writing concurring or dissenting opinions can write equally persuasive opinions, for each reasons from different premises. Nonetheless, despite the crucial importance of unstated premises, justices *are* affected by having to write opinions, by the expectation that they will justify their actions, will include certain material in their opinions, and will address certain problems.

The process of writing the opinions serves, to a greater or lesser degree, to constrain the unfettered operation of a justice's basic values. This means that the search for "neutral principles" or relevant precedent, or views about the virtues of self-restraint, even if not actually fully *governing* justices' opinions, do have some effect and thus can legitimately be called "considerations" in the justices' opinions. When those elements do not appear to constrain the majority, criticism is sure to follow, from inside the Court as well as from outside it. Thus Justice White recently complained in a major case involving the president's immunity from suits for civil damages, "The judgment in this case has few, if any, indicia of a judicial decision; it is almost wholly a policy choice, a choice that is without substantial support. . . ."[5]

In the course of arriving at the ultimate scope, content, and tone of an opinion, the Court must consider a number of major matters. One is the degree to which opinions will be based on "neutral principles"; another is the extent to which the Court will rely on precedent and will develop policy incrementally. Still another, subsuming these elements as well as others, is whether and how the Court, in attempting to achieve its goals, will engage in strategy—already an element in the Court's choice of cases for review and in the decision to give cases summary or full-dress treatment (see pages 156–158). An important aspect of strategy in the Court's relations with the other branches of government and in its relations with the states is whether and to what extent it should exercise its power of judicial review (see pages 59–64), a problem because of the tension between judicial review and democracy, discussed at some length in this chapter. Judicial review is an important —but not the only— aspect of the related concepts of *self-restraint* and *judicial activism*, at the heart of criticism of the federal courts for unnecessarily intervening in government activities (see pages 3–5). Those aspects, including the degree to which the Court should defer to the states as part of federalism, are treated here. We conclude the chapter with an examination of another way in which justices' role conceptions exhibit themselves—their off-the-Court activities concerning judicial and nonjudicial matters.

NEUTRAL PRINCIPLES

People who see the Court as finding law, and even many who recognize that it makes policy, expect of the Court that its decisions should be *principled.* Compromises deriving from pragmatism are for legislators and political executives; courts, on the other hand, must stand for principle, deliberateness, the use of rationality and logic, and detachment from the turmoil and passion of political conflict. As former Solicitor General Archibald Cox put it, "In expounding the Constitution, the Court's role is to discern 'principles sufficiently absolute to give them roots throughout the community and continuity over significant periods of time, and to lift them above the level of the pragmatic political judgments of a particular time and place.'"[6] Or, in Bickel's words:

> The root idea is that the process is justified only if it injects into representative government something that is not already there; and that is principle, standards of action that derive their worth from a long view of society's spiritual as well as material needs and that command adherence whether or not the immediate outcome is expedient or agreeable.[7]

In the most noted statement, Herbert Wechsler said judicial determinations should rest on "reasons that in their generality and their neutrality transcend any immediate result that is involved." Criteria for decisions had to be exercises of reason, "not merely . . . an act of willfulness or will."[8] But Wechsler had demanded too much even for some advocates of the Court's "passive virtues." Bickel argued that if the Court were to have to rest its decisions "only on principles that will be capable of application across the board and without compromise, in all relevant cases in the foreseeable future," with any flexibility built into the principle itself "in equally principled fashion," there would be few such principles; few cases would be decided, and the Court would thus fail to meet the public's demands that it resolve issues. As some judges are fond of saying, it is better that some cases be decided than that they be decided right. It should be enough, Bickel said, to have "an intellectually coherent statement of the reason for a result which in like cases will produce a like result, whether or not it is immediately agreeable or expedient," or a "principled process of enunciating and applying certain enduring values of our society," with the values having "general significance and even-handed application."[9] However, new principles might arise when there is a conflict between values, for example, between the right of people to associate—which Wechsler thought must have been the basis of the decision in the school desegregation cases, the opinion in which he criticized—and the right of others not to associate, or the right of free speech and the right to a fair trial.

A serious problem with the demand for "neutral principles" is that, while initially appealing, they might turn out to be rigid and thus prevent the Court from reaching publicly acceptable results: people want principles but they also want decisions with which they can live. For example, the statement of Justice Harlan, dissenting in *Plessy v. Ferguson*, that "the Constitution is colorblind," sounds marvelously unbiased but, taken literally, would prevent most programs to remedy results of past racial discrimination. Thus the Court is faced with the dilemma of having simultaneously to reach toward principle and reasoned judgment as the basis for its actions, while maintaining some flexibility in order to adjust to changing social conditions.

PRECEDENT

An even stronger expectation, particularly in the legal community, is that the justices will base their opinions on precedent and will adhere to the doctrine of *stare decisis* (literally, to stand on the decision) at the heart of the Anglo-American legal tradition. Precedent "not only plays an important role in orderly adjudication; it also serves the broader societal interests in evenhanded, consistent, and predictable application of legal rules."[10] Moreover, "the holy rite of judges consulting a higher law loses some of its mysterious power" when precedent is overruled or the Court "makes new law out of whole cloth."[11]

The expectation that courts base their decisions on precedent, which involves taking the present case, finding past cases that are similar, and then applying the rules from those past cases, creates a number of problems. How does one know which cases are "similar"? On what competing precedents should one rely? How should legal doctrine of the relevant cases be interpreted? And, at the level of the Supreme Court, should precedent be followed as closely as lower courts are expected to follow it? The Court's place as the nation's highest and last court has led it to feel *less* bound by precedent than do the lower courts. This is particularly true when the Constitution is being interpreted, because changes in constitutional rulings can be overturned only through the very difficult process of amending the Constitution itself. Because Congress has the power to rewrite statutes and thus correct the Court's interpretation of those statutes (see pages 248–250), the justices are more reluctant to alter precedents based on statutory interpretation even when they recognize that those precedents may be in error.

Illustrating this point is the Court's disposition of Curt Flood's challenge to the reserve clause in professional baseball, the only major professional sport exempted from antitrust coverage (Hi there, sports fans!). The baseball exemption stems from the Court's 1923 ruling, based on a narrow interpretation of the Commerce Clause, reaffirmed in 1953, that baseball was not commerce and therefore was not subject to the Sherman Antitrust Act. Later, before Flood's antitrust challenge, other courts, on the basis of the Supreme Court's post-1937 broader definition of commerce, held other sports, particularly professional baseball and professional basketball, subject to the antitrust laws. In ruling on *Flood v. Kuhn* (1972), the majority agreed that professional baseball was a business in interstate commerce and that the antitrust exemption for baseball was "in a very distinct sense, an exception and an anomaly," with the earlier cases "an aberration confined to baseball." Nonetheless, said Justice Blackmun, "the aberration is an established one" recognized by Congress, which had "by its positive inaction" allowed the earlier baseball decisions to stand and had shown no intention of placing professional baseball within the scope of the antitrust laws. Thus "if there is any inconsistency of illogic in all of this, it is an inconsistency and illogic of long standing that is to be remedied by the Congress and not by this Court."[12]

The *Flood* case does not mean that the Court is invariably resistant to changing its interpretation of statutes when it reads legislative history differently from earlier readings. If the legislature has not relied on the Court's past rulings, if those past rulings are out-of-step with still earlier rulings, and if the challenged ruling is out of phase with more recent statements of legislative intent, the Court will be more willing to overrule precedents interpreting statutes. Most notable in recent years was the Court's decision in the *Monell* case, only 16 years after initially holding that municipalities could not be sued under the Civil Rights Act of 1871 (42 U.S.C. §1983) (see page 123) and only five years after reaffirming the initial decision, that the courts *would* entertain such suits; the reversal was justified both on the basis of inconsistency with other civil rights rulings and of the Court's having inadequately considered its earlier position before adopting it.

As suggested by Justice Rehnquist's comment in the *Monell* case that "this Court is surely not free to abandon settled statutory interpretation at any time a new thought seems appealing," when the Supreme Court overrules a precedent, criticism is likely, both from other justices and from outside the Court. Such criticism occurs whether the precedent is new or old: if old, the Court is said to be interfering with the "settled ways" of the law; if new, the Court is not allowing the law to develop properly. Particularly where departure from recently established precedent has not been explained well by the justices, such criticism is often more than merely a "cover" for opposition to the result the Court has reached.

An example of this situation is provided by the Burger Court's rulings on leafletting in shopping centers. The Warren Court had said in 1968 that picketing of a particular store in a large, privately owned shopping center had to be allowed. In 1972, without overruling that earlier case, the Burger Court, saying the cases were different, allowed antiwar leafletting to be banned because the protest was unrelated to the shopping center or its stores. Then in 1976 the Court banned picketing of a shopping center shoestore by workers whose basic dispute was with the store's warehouse. Here the Court explicitly overruled the 1968 case but in doing so said the overruling had really taken place in 1972 because the 1968 case had not "survived" the 1972 ruling. The inadequacy of this explanation, which conceded that the first opinion had been overruled *sub silentio*, was so obviously at variance with the majority's own 1972 statements that Justice Marshall was prompted to complain that the first case had "been laid to rest without ever having been accorded a proper burial."[13] Similarly, the Court's overturning of Congress's extension of the minimum wage law to state and local government employees, in which it overruled another 1968 decision upholding a closely related extension of the law, led Justice Brennan to argue that the Court had "discarded roughshod" a whole series of decisions.[14] Notwithstanding these examples, the effect of the Warren Court precedent on the Burger Court meant that the latter remained more liberal in many of its decisions than would have occurred if President Nixon's appointees had been able to write on a clean slate.

Distinguishing cases from one another, emphasizing their differences and limiting the application of precedents by saying new cases contain facts not identical to those in the older cases, is one way the justices try to avoid precedents without stirring up as much criticism as would an explicit overruling. As one can see from the leafletting cases, the Burger Court has used this technique in its erosion of Warren Court rulings, particularly in the criminal procedure area, and has done the same thing to some of its own cases. For example, the right to counsel at police-conducted line-ups, established by the Warren Court in the *Wade* and *Gilbert* cases, was held not to apply when a witness viewed a display of pictures rather than a line-up of people (*United States v. Ash*, 1973).

More recently, the Court distinguished two earlier cases in which it had invalidated searches of containers (a locked footlocker and a suitcase) taken from cars. The majority ruled in *United States v. Ross* (1982) that police with probable cause to believe an automobile contained contraband could conduct warrantless searches of those cars *and* any containers and packages that might contain the object of the search. In the earlier cases, said the majority, the police lacked probable cause to search anything but the footlocker and the suitcase, and the containers' connection with the automobile had been "purely coincidental." This effort to cut away at precedents by attempting to distinguish them provoked Justice Marshall to comment that by rejecting "all of the relevant reasoning" of one of the earlier cases and offering a "substitute rationale that appears inconsistent with [its] result," the Court now had "effectively overruled" rather than distinguished the earlier case.

Despite the Court's overturning and distinguishing of precedent, the expectation that precedent will be used has a considerable effect on at least some of the justices, even when they disagree with the past cases. For example, the Court's 1976 ruling in *Runyon v. McCrary*, invalidating discrimination on the basis of race in admission to private schools, involved an application of its 1968 *Jones v. Mayer* decision applying post–Civil War antidiscrimination statutes to private housing sales. Justice Powell went along with the majority in 1976 because the Court had considered application of the civil rights statutes to private acts "maturely and recently," while Justice Stevens indicated he would vote differently "were we writing on a clean slate." However, Stevens said that "the interest in stability and orderly development of the law" and the fact that the precedent "accords with the prevailing sense of justice today" had "greater force" than the argument that the earlier case was wrongly decided.

Stevens repeated the argument a few years later in talking "about the potential damage to the legal system that may be caused by frequent or sudden reversals of direction that may appear to have been occasioned by nothing more significant than a change in the identity of this Court's personnel."[15] In another case, Justice Rehnquist went further to call for reversal of a precedent, announcing that he would "be more than willing to participate" when "this Court is willing to reconsider" its decision in a major parental consent abortion case. However, he would join the majority because "unless and until that time comes, literally thousands of judges cannot be left with nothing more than the guidance offered by a truly fragmented holding of this Court."[16] Rehnquist has also joined Chief Justice Burger in making long arguments for overturning the exclusionary rule with respect to improperly seized evidence.

The Court does, despite all this effort at avoidance, overturn decisions. From 1958 through 1980, 57 decisions were overruled, all but three by closely divided votes. The average life of the precedents before overruling was just under twenty years, and in only a few cases did the overruling take place in less than five years from the date of the original ruling. At the other extreme, some cases that had stood for more than 70 years were overturned.[17]

If precedent and ways of interpreting previous cases have exerted a brake on the Court's actions, the Court has also seen the need to move gradually and to make its rulings appear incremental and to stress continuity even when considerable change is taking place. In general, because law develops in response to new circumstances, filling in gaps, abrupt turns (and overturnings) are seldom necessary. Too many sharp deviations and departures, too many unpredictable results disturb the general public and particularly those "opinion leaders" who watch the Court most closely.

Gradual movement might well characterize the Court's decisions even without precedent, as a result of deciding narrow questions before large ones or making summary disposition of appeals instead of rulings with full opinion. Most policymakers do not make radical departures from past policy but operate incrementally, developing policy a bit at a time and making changes "at the margin." As Shapiro has argued, "The theory of incrementalism may explain, or at least describe, the phenomena of stability and gradual change in law just as well as or better than stare decisis."[18] The school prayer decisions, where the Court first struck down a state-written prayer in *Engel v. Vitale* before eliminating all recitation of school prayer and Bible reading in *Abington School District v. Schempp*, provides an example of incremental action. So does reapportionment, where the Court first demanded equally populated districts for the U.S. House of Representatives (*Wesberry v. Sanders*) and invalidated the Georgia "county unit" system (*Gray v. Sanders*) before ruling, in *Reynolds v. Sims*, that both houses of all state legislatures had to be apportioned on the basis of population. In the area of criminal procedure,

> The Court would typically approach a new issue warily, issuing first a narrowly limited decision which contained a hint of the result that might finally be required. A few criminal lawyers would get that hint, cases would develop, and lower court decisions would result. These decisions would usually not be consistent with each other, which could be a boon to the Supreme Court; it could deny petitions for certiorari in all of these appeals, leaving the lower court rulings in effect without indicating whether it approved or disapproved of the results. Over the years experience would develop in the lower courts as to the best way to proceed with the problem, and any warning signs would be detected before the Supreme Court had to take its position.[19]

Although policy may be developed incrementally, it may also be developed in "big pieces" and *applied* incrementally, as successive litigation brings the various parts and pieces of a problem to the Court. Thus the Court first provided a broad definition for obscenity in its 1957 *Roth* decision, gradually adding elements to the definition in later cases.[20] After the Court said in *Brown v. Board of Education* that "separate but equal" was not to apply to education, the Court applied this rule to other public facilities (golf courses, swimming pools, and the like) through a series of *per curiam* opinions shortly afterward. These examples also show the incremental development of what *seems* to be a major policy change, as the important elements of the *Roth* obscenity definition were derived from earlier lower court rulings, and *Brown* built on *Sweatt v. Painter*, invalidating segregation in graduate education because "intangible" factors were not equal.

STRATEGY

Expectations that the Court seek neutral principles and rely on precedent are traditional, one might say conservative, considerations in developing opinions. Quite different is the possibility that the Supreme Court engages in strategy. Changes in the Court's positions—from liberal to conservative, from activism to self-restraint (see below), from the center of the political arena to the periphery and back—are not accidental. Those changes result in part from external forces, such as the arrival of new justices chosen for their ideological proclivities and cases brought to the Court, and in part from internal factors, such as individual justices' attitudinal changes. Through their strategies, individual and collective, the justices contribute another important element to the decision-making process.

Those who believe that justices find law or who seek to have them apply neutral principles find unseemly any talk of judicial strategy. Issues are to be confronted directly, regardless of cost to the Court, and not for other concerns is justice for litigants to be sacrificed. There is, moreover, no doubt that conflicts between strategy and "justice" do exist and can be quite disturbing. Examples are the refusal in the 1950s to decide a challenge to a cemetery's refusal to bury a native American or to rule on the validity of antimiscegenation (anti-mixed-marriage) laws—even when a black woman went to prison for marrying a white man—or, more recently, avoidance of persistent challenges to the constitutionality of the Vietnam War, despite the increasing death rate during that conflict.[21] Nonetheless, almost by definition the Court must act strategically, because it is a *political* body acting in an often hostile—or at least nonsupportive—environment.

Courts, no less than other governmental institutions, cannot ignore their environments and must understand them. Thus, "Support for civil liberties, as provided by the Supreme Court, is a commodity for which buyers' markets alternate with sellers' markets in some kind of cyclical pattern. Courts of law can be expected to 'read' their markets as well (hopefully) as any other producer of consumables."[22] If it is to survive and achieve some of its goals, the Court may have to avoid some controversies. To be avoided where possible are "self-inflicted wounds" like the *Dred Scott* decision legitimating slavery and, some would add, the Warren Court's criminal procedure rulings. A justice's 1954 comment, "One bombshell at a time is enough," made when the Court turned away a miscegenation case,[23] was a recognition of the need to concentrate on achieving school desegregation—affecting a large number of people—rather than damage that effort by angering the South with a decision on the mixed marriage laws, affecting relatively few individuals.

That the Court does take actions based on strategy is clear from the evidence provided by the justices themselves. For example, the decision in *Brown v. Board of Education* was delayed to get a vote that was unanimous or more nearly so.[24] When Justice Frankfurter was assigned to write the Court's opinion striking down the "white primary," the Chief Justice was told that, because the ruling was likely to be received negatively in the South, it would be wiser if the opinion were *not* written by a Jewish immigrant who had taught at Harvard Law School—and the case was reassigned to Justice Stanley Reed, a Kentuckian. Similarly Justice Byrnes, also a southerner, was assigned the opinion in *Taylor v. Georgia* (1940), holding that a Georgia statute violated federal prohibitions against peonage, in order to give it more force.[25]

The justices' demonstrated awareness of their political environment makes it quite likely that, acting on the basis of strategic considerations, they take that environment into account even when they claim not to do so. Justice Powell, upholding school financing through the property tax in *San Antonio School District v. Rodriguez* (1973), said, "Practical considerations, of course, play no role in the adjudication of the constitutional issues presented," but commented that to rule otherwise "would occasion . . . an unprecedented upheaval in public education." More recently, Justice Blackmun said he could understand his colleagues' abandonment of past positions concerning state assistance to parochial school education only in terms of "concern about the continuing and emotional controversy and to a persuasion that a good-faith attempt on the part of a state legislature is worth a nod of approval."[26] In the past, the Court has acted strategically in responding to threats, as in changing its policy position on economic regulation after FDR's attempt to pack the Court and on internal security matters (loyalty oaths and congressional investigations of subversives) after congressional efforts in the 1950s to limit its jurisdiction, by refusing to decide more cases on a controversial issue or by deciding cases with larger majorities.

Perhaps justices' taking into account the effect of their rulings has been most obvious in the field of criminal procedure. For example, Justice Stewart justified a new restriction on admissibility of seized evidence by pointing out that the FBI and the federal courts had remained effective although operating under the exclusionary rule for many years. In the 1976 death penalty decisions, several justices said that the fact that thirty-five states had reenacted death penalty legislation after statutes had been struck down in 1972 was an indication that the penalty was not "cruel and unusual punishment." And Justice Clark asserted that to apply the exclusionary rule of *Mapp v. Ohio* to past cases "would tax the administration of justice to the utmost."[27] One of several criteria the Court regularly used in deciding whether to apply its criminal procedure rules to past convictions was the effect such application would have upon the administration of justice. Indeed, the Court's approach to the retroactivity problem has been said to have been guided largely by strategic considerations such as placating those opposed to the Court's new rules.[28] In evaluating these particular instances, one should, however, keep in mind findings that, in the related matter of setting its agenda, that is, deciding what cases to review, the Court "does not respond to increases in the general level of public concern about crime" and does not use public opinion—"either general levels or increments"—as an input into that decision.[29]

To say that the Court acts strategically does not mean that the justices have a complete blueprint to guide their actions. It is more likely that individual justices act strategically than that there is a "strategy of the Court." Justices appear to share the goal of preserving the Court as an institution, and one may find that at least some justices share a general sense of direction. Nonetheless, the Court is perhaps best seen as a "mixed-motive" or "mixed-strategy" group. Strategy encompasses efforts to affect the political world outside the Court or to fend off attacks from outside (*external* strategy) as well as persuasion and bargaining among justices while a case is under advisement (*internal* strategy), necessary to achieve external effects.

A justice wishing to accomplish any external goal must attract enough colleagues to constitute a majority for affirmance or reversal and to constitute a majority supporting an opinion advancing that goal, a far more difficult task. The goal-seeker must be careful not to take so strong a position that the potential majority is lost, and if unanimity is sought, extended discussions—and particular caution to keep potential "mavericks" from "wandering off the reservation"—may be necessary to retain it. This was apparently true after the 1954 school desegregation ruling, when the justices were highly uncertain about the proper way to enforce it or even about its precise meaning. In this situation, unanimity as a conscious strategy "masked the uncertainty" and also "provided a more solid defense to critics," although, because it deprived the Court of the opportunity to be persuasive, unanimity "operated in time to obscure rather than enhance the Court's decisions"[30]—thus providing an illustration of the difficulties that can result from operating strategically.

A variety of tools are available to judges wishing to engage in strategy. Such tools, usually used in combination, are applied not only to a justice's immediate colleagues on the Court but also to the lower court judges so important in implementing the Supreme Court's opinions. At times a justice can assist in the process of selecting new colleagues. Most important, however, and most frequently used are devices necessary to the everyday resolution of cases before the Court. Of the available tools, perhaps force of intellect, demonstrated to lower court judges through carefully reasoned and written opinions and to colleagues through draft opinions and arguments in conference, is the one closest to "the law" and furthest from "politics." Personal intellect is, however, often not a sufficient strategic mechanism. Judges must thus resort to other strategems—including endearing themselves to colleagues, important in obtaining votes in cases of lesser importance to those colleagues, and threatening to vote against the majority. When dissenting views are stated strongly in public, it may damage the Court. Negotiation and compromise, at the core of internal strategy, are most upsetting to those who accept the myth of the Court as apolitical. One needs to ask, however, whether one could expect anything *other than* bargaining and compromise as part of the activities of the nation's highest court charged with interpretation of the Constitution, once that court is recognized to be a political actor acting in a political environment.

Strategy-related behaviors are brought to bear as the Court chooses issues for decision and the opinions to be written. *Issue fluidity*, a shift in the issues to which the Court gives its attention in a case, can occur in the process of granting review to a case (see page 156) and can occur as well during postargument consideraton of a case and development of the Court's opinion. For example, in a recent case, *California v. Grace Brethren Church* (1982), the issue changed from the constitutionality of collecting unemployment insurance taxes from religious schools not affiliated with a church—the issue on the basis of which the case was decided in lower court—to whether the Tax Injunction Act permitted declaratory judgments—the issue decided by the Supreme Court.

As they focus on a case's principal issues, the justices may decide not to deal with some issues that litigants have briefed and argued (*issue suppression*). However, as they examine briefs or listen to oral argument, the justices may be prompted to consider issues not earlier thought to be present in a case (*issue discovery*) as well as to alter their views of issues' relative importance. This occurs because lawyers' arguments may be based on any matter appearing in the record and appellants may use any appropriate arguments in support of the lower court's judgment. Thus arguments may be made on appeal that were not made in the trial court or lower appellate court. Although the Court does not often decide a case on the basis of an issue not presented, and particularly if it has not been presented in the lower courts, issues *are* added to allow the Court to decide a case the way a majority considers appropriate. Thus, "An order limiting the grant of certiorari does not operate as jurisdictional bar. We may consider questions outside the scope of the limited order when resolution of those questions is necessary for the proper disposition of the case."[31] Furthermore, if a precedent is thought necessary "to cover a large number of detailed questions being posed in the lower courts" when no case is available posing the question with appropriate breadth, the justices may use issue transformation to develop such a question and then decide it. As this suggests, "The question(s) to which the Court will respond in any given case cannot be known with certainty until the Court's opinion in the case is announced. . . . The Court can expand, contract, suppress or replace issues posed by the litigating parties at various points between initial issue framing and final issue resolution."[32]

Once it has been decided that the Court will issue a full, signed opinion, important additional elements in decision making come into play. Pragmatism, evangelism, and the milieu of advocacy are among the factors that diminish the effect of attitude and ideology, particularly with respect to the opinions the justices write. Pragmatism involves the question of "strategic judgments about what professional and lay traffics would bear." It can be seen when a justice withholds a dissent even when opposed to the result or limits himself to a concurring opinion rather than a dissent, perhaps so that the Court's decision can have greater force through a larger majority. Evangelism, the attempt to persuade publics outside the Court of the correctness of the Court's doctrine, certainly influences not only the justices' votes but also what they say. Thus "the demands of persuading colleagues and countrymen in trailblazing cases coalesce with professional habits and personal antagonisms to transform opinion-writing into argument and over-statement."[33]

There are a number of options for the Court and the opinion-writer. The Court may wish to avoid a broad opinion that looks more "legislative" as well as a ruling so narrow it does not illuminate the law for other lawyers and judges and thus leads to the filing of many more cases. However, narrow rulings may be useful as a delaying tactic or as a device to clear away the underbrush before an unmistakable direct attack is mounted on a particular practice. They may also be necessary because a broad opinion may also lose judges from the majority, with the ultimate opinion often the lowest common denominator the justices can produce. It is wise for the Court to sound as much as possible like a "law court," with the opinion drawing heavily on precedent and history where possible and avoiding social science evidence, which tends to provoke criticism.

Opinions vary in their clarity, in their breadth and narrowness, and in the directness with which issues are approached. Ambiguity may be used strategically, to help keep control of policymaking in the Court's hands because unclear decisions force others to come back to the Court to obtain the justices' clarification. Thus ambiguous decisions, while producing "repeater" cases that may cause docket management problems, allow the Court to "monitor" the action of lower courts.

With respect to the breadth of opinions, the Court can achieve its goals without broad opinions, particularly if negative reaction to a straightforward doctrinal ruling is foreseen; limited doctrinal grounds—basing a case on its facts or relying on statutory interpretation—can be used instead of dealing with larger, "tougher" constitutional questions. Yet there are times when reaching the principal issues directly is not only what the judges want to do but is also important strategically—to satisfy the demands and expectations of the Court's constituencies. If much of the Court's strategy seems based on avoiding issues or minimizing the degree to which they are confronted, one must remember that this is done so that on the issues the Court considers most important it can act forthrightly.

If a variety of tools are available to aid the exercise of judicial strategy, there are also numerous constraints on a judge's ability to accomplish strategic aims. Two basic constraints serving to limit the degree to which judicial policymaking can be explicit and to which strategy can be openly considered are the strongly held myth that the Court finds and does not make law and the special legal framework within which the justices operate. Beyond those constraints, even if all justices were simultaneously concerned about strategy, each might focus on different aspects of a case or wish to pursue different strategies. Moreover, although a "policy-oriented judge" is "aware of the impact which judicial decisions can have on public policy, realizes the leeway for discretion which his office permits, and is willing to take advantage of this power and leeway to further particular policy aims," not all justices may fit this description: "Probably relatively few justices have had a systematic jurisprudence; more but probably still relatively few have been so intensely committed to particular policy goals as to establish rigid priorities of action that dominated their entire lives; probably few have been able to act only rationally in seeking to achieve their aims." In addition, each judge "has only a finite supply of time, energy, research assistance, and personal influence."[34]

Strategic considerations often compete and there are standard operating procedures (SOPs) and "bureaucratic routines" that courts, like any other organization, follow. The justices respond to self-imposed deadlines like the one that all cases argued within a term are to be decided by the end of that term, as well as to rules for handling caseload, including technical ones on timely filing and judicial doctines on the standing of a party to raise an issue. These rules can be ignored when it is felt necessary, but if the Court is to function effectively, that cannot be done often. Other constraints on the Court's exercise of strategy include the judges' own positions, interpersonal relations within the Court, the Court's prestige at the time, and external pressures—from interest groups, Congress, and the president.

Requiring particular attention in the Court's exercise of external strategy, and thus constituting a serious potential constraints are lower court judges. A major strategic question is whether—and to what degree—the Court should defer to those judges, particularly state judges. Such deference, like that shown the legislative and executive branches, is necessary because the Supreme Court depends on the lower court judges to carry out its mandates, something the latter would be less likely to do if the justices interfered frequently with their work. The deference may allow the lower courts to move ahead of the Supreme Court in applying a new doctrine, creating a base on which the Court itself can later build. However, it may also produce delay or noncompliance, with the case being brought back to the Court for further action and thus interfering with docket management. Particularly when the Court has remanded a case with only limited instructions, evasion may also result. This allows the lower court to find an alternative basis for reaching the result it had reached earlier, while keeping the case out of the Supreme Court's hands.[35]

JUDICIAL REVIEW

Criticism of judicial review, like criticism of the "imperial judiciary" (see pages 3–5), is something judges must keep in mind when they are contemplating overturning statutes or executive actions, particularly because of fundamental arguments about the propriety of judicial review in a democratic system. There are, of course, other arguments aimed at limiting judicial review. One is that each branch of government should decide for itself what is constitutional and then should act on the basis of its own conclusions.

President Andrew Jackson, saying he had to make his own judgment, vetoed legislation for a national bank even though Chief Justice John Marshall, in *McCulloch v. Maryland*, had earlier sustained the validity of such a bank. President Jefferson thought Supreme Court determinations about statutes' validity were entitled to respect but were not binding on him as president. Similarly, after *Dred Scott*, President Lincoln said he would again vote to ban slavery in the territories: a ruling not embodying what he conceived to be the Constitution's basic or fundamental values was not a "political rule" he had to follow nor did it command permanent obedience but was to be challenged.[36] Such a position—based on the idea that legislators and executives as well as judges take an oath to support the Constitution and can be thought to be as committed as judges to that oath—is close to that taken by President Nixon's lawyer when he told the justices that the question of whether the Watergate tapes had to be surrendered was being submitted for the Court's "guidance and judgment with respect to the law." As we know, in *United States v. Nixon* (1974), the Court, quoting Marshall's *Marbury* opinion, rejected this position in favor of a broader conception of judicial review.

This view, in which judges' rulings would be potentially persuasive but not determinative for the other policymaking branches, would not prevent the other branches from taking actions they thought appropriate or from trying to enforce laws without the courts' assistance, but it would still allow judges to refuse to *enforce* policies they thought unconstitutional when those policies came before the courts in "cases and controversies." However, even under this view, the Court's ability to rule effectively on challenges to acts of the other branches might not be severely limited because the executive needs to seek judicial assistance in enforcing the law.

In another, related version of judicial review, each branch should have the final word as to matters directly affecting it or "naturally" falling within its respective special competence. In this view, we would have "judicial supremacy" only as to matters within the judiciary's particular bailiwick. Examples are the jurisdictional question in *Marbury*, the advisory opinion aspect of *Hayburn's Case*, and judicial remedies for constitutional violations, such as desegregation orders. Chief Justice Marshall, of course, went further, to establish judicial review over the acts of the legislative and executive branches affecting the entire government, not simply the judiciary, although after *Marbury* the Court took no further such action for more than fifty years. (This time lapse has, however, been "attributed to lack of provocation rather than to judicial self-restraint," because judicial review "had long since won general public acceptance."[37])

Judicial Review and Democracy

Among arguments that judicial review is undemocratic,[38] we find judicial review disparaged because justices appointed for life, who often remain on the Court long after they are out of tune with the nation's views, can overrule acts of periodically elected representatives and acts of the executive branch, whose head, the president, is also elected. One response is that when the Court strikes down statutes as "void for vagueness," Congress, because it is not being told that it cannot act, only that it must act more clearly, can rewrite the statutes with clearer prescriptions. Even when the Court invalidates statutes as unconstitutional, such rulings can be overturned. Although some Court actions can be reversed only by constitutional amendment, at times only a statute is necessary to do so. Thus when state action is invalidated for intruding on the federal government's domain in violation of the Commerce Clause, Congress can restore state authority through legislation.[39] Enacting constitutional amendments to overturn the Court is difficult but not impossible, as we see from the Eleventh (no suits against states by citizens of another state), Sixteenth (income tax), and Twenty-sixth (18-year-old vote) amendments and the post–Civil War amendments eliminating slavery, redefining citizenship, and protecting civil rights.[40]

Another response to the claim that judicial review is undemocratic is Alexander Hamilton's, that through judicial review, the Constitution—the people's will—is enforced over the will of the people's representatives. However, the people whose will is being enforced are long dead, with the ideas of constitution-makers of the distant past pitted against views of much more recent legislators. Frequent exercise of judicial review will also, we are told, make it less likely that those seeking policy changes will press legislators and political executives for action, and will put a damper on legislators' willingness to meet their responsibilities to deal with social problems. In Chief Justice Burger's words, "When this Court rushes in to remedy what it perceives to be the failings of the political process, it deprives those processes of an opportunity to function. When the political institutions are not forced to exercise constitutionally allocated powers and responsibilities, those powers, like muscles not used, tend to atrophy."[41] On the contrary, the Court's action can also help establish an agenda of issues given active consideration by the other branches and can stimulate activity to deal with otherwise ignored problems. For example, after the Court's reapportionment rulings, state legislatures learned to deal with redistricting; those rulings also opened up, rather than restricted, the political process.

At the center of the debate about judicial review and democracy is the argument that courts must protect the minority rights that are as much a part of democracy as is majority rule, and can make an important contribution to democracy by enforcing rights of free speech and press, assembly, and petition. In a particularly significant statement, Justice Harlan Fiske Stone suggested, in Footnote #4 in the *Carolene Products* case, that the usual presumption of validity for challenged statutes might be given less weight when the statutes affected the subject matter of the Bill of Rights. Moreover, heightened judicial scrutiny might be given legislation that "restricts those political processes which can ordinarily be expected to bring about repeal of undesirable legislation" and laws directed at "discrete and insular" racial, ethnic, and religious minorities who were the object of prejudice, because that prejudice would limit use of the political process. Examples are a city charter amendment requiring approval of open housing ordinances by referendum and passage of a state referendum that limited busing for desegregation (but not for other purposes). Both were held invalid for restructuring the political process to the disadvantage of minorities.[42]

Justice Stone's cautious statement recently became the focus of John Hart Ely's further-reaching "representation-reinforcing theory of judicial review."[43] Ely argued that, in the exercise of judicial review, judges should not search for fundamental values to be enforced, or substantive results to be imposed, but should focus on restrictions on "the opportunity to participate either in the political processes by which values are appropriately identified and accommodated, or in the accommodation those processes have reached." The Constitution, by seeing to it that "everyone's interests will be actually or virtually represented . . . at the point of substantive decision" and that application of substantive policy "will not be manipulated . . . to reintroduce discrimination," "has sought to assure that [an effective] majority not systematically treat others less well than it treats itself." Thus "unblocking stoppages in the democratic process is what judicial review ought preeminently to be about."[44]

This basic position that the Court must use judicial review, even if incompatible with majority rule, to protect individual rights, is at the heart of another recent argument that the Supreme Court should limit and better focus its exercise of judicial review. Because, "almost by definition," Jesse Choper asserts, "the processes of democracy bode ill for the security of personal rights and . . . experience shows such liberties are not infrequently endangered by popular majorities . . . the task of custodianship has been and should be assigned to a governing body that is insulated from political responsibility and unbeholden to self-absorbed and excited majoritarianism."[45]

Pragmatism is an important element of Choper's argument. Decisions on personal rights are likely to provoke and offend other political actors. Thus, by abstaining from exercising judicial review in other situations, the justices can "both reduce the discord between judicial review and majoritarian democracy and enhance their ability to render enforceable constitutional decisions when their participation is critically needed."[46] The Court, Choper believes, should avoid decisions on questions of federalism when the states allege that Congress has interfered with their authority, because consideration of the states' concerns are built into the congressional decision-making process. However, the Court should not abstain from reviewing state acts in violation of the Supremacy Clause; here, in any event, Congress can alter any balance struck by the Court. Choper does urge that the Court "should pass final constitutional judgment on questions concerning the permissible reach and circumscription of 'the judicial power'." However, conflicts between president and Congress should be avoided by the Court and should instead "be remitted to the interplay of the national political process," where proper balance will be maintained by each branch's concern for its own prerogatives. In an argument like Chief Justice Burger's (noted above), Choper says that absence of a judicial arena for resolution of such disputes "may well remove an existing disincentive to political settlement."[47] Judicial action concerning separation-of-powers conflicts may also distract Congess from taking action against the president. For example, lawsuits over the constitutionality of the Vietnam War may have increased congressional hesitation to assert itself.

Despite the effectiveness with which such positions have been developed, arguments that judicial review is undemocratic may be misdirected. For one thing, other governmental institutions may be no more responsive to the public than is the Court, with no one (except perhaps the president) accountable to a majority of the nation's voters. Moreover, our government's institutions operate by means of a system of checks and balances in which each participates in the work of the others and thus limits them. The Court's involvement in these political processes, engaging in strategic actions as a policymaker, thus makes it to some extent a democratic institution;

only if it were fully insulated from those processes and if it found the law in total independence of other government bodies would it be undemocratic.

Nonetheless, there are continuing fears that, no matter how long we have had the practice, judicial review is undemocratic. These fears appear in debates over whether, in fact, the Supreme Court interferes with the work of the other, elected branches of government. In the 1950s, Robert Dahl asserted that the Court does not block the legislature and executive but, as a part of the dominant national alliance, actually legitimizes their work. In making his argument, Dahl relied on the seventy-eight cases through 1957 in which the Supreme Court had exercised judicial review to invalidate eighty-six provisions of federal law. He also considered the timing of that review. Only half of the Court's actions came within four years of the legislation's enactment, with more than one-third of the "prompt" overrulings occuring during the Court's emasculation of the New Deal. In most instances when recent legislation was overturned, Congress reversed the Court or the Court itself did so somewhat later.

Seldom is the Court outside the dominant alliance for long, according to Dahl; moreover, the Court generally can do little without support from president and Congress. The Court might win small battles, but the justices are not likely to be successful "on matters of *major* policy, particularly if successive presidents and Congresses continue to support the policy the Court has called unconstitutional." When other political actors are unable to decide important questions, the Court can take action, but even then it does so at great risk and can succeed only if its actions are in tune with the norms of the political leadership.[48]

This position has been met directly. One argument is that Dahl overestimated the Court's ability to legitimize; another, that Dahl *under*estimated the Supreme Court's effectiveness. In arguing the first of these two positions, David Adamany says the Court cannot legitimize unless it strikes down the acts of other branches at least occasionally. If all statutes and administrative actions were sustained, the Court's ability to legitimize would be meaningless. During constitutional crises, the Court cannot grant legitimacy because at such times justices, having been appointed earlier, are of the party opposite to that controlling the elected branches; the Court's actions invalidating legislation, more likely when one political party has dominated Congress and nominees of the other party controlled the Court, certainly do not grant legitimacy to the new coalition. Instead, conflict between the Court and the elected branches after realigning elections—those in which party control of the presidency changes and there is substantial shift in the voters' partisan identification—has "somewhat discredited and sometimes checked the lawmaking majority." In each such situation, however, the result has been "a clash that left doubtful the Court's capacity ultimately to legitimize the new regime and its policies." One hardly has legitimization when as a result of changes in personnel or its own strategic movement the Court finally adopts the dominant coalition's position. Instead there is "more the appearance of surrender to superior force."[49]

The public also does not seem to know about the Court's legitimizing role; what little the public does know is principally about cases in which majorities have been checked, not legitimized (see page 277). The Court's decisions also do not eliminate substantial opposition to policies it has enunciated or prevented legislative attacks on the Court and efforts to reverse its rulings. It is important to note, however, that the Court's opinions do provide ammunition for those defending the Court's position. Moreover, the views of political elites, who know more than does the general public about the Court and its decisions (see pages 279–280), are largely conditioned by the elites' political attitudes, not the Court's actions. Thus the Court does not legitimize policy for the nation through the elites; elites confer legitimacy on the courts. The Court does not itself help create respect for the political system, but commands respect because it is part of the political system. This ultimately saves the Court when a new political coalition considers limiting the justices.

In a response to Dahl from another direction, Jonathan Casper noted that the Court has intervened decisively in the policymaking process, holding 32 provisions of federal law unconstitutional in 28 cases from 1957 through 1974—roughly one-fourth of the instances in which national legislation had been invalidated up to that time. Even when ultimately overturned, Court decisions delay implementation of policies for some years after they are enacted, further indication of the Court's effectiveness. (Prompt overrulings of legislation—within four years of enactment—occurred in only a few of the cases. In only one, on the 18-year-old-vote, and in no case involving older legislation, was the Court reversed.) Also important in evaluating the Court's effects are the Court's statutory interpretation rulings, which have produced important policy on a wide range of subjects. When one assesses the Court's effectiveness, its initiatives not involving invalidation of national legislation, such as Marshall's *McCulloch v. Maryland* and *Gibbons v. Ogden* rulings, must also be taken into account, as should the Court's introduction of new issues and new participants into the political process, which may assist actors' ability "to attract adherents, mobilize resources, and build institutions."[50]

ACTIVISM AND RESTRAINT

A major consideration in Supreme Court decisions, suggested by earlier discussion of Supreme Court deference to lower courts, is the extent to which the Court, in dealing with other actors in the political system, should be "self-restrained" or "activist." Because of the absence of clear definitions, controversy over whether the Court has been sufficiently "self-restrained" or too "activist" has been almost continuous; that each concept has several dimensions further complicates communication about them. Despite the absence of fixed definitions, there is some general agreement on some basic dimensions of the terms. There are "two major premises that serve as underpinning [for] . . . a limited role for the courts": that judicial policymaking "conflicts with the very essence of a democratic society" and "that courts simply are not equipped to make wise policy."[51] As the Chief Justice recently observed, "We trespass on the assigned function of the political branches under our structure of limited and separated powers when we assume a policymaking role." He added, "It is not the function of the judiciary to provide 'effective leadership' simply because the political branches of the government fail to do so."[52]

Judicial restraint has been said to involve one or more of the following elements:

- "deference to the other branches of government"
- "a lack of result-orientation," that is, a concern "with legal principles, not the social or economic effects of . . . decisions"
- reliance on precedent
- "avoidance of 'political' questions"[53]

A more elaborate set of dimensions has six components. One is Majoritarianism, "the degree to which policies adopted through democratic processes are judicially negated"; this involves deference to other branches of government and to policies enacted through initiative and referendum. Interpretive Stability is "the degree to which earlier court decisions, doctrines, or interpretations are altered," which is essentially the same as reliance on precedent. Interpretive Fidelity requires the Court to adhere closely to the intentions of those who drafted constitutional provisions or to the "clear implications of the language" the drafters used. Other dimensions concern the extent to which the justices "make substantive policy" instead of focusing on the process by which policy is made (the Substance-Democratic Process Distinction), leave the making of policy to others (Specificity of Policy), or "supercede serious consideration of the same problem by other governmental agencies" (Availability of Alternate Policymakers). In terms of these dimensions, the Supreme Court has demonstrated activism in different ways at different times. For example, the Warren Court showed primarily "jurisprudential changes," while the mid-1930s Court "was most activist on the Majoritarian dimension and also usurped the prerogatives of Alternate Policymakers to a greater extent than did other Courts."[54] Despite the belief that it is a restrained Court, limiting "activist" lower court intervention in matters of state policymaking, sidestepping new issues, and making challenges to government activity impinging on civil rights more difficult through a narrowing of rules on standing, the Burger Court has also shown a considerable degree of specificity.

Action that is activist on one dimension may be self-restrained on another. For example, if the Supreme Court, deferring to law enforcement officers' judgments about the use of improperly seized evidence, were to overrule the exclusionary rule of *Mapp v. Ohio*, the Court would be simultaneously activist, overruling precedent, and self-restrained, in deferring to the executive. Similarly, the Court would be self-restrained in following precedent by striking down state legislation mandating school prayer, but activist in not deferring to the legislative judgment.

There has also been a change over time in the meaning of self-restraint and activism. Fifty to seventy years ago, self-restraint meant not disturbing national and state legislation regulating the economy, and it produced "liberal" results, while "activism"—striking down statutes as unreasonable interference with "freedom of contract"—assisted the business community. In the last forty years, and particularly the last twenty, a "hands off" approach preserved statutes infringing individual freedoms, while "activism" has generally protected civil liberties. Richard Nixon, who pledged to appoint "strict constructionist" judges who would not encroach on areas belonging to Congress and the president, criticized judges for having "gone too far in assuming unto themselves a mandate which is not there, and that is, to put their social and economic ideas into their decisions."[55] Yet his remarks about Supreme Court decisions that set free "patently guilty individuals on the basis of legal technicalities" meant he did not want self-restrained judges when activism could aid the "peace forces" rather than the "criminal forces."

Nixon's appointees were able to defer to legislative and executive actions when his basic policy goals would be aided by so doing. For example, the Court talked of its "reluctance to review legislatively mandated terms of imprisonment" and asserted that "the basic line-drawing process . . . is preeminently the province of the legislature when it makes an act criminal" in deferring to legislative judgments about appropriate sentencing and upholding a life sentence under a recidivist statute even though the defendants' three felonies had netted a total of less than $250.[56] Similarly, the Court stated that "a prosecutor should remain free before trial to exercise the broad discretion entrusted to him to determine the extent of the social interest in prosecution."[57]

The Court, reversing a trend toward questioning the expertise of prison administrators, also moved back to the deferential (self-restrained) "hands-off" doctrine on prison policy. For example, Justice Rehnquist, sustaining prohibition of a prisoners' union, criticized the district court for "not giving appropriate deference to the decisions of prison administrators and appropriate recognition to the peculiar and restrictive circumstances of penal confinement." He also asserted, in a case involving conditions for pretrial detainees, that "prison administrators . . . should be accorded wide-ranging deference in the adoption and execution of policies and practices that in their judgment are needed to preserve internal order and discipline and to maintain institutional security." With respect to those engaged in training the mentally retarded, the Court also said that a decision concerning that training, "if made by a professional, is presumptively valid."[58]

The Court's basic operational rules of self-restraint were spelled out most explicitly by Justice Louis Brandeis in his opinion in the *Ashwander* case. The Court will not rule on challenged legislation in a nonadversary proceeding nor will it decide a complaint made by someone not injured by the statutes or by someone who has benefited from the action being challenged. A constitutional issue will not be decided if other bases for decision, such as statutory construction, are available; in short, the Court will not anticipate a constitutional question unnecessarily nor will it formulate a rule broader than required by the facts of the case. Thus the Court exercises self-restraint by approaching cases cautiously—by denying review to some cases and, perhaps more important, by developing rules as to who may bring cases and under what conditions they may be brought (see pages 123–135).

Considerable disagreement has, however, occurred over whether the Court has followed such "rules" of self-restraint and whether it has heeded Justice Stone's admonition that "the only check upon our own exercise of power is our own sense of self-restraint."[59] For example, Justice Stevens, citing Brandeis, recently felt it necessary to remind his colleagues that "constitutional lawmaking efforts" should not take place "unless (1) those efforts are necessary to the decision of the case at hand and (2) powerful reasons favor a change in the law."[60] Justices' votes also raise questions about whether they *practice* self-restraint to the extent they *advocate* it, whether it actually motivates those who make claims in its behalf or whether ideology is the actual determinant of their actions. For example, the breadth of the Court's criminal procedure doctrine has been related to the justices' goals. Confronting broad rules favoring law enforcement, liberal justices have argued that cases should be decided on the basis of the "totality of the circumstances," rather than in terms of broad rules they had earlier espoused when in the majority. In the 1969–1977 Terms of the Court, out of a possible 40 situations—ten justices deciding cases in four categories (regulatory commissions, federalism, access, and civil rights and civil liberties)—in only ten did activism or restraint influence justices' voting, and only Justice Douglas "manifested activism or restraint in more than a single category."[61]

Of particular interest is Justice Felix Frankfurter, the Court's foremost advocate of judicial self-restraint in recent times. He argued in the 1962 reapportionment case, *Baker v. Carr*, that the Court should stay out of the reapportionment issue because it involved "political entanglements" and the "clash of political forces in political settlements." Civil liberties and labor cases in which Frankfurter participated often included questions of jurisdiction and issues of deference to other units of government, questions closely related to self-restraint. With such Denial of Judicial Responsibility (DJR) matters present, Frankfurter's vote was always against the civil liberties claim in civil liberties cases and against the liberal position in 16 of 18 labor cases. However, with DJR-related cases removed, Frankfurter's position relative to that of the other justices remained to the right of center in civil liberties cases. Thus, even if the DJR factor, when present, appeared to control Frankfurter's civil liberties ideology, in other cases he was obviously a conservative rather than an apostle of self-restraint, posing the question of whether self-restraint explains even cases where the DJR issue was present.[62]

The argument for self-restraint has been made forcefully in recent years, but the argument for "affirmative activism" is also a strong one, particularly when such activism takes the form of "an effort by the Court to redress minimally the political imbalance between bureaucrats and those who are subject to bureaucratic power but are typically impotent to reform or influence it."[63] Such a position is closely related to Justice Stone's *Carolene Products* footnote and to use of the courts by those unsuccessful in achieving their goals in other political arenas or who need governmental assistance to prevent being deprived of their rights. The argument thus became particularly important with the Warren Court, the first Court seriously attending to providing protection for minorities and others whose civil liberties had been infringed. When the Court reviews administrative officials' actions, whether the administrators may act *at all* is not usually at issue. Because the question is instead what *types* of actions are or are not permissible, such cases may thus require extensive answers and thus greater "activism" than in straightforward rulings on the validity of a statute. Thus, just as government has grown, so has the possibility of challenges to government action and thus judicial activism to restrain that action.

Adoption of a strongly activist position with respect to individual freedoms is not, however, necessarily realistic for the Court as a political actor. Despite approval from some segments of the public, the Warren Court's decisions were frequently attacked and often disobeyed. Indeed the Court almost lost some of its jurisdiction and perhaps would have suffered severe damage had it not avoided some issues and retreated on other occasions. The absence of attacks on the Burger Court, a result of the greater congruence of its decisions with the nation's civil liberties orientation, suggests the virtues of judicial self-restraint. Those virtues could also be seen after 1937 when the Court changed its posture with repect to economic regulation to one of self-restraint.

Federalism

The question of deference to state decision making is a crucial element of self-restraint. When the Court considers challenges to congressional and presidential actions, questions of deference to elected officials are present, but when state actions are challenged, another element is injected—deference to the "sovereign" states, the federalism element—and justices may wish to take it into account. For example, should states, because of their "police power" over matters of health, welfare, and morals, be given more flexibility than the federal government? (The Court, in the *Roth* and *Alberts* cases, treated both levels of government the same, with only Justice Harlan arguing for the distinction.) Or does Congress have the power to lower the voting age to 18 in both national and state and local elections? (In *Oregon v. Mitchell*, the Court said it could in national but not in state and local elections, provoking passage of the Twenty-sixth Amendment.) The argument for flexibility for state legislatures has also been made concerning a number of other subjects, from capital punishment—so that data on the effect of differing statutes might be available to all states—to the discipline of lawyers.[64] When actions of state *courts* are under review, questions of federalism and of deference to other judges may reinforce each other. Thus justices have resisted having federal courts engage in close supervision of state courts, whether the issue is alleged racial discrimination in those court's actions (see *O'Shea v. Littleton*, 1973) or federal court review of state court criminal cases through federal habeas corpus (see pages 141–142). As Justice Stevens remarked concerning the latter situation, "To assign a single federal district judge the responsibility of directly reviewing, and inevitably supervising, the most routine work of the highest courts of a state can only undermine the morale and the esteem of the State Judiciary."[65]

Much of the history of the Supreme Court can be viewed as a history of the treatment of federalism-related concerns.[66] However, the Warren Court's tendency to nationalize the protections provided in the Bill of Rights—to make criminal procedure, for example, the same for the national and state levels of government—decreased significantly the role of federalism as a concern in Supreme Court rulings. As Justice Powell recently observed, "No trend of decisions by this Court has been stronger—for two decades or more— than that toward expanding federal jurisdiction at the expense of state interests and state court jurisdiction. . . . The effect . . . has been the erosion of federalism."[67]

If questions of federalism have *largely* been settled and thus are less frequently the source of conflict within the Court than they once were, they are not *completely* settled. They come into play beneath the surface in cases where the focus is on the substantive issue (abortion, obscenity, the death penalty) rather than on federalism itself but where an important aspect of the case is whether states may take certain action the national government is not permitted to take. Cases directly posing federalism questions are also still present on the docket. Particularly significant are cases, occurring throughout the Court's history, involving the question whether the national government has "preempted" state action on a particular subject. Especially controversial was the decision in *Pennsylvania v. Nelson* (1956), in which the Court set aside a state conviction of a person for attempting to overthrow the government of the United States because the national government had indicated its intention to preempt the field through enactment of the Smith and McCarran Acts. Intense negative reaction led the Court to rule in *Uphaus v. Wyman* (1959) that the states could regulate subversion directed at the states themselves.

That issues of this sort have been present did not, however, mean that conceptions of federalism were the primary influence in the Court's rulings generally. Examination of the 1969–1977 Terms shows that despite occasional statements about leaving matters to the states, the Burger Court was *not* "an overwhelming example of judicial restraint." The justices deferred less to the states on questions of economic regulation than they did to federal government regulatory actions, and some of the justices' decisions were definitely affected by whether the state policy they were reviewing was probusiness or antibusiness: of four justices who supported probusiness decisions most strongly (three being appointees of President Nixon), three "become remarkably unsupportive" when the state policy is antibusiness. Marshall and Brennan adopted converse positions, and only Justice Rehnquist "defers to the states enough to qualify . . . as an advocate of judicial restraint," although his "conservative economic bias" showed nonetheless. The pattern of greater support for the federal government than for state governments also appeared in civil rights and civil liberties cases extending through early 1979, whether the subject was the First Amendment, double jeopardy, or poverty law, with support for state policy roughly equal to support for the federal government only in search and seizure cases.[68]

OFF-THE-COURT ACTIVITY

The Court's opinions—and the justices' separate concurring and dissenting statements—may provide the principal mechanism by which the justices participate in policymaking, but they are not the only one. There is also judicial participation in matters outside the Court. That extrajudicial activity is related both to judicial administration and to broader political issues.

A justice who has been politically active is not likely to slacken interest in political issues once his or her Supreme Court nomination has been confirmed nor to sever all contacts with the political world, for example, to cease contacts with the president. Thus justices have informally continued as presidential advisers, as Chief Justice Vinson did with President Truman and Justice Abe Fortas did with President Lyndon Johnson on such topics as Vietnam, steel price increases, and strikes. It is not, however, clear whether, as alleged, Vinson advised Truman that the latter had the authority to order an emergency seizure of the steel mills, an action the Court later determined to be invalid (see pages 253–254). Even when prior personal contact has been limited, as in Richard Nixon's acquaintance with Warren Burger during Burger's Justice Department service, contact may later expand, particularly in the case of the Chief Justice. Thus Burger apparently met on occasion with the president or with Attorney General Mitchell, but whether these discussions went beyond matters of judicial selection and judicial administration to comments about the school busing cases is unresolved. Whatever its scope, the role of presidential advisor is likely to be submerged and kept screened from the public to avoid the considerable criticism generated by public knowledge of such relations.

By comparison with activities in the Court's early years, justices' present political activities, such as contacts with the president, are very limited. Over the course of the Court's history, roughly two-thirds of the justices have engaged in some such activity, "either informally or in response to official government requests."[69] There has, however, been considerable variation in the general level of that activity, with some, like Chief Justice Melville Fuller (1888–1909), taking the equivalent of the veil, even avoiding Washington social contact. There has also been variation in the norms about the extent of such activity and in justices' sensitivity to those changing norms. Changes in the norms are in part a function of public reaction to the extent of previous extrajudicial activity, with the norm generally moving toward lessened out-of-Court involvement, relaxing somewhat after criticism abates, and then, in something of a ratchet effect, tightening further in the next similar cycle. However, in times of war and crisis the norm of noninvolvement tends to recede to allow the justices to "undertake any necessary informal extra-judicial tasks that might be useful to the nation."[70]

Not until after the Civil War did judges themselves begin to look askance at justices' close ties to political parties or interest groups. Indeed, up to that time, justices had failed even to adhere to a norm of not talking about the Court's cases outside the Court; and until late in the nineteenth century, justices had regularly courted high political office from their positions on the Court. There have been few such instances in the twentieth century, with Charles Evans Hughes' departure from the Court to run unsuccessfully for president the best known; that his nomination came while he still sat on the Court was thought to injure its nonpartisan image. There was off-and-on-again discussion of the candidacy of Justice William O. Douglas, who also offered to resign from the Court to campaign for President Truman if Truman had decided to run in 1952, but an indication of changed norms is that the very discussion provoked criticism.

After the justices cut most political party ties, it took longer before they could be weaned from contacts with interest groups. Most twentieth century out-of-Court activity not concerning judicial administration has focused on issues rather than partisan elections. Examples are provided by the extrajudicial activities of Justices Louis Brandeis and Felix Frankfurter. Before he joined the Court, Brandeis had been committed to advancing a wide variety of political positions. Once he became a justice, he maintained his interest in those issues, both political (such as the concentration of big business) or more specifically religious (Zionism), and he continued to meet and to talk about them with those involved in politics and government. Did he wish to feed an insatiable appetite for knowledge of "current events," or did he continue to influence legislative policy indirectly, for example, pressing against what he thought was the New Deal's excessively pro-big business orientation? Did he simply express concerns to friends or orchestrate political battle plans? We cannot be sure.

We do know that between 1916 and 1938, Brandeis, an extremely wealthy man, provided to then Harvard law professor Felix Frankfurter regular payments totaling roughly $50,000 (worth many times that amount in current dollars) to assist Frankfurter's engaging in political activity. Because of Frankfurter's medical expenses for his chronically ill wife, such activity would otherwise have been difficult for him, and the payments did allow Frankfurter to remain politically active. Whether they made him a "paid political lobbyist and lieutenant" [71] is another conjectural matter, about which we may be properly dubious. Many communications passed back and forth between Brandeis and Frankfurter; Brandeis' political positions apparently appeared in print as editorials in *The New Republic*, for which Frankfurter regularly wrote; Frankfurter served as Brandeis' representative at Zionist conferences; and Frankfurter apparently worked on legislation of interest to Brandeis, including legislation on subjects that had been before the Court or would come before it. Moreover, a number of Frankfurter's proteges (the "Happy Hot Dogs") went to work for the Roosevelt administration and could there espouse Brandeis' positions as transmitted to them from Frankfurter, but they were politically active in their own right and hardly acted solely as Frankfurter's agents.

All this may indicate no more than a commonality of interests between the two men or the professor's working on matters of joint concern as a result of Brandeis' intellectual and personal influence, rather than Frankfurter's taking direction from Brandeis. Frankfurter also worked on matters of primary interest to himself, including some—most notably FDR's Court-packing plan—on which the two disagreed. Thus Frankfurter "cannot be viewed solely as Brandeis's agent, in that he became involved in a wide circle of issues and causes célèbres on his own and in which the justice expressed no strong interest."[72]

The question also remains of whether—and to what extent—Brandeis' actions, even if it is clear they could not be ethically acceptable for a Supreme Court justice in the 1980s, exceeded the bounds of propriety. His strong (if behind-the-scenes) efforts to correct the injustice of the Sacco-Vanzetti conviction put him in a position of having to disqualify himself when attorneys brought the case to him and then to the Court. It is, however, at best a matter of interpretation as to whether Brandeis took specific positions on New Deal policies that would have hindered his performance as a justice. Brandeis did deal with major political figures through intermediaries, perhaps as a matter of personal style, perhaps as a smokescreen to conceal his activity. When cases involving statutes on which he had given advice came before the Court we are told that he did not recuse but instead took "only a very minimal role in the ultimate judicial decision,"[73] perhaps a result of his view of the cases rather than a function of efforts to conceal political activity.

Frankfurter's political activity also did not cease when he became a member of the Court and indeed it was more open than Brandeis's. He continued his interests in affecting the staffing of particular government departments, and also put considerable effort into the American war effort and into helping develop the international order for the postwar years. After World War II, and particularly as a result of President Roosevelt's death, Frankfurter's ability to affect the executive branch declined, and so did his efforts, although his involvement in the political battle can be seen in his continuing conflict, off the Court as well as on, with the equally strong-minded Justice Douglas.

If Brandeis tried to limit public knowledge of his extrajudicial political interests, Frankfurter used "strong arguments, indignantly put" to stifle criticism.[74] He seems to have been far more concerned about his activities than Brandeis had been. Did this result from different personalities, with Brandeis simply more sure of himself, or did Brandeis not believe he had committed improprieties? Or did standards change between Brandeis' accession to the Court during World War I and Frankfurter's arrival there over twenty years later? Whatever our evaluation, we should be careful not to read 1981 standards—on matters of political activity and recusal, justices' financial interests, or their participation in judicial selection—back into an earlier era.

The involvement of justices in nonjudicial governmental positions has been a source of continuous controversy because their absence from the Court can produce an evenly divided Court, or it can involve a justice in a matter that would later come before the Court.[75] When the Court's workload was not heavy, outside activity did not interfere with the Court's work. Both Chief Justice John Jay and Justice Oliver Ellsworth were involved in treaty negotiations, and Jay, who was also a candidate for governor of New York, served as secretary of state. In the nineteenth century, Melville Fuller and David Brewer arbitrated a boundary dispute between Venezuela and British Guiana, five justices served on the commission to help resolve the disputed 1876 Hayes-Tilden presidential election, and Stephen Field served on a commission to revise state laws in his native California. Earlier in this century, Charles Evans Hughes served on a commission to determine second-class postal rates.

More recent "calls" from the president to take on extra-Court jobs have encountered more objections because such jobs interfere with disposition of the Court's increased workload and because it has been feared that the Court's independence would be injured if it appeared that justices would readily serve at the president's bidding. During Franklin Roosevelt's presidency, Justice Reed chaired a committee to improve the civil service, Owen Roberts conducted an investigation of Pearl Harbor, and Robert Jackson was chief U.S. prosecutor at the War Crimes Trials in Nuremburg. Jackson's extended absence brought conflict within the Court as well as criticism for thrusting a judge into a simultaneous prosecutorial position and led Chief Justice Stone to turn down Roosevelt's requests to assume other tasks, such as investigating the nation's rubber supply. (During Taft's chief justiceship, Stone, a former attorney general, had been willing to serve on the Wickersham Commission investigating crime, but Taft had resisted.) Most recently, Chief Justice Warren, who generally stayed away from most extra-Court activity as a matter of propriety, headed the commission to investigate the assassination of President Kennedy, but he did so only after resisting President Johnson's request. Subsequent questions about the commission's report, including Senate Intelligence Committee revelations that the FBI and CIA withheld information, reinforce the case against this type of extrajudicial activity.

Justices' off-the-Court activity has included teaching in law school (Justice Story taught at Harvard and both the first Justice Harlan and Justice Brewer taught at the predecessor to George Washington Law School) and at seminars for judges. The "flap" over Justice Fortas's receiving $15,000, raised by friends, to teach a law school seminar, plus judges' increased public speaking, led the Judicial Conference in 1969 to adopt rules prohibiting the acceptance of fees unless the circuit judicial council approved after determining that the services to be rendered would be in the public interest, were justified by exceptional circumstances, and would not interfere with judicial duties. Such Conference rules, however, do not bind Supreme Court members, although several justices said they would follow them voluntarily.

Drafting legislation affecting the courts and commenting on matters directly affecting the Supreme Court are activities more directly related to the justices' regular tasks. Justice Willis Van Devanter drafted the Judiciary Act of 1915 modifying the Court's appellate jurisdiction and Justice McReynolds, helped by Justices Van Devanter and Day, drafted the 1916 Judiciary Act. Chief Justice Burger, instrumental in initiating examination of the need for a new level of national appellate court (see pages 47–49), and his colleagues all responded to the Hruska Commission's preliminary proposal for a National Court of Appeals. Many of the justices have since given speeches concerning problems of judicial overload, but whether any of them has been otherwise involved in legislative activity concerning such alterations in court structure is not known. Judges' lobbying is likely to be more informal and more covert, the more it departs from matters of judicial administration. There are expectations that lobbying even on such matters be discreet; however, certainly it could be—and has been—more open and explicit than on other issues because of the justices' expertise on judicial administration. Yet because the Judicial Conference provides an institutionalized mechanism for conveying judicial views to Congress, there is a view that judges should restrict their comments to such channels.

Perhaps coming to be more and more expected as a form of extra-Court activity—and certainly permissible under the Code of Judicial Conduct—are the Chief

Justice's comments about the "state of the judiciary," and proposals have been made that such an address be made to Congress. Chief Justices William Howard Taft and Charles Evans Hughes appeared at bar association meetings and at the American Law Institute (ALI) to discuss the "state of the judiciary." Such presentations were revived by Chief Justice Warren, who preferred the ALI as his forum because of ABA criticism of the Court's decisions. Chief Justice Burger, in addition to making numerous appearances to stress the importance of court administration, has delivered an annual State of the Judiciary address at ABA meetings. In those speeches he has called for restructuring of the circuits; for elimination of three-judge district courts and of federal diversity of citizenship jurisdiction; and for congressional *court impact statements* indicating how many more judges and supporting personnel would be needed to handle litigation under new statutes. More recently, he has urged Congress to limit federal judicial power over state criminal cases, a position consonant with his votes in the Court's decisions.[76]

Few take issue with the propriety of the Chief Justice's public discussion of the administration of justice, although some of his proposals and his statements that half the lawyers are inadequate as trial advocates have provoked disagreements. (The statement on advocates' incompetence did lead to formation of a Judicial Conference committee and then to adoption, in a number of federal judicial districts, of pilot programs of special requirements for admission to practice before the federal courts.) What *has* drawn particular criticism is the Chief Justice's general inaccessibility despite his many formal public appearances. Although he is a major public official and uses that position as the basis for statements on major (judicial) policy issues, Chief Justice Burger apparently does not believe in making himself available to the press. For many years, he would not allow his addresses to the ABA to be televised. After at first acceding to Burger's wishes, only later did the ABA decide that he would not be allowed to control media coverage of *their* activities, and the Chief Justice adjusted his position, which he has tried to justify in terms of a First Amendment "right to be left alone."[77]

In December 1981, after John Ehrlichman's allegations of contacts between Burger and President Nixon about particular cases, when a CBS News reporter attempted to ask the Chief Justice for some response to the charge, Burger, ignoring the reporter, kept walking. When the reporter sought to question the Chief Justice as the latter got into an elevator, Burger pushed the television camera off the cameraman's shoulder. Whether or not provoked, the Chief Justice's resistance to responding to an important allegation was clear. It is also inconsistent with his lack of hesitancy to comment about major policy issues on which he may have to rule, for example, his negative—indeed, highly critical—comments about the media and about television in the courtroom. (He does not withdraw from cases related to such matters about which he has so directly and negatively commented.)

Chief Justice Burger is not, however, the only justice who has gone beyond statements concerning the judiciary to speak out on matters of general public policy, including policy issues before the Court. Before the Court's traditions were established, when justices were active participants in partisan activity, they spoke openly on partisan subjects. From 1810 to the Civil War, judges' extra-Court speeches and public letters were less partisan. Perhaps to help repair the damage from the *Dred Scott* case, they became even more quiet after the Civil War, but at the end of the nineteenth century, when the Court's prestige again improved, there was an "explosion" of speeches and writing. After the Depression, the level of oratory again fell and has generally remained low, but there are exceptions—perhaps the most extensive being Justice Douglas's book writing and statements on conservation and the environment.

Within the last few years, we have seen interviews with Justice Stewart, well before he left the Court, and Justice Blackmun. Although Justice Stewart's comments were general in nature and uncontroversial in their support of upholding the Constitution, Justice Blackmun talked of relations among the justices and alignments within the Court, and particularly about his relationship with the Chief Justice.[78] There has also been commentary on specific Court cases by some of the justices. In particular, in the aftermath of *Gannett v. DePasquale,* a decision that judges could close *pretrial proceedings* but where the Court's opinion talked of closing *trials,* Justices Stevens, Powell, and Blackmun all made public comments about the ruling's ambiguity and the need to clarify matters. Going further, Justice Marshall, speaking at the Second Circuit Judicial Conference in 1979, in open criticism of his colleagues, applauded important Second Circuit civil liberties rulings—on jail conditions for pretrial detainees and on access to newscasters' thoughts in libel cases—which Marshall's Supreme Court colleagues had reversed.[79] Despite these remarks and the end-of-nineteenth-century outpouring, there seems to have been no relation between the level of off-Court commentary by the justices and either the Court's prestige, the policy direction of its decisions, or the judges' own liberal or conservative tendencies.[80]

NOTES

1. The argument is that of S. Sidney Ulmer and John Alan Stookey, "How Is the Ox Being Gored: Toward a Theory of Docket Style and Innovation in the U.S. Supreme Court," *University of Toledo Law Review* 7 (Fall 1975):1–28.
2. Stephen C. Halpern and Kenneth N. Vines, "Institutional Disunity, The Judges' Bill and the Role of the U.S. Supreme Court," *Western Political Quarterly* 30 (Fall 1977):471–483.
3. See Thomas B. Marvell, *Appellate Courts and Lawyers: Information Gathering in the Adversary System* (Westport, Conn.: Greenwood Press, 1978), pp. 106–116.
4. The phrase is that of William Haltom, in a comment at the meetings of the American Political Science Association, 1982.
5. *Nixon v. Fitzgerald,* 102 S.Ct. 2690 at 2712 (1982).
6. Justice Powell, in the *Bakke* case, 438 U.S. 265 at 299 (1978), quoting Cox, *The Role of the Supreme Court in American Government* (1976), p. 114.
7. Alexander Bickel, *The Least Dangerous Branch* (Indianapolis: Bobbs-Merrill, 1962), p. 58.
8. Herbert Wechsler, "Toward Neutral Principles of Constitutional Law," *Harvard Law Review* 73 (November 1959):19, 11.

9. Bickel, *The Least Dangerous Branch*, p. 59. See also Bickel, "The Supreme Court's 1960 Term, Foreword: The Passive Virtues," *Harvard Law Review* 75 (November 1961):40–79.
10. *Thomas v. Washington Gas Light Co.*, 448 U.S. 261 at 273 (1980) (Justice Stevens).
11. Walter F. Murphy, *Elements of Judicial Strategy*, p. 204.
12. The first part of Justice Blackmun's opinion contains a history of baseball, "Casey at the Bat," and a list of Blackmun's favorite players, from which he may have omitted at least one. See Woodward and Armstrong, *The Brethren*, pp. 189–192. The second part of the opinion begins with Flood's batting and fielding averages. At the end of the opinion, there is the following notation: "The Chief Justice and Mr. Justice White join in the judgment of the Court, and in all but Part I of the Court's opinion." Did they have no sense of humor? Don't they like baseball (White played professional football)? Or did they have a different "All Star Team"?
13. The three cases are *Food Employees v. Logan Valley Plaza*, 395 U.S. 575 (1968); *Lloyd Corp. v. Tanner*, 407 U.S. 551 (1972); and *Hudgens v. National Labor Relations Board*, 424 U.S. 507 (1976).
14. *National League of Cities v. Usery*, 426 U.S. 833 (1976), overruling *Maryland v. Wirtz*, 392 U.S. 183 (1968).
15. *Florida Department of Health v. Florida Nursing Home*, 450 U.S. 147 at 154 (1981).
16. *Bellotti v. Baird*, 443 U.S. 622 at 652–653 (1979). The earlier case was *Planned Parenthood of Central Missouri v. Danforth*, 428 U.S. 52 (1976).
17. David Danelski, "Explorations of Some Causes and Consequences of Conflict and its Resolution in the Supreme Court," paper presented at American Political Science Association, 1982, p. 42.
18. Martin Shapiro, "Stability and Change in Judicial Decision-Making: Incrementalism or Stare Decisis?" *Law in Transition Quarterly* 2 (Summer 1965):155.
19. Fred Graham, *The Self-Inflicted Wound* (New York: Macmillan, 1970), p. 171.
20. See *Manual Enterprises v. Day*, 370 U.S. 478 (1962) (patent offensiveness); *Jacobellis v. Ohio*, 378 U.S. 194 (1964) (national standard); *Memoirs v. Massachusetts*, 383 U.S. 413 (1966) (utterly without redeeming social importance); *Ginzberg v. United States*, 383 U.S. 463 (1966) (advertising); *Mishkin v. New York*, 383 U.S. 502 (1966) (material aimed at specific group).
21. *Rice v. Sioux City Memorial Cemetery*, 349 U.S. 71 (1955); *Jackson v. Alabama*, 348 U.S. 888 (1954); Anthony D'Amato and Robert O'Neil, *The Judiciary and Vietnam* (New York: St. Martin's Press, 1972). Full discussion of this point and most of the argument in this section can be found in Stephen L. Wasby, Anthony A. D'Amato, and Rosemary Metrailer, *Desegregation from Brown to Alexander: An Exploration of Supreme Court Strategies* (Carbondale, Ill.: Southern Illinois University Press, 1977).
22. S. Sidney Ulmer, "Parabolic Support for Civil Liberties," *Florida State University Law Review* 1 (Winter 1973):149.
23. Murphy, *Elements of Judicial Strategy*, p. 193. Murphy's discussion of strategy remains the best available.
24. S. Sidney Ulmer, "Earl Warren and the Brown Decision," *Journal of Politics* 33 (August 1971):697.
25. Alpheus Thomas Mason, *Harlan Fiske Stone: Pillar of the Law* (New York: Viking Press, 1956), pp. 614–615; Chief Justice Burger, 409 U.S. xxxv at xvi (1972).
26. *Committee for Public Education v. Regan*, 444 U.S. 646 at 665 (1980).
27. *Elkins v. United States*, 364 U.S. 206 (1960) (search); *Gregg v. Georgia*, 428 U.S. 153 at

180 (1976) and *Woodson v. North Carolina*, 428 U.S. 280 at 299 (1976) (death penalty); *Linkletter v. Walker*, 381 U.S. 618 (1965) (*Mapp* retroactivity).

28. G. Gregory Fahlund, "Retroactivity and the Warren Court: The Strategy of a Revolution," *Journal of Politics* 35 (August 1973):570–593.
29. Gregory A. Caldeira, "The United States Supreme Court and Criminal Cases, 1935–1976: Alternative Models of Agenda Building," *British Journal of Political Science* 2 (1981):461; in italics in original. For an examination of the effect of public opinion on federal district court rulings in a particular policy area, see Beverly B. Cook, "Public Opinion and Federal Judicial Policy," *American Journal of Political Science* 21 (August 1977):567–600, concerning sentencing for draft resistance and showing very high correlations between public opinion and sentences.
30. See Dennis J. Hutchinson, "Unanimity and Desegregation: Decision-making in the Supreme Court, 1948–1958," *Georgetown Law Journal* 68 (October 1979):87.
31. *Piper Aircraft v. Reyno*, 102 S.Ct. 252 at 261 n. 12 (1981) (Justice Marshall).
32. S. Sidney Ulmer, "Issue Fluidity in the U.S. Supreme Court: A Conceptual Analysis," in *Supreme Court Activism and Restraint*, eds. Stephen C. Halpern and Charles M. Lamb, p. 322.
33. J. Woodford Howard, "The Fluidity of Judicial Choice," *American Political Science Review* 62 (March 1968):49–50.
34. Murphy, pp. 4–5.
35. See Note, "State Court Evasion of United States Supreme Court Mandates," *Yale Law Journal* 36 (1947):574–583, and Jerry K. Beatty, "State Court Evasion of United States Supreme Court Mandates During the Last Decade of the Warren Court," *Valparaiso University Law Review* 6 (Spring 1972):260–285.
36. Fehrenbacher, *The Dred Scott Case*, pp. 4–5, 442–443.
37. Ibid., p. 232.
38. For an extended treatment, see Howard Dean, *Judicial Review and Democracy* (New York: Random House, 1966).
39. For example, see the regulation of insurance: *United States v. South-Eastern Underwriters Association*, 322 U.S. 533 (1944) (interstate insurance a form of commerce); the passage of the McCarran-Ferguson Act confirming state authority to regulate insurance; and *Prudential Insurance Co. v. Benjamin*, 328 U.S. 408 (1946), sustaining the act.
40. Reversing, respectively, *Chisholm v. Georgia*, 2 Dall. 419 (1793); *Pollack v. Farmers Loan & Trust Co.*, 157 U.S. 429 (1895); *Oregon v. Mitchell*, 400 U.S. 112 (1970); and *Dred Scott v. Sanford*, 19 How. 393 (1857).
41. *Plyler v. Doe*, 102 S.Ct. 2382 at 2414 (1982).
42. *Hunter v. Erickson*, 393 U.S. 385 (1969) (housing ordinances); *Washington v. Seattle School District No. 1*, 102 S.Ct. 3187 (1982) (busing).
43. John Hart Ely, *Democracy and Distrust: A Theory of Judicial Review* (Cambridge, Mass.: Harvard University Press, 1980), p. 181.
44. Ibid., pp. 77, 100–101, 117.
45. Jesse Choper, *Judicial Review and the National Political Process* (Chicago: University of Chicago Press, 1980), p. 68.
46. Ibid., p. 2.
47. Ibid., pp. 382–383, 263, 307.
48. Robert Dahl, *Democracy in the United States* (Chicago: Rand McNally, 1972), pp. 201–202. The original statement was Dahl, "Decision-Making in a Democracy: The Supreme Court as a National Policy-Maker," *Journal of Public Law* 7 (Fall 1957):279–295.

49. David Adamany, "Legitimacy, Realigning Elections, and the Supreme Court," *Wisconsin Law Review* 1973:825, 822.
50. Jonathan D. Casper, "The Supreme Court and National Policy Making," *American Political Science Review* 70 (March 1976):3.
51. Charles M. Lamb, "Judicial Restraint on the Supreme Court," in *Supreme Court Activism and Restraint*, eds. Halpern and Lamb, pp. 9, 12.
52. *Plyler v. Doe*, 102 S.Ct. at 2408 (1982).
53. Daniel Novak, "Economic Activism and Restraint," in *Supreme Court Activism and Restraint*, eds. Halpern and Lamb, pp. 78–79.
54. Bradley C. Canon, "A Framework for the Analysis of Judicial Activism," in *Supreme Court Activism and Restraint*, eds. Halpern and Lamb, pp. 386–387, 412. See also Canon, "Defining the Dimensions of Judicial Activism," *Judicature* 66 (December–January 1983):236–247.
55. James Simon, *In His Own Image: The Supreme Court in Richard Nixon's America* (New York: David McKay, 1973), p. 227.
56. *Rummel v. Estelle*, 445 U.S. 263 at 275, 276 (1980). However, three years later the Court overturned a life sentence without the possibility of parole for a multiple offender. *Solem v. Helm* 103 S.Ct. 3001 (1983).
57. *United States v. Goodwin*, 102 S.Ct. 2485 at 2493 (1982).
58. *Jones v. North Carolina Prisoners' Labor Union*, 433 U.S. 119 at 125 (1977); *Bell v. Wolfish*, 441 U.S. 520 at 548 (1979), citing *Jones; Youngberg v. Romeo*, 102 S.Ct. 2452 at 2462 (1982).
59. *United States v. Butler*, 297 U.S. 1 at 79 (1936).
60. *Jackson v. Virginia*, 443 U.S. 307 at 328 (1979).
61. Harold J. Spaeth and Stuart H. Teger, "Activism and Restraint: A Cloak for the Justices' Policy Preferences," in *Supreme Court Activism and Restraint*, eds. Halpern and Lamb, p. 296.
62. Joel B. Grossman, "Role-Playing and the Analysis of Judicial Behavior: The Case of Mr. Justice Frankfurter," *Journal of Public Law* 11 (1962):285–309. See also Harold J. Spaeth, "The Judicial Restraint of Mr. Justice Frankfurter—Myth or Reality," *Midwest Journal of Political Science* 8 (February 1964):22–38.
63. Stephen C. Halpern, "On the Imperial Judiciary and Comparative Institutional Development and Power in America," in *Supreme Court Activism and Restraint*, eds. Halpern and Lamb, p. 225.
64. *Coker v. Georgia*, 433 U.S. 584 at 619 (1977) (Chief Justice Burger, dissenting); *In Re Primus*, 436 U.S. 412 at 441 (1978) (Justice Rehnquist, dissenting).
65. *Jackson v. Virginia*, 443 U.S. 307 at 337 (1979) (dissenting).
66. John C. Schmidhauser, *The Supreme Court as Final Arbiter in Federal-State Relations, 1789–1957* (Chapel Hill, N.C.: University of North Carolina Press, 1958).
67. *Foremost Insurance Co. v. Richardson*, 102 S.Ct. 2654 at 2660 (1982).
68. Spaeth and Teger, pp. 283, 296; data at pp. 288–294.
69. Bruce Allen Murphy, *The Brandeis/Frankfurter Connection: The Secret Political Activities of Two Supreme Court Justices* (New York: Oxford University Press, 1982), p. 7.
70. Ibid., p. 352.
71. Ibid., p. 10. This is one of several instances in which serious criticism has been raised about Murphy's use of source material and interpretations and inferences drawn from those materials; another is the question of judicial impropriety by Brandeis, discussed below. Murphy's account should thus be approached with caution. See, for example,

Robert Cover, "The Framing of Justice Brandeis," *The New Republic*, May 5, 1982: 17–21, and David J. Danelski, Review, *Harvard Law Review* 96 (November 1982): 312–330.

72. Murphy, p. 43.
73. Ibid., p. 55.
74. Ibid., p. 253.
75. Russell Wheeler, "Extra-Judicial Activities of the Early Supreme Court," *Supreme Court Review 1973*, ed. Philip Kurland (Chicago: University of Chicago Press, 1973), pp. 122–158.
76. See, for example, Warren E. Burger, "Annual Report to the American Bar Association by the Chief Justice of the United States," *American Bar Association Journal* 67 (March 1981):290–293, and "Isn't There a Better Way?", *American Bar Association Journal* 68 (March 1982):274–277. See also Arthur R. Landever, "Chief Justice Burger and Extra-Case Activism," *Journal of Public Law* 20 (1971):523–541.
77. Lyle Denniston, "Chief Justice Shuns TV Because He Wants 'To Be Left Alone,'" *Washington Star*, November 12, 1979.
78. Kingsbury Smith, "Supreme Court doing its job with 'honesty and integrity'," *Boston Herald American*, April 30, 1979; John A. Jenkins, "A Candid Talk with Justice Blackmun," *The New York Times Magazine*, February 20, 1983:20–24 ff.
79. "Justice Marshall: Dissenter Speaks Out," *National Law Journal*, June 11, 1979, p. 21.
80. Alan F. Westin, "Out-of-Court Commentary by United States Supreme Court Justices, 1789–1962: Of Free Speech and Judicial Lockjaw," in *An Autobiography of the Supreme Court: Off-the-Bench Commentary by the Justices* (New York: Macmillan, 1963), pp. 28–29.

Chapter 9

The Supreme Court and the Other Branches: Judicial Review and Response

The central aspect of judicial review is the invalidation by judges of acts of the other branches of government. The Supreme Court's judicial review of state action was crucial in establishing the authority of national government. However, in its more recent history the nation has seen greater friction between the Supreme Court on the one hand and both Congress and the president on the other. Judicial invalidation of the New Deal and FDR's effort at "Court-packing" was the principal but not only example of such friction. In this chapter, to place such incidents in context, we look at the Court's exercise of judicial review of acts of Congress, the president, and the regulatory agencies. First, we examine the Supreme Court's overall treatment of congressional actions. This is followed by an analysis of Congress's responses to those decisions and to other controverted Court rulings. We then turn to the Supreme Court's rulings on the presidency, with attention to incidents beyond the New Deal and particularly to the substantial litigation involving the Nixon administration, and finally to judicial rulings on regulatory agency decisions.

JUDICIAL REVIEW: CONGRESS AND ITS RESPONSE

Judicial Review of Congress' Acts

Despite the impression left by the conflict between President Franklin Roosevelt and the Hughes Court, neither before that time nor after has the Court frequently struck down congressional acts. Prior to the Civil War, decisions invalidating acts of Congress "occurred on an episodic, nonsystematic basis." Over the long run, "periods of aggressiveness toward Congress have not occurred on a very regular basis." Swings from intervention to passivity have, however, grown larger over time, in proportion to increases in the frequency of the exercise of judicial review. There has also been a "very high correlation" between invalidation of congressional acts and those of state legislatures. Interestingly, the greatest judicial activity concerning state legislation occurred not during Warren Court activity concerning civil liberties but early in the twentieth century as part of judicial resistance to state economic regulation.[1] Judicial review has also been "significantly shaped by such political considerations as the degree of party difference between Congress and the Court, the nature of the party in power in the national government, and the party affiliations of the individual judges deciding specific cases."[2] Reexamination of judicial review during periods of partisan realignment has, however, led to the finding that, with the New Deal period eliminated because of the extremely high rate at which the Supreme Court invalidated recent legislation, the Court was actually more likely to invalidate a law in periods of partisan stability than during partisan shift.[3]

Just as judicial review of state legislative acts has continued past midcentury, so the Court has continued since 1937, particularly after 1950, to invalidate a number of federal statutes. The Warren Court used prohibitions against bills of attainder (legislative punishment without trial) and cruel and unusual punishment to invalidate removal of a person's U.S. citizenship for such acts as desertion from the military or remaining abroad to avoid military service, and the Court prohibited courts-martial of civilians in a number of circumstances as well as of service personnel for offenses not service-connected.[4] Restrictions on the rights of Communist Party members were also struck down. The Fifth Amendment was used to void registration provisions that forced people to incriminate themselves under other federal laws or state law.[5] Social Security Act durational residence requirements for welfare benefits were set aside in *Shapiro v. Thompson* as an interference with the right to travel.

Burger Court acts of national judicial review, which at times occurred through summary affirmance of lower court decisions, were scattered across a wide range of policy areas. These included welfare (limits on who could receive food stamps and discrimination in benefits on the basis of gender and illegitimacy) and free speech (Post Office methods for screening obscenity, a ban on demonstrations on U.S. Capitol grounds, and a ban on displaying the flag on the grounds of the Supreme Court itself).[6] Interference with freedom of speech was also the basis, in *Buckley v. Valeo* (1976), for voiding Federal Election Campaign Act limits on individuals' expenditures on behalf of candidates of their choice. The Burger Court's invalidation of the extension of the minimum wage law to state and local government employees, in *National League of Cities v. Usery* (1976) was its most controversial exercise of national judicial review because it was the first time since FDR's 1937 battle with the Court that congressional regulatory legislation based on the Commerce Clause had been invalidated; in 1983, the Court, upholding application of the Age Discrimination in Employment Act (ADEA) to state employees, limited the reach of the *National League of Cities* ruling *(E.E.O.C. v. Wyoming).*

One of the most sweeping instances of judicial review of legislative action came in 1983, when the Court invalidated the *legislative veto,* a major point of friction between president and Congress, and thus affected both the trend toward increased presidential power and the countertrend of increased assertion of congressional authority. Under legislative veto provisions, enacted as part of over 200 statutes, executive branch actions can be rejected by a resolution of one house of Congress (the "one-house veto") or by a concurrent resolution passed by both Senate and House of Representatives. Some legislative veto provisions limit the president's authority to use American troops overseas (War Powers Act of 1973), reorganize the executive branch, or defer expenditure of funds appropriated by Congress (Budget and Impoundment Act of 1974). Many concern foreign policy matters such as foreign trade, international development, and export of defense technology; others allow Congress to reject regulations promulgated by agencies such as the Federal Trade Commission or the Department of Education.

The constitutional objection to legislative vetos is that they allow Congress to take legislative action not subject to presidential veto. If Congress could overturn executive action only by passing a new law, the president could veto the legislative ban and that veto could be overridden only by a two-thirds vote of both houses. One counterargument has been that the president has accepted legislative veto provisions in approving the statutes containing them. In 1983, the Supreme Court ruled that legislative vetos violate the separation of powers doctrine and the Constitution's specific provisions concerning enactment of legislation, including the requirement that legislation must be adopted by both houses of Congress *(Immigration and Naturalization Service v. Chadha).* Availability of the legislative veto allowed Congress to give the president broad authority while retaining controls over exercise of that authority; elimination of the legislative veto means that to limit the president's power or to overturn regulatory actions, Congress will have to legislate specific limits directly.

In addition to invalidating legislation Congress has enacted, the Court has also ruled on internal congressional matters, such as committee treatment of witnesses and Congress' refusal to seat an elected representative. In one of its most important internal security rulings, *Watkins v. United States,* the Warren Court invalidated a contempt citation resulting from a witness's refusal to answer the House Un-American Activities Committee's questions because the relationship between the questions and the committee's investigation had not been made clear; in his opinion for the Court, the Chief Justice severely criticized both the committee and Congress for failing to control the committee's activities.

In setting aside Congress's refusal to seat Representative Adam Clayton Powell—held not to be a "political question"—the Court ruled that the Constitution's Speech and Debate Clause (Art. I, Sec. 6), which provides immunity for legislators' official activities, prevented a suit against members of Congress for their votes not to seat Powell but not against Congress's employees. In the *Gravel* case (1972), the Court said that a grand jury could not question a senator's legislative assistant about activities related to the senator's legislative work, but also said that the act of arranging to have a private company publish the Pentagon Papers was *not* legislative activity and thus the senator's assistant, and probably the senator himself, could be questioned about that subject. The *Gravel* decision and the Court's holding in *United States v. Brewster* that acceptance of a bribe—by Senator Daniel Brewster (D–Md.)—was not part of a legislator's official duties and thus could properly be the basis for an indictment not only limited the meaning of "legislative activity" but also restricted the effect of an earlier ruling that a congressman's speech on the floor of the House could not be used against him in a bribery case. Going even further, the Court then held in *Doe v. McMillan* that circulation outside Congress of a House committee report that named specific school children in connection with an investigation of the District of Columbia schools was not part of the legislative process and could be the basis for an injunction.

The Court strengthened the protections of the Speech and Debate Clause when it said in the *Helstoski* case (1979) that evidence of a representative's legislative acts could not be used in a prosecution of that representative for accepting a bribe, nor had the legislator waived the clause's protection by testifying before the grand jury and voluntarily producing legislative documents. At the same time, in a case stemming from Senator William Proxmire's "Golden Fleece Awards" for what he felt were unnecessary expenditures, the Court, further limiting what constitutes a "legislative" act, ruled in *Hutchinson v. Proxmire* (1974) that senators and their assistants were not protected from libel suits for transmitting allegedly defamatory material in press releases.

Decisions invalidating acts of Congress or questioning Congress' internal procedures are most likely to cause friction between the Court and Congress. However, most of the Court's decisions affecting Congress involve statutory interpretation—"supplementary lawmaking" as the courts interpret, apply, and flesh out statutes—with the Court emphasizing different modes of statutory interpretation in different policy areas, depending on the number, specificity, and complexity of statutes in the policy area.[7] Statutory interpretation is judicial policymaking although not as explicit as when the Court rules in constitutional cases. Statutory interpretation is not easy work because the least clear statutes are more likely to be litigated, and justices do not agree as to how to interpret statutes. They talk of turning first to a statute's "plain meaning" but must often resort to unclear legislative materials (or *legislative history*) in a search for Congress' intent.

A statutory interpretation question frequently occupying the Court in recent years is who may bring a lawsuit to enforce a statute when Congress has failed to be explicit about the matter. The Court must then determine whether a "private cause of action" is implied, particularly in civil rights statutes, because of executive underenforcement of those statutes. The Court has allowed some private causes of action, for example, against a private university for sex discrimination under Title IX of the Education Amendments of 1972 (*Cannon v. University of Chicago,* 1979). Such action is usually met with the complaint that Congress, not the Court, ought to be making the determination. For example, Justice Powell charged in the Title IX case that the Court violated the separation of powers by allowing such suits: "When Congress chooses not to provide a private civil remedy, federal courts should not assume the legislative role of creating such a remedy and thereby enlarge their jurisdiction."

In the course of statutory interpretation, the Court may explicitly suggest what Congress must do to make a statute valid. Overturning a law regulating grain futures transactions, Justice Taft said that Congress could not regulate the transactions unless it saw them as directly interfering with interstate commerce. Congress then placed such an explicit declaration in the Grain Futures Act, which the Court upheld. Even more indicative of the Court's influence are statutes into which Congress has written language the Court has already approved. In enacting the surveillance provisions of the Omnibus Crime Control and Safe Streets Act of 1968, Congress used procedures for wiretapping under a warrant spelled out by the Court in *Berger v. New York.* Similarly, when the Court ruled in *McCarty v. McCarty* (1982) that property settlements in divorces could not include military pensions, but said that Congress could provide otherwise if former spouses were to receive more protection, both houses of Congress took the Court up on the invitation.

At other times, the Court engages in the "trap pass," interpreting a statute so rigidly that the statute looks ridiculous, in the hope that Congress will be provoked to change the law.[8] A recent example is *Tennessee Valley Authority v. Hill,* a ruling that under environmental protection law, a major dam, largely constructed but still incomplete, would have to be stopped to protect the snail darter fish. Congress then both specifically provided for completion of the dam *and* altered the statute to provide procedural flexibility—probably exactly what the Court had in mind. Of course, not all clear statements by the Court are "trap passes." Many are simply a result of the justices carrying out their function of giving particularity to general statutory provisions. As Justice Stevens recently observed about antitrust law, "Given its generality, our enforcement of the Sherman Act has required the Court to provide much of its substantive content. . . . By articulating the rules of law with some clarity and by adhering to rules that are justified in their general application," the Court would provide Congress with a clearer target and would thus "enhance the legislative prerogative to amend the law"; Congress could also provide any exceptions to the general rules adopted by the Court.[9]

Congressional Response

What has Congress' response been to judicial review and statutory interpretation? "Supreme Court abrogations of majority-sponsored activities have been the primary source of retaliation, real and seriously threatened, by the national political branches . . . against the federal judiciary."[10] However, as time has passed, there have been fewer broad-gauge congressional attacks on the Court. Action has usually been directed to particular rulings or sets of rulings. Even the efforts of the early 1980s to restrict federal courts' or the Supreme Court's jurisdiction stem primarily from the Court's "social issue" rulings—on school prayer, school desegregation, and abortion. In general, conflict between Congress and Court has been more likely to arise on matters where "constitutional language is unclear and . . . on which public sentiment has been largely unsettled"; where interest groups see vital interests at stake; and where the Court has threatened Congress's authority.[11] Action reversing the Court has, at least until the present, occurred more frequently in the economic sphere than in the civil liberties domain, undoubtedly a reflection of the focus of the Court's caseload. Economic regulation issues were involved in four of seven periods (excluding the present one) in which proposals to curb the Court were frequent, but civil liberties issues were involved in only two such periods. Moreover, the presence of intensely held economic or civil libertarian interests meant less success for Court-curbing than occurred in the areas of separation of powers or federalism, where Congress could take into account policy factors outside the Court's concern.[12]

There have also been important reversals with respect to issues of federal-state relations, although they tend to be quite case-specific. Congress acted to reverse the Court's ruling that the offshore oil lands belonged to the national goverment, passing "quitclaim" legislation giving the lands to the states,[13] and Congress kept state regulation of insurance in force when the Court held in the *South-Eastern Underwriters* case that insurance was part of interstate commerce and thus subject to national regulation. In both instances, the Court then sustained Congress' reversal action, explicitly acknowledging Congress' intent to overturn the Court's initial decisions. At times Congress has also allowed the states to act after the Court has said the federal government had "preempted" an area and prevented state regulation. For example, when the Court said a state could not regulate interstate labor disputes even in the absence of National Labor Relations Board action, Congress rewrote the law to allow such state activity.[14]

Negative congressional reaction to the Court's rulings has taken a wide variety of forms: criticism, attempts to overrule the Court by amending the Constitution or by limiting the Court's appellate jurisdiction, and refusal to provide compensation required by the Court's rulings. The latter occurred in the Yazoo land fraud case (*Fletcher v. Peck*) and much more recently after the Court had struck down, as a bill of attainder, an appropriations bill rider stipulating that three alleged subversives not be paid (*United States v. Lovett*, 1946). In addition, there have been proposals for such basic structural change as requiring that federal or state laws could be declared invalid only by a vote of at least seven justices, allowing Congress to override declarations that a federal or state law was constitutionally invalid, or limiting justices' tenure. Negative reaction is also evident in reluctance or refusal to provide additional judges for the federal courts or to increase the justices' salaries, in attempts to impeach justices—as in the unsuccessful effort to remove Justice Douglas—and in resistance to confirming presidential nominees to the Court.

The Eleventh, Sixteenth, and Twenty-sixth Amendments, as well as the post–Civil

War amendments on slavery and the status of blacks, were passed to override Court decisions. After the Court limited Congress' power to regulate the use of child labor either through the power over interstate commerce (*Hammer v. Dagenhart*, 1918) or taxation (*Bailey v. Drexel Furniture*, 1922), Congress submitted for ratification a constitutional amendment prohibiting child labor. The Court's post-1937 shift, which included upholding the Fair Labor Standards (minimum wage) Act with its child labor provisions in *United States v. Darby* (1941), eliminated the need for the amendment, still open to ratification because it contains no termination date (unlike later amendments, including the ERA).

Many more such efforts have also failed. These include attempts in the 1960s to overturn reapportionment and school prayer rulings, the latter effort renewed after 1980 in the drive to allow "voluntary" prayer in the schools. Continuous activity to limit school desegregation through constitutional amendment is part of a larger set of legislative efforts aimed at achieving that goal, including limits on federal judges' power to order busing and prohibitions on executive branch initiation of desegregation. Similarly, extensive effort to repeal the Court's 1973 abortion ruling through constitutional amendment—such as defining when life begins and turning over abortion policy to the states—is only one aspect of legislative action aimed at limiting abortions. Included are a statutory ban on funding under the Foreign Assistance Act for abortion as a method of family planning; a ban on fetal research; a prohibition on Legal Services attorneys' handling abortion-related cases; a "conscience clause" in the Hill-Burton Act declaring that no federal funds shall be denied to public or private hospitals that refuse on the basis of religious or moral beliefs to perform abortions or sterilizations; and, perhaps best known, the Hyde Amendment—a ban on Medicaid payments for abortions except in very limited circumstances, upheld by the Court itself in *Harris v. McRae*.

Attempts to limit the Court's jurisdiction have been less successful than efforts to overturn rulings by amending the Constitution. Only once has Congress successfully removed some of the Court's appellate jurisdiction. In the aftermath of the Civil War, the Reconstruction Congress, at odds with President Andrew Johnson and fearful of the Court's potential action concerning questionable detentions of citizens, passed a law removing the Court's jurisdiction over cases arising under the Habeas Corpus Act. The Court complied, in *Ex parte McCardle*, dismissing a case already argued. However, the Court examined congressional action before complying, and its compliance did not foreclose other Court actions to protect the individual. Moreover, when Congress removed the Court's jurisdiction in claims cases involving proof of former Confederate soldiers' present loyalty—ordering the Court to treat acceptance of a presidential pardon as proof of aid to the Confederacy but to ignore the pardon in determining loyalty—the Court struck down the limitation in *United States v. Klein* (1872). That case is said to stand for the proposition that Congress may not withdraw jurisdiction when the intent is to dictate a specific result, as some current congressional efforts are thought to do.

There is little question about Congress' power to withdraw jurisdiction over the lower federal courts, which Congress established, and the Supreme Court has sustained limited withdrawals of such jurisdiction, for example, upholding withdrawal of the power to issue injunctions in labor disputes (the Norris-LaGuardia Act) and approving Emergency Price Control Act procedures under which review of the Price Administrator's actions was routed through the Emergency Court of Appeals, which was deprived of the power to grant injunctions.[15] Removal of *all* federal court jurisdiction, however, like removal of the Supreme Court's appellate jurisdiction, leaves no final authority to resolve disputes over the affected subjects. It thus leaves standing divergent interpretations of constitutional provisions by the lower courts, either state (if all federal jurisdiction is removed) or both federal and state (if only Supreme Court appellate jurisdiction is withdrawn), without a judicial body to reconcile them. No definitive answer is now available to the question of whether such removal of authority, regardless of the subject matter or the effect of such action, is constitutional; and *McCardle*, the most relevant case, does not provide such an answer.

The late 1950s saw a serious attempt by Congress to restrict the Court's jurisdiction. Bills were introduced aimed at the Court's rulings on internal security matters such as legislative investigations, the executive's loyalty-security programs, state control of teachers and admission of lawyers to the practice of law, and federal preemption of state internal subversion legislation. None of these bills passed, although the Senate vote was very close (a one-vote margin) and the Court appeared to retreat in the face of the attack.[16]

The growth of conservatism, reflected in Ronald Reagan's election as president and particularly in Republican control of the Senate in 1980, led to another substantial attack on the Court's appellate jurisdiction and on all federal court jurisdiction over subjects like school busing, school prayer, and abortion. That effort was made difficult when President Reagan's attorney general argued that Congress cannot limit the Court's jurisdiction when the effect is to "intrude upon the core functions of the Supreme Court as an independent and equal branch in our system of separation of powers." However, the "core functions" language is not found In Article III, and the attorney general did approve a bill to limit judicial power over school busing because it would only limit particular federal judicial remedies.

Perhaps because of the lack of consensus about Congress' authority, most opponents of the jurisdiction-limiting bills—including some people who do not doubt Congress' power and who strongly oppose the rulings at which the legislation is aimed—attacked the legislation for violating the Constitution's spirit as well as for being unwise. For example, eliminating Supreme Court review while "punishing" the Court for disliked rulings would be short-sighted because it would leave those precedents in place and would eliminate the possibility that the Court itself, perhaps with new appointees, would rectify its "errors" by modifying or overruling them.[17] Opposition to limitations of jurisdiction has been voiced by legal scholars, the ABA, and the Conference of State Chief Justices; the last pointed out that limitations on Supreme Court jurisdiction seem premised on the idea that state judges will not honor the national Constitution, as the Supremacy Clause requires them to do. (In 1958, by contrast, the then far more conservative state chief justices strongly criticized the Supreme Court's internal security decisions, some of which restricted state authority to deal with subversion, as activist interference with states' rights.) None of the strong efforts by congressional (and particularly Senate) conservatives in 1982 prevailed. The press of budget concerns delayed "social issue" legislation until late in the session, President Reagan's support for the bills was not strong, and Senate liberals' concerted filibusters led to the leadership putting the issue aside. (In 1983, the first of the constitutional amendments to come to a vote was defeated in the Senate.)

Congressional efforts to rewrite or reenact statutes, although affecting only a small proportion of the Court's rulings, have been far more frequent, and far more successful, than efforts either to amend the Constitution or to limit the Court's jurisdiction.[18] Between 1944 and 1960, the Court's actions were revised 50 times. Among the decisions altered were 34 instances in which the Court overturned 60 statutes.[19] Among examples of congressional action to counter action by the Court are protection, provided in the Longshoresmen's and Harbor Workers' Compensation Act (1927), for longshoremen working on vessels and on gangplanks between the vessels and piers, and antitrust immunity for efforts to control activities of nonsigners of "fair trade" agreements, provided after the 1951 *Schwegmann Brothers* ruling that there was no such immunity.

Sponsors of bills introduced in reaction to Supreme Court rulings vary in their aims. Few bills are aimed at writing the judicial decision into law. Some supplement or clarify the Court's rulings, but most bills are intended either to reverse or to modify. However, only a small portion of such efforts are enacted; only 13 percent of 176 bills introduced between 1950 and 1978 to react to Supreme Court decisions handed down between 1950 and 1972 were the subject of any congressional action, and less than one-third of those were enacted.[20]

At times, after the judiciary has altered the law, Congress has returned the law to its original state. For example, the Court's 1908 ruling that the Interstate Commerce Commission could not compel testimony to secure information in order to recommend legislation to Congress was reversed, and the Supreme Court capitulated. When the Supreme Court held in the *Wunderlich* case that judicial review in certain government contract cases could be based only on a fraud by a government contracting officer, Congress responded by providing that government contracts must allow an appeal by the contractor to the court of appeals. This not only reinstated the status quo ante after the Court had disturbed a "pre-existing 'common understanding'" true in other instances as well, but provided a broader basis for judicial review than had existed before the Court's action.[21] There are, however, other occasions on which, subsequent to the Supreme Court's ruling, Congress has acted with the intent to restore an earlier situation but the result has been to leave intact the basic thrust of what the Court has done. For example, after the *Jencks* ruling that the government must make available to the defense all records used by a witness so that the witness's credibility could be tested, Congress in the Jencks Act said that only such records as a judge had determined were relevant to the witness's testimony had to be produced.

Congress takes some actions, including reenacting statutes with clarified provisions, because the legislators feel the Court has improperly interpreted the statutes. However, a changed balance of legislative power in favor of supporters of an interpretation of the law different from that initially intended can also result in enactment of new provisions. One revision of an intended statutory meaning came after the Court—perhaps as a result of lack of congressional clarity—defined "employee" in the National Labor Relations Act to exclude foremen from the act's coverage. Congress reversed that interpretation when it passed the Taft-Hartley Act. Congress' construction industry exception to the prohibition on "hot cargo" agreements (that workers would not have to handle nonunion goods) was a reaction to the Court's ruling that picketing a general contractor's entire project to protest the presence of a nonunion contractor was an illegal secondary boycott. (The ban itself resulted from the Court's upholding such agreements if entered into voluntarily by labor and management.)[22] When the Court ruled, in *General Electric v. Gilbert* (1976), that providing disability benefits to pregnant women was not discrimination based on sex, Congress, after a strong campaign by women's groups, overturned the ruling and made clear that Title VII of the 1964 Civil Rights Act (concerning employment discrimination based on race or sex) covered that situation.[23]

These instances suggest that Congress has the last word, but even when the Court's rulings permit further legislative action, there are instances when Congress does nothing—perhaps because the forces there are so evenly balanced that no agreement can be reached on a new statute but also perhaps because of lack of concern. Such nonaction can itself have consequences. For example, the *Toth* decision preventing courts-martial of ex-servicemen for in-service offenses did not preclude a statute allowing them to be tried in federal district court, but such a law was never enacted, allowing some of those involved in the My Lai massacre to remain beyond the government's reach because their involvement was not discovered until after they were discharged from the service. Another example was provided by *Branzburg v. Hayes*, in which the Court said that although the First Amendment directly did not provide protection for news media personnel refusing to reveal confidential sources to a grand jury, federal and state "shield laws" were permissible. Although legislation to provide such protection was introduced in Congress, none has yet been enacted. Nor as of 1982 had Congress taken action after the decision in the *Flood* case that Congress would have to act if professional baseball were to be subject to the antitrust laws, although a few representatives, perhaps hoping to force the return of baseball to Washington, D.C., did introduce bills on the subject. (Yes, sports fans, Washington once did have a team, the Senators, whose performance led to the saying, "Washington: First in War, First in Peace, and Last in the American League.") Similarly, Congress has not reenacted a federal death penalty to replace the provisions of the Lindberg (Kidnapping) Act invalidated in *United States v. Jackson* (1968) as interfering with the right to a jury trial; this inaction is, however, largely a result of the difficulty of enacting a new federal criminal code, in which the death penalty was only one element. Congress' failure to respond to the Court's invalidation of the new bankruptcy statute resulted from disagreement both over the proper status of bankruptcy judges and over whether further changes in the substantive provisions of bankruptcy law were needed (see pages 38–39).

Congress's *reaction* to the Court should not make us forget its *use* of judicially developed doctrine. Both point to the question of whether and to what degree Congress should defer to the Court's judgment. Here it is important to remember that although attacks on the Court are not prevented, "reversal bills" have been less likely to pass when arguments about the Court's sacrosanct nature have been used frequently; broad attacks on the Court also produce more arguments that the Court should remain inviolate than do "decision-reversal" proposals.[24]

Members of Congress, in addition to using the Court's legitimacy to support their positions, may find it useful to rely on the Court to resolve difficult problems. They seem divided between a "judicial monopoly" position, according to which questions of constitutionality should be referred to the courts for decision by experts (judges), and a "tripartite" position in which they feel that Congress itself should decide matters of constitutionality. On questions about which the Court has not ruled, believers in the "judicial monopoly" theory see little need to think in terms of constitutionality. Those favoring referral of constitutional questions to the courts have been more likely to think that those issues were raised in the legislature primarily as political maneuvers. On the other hand, those who have wanted Congress to make its own decisions thought the questions were seriously raised in the legislature. The more junior members of Congress and those from the Middle Atlantic and Midwest were more likely to support the "judicial monopoly" approach, while those of greater seniority and those from the South and Southwest thought the courts should defer to Congress's constitutional interpretations.[25]

Congressional reliance on the Court also varies from one policy question to another. When an issue is particularly complex, Congress may stop when it has made a general policy statement—also a result of legislative compromise —and thus leave it up to the justices to make policy as the Court passes on applications of the law. Congress has been more likely to leave matters of judicial procedure up to the courts, which participate directly in rule development, although, as noted earlier, in the last few years Congress has been reluctant to approve those rules without its own examination.

THE COURT AND THE PRESIDENCY[26]

Beyond occasional informal contacts between the president and members of the Court (and their presence at state dinners or at the State of the Union message), most interaction between the president and the Court has been indirect, occurring when the justices have ruled on executive department actions and on challenges to presidential policies after Congress has enacted them into law. The Court's decisions concerning statutes usually come only after a private citizen has challenged executive branch action, promulgation of implementing regulations, or actual or imminent enforcement of the statute or regulations. An increasing number of lawsuits against the executive branch are being brought by members of Congress, particularly over exercise of the war and appointment powers and certain agency activities. Such lawsuits lead to confrontations in which the two elected branches are the primary contestants and the Court an actively involved umpire.

The subject of this section is direct disagreement in the formal relations between Court and president. Famous confrontations between president and Court—which include President Lincoln's rejection of Chief Justice Taney's order to release a prisoner imprisoned by Lincoln after his suspension of habeas corpus—have been few. Even President Andrew Jackson's famous statement, "Mr. Justice Marshall has made his decision; now let him enforce it," seemingly the epitome of resistance, involved not direct defiance but reluctance to assist in enforcing a Supreme Court mandate directed at the State of Georgia. Only five presidents (Jefferson, Jackson, Lincoln, Franklin Roosevelt, and Nixon) have been engaged in direct conflict with the judiciary, and the administration of only one (Nixon) was frequently involved in litigation.

President Reagan has not been in direct conflict with the Supreme Court, but as a candidate he inveighed against its "abuse of power." As president, he endorsed a constitutional amendment allowing "voluntary" prayer in the public schools and bills to limit abortion, thus undercutting major Supreme Court precedents which were also regularly and directly questioned by his administration, as were the Court's decisions on affirmative action programs in industry and tax exemptions for private schools discriminating against minorities.

Appointment Power

Franklin Roosevelt's administration was the first in this century during which the Court dealt with important questions of presidential power. The Court first ruled adversely to the president on the question of his right to dismiss employees. Relying on *Myers v. United States* (1926), in which the Supreme Court, speaking through Chief Justice (and former President) William Howard Taft, had upheld the president's authority to discharge a postmaster, FDR tried to assert his authority to remove Federal Trade Commissioner William Humphrey. Upon Humphrey's refusal, FDR removed him anyhow, but the Court ruled, in *Humphrey's Executor v. United States* (1935), that Congress could limit the president's power to discharge members of regulatory commissions simply because he disagreed with them politically, as the commissioners were expected to play a quasi-judicial role requiring independence of the one who appointed them. President Eisenhower produced the same response, in *Weiner v. United States* (1958), when he removed a member of the War Claims Commission to replace him with someone of his own choosing. The Court has also ruled that, although the president cannot insist on the right to remove members of a commission, he is entitled to be involved in the appointment process when commission members have enforcement and administrative powers making them "officers of the United States." As part of its ruling in *Buckley v. Valeo* (1976), the Court therefore overturned the original method designated by Congress for selection of members of the Federal Election Commission.

Delegation of Authority

In the 1930s, Congress turned over considerable policymaking authority to those administering the law. The issue of whether Congress could do so without specifying standards to guide the president's actions reached the Court during Roosevelt's first term. In the *Panama Refining* case, with liberals and conservative justices agreeing, the Court overturned Congress's grant of authority to embargo shipments of oil produced in excess of state quotas ("hot oil") because Congress had not provided standards by which the president could determine when to act. "This is delegation run riot," said Justice Cardozo. The Court also ruled in the *Schechter Poultry Corporation* case that the National Industrial Recovery Act, under which "codes of fair competition" were developed by industry groups and promulgated by the president, was infected by improper delegation. Recognizing Congress's need to delegate certain tasks to the executive branch, the Court said, however, that "Congress cannot delegate legislative power to the President to exercise an unfettered discretion to make whatever laws he thinks may be needed or advisable for the rehabilitation and expansion of trade or industry." Because the NIRA was at the heart of Roosevelt's economic program, the ruling was even more important than *Panama Refining*, but as his attention had shifted to other programs by the time of the ruling, he may not have been particularly distressed by the Court's action.

At almost the same time, the Court upheld delegation without standards in the foreign affairs area. In the *Curtiss-Wright Export Corporation* case, the justices were faced with a challenge to another presidential embargo (on the sale of arms to warring Latin American countries) imposed pursuant to a congressional grant. Justice Sutherland's opinion for the Court sustained the president's action on the basis of both executive independence in foreign policy under the Constitution and pragmatic considerations:

> In this vast external realm, with its important, complicated, delicate or manifest problems, the President alone has the power to speak or listen as a representative of the nation. He *makes* treaties with the advice and consent of the Senate; but he alone negotiates. Into the field of negotiation the Senate cannot intrude; and Congress itself is powerless to invade it. . . . The very delicate, plenary, and exclusive power of the President as the sole organ of the federal government in the field of international relations . . . does not require as a basis for its exercise an act of Congress. If, in the maintenance of our international relations, embarrassment—perhaps serious embarrassment—is to be avoided and success for our aims achieved, congressional legislation which is to be made effective through negotiations and inquiry within the international field must often afford to the President a degree of discretion and freedom from statutory restriction which would not be admissible were domestic affairs alone involved.

Curtiss-Wright is still the law, but *Panama Refining* and *Schechter* are not; in fact, those two cases, for all their strong language, were the Court's only two invalidations of delegation of authority. The Court has repeatedly accepted delegations of authority couched in terms at least as broad/vague as those involved in *Panama*, for example, in *Yakus v. United States* approving the delegation of authority to the administrator of the Office of Price Administration (OPA), under the Emergency Price Control Act, to fix "generally fair and equitable" prices that would carry out the purposes of the law. More recently, the Supreme Court overturned lower court rulings against the president and sustained actions by Presidents Nixon and Ford increasing fees on imported oil. The statute had authorized the presidential action; standards had also been provided; and the president's actions were limited so that he could do only what was necessary to prevent damage to the national security.[27]

War Powers and Foreign Policy

Unlike its rulings on the president's appointment powers and its mid-1930s rulings on delegation of authority, the Court's decisions on the president's authority as commander-in-chief have been favorable. Judges have generally been quite unwilling to challenge the president's war-making authority, at least until after a war is over. As Rossiter observed, "Whatever limits the Court has set upon the employment of the war powers have been largely theoretical, rarely practical."[28] For example, although *Ex parte Milligan*, invalidating the practice of trying civilians at courts-martial when the civilian courts were operating, contained stern words applying the Constitution to the president (Lincoln), it came after the Civil War had ended. Moreover, in *The Prize Cases*, involving the blockade of the South, the Court sustained Lincoln's ability to wage war without a congressional declaration of war, and later, in *Texas v. White*, it upheld his theory of the relation between the seceded states and the Union. President Franklin Roosevelt's relocation of the Japanese-Americans was held valid in the *Korematsu* case despite the dissenters' claims that the relocation was racist. In fact, the Court sustained the action not only on limited grounds of "military necessity" (the idea that the Court did not have jurisdiction to review military judgments) but also specifically held the action constitutional. (The Court did, however, say in *Ex parte Endo* that, once found to be loyal, a relocated citizen must be released.) Certainly such rulings would leave the impression that "as in the past, so in the future, President and Congress will fight our wars with little or no thought about a reckoning with the Supreme Court."[29]

President Truman's 1952 seizure of the steel mills to avoid their shutdown as a result of a labor dispute tied to wage-price control problems was founded in part on the war power; the government's claim was that if the mills closed, our national security would be endangered. In response to the challenge of the seizure, the government also argued the president's "inherent power" to make the seizure. Insistence on such authority not grounded in specific statute or constitutional provision, particularly where there was no real emergency, led the Court to invalidate the seizure in *Youngstown Sheet & Tube Co. v. Sawyer* (1952): Congress had provided means for handling such situations and moreover had refused to enact the broader provisions Truman had requested. Justice Black, in his opinion for the Court, directly rejected the president's "inherent powers" argument, but if one takes the concurring and dissenting opinions together, a majority of justices did not denounce such powers outright, leaving the possibility of their use where Congress had not spoken. Of the president's four appointees to the Court, only two (Minton and Chief Justice Vinson), joined by FDR appointee Stanley Reed, supported his action. Truman's compliance was immediate; the mills were returned to private hands the day after the Court's ruling, which may have taught the president to use with business and labor "several lesser sanctions none of which is as potent as seizure but the cumulative impact of which enables the President to prevail."[30] (When President Carter enforced wage-price guidelines through government procurement policy—canceling contracts or debarring businesses from bidding if they did not comply with the guidelines—the Court of Appeals for the District of Columbia ruled that there was an adequate statutory basis for his action, and the Supreme Court refused to grant review.[31])

Because Congress had not declared war in Vietnam and because the war was said to violate international law, many efforts were made to challenge its constitutionality. Using the "political question" doctrine or ruling that by making appropriations Congress had acquiesced in the war, lower courts refused to interfere.[32] Despite consistent dissents by Justice Douglas, joined occasionally by Justice Stewart and once by Justice Harlan, the Supreme Court consistently refused to grant review, even refusing to do so in *Massachusetts v. Laird*—over dissents from all three—when pursuant to state legislative action Massachusetts's attorney general sought adjudication of the war's constitutionality.

The Supreme Court also avoided a ruling after Repesentative Elizabeth Holtzman (D-N.Y.) obtained an injunction against further bombing of Cambodia because the bombing lacked congressional authorization. As circuit justice, Justice Marshall would not lift an appeals court stay of the injunction but did say both that the issue might be justiciable and that the president could not wage war "without some form of congressional approval" except in extreme emergencies. He added that "the decision to send American troops 'to distant lands to die of foreign fevers and foreign shot and shell' [quoting Justice Black] . . . may ultimately be adjudged to have not only been unwise but also unlawful." When the plaintiffs persuaded Justice Douglas to vacate the stay, the Defense Department threatened noncompliance, and the entire Court overruled Douglas *the same day* and directly stayed the district court injunction. The result of this maneuvering was the usual one of judicial noninterference in war matters.[33]

President Carter's foreign policy actions were challenged on several occasions. The unilateral termination of the 1954 Mutual Defense Treaty with Taiwan provoked a suit by members of Congress. After passage of a "sense of the Senate" resolution that Senate approval was required to terminate a mutual defense treaty, a district judge ruled that a defense treaty could be terminated only by two-thirds of the Senate or a majority of both houses of Congress. The court of appeals promptly ruled in the president's favor, however, and the Supreme Court upheld the president's action without ruling on it directly by ordering dismissal of the suit (*Goldwater v. Carter*, 1979). Four justices said the case posed a "political question," and one said the question was not ripe because Congress had not taken appropriate formal action. Only one justice voted to affirm the appeals court and two more would have heard argument.

The Iran hostage crisis produced litigation on the administration's decision to conduct special immigration checks on Iranian students, with the appeals court ruling for the president, and on the hostage agreement. The agreement provided mechanisms for resolving claims and obligated the United States to terminate all legal proceedings in U.S. courts involving claims against Iran and its state enterprises and to nullify attachments against Iranian property. Implementing regulations prohibited any attachment of Iranian property in this country or other nonapproved judicial action. The president then allowed judicial proceedings against Iran but no entry of judgment. When a district judge nonetheless issued orders of attachment, the case—*Dames & Moore v. Regan* (1981)—reached the Supreme Court on an expedited schedule and was decided eight days after oral argument and thus more than two weeks before the deadline for transfer of Iranian assets.

The Court, unanimous except for Justice Powell's limited partial dissent, said the question whether nullifying the attachments was a "taking" (subject to compensation) was presented prematurely but upheld the president's broad authority under both the Trading with the Enemy Act and the more recent International Emergency Economic Powers Act. The ruling was confined "only to the very questions necessary to decision of the case," with Justice Rehnquist "freely confess[ing] that we are . . . deciding only one more episode in the never-ending tension between the President exercising the executive authority in a world that presents each day some new challenge with which he must deal and the Constitution under which we all live and which no one disputes embodies some sort of system of checks and balances." The Court, he continued, would not find the president without authority to settle claims when their settlement "has been determined to be a necessary incident to the resolution of a major foreign policy dispute between our country and another, and where Congress acquiesced in the President's action." The ruling is significant not because the Court again did not interfere with the president, but because the Court sustained his action even though that action had restricted judicial power in the name of dealing with a foreign policy emergency. The justices were, however, careful to note that courts were not being stripped of their jurisdiction.

The Court also did not interfere when an individual's passport was revoked on the grounds his activities—revealing the identities of present and former CIA agents—had caused serious damage to the national security and U.S. foreign policy. Although the Passport Act did not explicitly confer such authority, the Court showed its typical deference to the president, saying that "matters intimately related to foreign policy and national security are rarely proper subjects for judicial intervention" and affirming the president's action (*Haig v. Agee, 1981*).

This is hardly the last litigation over the president's war powers and foreign policy authority. For example, members of Congress claimed that the presence of military advisers in El Salvador without Congress having been informed violated the War Powers Act. When district courts sustained challenges to detention of Haitian refugees, based on claims of improper procedure and racial discrimination, the government almost defiantly asserted that only the executive branch had the authority to determine appropriate procedures for considering release of detainees. This would seem to provide further evidence that "the rare decision" in which the justices "shout 'Check!' at the President" has not "had the presumably salutary effect of keeping the Presidency in rein, to say nothing of rendering it [check]mated. The most effective restraints upon both the Presidency and the Congress have been those imposed by other components of the national political system."[34]

The Nixon Administration

Judicial challenges to actions of the president had been relatively infrequent until the Nixon administration, when the courts regularly were asked to invalidate the president's acts or to force him to do what he had not done. Many of these controversies never reached the Supreme Court because the administration did not appeal adverse lower court decisions, hoping thus to limit their legal effect. Among these cases was a ruling that the president had unconstitutionally failed to submit to the Senate the name of his nominee to be director of the Office of Economic Opportunity (OEO); invalidation of his attempt to terminate the Community Action Program (CAP) element of the War on Poverty because he had not given Congress the statutorily required opportunity to act on a reorganization plan; and the overturning of the president's pocket veto of a bill (the Family Practice of Medicine Act) during a five-day Christmas recess, because Congress had ample opportunity to consider his objections when it returned from the recess.[35]

When the president impounded funds either allotted or appropriated by Congress, that issue did reach the Supreme Court. The president had said that priorities must be given to other programs or that because the expenditures would be inflationary, he would exercise restraint if Congress would not. A large number of cases were generated, each over a specific withholding of funds, and the government lost over *thirty* decisions in the lower courts involving funds for state and local education programs, community mental health centers, highways, and a variety of environmental programs. After the Supreme Court denied an attempt by the State of Georgia (*Georgia v. Nixon*) to bring a complaint against impoundment on behalf of its citizens directly in the Court's original jurisdiction, the justices unanimously ruled against the president in early 1975 in *Train v. City of New York* and *Train v. Campaign Clear Water*, involving $9 billion for waste water treatment plants. On the basis of statutory interpretation, the Court said that President Nixon had exceeded his authority in refusing to allot 55 percent of the 1972 Water Pollution Control Act funding. Justice White said that Congress had clearly intended to "provide a firm commitment of substantial sums within the relatively limited period of time in an effort to achieve an early solution of what was deemed an urgent problem" and would not have intended to undercut its own program by giving the president unlimited impoundment power. Although the president lost, the decision was in a way anticlimactic, in large part because of enactment of the Impoundment Control Act of 1974, which provided for impoundment or deferral of appropriate funds only after congressional consideration.

Far more serious than impoundment were the continuous confrontations over the release of the Watergate tapes. Prior to the Watergate cases but relevant to them, the administration had been embroiled in litigation over who—the Department of Justice or the courts—should determine the relevance to a prosecution of conversations overheard during electronic surveillance. When the Supreme Court refused to accept the department's own determination of nonrelevance and held, in the *Alderman* case (1969), that a defendant alleging improper interception of conversations was entitled to inspect the "logs" of those conversations, the administration asserted that the Court's ruling would damage the national security and threatened not to tell the courts of the existence of foreign intelligence surveillance the department thought irrelevant. Not intimidated, the Court refused to change its position.

When the administration used electronic surveillance without a court order in a *domestic* security case (the Omnibus Crime Control Act of 1968 allowed it in national security cases), the Court handed the administration another defeat. The Court unanimously ruled in *United States v. U.S. District Court* (1972) that such surveillance could not be conducted without a proper warrant, because Congress had meant to restrict the law's exceptions to the warrant requirement. Perhaps more important, the Court said that surveillance had to be controlled by judges: the executive branch could not be the sole judge of whether surveillance should take place. Responding to the administration's argument that "internal security matters are too subtle and complex for judicial evaluation," Justice Powell stated flatly:

> Courts regularly deal with the most difficult issues of our society. There is no reason to believe that federal judges will be insensitive to or uncomprehending of the issues involved. . . . If the threat is too subtle or complex for our senior law enforcement officers to convey its significance to a court, one may question whether there is probable cause for surveillance.

When the administration again failed to follow statutory procedures for authorization of surveillance orders, the Court also ruled against the government in some cases but for it in others, although with the reminder "that strict adherence by the government to the provisions of Title III [of the Omnibus Crime Control Act] would . . . be more in keeping with the responsibilities Congress has imposed upon it."[36]

In the first stage of the Watergate tapes litigation, the Court did not hand down a ruling but did affect the subsequent course of events; its ruling in the second stage helped send President Nixon from office. The cases began when the president resisted requests to supply material for the Watergate grand jury, the Senate Watergate Committee, and the House Judiciary Committee, and for use in the cover-up trial and the trial of those involved in the burglary of Daniel Ellsberg's psychiatrist's office. Judge John Sirica ruled that, because the need for information for criminal proceedings—specifically the grand jury—was superior to the president's claims of authority to withhold material, a *judge*, not the executive acting alone, must decide the president's claims. He ordered tapes turned over for his screening, with only necessary material to be given the grand jury. After the judges of the court of appeals unsuccessfully tried to avoid a constitutional confrontation by suggesting a compromise—inspection of the tapes by the president (or his designee), his counsel, and the special prosecutor—they sustained Judge Sirica's ruling, with slight modification.[37]

The president at first said he would comply only with a "definitive ruling" from the Supreme Court, which he later indicated meant one with a vote of at least 7–2. (Such a position also clearly meant the president reserved to himself the power to accept or reject matters of constitutional interpretation—an argument rejected by the Court shortly thereafter in the next stage of the tapes litigation.) Having ascertained that apparently only Justice Rehnquist and possibly Chief Justice Burger would have voted for his position, the president chose not to appeal to the Supreme Court. Compliance with the lower court ruling came only after an abortive attempt to furnish a summary of relevant portions of the tape and the "Saturday night massacre" in which Special Prosecutor Archibald Cox and the attorney general were fired. (Even the firing of the special prosecutor was found illegal by a lower court because the president had violated Justice Department regulations "having the force of law."[38])

The Supreme Court's definitive ruling in the Watergate tapes matter came when the president refused to comply with Justice Sirica's subsequent order for production of a much larger number of tapes for the Watergate cover-up trial. In *United States v. Nixon,* a unanimous Court, speaking through Chief Justice Burger, rejected the president's arguments and ruled that the special prosecutor had made a showing sufficient to justify the subpoena. (It did, however, decline to rule on whether the grand jury had acted properly in naming the president as an unindicted coconspirator in the cover-up.) The justices, while asserting that in a case involving the president "appellate review . . . should be particularly meticulous," emphasized their power to determine the constitutionality of claims made by other branches of government, whether pursuant to express or implied constitutional provisions. Chief Justice Burger twice used Chief Justice Marshall's *Marbury v. Madison* language that it is "emphatically the province and the duty" of the Court "to say what the law is."

The Court did legitimize "executive privilege" by recognizing that the president needed "complete candor and objectivity from advisers," which confidentiality of communications would assist. However, balancing that interest against the requirements of the criminal process, the Court struck the balance against the president, who could not be above the law. An undifferentiated claim of privilege not involving protection of special types of secrets "cannot prevail over the fundamental demands of due process of law in the fair administration of criminal justice" because such a claim would interfere with the judiciary's ability to handle criminal cases properly, and would "upset the constitutional balance of 'a workable government.'" The decision, with which the president complied, was important in leading to his departure from office. The recognition of executive privilege—even though its application in the context of a criminal trial was not in the president's favor—may, however, have been a more far-reaching result of the case.

Closely related to the recognition of executive privilege was the Court's legitimation of absolute immunity for the president from civil damage suits. A result of

President Nixon's involvement in the removal of "whistleblower" Ernest Fitzgerald from his Pentagon job, this ruling did not come until long after Nixon had left office. By a 5–4 vote the Court ruled in *Nixon v. Fitzgerald* (1982) that the president had absolute immunity from civil suits for damages for acts within the "outer perimeter" of his official responsibility, unless Congress authorized such lawsuits. The energies of the president who had to defend himself against such suits, said Justice Powell for the Court, would be diverted from the goverment's effective functioning; moreover, our system of checks and balances, including impeachment, was available to constrain the president. Because of his "unique status," the president could be treated differently from other executive officials. In the companion case of *Harlow v. Fitzgerald*, on the liability of presidential assistants, the Court, by an 8–1 vote, extended earlier rulings concerning Cabinet members' immunity, holding that most such assistants were entitled to only qualified (limited) immunity from suit, but left open the possibility of absolute immunity for those involved in national security and foreign policy work. Justice White, dissenting in the *Nixon* case, attacked absolute presidential immunity for placing the president above the law and allowing him "deliberately [to] cause serious injury to any number of citizens." It was, said White, "a reversion to the old notion that the king can do no wrong."

After President Nixon's resignation, the issue of his pardon by President Ford did not reach the Supreme Court. A federal judge in Michigan, however, did rule the pardon constitutional, saying it was within the letter and spirit of the presidential pardon power as well as a "prudent public policy judgment."[39] The Supreme Court had also said in late 1974 in *Schick v. Reed* that the president had broad discretion to treat individually each commutation and pardon he chose to issue and to attach conditions, even those not mentioned in the statutes.

Litigation over President Nixon's tapes and papers continued after he left office. Congress set aside his agreement with the General Services Administration (GSA) on disposition of his presidential papers in the Presidential Recordings and Materials Preservation Act, which provided for screening of materials by archivists and return of purely private material, and included safeguards against disclosure of materials affecting confidential communications with the president. There was to be no more intrusion, the Court said in sustaining the act in *Nixon v. Administrator of General Services* (1977), than in Judge Sirica's *in camera* inspection of the tapes. The Court swept aside the ex-president's barrage of objections one by one: the act did not violate the separation of powers nor the president's privilege to have confidential communications; it did not improperly invade his privacy or association rights (as head of the political party); nor was it a bill of attainder. On this last point, the president was a legitimate "class of one" on which Congress could legislate; Congress had engaged in nonpunitive lawmaking to protect materials, not in punishment. Justice Stevens, more forthright, said the statute did implicitly condemn Nixon as an unreliable custodian of his papers, but he approved the legislation because of Nixon's resignation from office and acceptance of a pardon. In dissent, the Chief Justice argued vehemently that the Court was repudiating 200 years of judicial precedent and historical practice, with fundamental principles subordinated to the needs of the situation, and Justice Rehnquist thought the Court's ruling would hinder future presidents from obtaining confidential advice.

In reviewing lower court rulings concerning the president's authority to prevent access to the portions of the tapes received into evidence at the cover-up trial, the Court, relying on procedures in the Presidential Recordings Act, ruled in *Nixon v. Warner Communications* (1978) that neither a common law right of access nor the First Amendment required release of the tapes; the lower courts could use their informed discretion in providing procedures for release of materials that had been used in judicial proceedings and in limiting release of those materials. Even this ruling did not end Nixon's resistance to release of materials, but in 1982 the Court of Appeals for the District of Columbia upheld allowing the public to listen to the president's tapes, including those from the cover-up trial, after archivists had reviewed them in accordance with statutory procedures.

THE COURTS AND THE REGULATORY AGENCIES

The regulatory commissions and executive branch departments performing regulatory tasks handle many more cases than do federal district courts. In the commissions' early years, courts were often hostile to them, but later the lower courts and the Supreme Court have allowed them and executive agencies considerable discretion.

The Supreme Court's earliest response to some agencies was to restrict both their jurisdiction and the weight judges were to give the agencies' determinations. Decisions like the one stating that the Interstate Commerce Commission could only determine whether railroad-proposed rates were reasonable led the ICC to concede that "by virtue of judicial decisions, it has ceased to be a body for the regulation of interstate carriers."[40] Similarly, the ruling in the *Gratz* case that methods of unfair competition unknown before passage of the Federal Trade Commission Act were not within the FTC's jurisdiction and that the courts would identify those methods led the commission to stop trying to prohibit new unfair trade practices. However, when the Court held in the *Winstead Hosiery* case that the FTC could deal with false advertising and misbranding, the commission's level of activity on those subjects increased. The Court's later limitation of the commission through the decision that the FTC could deal with only false advertising that was both unfair *and* a method of competition had to be overruled by Congress. Only in 1934 in the *Keppel Brothers* case did the Court say that it would give weight to the FTC's determination of what practices would be considered unfair. The agencies were also restricted procedurally by the Court. While the Court finally came around to giving administrators greater freedom of action, the Court's restrictive rulings caused reexamination of the agencies' procedures and helped lead to their codification in the Administrative Procedure Act of 1946.

The courts' more deferential approach to agency action resulted both from judges' greater familiarity with the agencies, new judges' more favorable attitudes toward regulation, and a greater recognition of the necessity of letting the agencies operate with less supervision lest the courts be swamped with cases appealed from the agencies. Instead of reviewing agency action with a fine-toothed comb, that is, subjecting even the agencies' factual determinations to *de novo* review, doctrines were developed by Congress and enforced by the courts that decreased judicial oversight of the agencies' work. Judicial review has been ruled unavailable in some situations; in others, courts have insisted that various steps must be followed prior to judicial review (*exhaustion of administrative remedies*); and courts examining agency rulings have generally limited themselves to determining whether "substantial evidence" supports agency actions.

Courts continue to interpret the law applied by the agencies and commissions, so courts determine whether agencies are acting within the scope of authority granted them by Congress. For example, the Supreme Court ruled, in the *Hampton* case, that the Civil Service Commission's exclusion of aliens from federal government employment, far from the commission's core duties, had not been explicitly authorized. Because agency and court jurisdictions overlap at times, the courts also have to help distribute responsibilities among agencies, or, as in the field of labor law, among agencies, arbitrators deciding cases closely related to agency jurisdiction, and courts.[41]

Courts have available a battery of rules to assist them in sustaining agency actions that are challenged in court, and the courts sustain agency actions in a high proportion of these cases. One rule is to give great weight to agency interpretations of the statutes under which they operate. Thus, in holding that the Federal Power Commission did not have jurisdiction over thermal-electric power plants but only over hydroelectric ones, the Supreme Court relied on "a longstanding, uniform construction by the agency" of the statute; this interpretation deserved "great respect," particularly when it had been first developed contemporaneously with the statute's passage and where the interpretation had not been altered by Congress.[42]

In reviewing Department of Justice "preclearance" decisions under the Voting Rights Act of 1965, concerning changes in voting procedures to determine whether they have the purpose or effect of discriminating against minorities, the Court has also shown substantial deference to the attorney general's rulings on the scope of coverage (what types of changes are subject to preclearance). With limited exceptions, the Court has tended to adopt Justice Department standards. When the department failed to object to proposed changes, the Court also deferred, holding such inaction not subject to judicial review. That the Court's position and the agency's stance *converged* through interaction made it easier for the Court's majority to draw upon the executive's position. This is similar to the pattern found in appeals court rulings on the Federal Power Commission. In that pattern, the agency, although trying to anticipate the courts' reaction from accumulated judicial rulings, initiates policy changes, and the courts decide whether to accept those changes intact or to require modifications. Throughout, "the typical pattern of interaction . . . has been one of adjustment and accommodation to divergent viewpoints," with cooperation rather than conflict predominating, as the courts learn from the agencies and do not simply tell them what to do.[43]

The Administrative Procedure Act's "substantial evidence" standard and closely related tests, such as whether agency actions are "arbitrary and capricious," generally produce deference to the agencies. As Justice White remarked when the Court sustained a National Labor Relations Board (NLRB) ruling, "Assessing the significance of impasse and the dynamics of collective bargaining is precisely the kind of judgment that [we earlier] ruled should be left to the Board. We cannot say that the Board's current resolution of the issue is arbitrary or contrary to law."[44] Similarly, in ruling on a challenge to a Federal Elections Commission decision concerning expenditure agreements between state party organizations and the national party's senatorial campaign committees, Justice White wrote that a court's task in acting against the background of an agency ruling—not the same as acting initially in a judicial proceeding—"was not to interpret the statute as it thought best but rather the narrower inquiry into whether the Commission's construction was 'sufficiently reasonable' to be accepted by a reviewing court." He did, however, concede that "the thoroughness, validity and consistency of an agency's reasoning are factors that bear upon the amount of deference to be given an agency's ruling."[45]

Application of the Freedom of Information Act (FOIA), which has a general policy of disclosure but contains many exemptions, has provided recent tests of the Court's deference to agencies, which use the exemptions to withhold information, particularly informal policies and information on which ultimate decisions have been based. In its first FOIA ruling, *Environmental Protection Agency v. Mink* (1973), the Supreme Court upheld the Environmental Protection Agency's refusal to provide members of Congress information about an underground nuclear test because the relevant documents, classified Secret or Top Secret, were exempted from disclosure. (The FOIA was amended to allow challenges to classification of documents.) The Court has strengthened the agencies' hand by ruling that they need not release documents that were not final opinions. However, the justices have also ruled in favor of disclosure of final opinions and of materials that would not produce a "clearly unwarranted" invasion of privacy, and have decided that private companies, such as government contractors, could not prevent release of information otherwise obtained by the government.[46] By and large, the Court has continued to reinforce agencies' FOIA positions. For example, the Court ruled that the NLRB need not disclose the statements of witnesses it intended to call at an unfair labor practice hearing and that information contained in records originally compiled for law enforcement purposes does not lose its exemption from disclosure when reproduced or summarized in a new document prepared for other purposes.[47] The Court has also ruled that when material subject to disclosure is no longer in the agency's possession because an official—in this instance, Secretary of State Henry Kissinger—treating the documents as his own, has taken the documents from the agency, it did not "improperly withhold" them. In the same case the Court also ruled that Kissinger's notes of telephone conversations made when he was the president's assistant for national security were not State Department "agency records" and thus were not subject to disclosure even after Kissinger brought those notes to the State Department when he became Secretary of State.[48]

The court's deference to agencies does, however, have limits. For one thing, the Court does not always follow agency interpretations of statutes, for example, refusing in the previously noted *Gilbert* case to follow Equal Employment Opportunity Commission guidelines treating pregnancy as a disability. Of particular significance is the Court's invalidation of Occupational Safety and Health Administration's (OSHA) rules on occupational exposure to benzene. Because the Secretary of Labor had not made the threshold determination required by the statute that the particular toxic substance posed a significant workplace health risk and that under the statutory standard of "reasonably necessary or appropriate to provide safe or healthful employment and places of employment," the agency rulings had to fall.[49] Generally, the Court has said that agencies need to explain how they have reached their conclusions, even if they do not produce the ultimate in clarity, and the justices have invalidated agency orders not linking findings and conclusions. (However, the Court often asks the agency to try again.)

The Court says that it does not weigh the evidence presented to an agency, except to see whether there is enough (under the "appropriate" standard) to support the agency's result, and that it does not judge the "wisdom" of the agency's action. Sometimes, however, the justices manage to send an agency "multiple messages" by saying they support the agency position while indicating strong misgivings. In the labor cases noted above, Justice White said, "The Board might have struck a different balance from the one it has, and it may be that some or all of us would prefer that it had done so . . . " In voting to sustain a Federal Communications Commission order, Chief Justice Burger said he was unsure that the FCC had made the right decision, but that as a justice of the Supreme Court, he could not "resolve this issue as perhaps I would were I a member of the . . . Commission."[50]

The Court can also limit agency discretion by requiring due process protections for those affected by agency actions, but the Court has not done this frequently. Perhaps the most notable application of due process came in the Court's 1970 *Goldberg v. Kelly* and *Wheeler v. Montgomery* rulings that welfare benefits could not be terminated without a prior evidentiary hearing even though a full HEW "fair hearing" need not be held until after termination. However, in *Mathews v. Eldridge* (1976) the Court refused to extend its earlier rule to termination of disability benefits. More typical are procedural rulings in which the Court refused to require full hearings for all aspects of new drug applications, allowing summary proceedings instead; said that, while the Federal Power Commission (FPC) had to consider the anticompetitive effects of a utility's securities issue, the agency did not have to hold hearings in every case; or did not require the Secretary of Transportation to make formal findings even though he had to follow certain procedural requirements in making his determination that there was no "feasible and prudent" alternative route for an interstate highway scheduled to go through a park. There are, however, limits to even this sort of requirement, and the Court will not allow lower courts to demand more procedurally than the Administrative Procedure Act requires.[51]

Deference to Lower Courts

Related to deference to administrative agencies is deference to the lower courts, particularly the courts of appeals, that rule initially on agency actions. In recent controversial cases involving OSHA standards for exposure to "cotton dust," which results in byssinosis ("brown lung"), the Court remarked, in upholding the agency, "Our inquiry is not to determine whether we, in the first instance, would find OSHA's findings supported by substantial evidence. Instead we turn to OSHA's findings and the record upon which they were based to decide whether the Court of Appeals 'misapprehended or grossly misapplied' the test for evaluating agency decisions."[52]

In other cases, the Court has not hesitated to overturn lower court rulings on the basis of its own examination of the relevant statute and administrative action—even when the lower court is the U.S. Court of Appeals for the District of Columbia, the most important court of appeals for administrative law because of the high proportion of administrative agency cases it reviews. The D.C. court's posture toward the agencies—essentially liberal and activist—has led it on a path different from the Supreme Court's, particularly in the 1970s, making deference by the Supreme Court less likely. For example, after the Federal Communications Commission decided that market forces should prevail and that it would not consider changes in program format (from rock to jazz or from jazz to classical music) in a license renewal application, the D.C. Circuit held that the FCC's policy violated the Federal Communications Act. "Unconvinced" that the lower court's doctrine was "compelled by the Act," the Supreme Court sustained the commission, which had "provided a rational explanation for its conclusion that reliance on the market is the best method of promoting diversity in entertainment formats."[53] As this case indicates, where agency and lower court differ, the Supreme Court can "have its pick" of policies, dressing up its conclusion in the language of deference—to the agency or to the lower court as appropriate.

Overall Support

The Supreme Court's rate of affirmance of agency rulings has usually been in the vicinity of 70 to 80 percent. During the 1947–1956 Terms, average support for the agencies was 69 percent; for the 1960–1965 Terms, it was 78 percent; for the 1967 Term, the rate went to 84 percent, a further indication of term-by-term variation. Even with the Burger Court's conservative tendencies in economic regulation, 76 percent of agency actions challenged in the Supreme Court were sustained there in the 1971–1973 Terms,[54] but this may reflect a change in the types of cases being appealed. The high level of support is particularly striking because only a very small percentage of the regulatory agencies' rulings are appealed to the courts and even fewer—the "difficult" and controversial decisions—to the Supreme Court, which denies certiorari in most cases. This means that the support level for the agencies is extremely high, with very, very few of their decisions overturned.

Not all agencies have been supported at the same level, however. During the Roosevelt Court, although the FCC won fewer than half its cases before the Court, the basic range of support ran from a high of 86 percent (NLRB) to a low of 60 percent (FTC). The Federal Power Commission and the Federal Trade Commission were supported at rates of over 90 percent during 1957–1968, and the NLRB and Internal Revenue Service won about three-quarters of their cases, but the ICC was supported less than two-thirds of the time and the Immigration and Naturalization Service won only 56.3 percent of its cases. These differences are explained largely in terms of the agencies' substantive policies. At least through the Warren Court, Schubert has argued, the Court supported the agencies because the agencies decided cases in the same liberal direction to which the justices were favorably inclined. Thus, where agency results were conservative, the Court was more likely to overturn the decisions.

A different look at Warren Court agency support scores shows that when the agency decisions were probusiness, the Court supported the agency just slightly more than half the time (52 percent), but when the agencies were antibusiness, support increased to almost two-thirds (65 percent). The Court supported two-thirds of prolabor agency decisions, but only 53 percent of antilabor rulings. The Burger Court, although supporting the agencies over 70 percent of the time—more when unanimous than when divided in the 1969–1977 Terms—was more likely to overturn liberal agency actions. When the NLRB was prolabor, the Burger Court supported it only 53 percent of the time, but did so in *89 percent* of the board's antilabor cases. Support for probusiness or antilabor agency decisions was higher than for prolabor and antibusiness decisions (63% to 51%).[55]

The Court's overall supportive position toward the agencies masks differences among justices. For the 1947–1956 Terms, all except Black were consistent in overall support for the agencies. However, justices' value preferences appeared to affect their voting in some situations, for example, Black and Douglas (prounion) and Chief Justice Vinson (antiunion) in labor cases and Black and Douglas in business competition cases. Black, Douglas, and Frankfurter were more likely to oppose an agency ruling when a person's freedom was involved than when it was not. All the justices were more likely to support the agencies when evidentiary questions were involved than when they were not, but some (Jackson, Reed, Burton) were particularly likely to do so; questions of statutory authority and due process of law also affected some voting in the Court. During 1957–1968, differences between justices followed the Court's overall pattern. The justices' basic substantive policy attitudes had a greater effect on their voting than "due process" and "statutory authority and interpretation" dimensions of cases.[56]

In the Burger Court, one could also find differences among the justices; even among the four Nixon appointees, two (Burger and Powell) showed a relative lack of deference to the agencies, while Blackmun and Rehnquist were more deferential. Looking at the entire Burger Court membership, one can see that some justices are deferential in particular categories of cases—Powell when agency decisions are probusiness, Marshall when they are prolabor—while only two (Blackmun and White) seemed restrained or deferential across all categories of cases.[57]

Agency Response

That the courts generally sustain agency rulings does not necessarily mean that the agencies eagerly follow the courts' rulings when those rulings go against them.

Indeed, there is agency resistance, followed by judicial reversal of the agency, with Supreme Court action part of a stream of continuous policymaking. Much judicial activity concerning the regulatory agencies has taken place in the appeals courts rather than in the Supreme Court. An agency, although trying to anticipate the courts' reaction from accumulated judicial rulings, initiates policy changes, and the courts decide whether to accept those changes intact or to require modifications. Throughout, "the typical pattern of interaction . . . has been one of adjustment and accommodation to divergent viewpoints," with cooperation rather than conflict predominating, as the courts learn from the agencies and do not simply tell them what to do.[58]

We can see the relation between the Supreme Court and the agencies in the area of patent law, where the Supreme Court's impact has come less from individual decisions than from their collective force, as the decisions have been reinforced by rulings of the lower federal courts. During the 1930s the Supreme Court quietly changed its standards concerning the patentability of inventions by substantially increasing the rate at which it invalidated patents; it was the results rather than the Court's language that mattered. Those decisions from the 1930s and further Supreme Court rulings in 1941, 1949, and 1950 were frequently cited by both the lower courts and others interested in patent policy. However, without a "clear command" from the Court, the Patent Office chose to follow the Supreme Court's doctrine rather than its actions. The agency thus did not change its decision making even when it was criticized by the Supreme Court for departing from the Court's standards.[59]

One reason for Patent Office resistance was that, although some lower court judges recognized the Supreme Court's change in posture and shifted their positions accordingly, others, among them the Court of Customs and Patent Appeals, resisted the change. This lower court reluctance to recognize what the Supreme Court had done meant that the justices, to try to make their point, had to reverse those courts frequently. When either the appeals courts or district courts found a patent valid, the likelihood of reversal by the Supreme Court was very high. Even when a new patent statute was enacted—partly a result of the Supreme Court's actions—little appeared to change. The Supreme Court's declaration that the new law was in fact a codification of the old law reinforced the pattern of divergent interpretations: some courts of appeals applied Patent Act language, others applied a different standard, and some appeared to apply no particular standard.

Another instance of Justice Department difficulty with the Court and of limits to the Court's deference to the executive came in the antitrust field when the department settled a case in which the Supreme Court had earlier ordered one company to divest itself of another. Justice Douglas, saying, "No one except this Court has authority to alter or modify our mandate," made clear that the Court was not questioning the attorney general's power to settle suits but that the power had to be exercised within the bounds established by the Court's doctrine. When the department later agreed to dismissal of an appeal from a new lower court order in the same litigation, the Supreme Court also set aside the new order despite Justice Harlan's complaint that the Court had set out "to thwart the Department of Justice when it decides to terminate an antitrust litigation."[60]

Overall, the picture we find in examining Supreme Court judicial review at the national level is that the Court only infrequently reverses the actions of Congress, the president, or the regulatory commissions and executive branch agencies. However, it is not hesitant to do so and can have considerable effect when it does. Yet, despite an apparent lack of reaction to many of its decisions and more willing compliance in other instances, Congress rewrites statutes and at times takes more severe reversal action, and the regulatory agencies have shown themselves quite capable of resisting the High Court through delay and persistence. Judicial review certainly did not cease after 1937, although the focus of such actions shifted from economic regulation to other matters, most notably in areas of civil liberties policy. These actions and their aftermath show the Court important but not all-powerful.

NOTES

1. Gregory A. Caldeira and Donald J. McCrone, "Of Time and Judicial Activism: A Story of the U.S. Supreme Court, 1800–1973," in *Supreme Court Activism and Restraint*, eds., Stephen C. Halpern and Charles Lamb, pp. 111–113, 120–121.
2. Stuart Nagel, *The Legal Process from a Behavioral Perspective* (Homewood, Ill.: Dorsey, 1969), pp. 248, 259.
3. Bradley C. Canon and S. Sidney Ulmer, "The Supreme Court and Critical Elections: A Dissent," *American Political Science Review* 70 (December 1976):1215–1218; Richard Funston, "The Supreme Court and Critical Elections," *American Political Science Review* 69 (September 1975):795–811.
4. *Trop v. Dulles*, 356 U.S. 86 (1956) and *Kennedy v. Mendoza-Martinez*, 372 U.S. 144 (1963) (citizenship); *Reid v. Covert*, 354 U.S. 1 (1957), *United States* ex rel. *Toth v. Quarles*, 350 U.S. 11 (1955), and *O'Callaghan v. Parker*, 395 U.S. 258 (1969) (courts-martial).
5. For example, *Marchetti v. United States*, 390 U.S. 39 (1968) (gambling) and *Leary v. United States*, 395 U.S. 6 (1969) (marijuana tax).
6. *U.S. Department of Agriculture v. Murry*, 413 U.S. 508 (1973), and *U.S.D.A. v. Moreno*, 413 U.S. 529 (1973) (food stamps); *Weinberger v. Wiesenfeld*, 420 U.S. 630 (1975), and *Jimenez v. Weinberger*, 417 U.S. 628 (1974) (benefits); *Blount v. Rizzi*, 400 U.S. 419 (1971); *Chief of Capitol Police v. Jeannette Rankin Brigade*, 409 U.S. 972 (1973); and *United States v. Grace*, 103 S.Ct. 1702 (1983) (free speech).
7. See Beth Henschen, "Supreme Court–Congressional Interaction in the Interpretation of Statutes," paper presented to Midwest Political Science Association, 1980.
8. Walter Murphy, *Elements of Judicial Strategy*, pp. 129–131.
9. *Arizona v. Maricopa County Medical Society*, 102 S.Ct. 2466 at 2478–2479 (1982).
10. Jesse H. Choper, *Judicial Review and the National Political Process*, p. 143.
11. Nagel, p. 275; Walter F. Murphy, *Congress and the Court* (Chicago: University of Chicago Press, 1962), pp. 257–258.
12. Nagel, p. 266.
13. Lucius J. Barker, "The Offshore Oil Cases," in *The Third Branch of Government*, eds. C.

Herman Pritchett and Alan F. Westin (New York: Harcourt, Brace, and World, 1963), pp. 234–274.

14. *Guss v. Utah Labor Relations Board,* 343 U.S. 1 (1957).
15. *Lauf v. E. G. Shinner & Co.,* 303 U.S. 323 (1968); *Yakus v. United States,* 321 U.S. 414 (1944).
16. Murphy, *Congress and the Court,* is an account of Congress' action.
17. For a discussion of some of these points, see Kenneth R. Kay, "The Unforeseen Impact on Courts *and* Congress," *Judicature* 65 (October 1981):185–189; Charles E. Rice, "The Constitutional Basis for the Proposals in Congress Today," ibid., 190–197; Telford Taylor, "The Unconstitutionality of Current Legislative Proposals," ibid., 198–207; and Carl A. Anderson, "The Government of Courts: The Power of Congress," *American Bar Association Journal* 68 (June 1982):686–690.
18. An earlier version of part of this material appeared in Stephen L. Wasby, *The Impact of the United States Supreme Court: Some Perspectives* (Homewood, Ill.: Dorsey Press, 1970), pp. 203–213.
19. Samuel Krislov, *The Supreme Court in the Political Process* (New York: Macmillan, 1965), p. 143.
20. Henschen, pp. 20–23.
21. Note, "Congressional Reversal of Supreme Court Decisions: 1945–1957," *Harvard Law Review* 71 (May 1958):1336. See *S & E Contractors v. United States,* 406 U.S. 1 at 13–14, 25–26, 48–51, and 69–90 (1972).
22. The cases are, respectively, *N.L.R.B. v. Denver Building Construction Trades Council,* 341 U.S. 675 (1951) and *Local 1976, United Brotherhood of Carpenters v. N.L.R.B. (Sand Door),* 357 U.S. 93 (1958). See *Woelke & Romero Framing v. N.L.R.B.,* 102 S.Ct. 2071 (1982).
23. On the campaign to overturn *Gilbert,* see Joyce Gelb and Marian Lief Palley, "Women and Interest Group Politics: A Comparative Analysis of Federal Decision-Making," *Journal of Politics* 41 (May 1979):385–387.
24. Harry Stumpf, "The Political Efficacy of Judicial Symbolism," *Western Political Quarterly* 19 (June 1966):293–303, and "Congressional Response to Supreme Court Rulings: The Interaction of Law and Politics," *Journal of Public Law* 14 (1965):376–395.
25. Donald G. Morgan, *Congress and the Constitution: A Study of Responsibility* (Cambridge, Mass.: Harvard University Press, 1966), p. 367. See pp. 10–11 for an exposition of the theories.
26. For greater detail, see Stephen L. Wasby, "The Presidency Before the Courts," *Capital University Law Review* 6 (December 1976):35–73, in which some of this material was first presented.
27. *Federal Energy Administration v. Algonquin SNG,* 426 U.S. 548 (1976).
28. Clinton Rossiter, *The Supreme Court and the Commander in Chief* (Ithaca, N.Y.: Cornell University Press, 1951), pp. 127–128.
29. Ibid., p. 131.
30. Arthur S. Miller, *The Supreme Court and American Capitalism* (New York: Free Press, 1970), p. 100. For a complete account of the case, see Maeva Marcus, *Truman and the Steel Seizure Case: The Limits of Presidential Power* (New York: Columbia University Press, 1977).
31. *A.F.L.-C.I.O. v. Kahn,* 618 F.2d 784 (D.C.Cir. 1979), cert. denied, 443 U.S. 915 (1979).
32. See Anthony D'Amato and Robert O'Neil, *The Judiciary and Vietnam* (New York: St. Martin's Press, 1972).

33. *Holtzman v. Schlesinger,* 414 U.S. 1304 and 414 U.S. 1316; *Schlesinger v. Holtzman,* 414 U.S. 1321 (1973).
34. Glendon Schubert, *Judicial Policy-Making* (Glenview, Ill.: Scott, Foresman, 1965), pp. 59–60.
35. *Williams v. Phillips,* 360 F.Supp. 1363 (D.D.C. 1973), aff'd, 482 F.2d 669 (D.C. Cir. 1973); *Local 2677, American Federation of Government Employees v. Phillips,* 358 F.Supp. 60 (D.D.C. 1973); *Kennedy v. Sampson,* 364 F.Supp. 1075 (D.D.C. 1973).
36. *United States v. Chavez,* 416 U.S. 562 at 580 (1974); see also *United States v. Giordano,* 416 U.S. 505 (1974).
37. *In Re Subpoena to Nixon,* 460 F. Supp. 1 (D.D.C. 1973), 487 F.2d 700 (D.C. Cir. 1973).
38. *Nader v. Bork,* 366 F. Supp. 104 (D.D.C. 1973).
39. *Murphy v. Ford,* 390 F. Supp. 1372 (W.D. Mich. 1975).
40. Quoted in Merle Fainsod, Lincoln Gordon, and Joseph Palamountain, Jr., *Government and the American Economy,* 3rd ed. (New York: W. W. Norton, 1959), p. 260.
41. See *Vaca v. Sipes,* 386 U.S. 171 (1967); *Barrentine v. Arkansas-Best Freight System,* 450 U.S. 728 (1981); *Clayton v. Auto Workers,* 451 U.S. 679 (1981).
42. *Chemehuevi Tribe of Indians v. F.P.C.,* 420 U.S. 395 (1975). For an earlier ruling on this doctrine, see *Udall v. Tallman,* 380 U.S. 1 (1965).
43. Daniel J. Fiorino, "Judicial-Administrative Interaction in Regulatory Policy-Making: The Case of the Federal Power Commission," paper presented to the American Political Science Association, 1975.
44. *Charles D. Bonanno Linen Service v. N.L.R.B.,* 102 S.Ct. 720 at 725 (1982).
45. *Federal Election Commission v. Democratic Senatorial Campaign Committee,* 102 S.Ct. 38 at 44–46 (1981).
46. *Renegotiation Board v. Grumman Aircraft,* 421 U.S. 168 (1975); *N.L.R.B. v. Sears, Roebuck,* 421 U.S. 132 (1975); *Department of the Air Force v. Rose,* 425 U.S. 352 (1976); *Chrysler Corp. v. Brown,* 441 U.S. 281 (1979).
47. *N.L.R.B. v. Robbins Tire & Rubber Co.,* 437 U.S. 214 (1976); *Federal Bureau of Investigation v. Abramson,* 102 S.Ct. 2054 (1982).
48. *Kissinger v. Reporters Committee for Freedom of the Press,* 445 U.S. 136 (1980).
49. *Industrial Union Department v. American Petroleum Institute,* 448 U.S. 607 (1980).
50. *United States v. Midwest Video Corp.,* 406 U.S. 649 at 676 (1972).
51. *Weinberger v. Hynson, Westcott & Dunning,* 412 U.S. 609 (1973) (drug application); *Gulf States Utilities Co. v. F.P.C.,* 411 U.S. 747 (1973) (antitrust); *Citizens to Preserve Overton Park v. Volpe,* 401 U.S. 420 (1971) (interstate highway); *Vermont Yankee Nuclear Power Corp. v. Natural Resources Defense Council,* 435 U.S. 519 (1978) (procedural requirements).
52. *American Textile Manufacturers Institute v. Donovan,* 452 U.S. 490 at 523 (1981).
53. *Federal Communications Commission v. WNCN Listeners Guild,* 450 U.S. 582 at 593, 595 (1981).
54. Joseph Tanenhaus, "Supreme Court Attitudes Toward Federal Administrative Agencies," *Vanderbilt Law Review* 14 (1960–1961):473–502; Bradley C. Canon and Micheal Giles, "Recurring Litigants: Federal Agencies Before the Supreme Court," *Western Political Quarterly* 25 (June 1972):183–191; Glendon Schubert, *The Constitutional Polity* (Boston, Mass: Boston University Press, 1970), pp. 37–38.
55. Harold J. Spaeth and Stuart H. Teger, "Activism and Restraint: A Cloak for the Justices' Policy Preferences," in *Supreme Court Activism and Restraint,* eds. Halpern and Lamb, pp. 299, 278–280.

56. Tanenhaus, "Supreme Court Attitudes"; Canon and Giles, pp. 189–190.
57. Spaeth and Teger, p. 282.
58. Fiorino, pp. 28, 30. An extremely helpful discussion of the ability of regulatory agencies to avoid full compliance with court decisions can be found in Robert Rabin, "Lawyers for Social Change: Perspectives on Public Interest Law," *Stanford Law Review* 28 (January 1976):esp. 242–252.
59. On patent law, see Martin Shapiro, *The Courts and the Administrative Agencies*, pp. 143–226; Lawrence Baum, "The Federal Courts and Patent Validity: An Analysis of the Record," *Journal of the Patent Office Society* 56 (December 1974):758–787.
60. *Cascade Natural Gas v. El Paso Natural Gas*, 386 U.S. 129 at 136 (1967); *Utah Public Service Comm. v. El Paso Natural Gas*, 395 U.S. 464 at 476 (1969). The earlier case is *United States v. El Paso Natural Gas*, 376 U.S. 651 (1964).

Chapter 10

The Supreme Court's Impact

The expectation of immediate, unbegrudging, and total obedience to the Supreme Court's rulings is widely held, particularly by those who fail to recognize that the Court is an actor in a political system. Compliance receives little attention and noncompliance is newsworthy—a further indication of the expectation that compliance should be the norm and the belief that it is. Recognition of the Court's political role should carry with it an understanding of the inevitability of negative reaction to its rulings, including noncompliance with them, particularly when important constitutional questions are at stake or controversial issues are being decided. Yet abundant hostile rhetoric aimed at the Court's rulings interpreting, sustaining, or overturning federal and state statutes is not always consonant with broader response, and those rulings do produce results. For example, one gets two very different estimates of reaction to the abortion rulings by looking at (a) the hate mail received by Justice Blackmun after he wrote the opinion, demonstrations at the Court against the rulings, and efforts to amend the Constitution to prohibit abortions and (b) public opinion polls, which show increasing support for a woman's right to obtain an abortion, not to mention (c) the increase in the number of abortions performed —even if only part of that increase is attributed to the Court's rulings.

Individually or cumulatively, Supreme Court decisions have had definite impact (effects). Some rulings have produced support and compliance; others have resulted in opposition. Search warrants are now obtained where police would not have bothered to do so earlier; police now give the "*Miranda* warnings." Despite such clear effects, because the Court's rulings are often only one of multiple causes of events, it is often difficult to tell whether the Court has produced social change, increased its pace, merely served as a catalyst, or had no effect. Southern schools are desegregated, but it is hard to tell how much as a result of *Brown v. Board of Education* and how much as a result of the statute providing for the cutting off of federal funds to government units that discriminate. Except in the Deep South, changing public opinion, itself a result of World War II, might have led to some change without court rulings, but changed national opinion certainly made it easier for the Court to rule as it did. *Brown* itself had not produced much activity except resistance in the Deep South before Congress acted, but the statute and the desegregation guidelines issued by the Department of Health, Education, and Welfare might not have occurred without the Court's action.

Decisions on desegregation and the perhaps even more widely disobeyed school prayer rulings were highly visible and affected many people, average citizens as well as officials. Other rulings, such as those on reapportionment or criminal procedure, have their basic direct effect on government officials, through structural or organizational changes, although changes in policy may ultimately affect the citizens. Still other decisions may serve to alter our federal system of government. As Charles Warren stated years ago, "To untrammeled intercourse between its parts, the American union owes its preservation and strength. Two factors have made such intercourse possible—the railroad, physically; the Supreme Court, legally."[1] Most decisions have an economic effect, although the visibility of that effect may differ and sometimes it may come through costs imposed, for example, by increasing the number of people eligible for welfare, at other times by costs removed, as in the 1976 invalidation of the federal minimum wage for state and local employees. If some effects are specific, others can be relatively diffuse, as when the Court affects the nation's political agenda by helping focus attention on a subject like abortion. The increase in the number of abortions obtained and the wide variety of "Right-to-Life" activities following the Court's 1973 rulings also demonstrate that a decision can have both specific and diffuse effects.

Despite this variety of impacts stemming from the Court's decisions, we must be careful not to attribute to it more power than it may actually have when put to the test, as we do at times in our tendency to make the Court a scapegoat for phenomena like increased crime rates that we can't easily explain. Thus the Court's decisions have been said to have produced desegregation—or retarded it; to have increased crime—or protected people's rights; to have expanded free speech—or allowed our morals to sink by facilitating the sale of indecent literature. As this suggests, one ruling may produce competing or opposite effects, as when we note that the Court helped force a president from office, while increasing the president's power by recognizing executive privilege.

We begin this chapter with a brief look at some historical instances of impact. This is followed by an examination of the Supreme Court's place in public opinion, both historically and especially in recent years. Then we turn to a discussion of terms like "impact" and "compliance," followed by a detailed look at channels through which decisions might be communicated to those expected to know about and follow them, and at some of the factors that help to explain both communication and impact across different policy areas. We conclude with a more detailed discussion of the Supreme Court's impact concerning church-state relations and criminal procedure.[2]

Impact in History

Supreme Court decisions have produced controversy (one type of impact) and other substantial effects throughout the nation's history, perhaps starting with the Eleventh Amendment, a direct and immediate result of *Chisholm v. Georgia* (1793), allowing a suit against a state. The growth of a national economy was aided by Chief Justice Marshall's broad interpretation of national government power, for example, in sustaining the National Bank against state efforts to tax it (*McCulloch v. Maryland*, 1819) and of commerce when striking down a state steamboat monopoly in *Gibbons v. Ogden* (1824). The economy was also affected by the *Dartmouth College* case (1819) on the sanctity of contracts, which states could not abridge, and the *Charles River Bridge* case (1837), allowing establishment of competing transportation companies.

The Court has also had long-term effects on American federalism, particularly when the states as states resisted national supremacy. In the controversy over the fugitive slave laws, the Court ruled that Congress' jurisdiction over fugitive slaves was exclusive, with a federal statute on the subject preempting conflicting state law, and the Court also denied a state court the authority to order federal officials to commit an act in conflict with a federal court decision.[3] Indeed, conflict has been quite likely whenever the Court has ruled that federal activity prevents the states from taking action.

Another important ruling on federalism that stirred the anger of those supporting "states' rights" was the 1920 decision in *Missouri v. Holland* that a federal treaty (with Canada) concerning migratory waterfowl supplanted Missouri's hunting regulations. The Court's statement that in implementing a treaty the national government could go beyond the constitutional powers it would have in the treaty's absence led to later attempts to amend the Constitution to limit the president's treaty-making power.

One of the most important instances of impact was *Dred Scott*. By saying that Congress could not limit slavery in the states, the Court destroyed congressional compromise. The decision had a number of other impacts, one of which is said to have been that the Court badly damaged itself. However, the extent to which the ruling "undermined the Court as an institution has in fact been greatly exaggerated": Those opposed to the decision wanted to change the Court's membership (and decisions) but "not its structure and functions"; moreover, "hostility to the Supreme Court as a whole . . . was confined to a small though at times highly vocal minority."[4] As is often the case, "the response to the decision proved to be much more important than its direct legal effect." Because of the Civil War itself, the expansion of slavery permitted by the decision did not occur; the owner of the slave whose freedom the Court had denied manumitted him (set him free). However, by legitimating the South's proslavery argument, thus increasing its confidence and making it more inflexible, and by increasing Northern hostility to the *South* (instead of to slavery as such), "as a public event, the decision aggravated an already bitter sectional conflict and to some degree determined the shape of the final crisis."[5]

As these few historical instances indicate, the Court not infrequently has created adverse reaction on questions bearing on the structure of the federal system, "particularly when it has validated exertions of national power against the plaint of states' rights," perhaps thus helping create enemies willing to join those "who oppose judicial activism in defense of personal liberties"[6]—the area in which most recent noncompliance has occurred.

THE SUPREME COURT AND PUBLIC OPINION

One effect of the Supreme Court's decisions is opinions about them, whether held by newspaper publishers, political elites, members of the "attentive public," and "average citizens." Public opinion about the Court itself, for example, the confidence that people express in it, is both another impact of the Court's decisions and a more general reflection of the impact of the Court's individual rulings. In this section, we examine a number of aspects of public opinion regarding the Supreme Court. After brief treatment of editorial reaction to some of the Court's major rulings, we turn to extended treatment of public opinion polls—both those of the general public and more specialized and focused surveys. Through such polls, we examine the Court's overall rating in the eyes of the public, the public's confidence in the Court, and public reaction to specific decisions. We also can learn the extent to which people have information about the Court on which their opinions might be based; their belief (or disbelief) in the "myth" that the Court finds rather than makes the law; and elements—apart from information—that underlie the extent of their general and specific support of the Court.

Early History and Editorial Reaction

The Supreme Court's decisions produced effects on public opinion long before the days of public opinion polls. Public reaction to the decisions was often mixed. When the Court invalidated state fugitive slave statutes, "the decision was equally unsatisfactory to both pro-slavery and anti-slavery men" because the former were upset at the blow to states' rights and the latter, who disliked the federal fugitive slave law, thought the Court was backing the South.[7] The Court also suffered in the public eye when, shortly after being enlarged and only a year after it had held in the first Legal Tender Case that the Union government could not require that debts made before the passage of the Legal Tender Act be paid in paper money, it reversed itself. Although the legal community felt that the Legal Tender Act was constitutional, the reopening of the case was "a mistake which for many years impaired the people's confidence, not in the honesty, but in the impartiality and good sense of the Court."[8]

In the New Deal period, divided reaction was again evident. When the Court invalidated the National Industrial Recovery Act, "the more conservative sections of the press welcomed it as putting an end to unsound experiments in government regulation of industry," labor opposed the decision, and the business community was divided.[9] However, more and more elements of the public were alienated by the Court's continued striking down of New Deal legislation, and "each new adverse decision in the winter and spring of 1936 brought new bursts of hostility."[10] The farmers were upset about invalidation of the Agricultural Adjustment Act, the voiding of the Bituminous Coal Act irritated workers, and the minimum wage rulings "alienated nearly everybody"—including supporters of eariier decisions. Only 10 of 344 editorials approved the decision on the minimum wage, with some sixty papers, including a number of conservative ones, calling for a constitutional amendment on the subject.

Editorial reaction to decisions is one measure, although an indirect one, of public opinion, and it has thus received some attention. Twenty-four large-circulation newspapers generally favored separation of church and state after three of four major Supreme Court church-state decisions; the exception was the *Zorach* ruling upholding New York's released time program, which the papers favored. The *McCollum* ruling striking down religious classes on school property was the most favorably received (eight papers favoring and two opposing), with editorials on the school prayer case closely divided (thirteen favoring, nine opposing). Support for the released time ruling may have resulted from that program's milder link between church and state, more conservative public attitudes toward civil liberties in 1952, liberal Justice Douglas's authorship of the Court's opinion, and the general tendency of newspapers to support the Court. Newspapers' editorial positions on church-state matters were affected by a city's political climate (the more Democrats, the more likely a paper to favor church-state separation), the publisher's politics (same relationship, but stronger), and the publisher's religion (higher support for the Court if Catholic or Episcopalian).[11]

More in line with general public opinion was the editorial and cartoon reaction of 63 papers of a wider range of circulation. Opposition to the school prayer ruling was stronger in those papers in the upper Midwest, with more Southern papers neutral or favorable. Editorial reaction among these same papers to the Court's first reapportionment decision was generally favorable, and the papers' editorial position affected news coverage: those supporting the Court presented a more restrained account of the Court's rulings in both headlines and reportage of critical reaction to the decisions than did papers opposing the decision.[12]

Public Opinion Polls

Despite the frequency with which public opinion polls on a wide variety of topics appear, no unified statement about public opinion about the Supreme Court has yet been developed. We can, however, provide a basic picture from scattered items in the Gallup and Harris surveys and from more intensive studies conducted by political scientists.

In the 1960s, national polling organizations began to ask how people rated the Supreme Court. Overall ratings remained fairly constant in the mid-1960s. A November 1966 Harris Poll showed the public giving the Court an overall negative rating (46 percent–54 percent). Younger people, the better-educated, and blacks backed the Court, while southerners, older people, and the less well educated were the Court's severest critics. Similar results appear in a 1967 Gallup Poll. The Court's work was rated excellent by 15 percent, good by 30 percent, fair by 29 percent, and poor by 17 percent, resulting in an almost even balance between favorable and unfavorable reactions. The June 1968 Gallup Poll rating showed how quickly opinion can change. Evaluations had shifted to 36 percent favorable, 53 percent unfavorable, with only 8 percent rating the Court's work as excellent. Republicans were most critical of the Court, and those with less than a college education were also negative; Democrats and those with a college education were evenly divided.

Although the Burger Court's criminal procedure rulings were more in tune with public opinion, they did not produce an improvement in the Court's overall rating. The Court received only a slightly higher Gallup Poll rating in 1973 than it had received in 1969—a rating much lower than the Court's mid-1960s ratings. In 1973, 37 percent rated the Court's work good or excellent, but only 6 percent rated it excellent. Thirty-five percent thought the Court too *liberal*, while 26 percent thought it too conservative. Who liked the Court had also changed. Decreased approval of the Court was shown by the college-educated, those twenty-one to twenty-nine years old (who showed the greatest drop), westerners and easterners, and Democrats, but ratings were up among those age fifty and over, southerners, and Republicans (up 12 percent).[13]

The polls also showed shifts in the public's confidence in the Court as an institution. In 1966 a Harris Poll majority (51 percent) expressed a great deal of confidence in the Court—almost 10 percent more than did so for either Congress or the executive branch but less than for medicine, colleges, or the military. A 1967 Gallup Poll indicated that almost half the American public thought the Court had been impartial, but 30 percent—particularly older citizens, Republicans, and southerners—believed the judges showed some group favoritism.

By 1972, confidence in the Court decreased noticeably, part of the overall decrease in the public's confidence in its leaders; only 21 percent of Harris survey respondents expressed a great deal of confidence in the Court. Starting with 1972, confidence in the Court rose for three years (to 40 percent in 1974) but then dropped substantially to 28 percent in 1975 and 22 percent in 1976, where it remained the following year before rebounding in early 1978 to 31 percent. This was a higher percentage of the public than had a great deal of confidence in other government institutions; the Court had maintained such a position in public opinion since 1973. The Court also showed a bigger gain in the proportion of those expressing confidence than did the president and Congress, an indication that the Court's place in public opinion, although partly a function of confidence in all government institutions, is to some extent independent of the public's view of the other institutions.

Another indication of the Court's position in public opinion is the 1975 Harris survey finding that 38 percent of the respondents felt that those in charge of the Supreme Court "really know what most people they represent or serve think and want," somewhat better than Congress, the White House, or the executive branch. However, more—43 percent—said the Court was out of touch with those it served, and 19 percent did not know, higher than for any other institution. By 1977, the percent saying the Supreme Court was "mostly out of touch" had risen to 47 percent.

In addition to their general evaluation of the Court, the public expressed reaction to specific decisions. Thus the 1966 Harris survey showed the public, despite its overall negative rating of the Court, favoring rulings on reapportionment (76 percent–24 percent) and desegregation of schools and public accommodations (both 64 percent–36 percent). Only reapportionment received approval in the South, where only 44 percent of the public supported school desegregation. Opinion was evenly divided on the Court's having forbidden the State Department to deny passports to Communists, but the school prayer and *Miranda* rulings were disliked (30 percent–70 percent and 35 percent–65 percent). A 1973 Gallup Poll revealed that 58 percent favored the Burger Court's conservative ruling on obscenity, but roughly the same percentage disapproved of the Court's 1972 invalidation of the death penalty. (President Nixon's appointees, who had dissented, were closer to public opinion.) The rulings denying news reporters a First Amendment right to protect confidential sources and invalidating aid to parochial schools were also opposed by majorities of those questioned.

Recent polls reveal potentially conflicting findings. In early 1981, 74 percent of the public opposed busing their children to another part of town for desegregation, but a year later, a majority opposed a federal law prohibiting the Department of Justice and federal courts from ordering school busing to achieve racial balance. At the same time, only 17 percent said the Supreme Court had too much power, with more than twice that proportion (39 percent) saying the Court was carrying out proper responsibilities. This illustrates the difficulty of predicting public opinion about how to respond to the courts from surveys about specific rulings.

What about the opinion of those in the legal community? A 1970 poll of Providence, Rhode Island, lawyers showed they were more dissatisfied with the Court than was the Gallup Poll's national sample. They were also more undecided than the national sample's college-educated and business and professional groups, with their indecision coming from indifference rather than ambivalence. The criminal procedure decisions seemed most important for the lawyers who criticized the Court; they tended to hold a "traditional" attitude toward the Court—including the idea that the Court only finds law—and wanted "strict constructionist" judges. Those favoring the Warren Court were more likely to approve of judges engaging in lawmaking.[14]

In 1967, four-fifths of the police officers in four medium-sized Wisconsin cities disapproved of *Miranda*. There was no relationship between attitude and amount of formal education, but those with least police experience approved of the decision the least.[15] Five years later, Illinois and Massachusetts small-town police chiefs did not show this same resistance to *Miranda*, as most officers had learned to live with the ruling. However, although Massachusetts officers generally favored the (*Mapp*) rule excluding illegally seized evidence from trials, it was hard to find an Illinois officer who could say anything good about that doctrine. The chiefs' views were not related to their formal education, but those who had had law enforcement training before becoming officers were somewhat more likely to view the rule positively.[16] A study of officers in twenty-nine St. Louis area police departments carried out at the same time, however, showed weak relationships between training and attitudes. Officers with a college education were somewhat less likely than others to see the Supreme Court's criminal procedure rulings as harmful, but some findings ran counter to the hypotheses that officers with higher levels of education and training would "have a view of the goals of law enforcement which includes the protection of civil liberties even of persons suspected of criminal acts" and would "be less critical of Supreme Court decisions."[17]

More than three of four federal judges, state supreme court judges, and lawyers responding in early 1977 to a *U.S. News & World Report* survey preferred the Burger Court to the Warren Court. Almost all (98.8 percent) thought the Burger Court was more conservative than the Warren Court, and 78.4 percent approved of this conservative position. Although two-fifths thought the Court was still taking questions the respondents felt better left to the legislative or executive branches of government, 84.2 percent thought the Burger Court less likely to do so than the Warren Court, and only 2.4 percent thought the Burger Court *more* likely to do so. Over half of those in the poll approved of the Court's making it more difficult for citizens to use the federal courts to obtain redress of grievances and just under half (48.4 percent) said that the Court *was* making it more difficult. A majority of those surveyed approved of the Burger Court's decisions and direction in all areas except obscenity and pornography, where just more than half disapproved. Highest approval (80 percent) came in the area of racial discrimination. Also receiving over 70 percent approval was the Court's work on criminal defendants' rights, sex discrimination, labor union law, environmental protection, and freedom of speech and press. Almost two-thirds approved the abortion rulings, and just over two-thirds, those on states' rights and federalism. However, the death penalty decisions were approved by only 57.5 percent, and the smallest favorable majority (51.1%) approved rulings on mandatory busing to alleviate segregation.

More Extensive Surveys

These polls do not provide information about the public's knowledge of the Court or reveal deeper orientations toward it. Detailed local, state, and national surveys indicate low levels of knowledge, broad general support, and low specific support.

Information

People have relatively little information about the Court and "only a few cases are sufficiently dramatic to rise above the public's threshold of attention."[18] This is clear from a 1965 survey of Seattle residents and from respondents' inability in 1964 and 1966 University of Michigan Survey Research Center (SRC) national postelection surveys to name good or bad things the Court had done and their attribution to the Court of cases it had *not* decided. It is also clear from the fact that one-fourth of a 1968 Missouri sample declined to comment on the Court or pleaded ignorance. In a 1966 Wisconsin survey test of knowledge about decisions, only two percent of respondents had all items correct and only 15 percent had more than half correct; 12 percent had every answer wrong. This lack of awareness extended even to criminal procedure decisions about which there had been open controversy and to reapportionment despite redistricting in the state, indicating that people have difficulty relating decisions to their personal lives.[19] Less than half (45.2 percent) of those in the 1964/1966 national SRC survey could name any Supreme Court decision they liked or disliked, although by 1975 over 60 percent of those in the same sample who had been located indicated specific knowledge of Supreme Court decisions. Despite this improvement, in both years less than half could answer open-ended questions about specific likes and dislikes.[20]

By comparison, more than three-fourths of the attentive public (those generally better informed about public events) could indicate specific likes and dislikes among Supreme Court rulings. Elite groups—congressional administrative assistants and Princeton students—had still higher recall levels: 86 percent could name a recent Supreme Court policy they liked or disliked; not surprisingly, 99 percent of lawyers could do so.[21] Similar differences between the general population and those politically active were evident in a 1976 Wisconsin survey. Overall, only one-third could identify a Supreme Court decision; over half of those politically active had such knowledge, while only one-fourth of the inactives did. Yet only slightly more than one-fifth of the activists identified more than one subject on which the Court had ruled, support for the proposition that likes and dislikes about the Court are based on limited aspects of the Court's work.[22]

School prayer rulings have been among the most salient of the Court's decisions and, along with civil rights rulings, accounting for more than two-thirds of the 1964 likes and dislikes about the Court; by 1966 most likes and dislikes were accounted for by criminal procedure decisions, indicating volatility in the public's views. In the 1975 reinterviews, references to school prayer had decreased but other issue-areas salient in 1966 (civil rights, school prayer, criminal defendants' rights) were still salient; specific references to capital punishment (on which the Court had begun to rule in 1972) had increased. The school prayer decisions were "unknown only to the same seemingly irreducible number of persons who have managed to remain unaware of the segregation decisions."[23] However, because some in the Missouri survey who did not read newspapers knew of at least one Court decision, it appears that "issues which gain the court renown (or notoriety) are so salient that they come through even to people virtually isolated from the printed word."[24]

Support

What about support for the Court's actions? A recent summary suggests:

> There is . . . little evidence of widespread public support for the justices' specific decisions; and the Court does not appear to command sweeping generalized approval. Indeed, it often appears to win lower support than other policy makers.[25]

In the earlier national surveys, those giving the Court diffuse (general) support outnumbered four-to-one those giving it specific support (that based on particular decisions). Only about 20 percent were negative as to diffuse support, but one-third were negative on specific support; moreover, almost three times as many people named only decisions they *dis*liked as named only those they liked.

Putting together the data on general support and that on specific support shows that some of those opposing particular decisions provided general support, as did some of those least knowledgeable about the Court—who also seemed most trusting of government. Among 1966 SRC respondents reinterviewed in 1975, support for the Court decreased, on almost every measure, although by modest amounts, so that support levels, overall, were not substantially different from 1966 levels: "In the aggregate, diffuse support for the Supreme Court, despite tremors that shook the entire political system, proved comfortingly resilient."[26] This is further evidence for the view that "public orientations toward courts apparently change slowly over time if at all, as decisions and popular policy preferences (and other factors) interact."[27] Such interaction is evident in the responses to civil rights matters, particularly busing, where from 1966 to 1975 we find the proportion of negative mentions had increased, with the proportion of positive references decreasing by an even greater amount (from 46.5% to 25.8%); far higher proportions of whites than blacks oppose busing, but not all blacks support it.

What produces opposition to busing? "It is apparently the *symbolism* evoked by the prospect of *any* white children's forced intimate contact with blacks, rather than the *reality* of one's own children's contact, that triggers opposition to busing." In short, self-interest did not affect attitudes toward busing, and the 1972 election revealed an absence of self-interested antibusing voting. Symbolic political attitudes are much more strongly correlated with antibusing attitudes than are measures of self-interest.[28] This is consistent with results of a Florida survey that indicate that "even if it were possible to reduce the objective costs placed on children by the local desegregation policy, little improvement in their parents' approval of the handling of desegregation would follow" because "policy support is far more contingent on parents' diffuse attitudes and their perceptions of political conditions within their districts" than on utilitarian (self-interest) considerations.[29]

Explaining Support

What explains support for the Court? Higher knowledge about the Court has regularly seemed to correlate with greater *dis*approval of the Court, although the relationship might be complex. For example, a person's support for procedural rights might affect what that person heard and read about the Court, which in turn would affect support for the Court. Level of knowledge of the Court and race are related, affecting blacks' support for the Court. The 1966 SRC survey showed a majority of blacks to be among those unaware of even the desegregation decisions. Waterloo, Iowa, surveys in 1970 produced similar results: for 49 percent of blacks but only 32 percent of whites, the Supreme Court "as a regime institution is not salient."[30] A 1975 survey of students at Kentucky universities showed that blacks attributed more legitimacy to the Supreme Court than did whites but were more likely to be found in the midrange of support for the Court than were whites, a result of blacks' having less knowledge about the Court's decisions. Whites, aware of more decisions, favored and disfavored them about equally.[31]

What about partisanship and ideology? Degree of political activity seems to correlate with support. Wisconsin activists indicated opposition to most major Supreme Court decisions but nonetheless provided higher levels of specific support than those politically inactive.[32] Political party identification affected attitudes toward the Court in some but not all surveys; in some situations, the relationship was indirect, for example, being a Democrat influenced what one heard, affecting current attitudes. In the 1966 Wisconsin survey, approval of the president and approval of the Court were positively related regardless of one's party, but part of Republicans' unhappiness with the Court seemed to stem from Democratic control of the White House.[33] However, 1975 SRC reinterviews produced no evidence that the public evaluated the Court in terms of who was president, and, more important, showed party identification "useless in explaining change in diffuse support."[34] Among those surveyed in Wisconsin in 1976, among the politically inactive the level of hostility exceeded 80 percent for both Republicans and Democrats, with Republicans somewhat more hostile. Differences between Democrat and Republican activists were much greater, with the Democrats far more favorable to the Court's decisions (59.3%–39.5%).[35]

Respondents' attitudes (liberal/conservative) best explained support for the Court in the SRC national surveys. Congruence between liberals' political positions and the Warren Court's decisions meant that liberals gave the Court more support at that time. Strong effects of ideology also appeared in the 1976 Wisconsin survey. Although activists supported the Court much more strongly than inactives, it was the combination of liberalism *and* activism, not activism alone, that operated to provide strong commitment to the Court.[36]

Related to diffuse and specific support is public belief in the myth that the Court is a legal rather than a political body. Less than 10 percent of the Missouri sample associated the Court directly with the Constitution, although respondents' references to constitutionality increased the proportion to one-sixth. Just under one-third referred to law and a similar proportion to courtlike functions. Although 60 percent saw the Court in terms of symbols and beliefs, less than half the comments (46.7%) contained positive symbols regarded as legitimators of the Court's authority. In less than one-fourth of all responses was the Court seen primarily as a political institution. This led to the conclusion that "the Court's myth enjoys widespread diffusion," although members of the public were not fully dependent on external symbols to legitimate their belief in the Court. Particularly important is that education *increased* rather than reduced belief in the myth: those who did not believe in the myth were not more politically sophisticated but actually were less well socialized into prevailing norms.[37] Similarly, in the 1975 survey in Kentucky universities, whites, who "exhibited a greater mythical belief" than did blacks, and those from higher status families "seem to accept conventional political values and attribute fine qualities to the Court" more than blacks and lower-status whites.[38] The continuing strong hold of myth is also shown in the 1976 Wisconsin survey: although one-half the respondents held a "realist" perspective, one-third were classified as myth-holders, with a higher proportion among the more politically active.

A question following from people's myth-holding, related to functions thought appropriate for the Court to perform, is whether people can think it proper for the Court to produce changes in governmental structure or process, such as those required by the reapportionment decisions, that is, whether the Court could "legitimate regime change." A Supreme Court ruling can perform such a function only for those who satisfy three conditions: they must perceive, that is, be aware of, the Court, recognize that it may properly interpret and apply the Constitution, and feel that the Court was acting competently and impartially. According to the 1964/1966 surveys, 40 percent satisfied neither of the first two conditions, while roughly one-fourth satisfied both; only about one-eighth satisfied all three. Ten years later, asked to indicate their preference as to whether Congress or the Supreme Court should resolve disagreements over national policy, more Wisconsinites chose Congress (40.4%–35.3% overall), although the politically active chose the Court by a 6–5 ratio. Perhaps a reflection of Watergate, far more respondents picked the Court over the president (54.2%–19.4%); activists were even more likely to choose the Court.[39]

Action from Opposition?

If we wish to know more fully about the Court's place in public opinion, we need to know whether those opposed to the Court will act on their beliefs. Those who think the Court's performance is poor are "most likely to act to change a decision" but "they are neither numerous nor particularly rebelliously inclined."[40] In Wisconsin only a few of those who said they would do something to change a Supreme Court decision they disliked would try to develop further opposition to those decisions among the public. Half would work through members of Congress, and another one-fourth would "act within the established legal processes." Virtually no Illinois or Massachusetts small-town police chiefs said they would refuse to go along with a court ruling. Over half the Illinois officers said, however, that they would do something about a decision they disliked, but for most, this was only to talk about the disliked decisions, complain, and "gripe." In Massachusetts, most spoke of writing to the authorities, including their commanding officers or other chiefs, in order to express their opinions, while a couple would have acted through the legal system.

These responses lead to the remark made about the Wisconsin sample: "This is quiescence indeed" and to the conclusion that "the decisions of the Supreme Court have had more effect on the reputation of the Court than the activities of its antagonists."[41] Yet we have seen repeated attacks on the Court, from the conservative end of the political spectrum, in the 1970s and 1980s. What then protects the Court? A distinct possibility is "the complex interaction between ideological activists, ideological elites, the nation's institutional and structural arrangements, and the character of dominant political majorities in the United States."[42] Liberal activists provide support for the Court. That support reinforces liberal office-holders' will to resist attacks and to use the complexity of the policymaking process (such as the number of points that a proposed statute or constitutional amendment must "clear") to delay and defuse opposition attacks. The requirement of extraordinary legislative majorities and strong executive support to enact anti-Court policy works to liberals' advantages as they seek to protect the Court, evident in the 1982 filibusters by liberal senators against school prayer and abortion measures.

IMPACT AND COMPLIANCE

The terms *impact* and *compliance* are both used to refer to effects of Supreme Court rulings, but they do not have the same meaning.[43] *Compliance* may mean several things. One can distinguish between impact and compliance by saying that impact stands for the consequences of a policy—including but not limited to compliance—while compliance refers to the process, which occurs prior to impact, by which individuals accept decisions. Or one can define compliance differently, saying that a person cannot comply with a law unless he knows of its existence. In this definition, compliance is obedience to a ruling *because* of that ruling, particularly when a person through either opposition or neutrality did not previously intend to take the action required by the decision. One *can* also say that a person is compliant when the person's behavior is parallel to the requirements of the Court's ruling—when the person would, in any event, have done what the Court requires—but that weakens the meaning of compliance; at best one can say the person is *not noncompliant.*

Compliance is relevant when decisions *demand* or *require* certain actions; other *permissive* decisions *allow* governments or private actors to take certain actions, called *adopting* behavior. With the latter, because no one is required to do anything, there can be no noncompliance. Thus, after the Court, in *Ginsberg v. New York*

(1968), upheld New York's statute prohibiting the sale to children of materials "harmful" (a standard less strict than "obscene") to them, several states adopted that type of statute. Cases on jury size and unanimity are other examples of permissive decisions: when the Court ruled that state noncapital criminal juries could be smaller than twelve people (*Williams v. Florida*, 1970) and nonunanimous (*Johnson v. Louisiana*, 1972), the Court was saying only that nonunanimous juries and juries of less than twelve were acceptable, not that they were required, so a state retaining unanimous, twelve-person juries was *not* disobedient.

Even when part of a ruling is mandatory, some implications may be permissive, leaving certain actions optional. For example, *Roe v. Wade* told states to stop criminalizing abortions, at least during the first trimester of pregnancy if the woman and her doctor thought an abortion appropriate, and placed strict limits on regulation of abortions during the second trimester. Because the Court did not order doctors or hospitals to participate in abortions, on this score the ruling was permissive for hospitals. Nonetheless, the decision "appears to have had a substantial impact on hospital abortion policies," with almost half changing their policy. Most expanded abortion services to include elective as well as therapeutic abortions, with a smaller number changing from no abortion services to providing elective abortions.[44]

Determining what is compliant is difficult, but there is little question that noncompliance exists. By any standard, some resistance is obvious, for example, Virginia's plan of Massive Resistance to school desegregation and its closing of schools in Prince Edward County. Other types of resistance, such as attempts to override the Court by constitutional amendment, may be accompanied by compliant behavior. This mix of compliant and defiant behavior, which when combined appears to fall between outright defiance and full acceptance, is *evasion*. Evasion also occurs when the Court's ruling is accepted, but only literally and narrowly while other ways are sought to achieve goals with which the ruling has interfered. For example, after the Court said in 1917 that whites could not enact laws to prevent blacks from residing in particular neighborhoods (*Buchanan v. Warley*), they developed private racially restrictive covenants and enforced those covenants in state courts. Another type of evasion is the misapplication of Supreme Court standards or the substitution of other standards for the Court's, particularly when those doing so (for example, state supreme court judges in establishment of religion cases) do "not admit their noncompliance but rather attempt to portray their decisions as consistent with previous Court decisions and the standards enumerated in them."[45] When those affected move only a small distance from invalidated statutes, evasion is close to disobedience. Many statutes enacted after the 1973 abortion ruling, particularly those that outlawed the use of saline solution for abortions and thus interfered with medical decisions, fell in this category.

Impact includes all effects resulting from a decision regardless of whether people knew about the decision. There may, of course, be situations of "nonimpact" in which nothing happens. For example, after the Court upheld Illinois' "group libel" statute prohibiting unfavorable references to minority racial or religious groups (*Beauharnais v. Illinois*, 1952) no other states adopted a similar statute. More recently, when the Court in *Cox Broadcasting Co. v. Cohn* (1975), allowed the use of the name of a rape victim by the media if that name was in public court records, newspapers for the greatest part continued to adhere to the older ethic of not reporting the name: nothing much changed as a result of the decision.

Impact may well begin *before* the Court hands down a decision, perhaps even before litigation commences, as a controversy produces a series of effects on those involved. Impacts may also be unintended, such as extra work for federal district judges as a result of new standards for deciding habeas corpus petitions; "white flight" after desegregation rulings; or a complete stop in the building of public housing in Chicago after the Court in *Hills v. Gautreaux* (1976) ordered a desegregation of public housing in the Chicago area.

Impact includes a wide variety of behaviors. When a statute from one state is struck down, officials elsewhere may reexamine their own laws to determine whether they remain valid. If it is not clear whether the statutes or regulations differ in significant particulars, uncertainty will result, as it does when the Court's ruling is not comprehensive and thus does not encompass laws elsewhere. For example, when the Court ruled in the 1982 *Rowley* case that a school district did not have to provide a sign-language interpreter for a deaf fourth-grade child, school administrators were unclear what services school districts would have to provide to handicapped children. An important element of uncertainty is fear of litigation. When the Court held municipalities not acting under policies directly approved by state government open to antitrust lawsuits, there was considerable concern that a wide range of local government actions would prompt lawsuits.[46]

Fears of a Court ruling's effects, which are often highest immediately after the decision, may be shown to have been exaggerated and to have resulted from claims made in defending the challenged action. For example, fears that the Court's ruling requiring Texas school districts to provide tuition-free education for children of illegal aliens (*Plyler v. Doe*, 1982) would result in substantial enrollment increases were not borne out at the beginning of the 1982–1983 school year. Similarly, when the Court ruled in *Baxstrom v. Herold* (1966) that prisoners could not be retained in an institution for the criminally insane beyond the end of their maximum prison sentence unless they were provided a hearing to determine their dangerousness, the state feared that dangerous individuals would create violence in mental hospitals outside the prison system or would be assaultive if released into the community. Again, none of these fears was borne out: levels of violence in civilian mental hospitals were less than expected, and there was less assaultive behavior, both there and "outside," than expected.[47]

There are both first order and second order impacts, which parallel the distinction between impact and outcomes. For example, the *impact* of a judicial ruling ordering desegregation would include not only immediate resistance to or acceptance of the decision but also the actual desegregation of schools. Second-order impact or *out-*

comes would include desegregation's effect on children's education, including increased disciplinary action against black children; removal of black teachers and administrators; and population movement, such as "white flight" to the suburbs. If the impact of reapportionment is redrawn legislative districts and increased numbers of minority legislators, outcomes would include public policy changes enacted by the newly constituted legislature, such as increased welfare benefits or general state expenditures that were not as substantial as some anticipated.[48] If the impact of the Court's 1973 abortion ruling was invalidation of most criminal abortion statutes and changes in hospital policy, outcomes included a substantial increase in abortions: the Court's ruling did not command but only facilitated abortions for women desiring them.

This range of impacts involves several relevant "populations": an "interpreting population," usually a lower court, that refines—makes clearer—the higher court's policy; an "implementing population" that applies the Court's basic policy directive; a "consumer population" for whom the directive was intended and to whom it is applied; and a "secondary population." This last group includes the general population not included in the consumer population—for example, for school desegregation, perhaps those without children in school, as well as both governmental and nongovernmental "attentive publics"—those interested in but not directly involved in the particular policy and its implementation.[49]

Not only are several populations involved, but to get a full picture of impact one must look at both short-term and long-term effects of cases and at the effects of *sets* (or a "line" of) decisions in a policy area. Thus to determine impact in the criminal justice area, we would not look only at *Mapp* or *Miranda* but at the whole set of rulings "nationalizing" defendants' rights, which as one effect led state court judges to master federal law. Looked at this way, impact involves not only one-way effects of Court on relevant populations but also feedback, the transmission of reactions back to the Court, in short, reciprocal interaction over time between the Supreme Court, lower courts, legislatures, and executive branch agencies. An important part of the feedback is *anticipatory compliance*, in which lower courts, in an example of inter-level interaction, see the direction in which the Supreme Court is heading and hand down rulings that take the law beyond the last Supreme Court decision, with the Court then adopting this forward movement as its own. Evidence of this behavior is quite clear in libel law where the Supreme Court itself invited lower courts to extend the test it had developed in *New York Times v. Sullivan* (1964), limiting public officials' ability to obtain libel judgments.[50]

COMMUNICATION OF DECISIONS

Communication and response or impact are intimately related. In some instances, people may not know much about the actual outcomes that result from the Court's rulings but may respond to the Court because of effects the media have attributed to a decision. Those expected to respond to a decision cannot do so if they do not learn of the ruling. If they receive an incomplete or otherwise distorted version of the ruling, their response may diverge from what the Court anticipated. Because compliance or impact will vary even if justices' opinions come through "loud and clear," communication and compliance are related but communication does not control compliance. The means by which decisions—or information about them—are communicated are quite important, particularly because few among those who might be affected by rulings—whether police affected by criminal procedure decisions or booksellers by decisions on the meaning of "obscenity"—seek out that information. Thus it must be brought to them if they are to obtain it.

Only a "small minority" of booksellers questioned in one multistate survey knew about the Supreme Court's obscenity decisions, and only 3 percent of those responding sought legal advice on more than "isolated occasions" about sexually explicit books they sold. In a study of 18 communities that had experienced censorship campaigns, newsdealers did know the Supreme Court had handed down rulings on obscenity and that those rulings "restricted 'obscenity' to a very narrow class of publications," but they were nonetheless "generally unclear about specifics."[51] These studies also indicate the complexities of the relationship between information about the Court's rulings and other factors. For example, in the former study, those who did know and who allowed their activities to be regulated were the most restrictive in their attitudes toward what they would sell, that is, they engaged in "self-censorship." In the eighteen-community study, however, "attitudes of the wholesalers and retailers toward sexual speech yield[ed] very limited insight into merchandising practices." One reason was that some retailers did not have to self-censor because their wholesalers did so; another, pointing in the opposite direction, was that customer demand for sexually explicit material made it difficult for retailers to limit the items they made available for sale; moreover, publishers exerted pressure on sellers to stock disputed items. Quite relevant to wholesalers' and retailers' actions was their view of "whether their rights . . . could be defended without great cost or anguish" and their recognition that if they cooperated with censorship groups, the demands of those groups often became excessive—requiring resistance by those in an economically marginal situation.[52]

What *are* the ways in which the Court's decisions are communicated?[53] Figure 10.1 depicts the basic channels through which information about the decisions might flow. One obvious means would be the Court's own opinions, available in several forms, including the "slip opinions" handed out on Decision Day, the advance sheets published by private companies soon thereafter, and, in due course, bound volumes. These circulate among at least some attorneys and others interested in the Court's work. The actual availability of the decisions at the local level where people might want to use them is generally unsatisfactory, particularly in the more rural states, where a set of the *United States Reports* may be found only in the few larger cities. In many counties in the United States, a set is simply not available, and the reported decisions of the courts of appeals and district courts are even less likely to be accessible. However, even in larger cities, only a few of the larger law offices—and the county law library—may have copies.

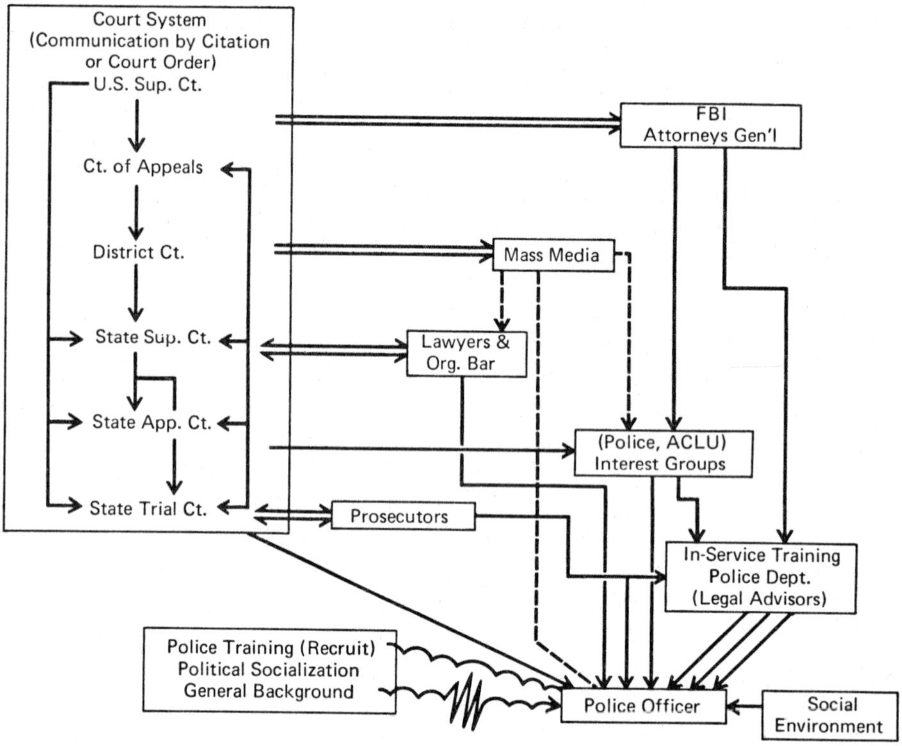

FIGURE 10.1

Source: Stephen L. Wasby, *Small Town Police and the Supreme Court* (Lexington, Mass.: Lexington Books 1976), p. 43.

Lower Courts

The court system itself can serve as a means of communication. The decision in a case is generally sent to a lower court for "proceedings not inconsistent with this opinion." As a result, "the formal judicial structure . . . provides an important channel through which a ruling is transmitted to those directly under obligation to act."[54] But Supreme Court decisions often are not communicated directly to others, instead slowly working their way down to implementing populations through intervening layers of federal and state courts. The relationship of the highest court and the courts below it, despite the court system's official structure, is not hierarchical and bureaucratic. Indeed, "communication channels may be so poor that subordinates do not become aware that a superior has issued a directive," particularly the further away they are from the Supreme Court.[55]

Notwithstanding these difficulties, major changes in law can be heard and understood by the lower courts, particularly if they are clear. When the rulings are not clear—true of Burger Court rulings weakening *Miranda*—there will be less effect; as a result, those rulings "did not result in as much erosion of the *Miranda* principles by state supreme courts as observers seemed to expect."[56] When the Supreme Court ruled that pretrial proceedings could be closed to the public, judges closed their courtrooms much more frequently, an indication—although not proof—that they were well aware of the ruling, one to which they were likely to pay more attention because it directly affected their control of the courtrooms.

Appellate judges also obviously hear the Court's rulings. For example, the U.S. Courts of Appeals and state supreme courts, despite the major change in libel law the Supreme Court directed in *New York Times v. Sullivan,* complied in *86 percent* of their relevant cases, with federal courts complying somewhat more than the state courts. This compliance by the appellate courts was particularly important, because, although the present evidence is mixed, in those libel cases that went to trial, the press was likely to lose there, with the juries, despite Supreme Court statements disfavoring punitive damages, often adding punitive damages to the general damage award. Whatever impact the Supreme Court may have had on lower appellate courts, its libel decisions did not have the same impact on lawyers (who could prove the "actual malice" required by the Court) and juries, who are said to "have disregarded legal and constitutional niceties and decided as they pleased."[57]

Lower courts' acceptance of Supreme Court rulings can also be seen in their response when the Supreme Court remands a case after reversing the lower courts. Somewhat more than a majority of those who have won in the Supreme Court in civil as well as criminal cases were able to preserve that victory on remand. Civil liberties and criminal procedure cases received less support than economic regulation decisions, partly because the Supreme Court gave the lower courts considerable discretion in criminal procedure cases. There were no differences in outcomes on remand between federal and state courts, but courts two levels away from the Supreme Court were less supportive than were those only one level away, such as the U.S. Courts of Appeals. In addition, the longer the time after the Supreme Court's ruling, the less likely was the Supreme Court victor to prevail on remand.[58]

If the high state courts often follow the Supreme Court's rulings, state judges have nonetheless engaged in sarcasm or injected "organizational contumacy" into communication channels by criticizing the rulings, by stating concern for the effect of those decisions on the public's safety, and by challenging the factual premises underlying the rulings. At times they have gone beyond criticism to urge lower state courts not to extend disliked Supreme Court rulings beyond absolute necessity so as not to unsettle the state judiciary. When enforcement is thus based less on "genuine enthusiasm" than on "a sense of hierarchical duty," with courts indicating they are acting because they have to do so, they are not likely to kindle much enforcement activity by implementing populations.[59]

Trial court judges are crucial in the transmission of the Supreme Court's rulings to particular recipients, such as the police. "To the average officer 'the law' concerning arrest, search, and other police practices is in large measure represented by his direct and indirect knowledge of the attitudes of the local judiciary."[60] Yet the trial judge seldom explains his decision, most trial court decisions are either unwritten (announced from the bench) or unpublished, and few local government units have established methods for systematically gathering and transmitting information from the courts.

Most trial court judges are not likely to obtain information about Supreme Court rulings through vertical channels. They are more likely to learn about them "horizontally" or laterally from other judges at the same jurisdictional level, who thus can be crucial in the transmission of the rulings. However, even when they correctly apply the Supreme Court's rulings, they may do so narrowly, taking their lead from the higher state courts to which they are likely to pay more attention. Lower court judges who did not like the *Escobedo* ruling—that a suspect being interrogated had to be allowed access to his lawyer—refused to apply *Escobedo* to anyone who did not already have a lawyer. Similarly, judges who did not like the *Miranda* ruling did not require warnings to be given to those not in custody, and then defined "in custody" as narrowly as possible. They were thus much like state supreme court justices in their interpretation of *Escobedo.* Only four state supreme courts followed the letter and spirit of *Escobedo,* while thirty-seven followed the letter but violated the spirit by refusing to extend the ruling beyond its specific facts; five openly criticized the decision. On the other hand, all but two of the courts interpreting *Miranda* complied, with fourteen classified as "liberal" in their interpretations.[61]

In evaluating state judges' performance, we should not assume that all lower courts—even those at the same jurisdictional level—are the same. They may vary in general orientation to legal matters, to their local community, and to important "relevant others" with whom the judges interact. For example, in the area of juvenile justice, courts differ in the extent to which proceedings are adversary in character and emphasize treatment. Some local criminal courts are characterized more by "community mediation" than by imposition of formal penalties. One would expect Supreme Court rulings requiring increased due process requirements to be more readily accepted and implemented in those courts with a more formal orientation—although the judge's ideology about defendants' rights would also have an effect.

At times the pressures from their local "constituency" under which lower courts operate—whether or not the judges are elected—can be severe, as it was on Southern judges, both state and federal, asked to enforce desegregation in the decade and more after *Brown v. Board of Education.* Some were aggressive, active enforcers of individual rights; others, more gradualist, although probably having personal attitudes not congruent with the rights required by the Constitution and statutes, would enforce the law if they were given enough evidence. Similarly, although some state supreme court judges (States' Righters) have emphasized local needs and problems and stressed the primacy of state law and state judicial processes, others (Federals) have been willing to take their cues from higher federal courts and from the Supreme Court's interpretation of the national Constitution.[62] If some local judges were to do what the Supreme Court wanted and to resist pressures from the communities to which they had ties, they needed a "hierarchy of scapegoats" as well as more specific guidance as to how to achieve desegregation.[63] It was also easier for state judges to sustain civil rights when they could avoid mentioning the U.S. Constitution and could emphasize state legal symbols (the state constitution and state cases). If constituency pressure can work against acceptance of Supreme Court rulings, it can also support it. Liberal lower court judges, particularly if elected, may be hesitant to diverge from Burger Court criminal procedure rulings for fear of being labeled "soft on crime."

Lower courts' resistance to a controversial set of Supreme Court civil liberties decisions undoubtedly overstates the degree to which the judges react negatively to the Court's rulings overall. Lower court judges' preferences and interests do run in opposite directions from Supreme Court rulings from time to time, particularly in new areas of the law. Also, some trial judges may not pay much heed to the Supreme Court—particularly if they have adopted a position on an issue before the Court has spoken or if their attitudes are "unfavorable to the intrusion of 'law' into court proceedings which are highly routinized."[64] Yet in the broad range of cases, resistance occurs relatively seldom. Most policies enunciated by the Supreme Court fall within lower court judges' "zone of indifference," the area in which their feelings are not strong; because the judges have been socialized to accept the authority of higher courts—coupled with the potential sanction of reversal—they usually do what is expected of them.[65]

Lawyers

With few judges monitoring higher court decisions, a Supreme Court ruling may come to a judge's attention only when a lawyer presenting a case cites it. Indeed, many judges, partly because of work pressures that limit their reading, intentionally wait until attorneys bring new legal doctrine to their attention. Yet if attorneys are unaware of cases and thus do not cite them, the judges may never be apprised of new rules, and trial lawyers' negative feelings about their clients do serve to limit their learning about the rulings. Where a substantial number of attorneys practice a particular specialty, they may have an informal organization for circulating information about relevant cases, and lawyers arguing appellate cases are particularly likely to know about relevant higher court decisions. (Nonlawyers generally must rely on the interest groups to which they belong to provide such information, but most interest groups do this only sporadically.[66])

Attorneys general and prosecuting attorneys are among the lawyers playing a most important role in the process of communication and impact. We can see this from another study of the disposition of cases on remand after the Supreme Court has ruled. Of the over 1,100 criminal cases in fiscal years 1975–1979 that resulted in reprosecution, a majority led to results different from the original trial; however, the changes resulted largely from actions of prosecutors, not the judges, with motions filed by U.S. Attorneys producing most of the changed results. In those instances where there was a retrial to final verdict, however, only one-fourth resulted in acquittals.[67]

The advisory opinions of state attorneys general, which may incorporate Supreme Court rulings, do not have the force of law but are often given great weight by officials contemplating the legal ramifications of proposed actions. However, the advisory opinions usually are issued only on request by a public official and are not widely circulated, thus limiting their use as a means of communication. More important are informational meetings on new developments in the law and bulletins published for law enforcement officials, in which Supreme Court decisions are related to state statutes and judicial rulings and thus made more relevant to local officials' immediate concerns.

Local prosecutors, although they could play a large role in the communications process, may not be knowledgeable even on the subjects of cases they have tried. For example, Wisconsin district attorneys involved in obscenity cases felt some books and magazines "cleared" by the Supreme Court were obscene and other prosecutors gave many wrong answers to factual questions about Supreme Court obscenity cases. Only 20 percent of the prosecutors were rated as having high perception of Court policy (medium perception: 42 percent; low: 20 percent).[68]

Regardless of their knowledge, however, even where the police would like them to do so, prosecutors rarely undertake the task of telling the police about Supreme Court decisions or about how police practices might be altered to comply with those decisions. Similarly, a regular link with local police departments through which the information could be transmitted is likely to be lacking, so officials who obtain legal information from the prosecutor usually must do so informally. This lack of legal information from the prosecutor has led an increasing number of large police departments to hire police legal advisers—lawyers whose task includes interpretation of Supreme Court decisions, the development of teaching materials, and training within the department.[69] Small departments, which cannot afford to hire these advisers, are thus left without systematic means of acquiring appropriate legal information.

Media

Although sources of legal information inside the legal community are important, there are other sources outside the judicial system and legal community. There is no radio or television coverage of the Supreme Court's oral argument or its announcement of decisions: Chief Justice Burger has said it would not occur "until after my funeral." Nonetheless, the mass media serve as an important initial source of information about cases. Television is the principal source for the general public, as well as the one given most credibility, although newspapers provide greater detail.

In the 1960s, reporters covering the Supreme Court were frequently criticized for not being well trained, and for being passive and uncritical in their reporting of the Court.[70] Since then, however, the accuracy of reporting has increased; most reporters covering the Supreme Court for major newspapers, the wire services, and the television networks either have law degrees or have spent some time studying law. This results in greater legal sophistication in coverage of the Court, and one now seldom finds such errors as reporting a denial of review as a full decision of the Court.

Nonetheless, reporters covering the Court operate in a situation where the public seems not to have an expectation of accurate reporting about the Supreme Court, or perhaps the public's low level of knowledge about the legal system makes it difficult for the newspaper reader or television viewer to know whether information presented is accurate. Nor does there appear to be an expectation of complete reporting about the justices' activities, unlike expectations that the media will report the work of Congress and the president and of the president's activities fully and *accurately.* For example, reporters covering the Court did not mention a speech problem (stammering, slurred words) exhibited by Justice Rehnquist in 1982 until after he was hospitalized. Only from George Washington University Hospital's spokesman were other doctors able to identify the drug (for a back problem) that had probably caused the difficulty. Nor did reporters seem to complain when the Court's Information Officer was typically uncommunicative on the matter, and the Court did not issue a clear or full statement of the sort the reporters would *demand* of the president's press secretary. Some commentators actually defended the silence, saying the Court was sufficiently close-knit to take care of the problem. However, such statements ring false, given the Court's difficulty in getting a disabled Justice Douglas (like other disabled justices before him) to leave even when the Court's work was being affected.

The media do not transmit Supreme Court decisions intact; few newspapers even print portions of the most important cases. Nor could they, not only for reasons of space but because the Court's opinions are too complex in their original form to be understood by most people. The wire services have been and continue to be the principal source of information about the Court for newspapers and to some extent for television as well. A study of *Baker v. Carr* and the School Prayer Cases in the early 1960s showed that twenty-three of twenty-five papers carried reports of the reapportionment ruling on Decision Day, with fourteen stories coming from AP, five from UPI, one from the *Herald Tribune* News Service, and only two from the papers' staff writers. The picture was roughly the same for the school prayer rulings. However, starting with the second day after the opinion, although wire service domination continued, more stories were written by staff writers.[71]

In addition to not communicating decisions intact, the media's reporting filters the Supreme Court's rulings in other ways. This is particularly likely when the Court's decisions affect the media themselves, because the media do not remain objective about those decisions. (The media's attacks on those rulings have even been criticized by Justice Brennan, whose votes indicate he is no enemy of the media. Brennan suggested that the criticisms are unreasonable, unintelligent, and inaccurate, and fail as well to separate decisions definitely imposing restraints on the press from those, like rulings on free press and fair trial, that balance the press's interests with other social interests or other civil liberties.[72]) The media's views affect the way opinions are condensed and summarized generally. As Justice O'Connor has observed, "The summaries of the opinions of this Court carried in the media . . . frequently provide a perspective, not only on the work of the Court, but also on the perceptions and judgment of the reporters and their editors."[73] One can see this in a humorous vein in the accompanying "Supreme Court Roundup," a parody of typical wire-service summaries of the Court's decisions.

The media deal with some decisions more carefully or more sympathetically than with others. Some rulings are not treated at all, being lost in the deluge of rulings, particularly toward the end of each term of Court. Because the rulings are not

SUPREME COURT ROUNDUP

by *Veronica Geng*

Washington, May 8—*The Supreme Court took the following actions today:*

First Amendment

In a landmark decision, the Court ruled unanimously in favor of a twelve-year-old plaintiff who sought damages on account of being denied the chance to audition for the Clint Eastwood role in the motion picture "Maddened Rustlers." The Court's opinion, written by Chief Justice Happ, argued that exclusion of the little girl was "rotten, beastly, a crying shame—really makes the Court sick." The case was not decided, as had been expected, on the ground of sex discrimination; rather, the Justices invoked the First Amendment's guarantee of freedom of expression. The Court thus affirmed for the first time the constitutional right to a screen test.

Search and Seizure

Overturning the "dog's breakfast" doctrine of search and seizure, the Court held unconstitutional the Drug Enforcement Administration's system of obtaining search warrants, under which a judge who issues a warrant receives the rest of the afternoon off, while a judge who refuses a warrant is reclassified as a Controlled Substance. Justice Happsberger, writing for the majority, said that such procedures "lean upon the delicately coiffed maiden of the Fourth Amendment with the great ugly brutish heavily muscled shoulder of procedural error," and cited Judge Cheerful Hand's famous dictum "I shall keep at it with these metaphors until I'm very old and it's unbecoming."

Taxes

Without hearing arguments on the issue, the Court ordered the Internal Revenue Service to desist at once from collecting personal income taxes—a practice that Justice Hapenny defined in his opinion as "inconsiderate" and "the product of diseased minds." He pointed out that the government could easily collect the same amount of money by manufacturing and selling wall plaques that say "UNCLE SAM LOVES YOUR FIRST NAME HERE."

Controversy

In one of their occasional "piggy-back" decisions, the Justices resolved some of the long-standing issues that clog the Court calendar. They ruled that nurture is more influential than nature, that men make history, that Iago is driven by motiveless malignancy, that one isn't too many and a thousand is enough, that there is an earthly paradise, and that Don Bucknell's nephew Ed doesn't look anything like John Travolta. Justice Hapworth dissented but was too polite to say so.

Moral Blight

Citing "want of attractiveness" as a reason, the Court declined, 7–2, to hear an

directly reproduced, much of the "richness"—including the rationale or reasoning—of the Court's opinions is lost during transmission. The media are thus part of a translation process in which changes are introduced and different elements of a decision and its context are emphasized. Each medium differs in what it emphasizes about what happens at the Court. The wire services, which cover the Court on more days than the newspapers (relatively close behind) or the television networks, appear appeal by the publisher of two so-called men's magazines, *Rude Practices* and *Men's Magazine*. In the majority opinion, Chief Justice Happ explained that appellant's arguments were "unprepossessing and—let's be frank about it—just incredibly disingenuous." Dissenting, Justices Happer and Happner said they wanted to pretend to hear the case and then rule against appellant for "putting out such a clumsily edited and typographically unappetizing publication."

In a related decision, the Justices unanimously refused to hear a song written by a Kleagle of the Ku Klux Klan.

Criminal

By a 9–0 vote, the Court held unconstitutional a New York City statute that would have mandated criminal convictions for suspects who fail to take policemen aside and "read them their duties." The statute had required that suspects deliver these "Caliban warnings" to policemen in order to remind them of their power of life and death, their obligation to attend to personal hygiene, etc. The Court, in an opinion by Justice Happell, contended, "Who can doubt that this would be the first step toward compelling suspects to serve their arresting officers creamed chicken on toast points?"

Greed

Splitting 8–1, the Court upheld the constitutionality of a federal program for the redistribution of wealth. Under the program, which is known as "horizontal divestiture," rich people are asked to lie down, and poor people then divest them of their money. Justice Happold, dissenting, said that the program would diminish the impact of a standing Court order requiring that income in excess of $8,000 a year be bused across state lines to achieve bank-account balances.

Gibberish

The Court voted unanimously not to review a case in which a court of appeals struck down a lower federal court's decision to vacate an even lower court's refusal to uphold a ruling that it is not unconstitutional to practice "reverse discrimination." Chief Justice Happ, who wrote the opinion, said that the Court "is not, nor will it consent to be, a body of foolosophers easily drawn into jive baloney-shooting." A brief was filed by the Modern Language Association as *amicus curiae* ("curiosity about Don Ameche").

•

As is their custom, the Justices closed the session with an informal musicale, playing a Corelli *gigg*. Justices Hapgood, Hapworth, Happner, and Happer performed on violin, Justice Happell on bassoon, Justice Happsberger on harpsichord, Justice Happold on oboe, Justice Hapenny on flute, and Chief Justice Happ on viola d'amore.

to have the greatest capacity to handle "raw word flow." Although individual newspapers vary considerably, wire-service and newspaper coverage is closely related to the Court's output, but television coverage is not. When output increases, changes in the pattern of coverage occur, with more attention paid to impact and somewhat less to legal principles; television is more affected by increase in output than are the other media. However, when output reaches a certain level, the ability of the media to expand coverage to match that output ceases and coverage loses most of its "depth," tending to summaries of individual cases.[74]

Each medium also seems to have a different "profile" in relation to "Court time": wire services and television give relatively greater emphasis to predecision coverage; newspapers, more to postdecision coverage. Television seems to add more "contextual information" than do the other media, and to report "informational content" about the decisions least; the newspapers, on the other hand, seem to be most balanced in coverage of various elements—including not only predecision material and the decision itself, but also material on the Court as an institution and trends in the Court's decisions. The inclusion of all this other material makes it difficult for people to find out what the Court has said: they may be able to read about the decision's impact without knowing what it is that is having the impact. Yet if a decision is to be applied to a variety of circumstances, its rationale—not merely the facts and the holding—must be communicated.

For specialized audiences, television is clearly inadequate as a source of needed operational information, and even newspapers are likely to have insufficient material about the Court's decisions. Because of these inadequacies, specialized magazines must perform an information-communication function about judicial decisions. However, while most occupational groups' trade journals can carry such information and some do, it usually is not well developed and is available only sporadically. Another, related source of information about legal decisions is the specialized material prepared for use in training. An advantage of such material is that the law is related to problem situations that those who must implement the rulings will face. Such details, although quite necessary, are not likely to have been provided by the courts. Such material must be written so that it can be understood; for example, materials for police officers must be written without a "dumb cop" image but so that those with a high school education or at most a couple of years of college can understand it.

As this suggests, training serves as a major means of communicating the law (statutory materials as well as court cases) to specific occupational groups like police officers, who tend to rank training as the most effective means of learning about the law. Training takes a variety of forms, including degree programs at two-year and four-year colleges and much shorter two-day or three-day or one-week in-service programs. These education and training programs must cover many subjects, so that coverage of legal matters is likely to constitute only a very small percentage of a total program unless, as is rarely the case, it is devoted solely to the law.

FACTORS AFFECTING COMMUNICATION AND IMPACT

Communication of the Supreme Court's rulings and the impact of those rulings are affected by a variety of factors that alter messages before they reach their intended audience and by the ways in which those audiences respond to the rulings. At times such factors are strong enough to "wash out" most of a decision's intended effect.

There is, however, no clearly developed "theory of impact" to tell us the exact effects or relative importance of these factors.

Attitudes

Attitudes of those affected by decisions appear to play a particularly important role in the decisions' impact. Relevant attitudes include views of the Court's legitimacy, with distaste for the Court leading people to pay less attention to its decisions. Similarly, a feeling that the Court is not ruling fairly on a subject or is not ruling on the basis of adequate knowledge can interfere with the reception given its decisions. For example, the Court's competence and hence its legitimacy was questioned in the police area when the Court in *Miranda* seemed, at least to law enforcement officers, to be acting without reference to the actualities of police work. This perceived action of the Court made it increasingly likely that the personal and organizational goals of the police would differ from the goals embodied in the Court's ruling. On the other hand, when the Court showed recognition of the dangerous situations in which police find themselves, as in the *Terry* "stop and frisk" case, there was less hostility to the decision in the law enforcement community.

Another attitudinal element is an individual's general commitment to "obeying the law." However, "obeying the law," including the dictates of the Supreme Court, plays a limited role when other factors enter the picture. Some people alter their attitudes to bring them more in line with the Supreme Court's position, but many others develop a variety of techniques that allows them to retain their policy preferences without adhering to the Supreme Court's doctrine. Among these techniques are attacks on those who are seeking to enforce the decisions (condemning the condemners); appeals to a "higher morality" (an authority higher than the Supreme Court); denial of responsibility for the present situation, perhaps coupled with a claim that others are preventing compliance from coming about; and beliefs that those the decision is intended to protect (whether blacks or criminal defendants) have not really been injured or are instead the *real* menace to society.[75]

Attitudes of community leaders, at least as perceived by those implementing Supreme Court rulings, also affect impact. Such attitudes were related to post–*Roe v. Wade* changes in hospitals' abortion policies and played a larger role in such changes than did demands for abortions or the activities of interest groups. Similarly the attitudes of hospital governing boards and of doctors and nurses working in the hospitals heavily determined hospital abortion policies.[76]

Basic attitudes help explain parental resistance to desegregation, and the attitudes of decision makers can somewhat moderate local opposition to desegregation. However, sometimes attitudes are superceded by judgments of whether "the utility of noncompliance is greater than the utility of compliance, that is, of engaging in the available alternative activity expected to yield the greatest net gratification." Indeed, desegregation of Georgia school districts provided strong evidence to support a cost-benefit explanation: "In communities in which the costs of compliance were perceived to be high and rewards low, the most severe coercion was required."[77]

Clarity

Characteristics of the Court's ruling itself and the place of the ruling in a pattern of decisions are also important. If those who are expected to implement decisions are to hear about them, the decisions must be highly visible. Because at times people become aware of rulings only after they have been cited by lower courts or commented on in an attorney general's bulletin, that is, only after they have traveled through lengthy communication channels, the initial signal must be strong to overcome interference and delays. Otherwise the message becomes garbled, as in the game of "Gossip." A unanimous opinion is thought easier to transmit than are several opinions from a single case, and thus increases impact. However, if unanimity is achieved at the cost of a murky, unclear compromise, communication will be more difficult and impact may be lessened. Concurring and dissenting opinions not only increase the information to be transmitted but also make it easier for potential opponents of the majority's view to resist compliance. A plurality opinion makes it particularly difficult for others to determine the Court's intent.

As this discussion indicates, the relative clarity or ambiguity of even a single opinion also affects its communicability. There are few decisions that, like *Miranda*, can be reduced to four or five warnings to be put on a "Miranda card." Even when a decision is clear initially, it may become less clear as the Court later explicates or limits it. Thus, the initial clarity of *Miranda* was blurred by rulings on use of confessions obtained without warnings or resumption of questioning after it had been stopped. Greater clarity is generally thought to produce greater compliance; ambiguity, more noncompliance. However, state supreme court reaction to establishment of religion cases did *not* show a relationship between Supreme Court clarity and lower court compliance.[78]

The addition of more and more cases will by itself increase the amount of "noise" in the communication system, particularly if they are decided on the basis of the "totality of circumstances" in the case—the Burger Court's initial preference in the field of criminal procedure—rather than a broad rule such as the Warren Court tended to use. Just as a large number of cases increases distortion, gaps in doctrine may also create ambiguity. Such gaps are inevitable because the number of cases decided by the Supreme Court is very small in relation to the total number of issues on which it is asked to rule. Thus courts can develop a "clear policy line" on only a few issues at any one time, if they can do so at all.

The Court may set off far more of a furor when it first approaches an area of policy, even if its first case in that area has limited scope, than it does later with more far-reaching cases, because its initial action may be unexpected. Thus *Engel v. Vitale*, although invalidating only state-written prayers in schools, drew far more heated reaction than *Abington School District v. Schempp*, which outlawed school prayer and Bible reading, which were far more prevalent. Affecting reaction to these cases was the Court's greater care in delineating its second holding—in saying that not all teaching about religion had to be excluded from the school—than it had been in its first opinion, where important qualifications appeared only in a footnote. Similarly, less negative state court reaction to *Miranda* than to *Escobedo* may have come both from a realization that *Miranda* was likely to follow and from the *Miranda* opinion's greater clarity.

Situation

The ongoing situation into which a Supreme Court decision is injected is another factor affecting the receipt of communications and the decision's impact. A decision handed down in the midst of a crisis is likely to receive less coverage than one announced in "normal" times, unless the decision is perceived as contributing to the crisis or producing one. Compliance with an appellate court decision is assisted because such a ruling "often comes well after the deep feelings in the community [provoked by the litigation] have subsided."[79] However, if a substantial change in the law has taken place immediately prior to the Court's ruling, obtaining further change soon is difficult. Similarly judges are less likely to go along with the Supreme Court when invalidating local practices is thought likely to be disruptive. Getting people to pay attention to the courts is also difficult when the law is well settled, making it less likely that further substantial change will occur in the short run.

Both a community's long-term history and events of the immediate past may attune potential recipients to what the Court has said; a community with few major crimes is less likely to be "up" on criminal law than one in which a murder has recently occurred or in which the police want to make a major drug "bust." A community's general belief system also affects communication of decisions and receptivity to them. Officials in communities that pride themselves on being "up-to-date" or "professional" might be more likely than other communities to seek out information about court decisions and to work to bring local government action into accord with those rulings.

Organizational structure and location play a part in the communication of and compliance with court decisions. An organization may be so large that what specialists or others at the "top" of the organization learn about judicial rulings cannot be effectively transmitted to the "bottom." Where units are small, division of labor and specialization may be insufficient to have a person assigned to monitor judicial rulings. A small unit located near other units may acquire information from those units "horizontally"; however, when the small unit—like a rural police department—is geographically isolated, it may have few contacts through which to acquire information. Political isolation may be as important as geographical isolation in determining communications received, with community influence in the form of daily pressure affecting how an agency responds to a judicial ruling. Community pressures vary with the size and homogeneity of the community and are particularly severe in small, homogeneous communities where role expectations reinforce each other. And an agency operating in a supportive environment may be more resistant to outside rules that demand change than an agency that is politically vulnerable and may comply to protect its position.[80]

"Follow-up"

Another important part of the postdecision situation is the "follow-up" to a ruling—*who* responds and how they respond. Average citizens and government employees may pay greater attention to subsequent communications about a ruling if elites support it. Even the absence of criticism—when relevant officials merely maintain a neutral posture—may be important. However, communities with homogeneous populations may prove immune to officials' support of a disliked Supreme Court ruling such as school prayer. And if prominent officials immediately oppose a ruling, further communication about it may well fall on plugged if not deaf ears. Agency officials' reactions to the Court's rulings are likely to be a function of the distance between the organization's policy and what the Court suggests, as well as of the agency's commitment to its own program; the greater the change the agency thinks the Court requires, the greater the likelihood the agency will search for alternative policies. Here organizational norms can come into play forcefully; the norm that the organization should make decisions independently, not subject to an external "superior," would encourage noncompliance.[81]

Because the Court's rulings are usually not self-enforcing, the degree to which government officials enforce or attempt to enforce those rulings, part of "follow-up," is critical. (Even where the decisions are self-enforcing, such as decisions allowing sale of material of greater sexual explicitness, officials' actions in responding to or rejecting demands from community groups opposed to the rulings or abstaining from taking action themselves are important in that situation as well.[82]) Executive branch officials do not often directly attack Supreme Court decisions, but they may severely damage the possibilities for compliance by refusing to take firm action to implement them. This was true with respect to school desegregation in the Eisenhower, Nixon, and Ford administrations. Eisenhower "declined to state publicly his personal view of the *Brown* decision, thus giving rise to speculation that he disapproved of compulsory desegregation." Although his attorneys general supported desegregation in the courts, "the President's ambiguity and the administration's general inactivity . . . encouraged white Southern leadership to believe that the federal executive branch would take no forceful action to enforce the courts' orders." The role of southern governors was also vital; the increase in the number of militant segregationist governors after *Brown* certainly did not facilitate compliance.[83]

At the local level, prosecutors' inaction concerning police violations of search and seizure rules does little to encourage compliance. Prosecutors may even approach the Court's rulings negatively, talking to police (in what is called "negative advocacy") about how to "get around" a ruling. People are not encouraged to learn about or to follow the rules if there are no sanctions or only limited ones for not knowing the law, with little if any reward for following Court-established rules. Thus, if new rules are to be carried out, there must be active supervision, not just executive passivity.

Follow-up is also affected by the community pressures that are an important part of an official's "work situation."[84] That work situation also includes the people from whom the official takes cues as to how to behave—his "reference group"—that is particularly important when community expectations are contradictory, thus allowing the individual more discretion as to how to act. Some government employees ("locals") take their cues primarily from their own communities, while others ("cosmopolitans," particularly professionals), such as lawyers and doctors, look to those in the same occupation. If, like police officers, individuals spend much time in the company of colleagues and feel the Supreme Court is hurting their work, they may wish to avoid becoming "sore thumbs" or deviants and thus will not attempt to follow rules adhered to by their fellow workers. Such social pressure is increased when the work subculture becomes organized into unions or comparable interest groups.

IMPACT IN PARTICULAR POLICY AREAS

Church-State Relations

The Court's rulings on released-time programs (in which children are released from public school classes to receive religious education) and those on prayer in the public schools attracted much attention and produced much controversy, which has continued to the present concerning school prayer. Resistance to the Court's school prayer ruling, not typical of reaction to decisions on other church-state issues, has come close to matching resistance to school desegregation in both intensity and openness. For example, when the Supreme Court in 1981 invalidated a Kentucky law that required the posting of the Ten Commandments in public school classrooms, many school districts left them posted despite a state attorney general's opinion that this was improper even if the Commandments were donated by a private group.

Released Time

When the Supreme Court in the 1948 *McCollum* case invalidated a program of religious instruction operated on school property by religious personnel, those operating other programs attempted to differentiate theirs, and some were modified. Programs most likely to continue were those with long-standing enabling legislation. Some on-premises programs continued, with state attorneys general doing little to stop them; opponents of the programs tended to be religious minorities who lacked the political weight necessary to produce change.[85]

After the 1952 *Zorach* decision sustained religious programs held *off* school grounds during school hours, attendance at such denominational activities returned to pre-*McCollum* levels, but subsequent growth was small. Some people interpreted *Zorach* to require, rather than merely to permit, released time programs, but states did not enact new programs, a fact that raises further questions about the force of the Court's power to legitimate a policy. Nor was much done to eliminate continuing noncompliance with *McCollum*, even though off-premises programs could have been adopted with relative ease to produce compliance.[86] (Another impact of *Zorach* stemmed from Justice Douglas's dictum, "We are a religious people whose institutions presuppose a Supreme Being": it was often quoted subsequently by those favoring a variety of programs supporting religion.)

School Prayer

The school prayer decisions of 1962 and 1963—*Engel v. Vitale,* invalidating a state-composed prayer, and the *Schempp* case, striking down recitation of the Lord's Prayer and readings from the Bible—produced far more outcry than the released-time rulings. Local and state officials played a key role in deflecting the requirements of the school prayer rulings. Where a superintendent opposed the practices, he was able to use the Supreme Court's ruling to change local practices but needed the decisions to do so. However, far more numerous were officials who wanted to avoid conflict with small-town local power structures, often because the officials had other, more important goals to achieve. The large number of local districts provided necessary *opportunities* for noncompliance that must accompany depth of feeling before noncompliance can actually occur. Local officials' claims that their districts were in compliance when the truth was otherwise also made it difficult to constrain disobedience. The officials either presumed that compliance was taking place and did not check for violations or turned their heads after making a perfunctory statement that prayer and Bible reading were to be stopped, thus allowing teachers to continue the practices. Lawsuits were the only practical way of challenging the practices, but little litigation occurred because it was extremely expensive and often had few supporters and because, as in the post-*McCollum* period, those in the minority on this emotional issue were unwilling to subject themselves to the pressure they would have felt had they attacked local practices.[87] Where policy was made primarily at the state level, compliance was more likely both because there were fewer actors to be constrained and because the education "establishment" actively enforced compliance.[88]

There were major regional differences in compliance. Where the practices had been most widespread, in the East and particularly the South, they were least likely to be given up, but school prayer was far more likely to be discontinued in the Midwest and West. Some areas had had long-standing prohibitions against such devotional activities; areas that had adopted the practices without explicit requirements found it easy to give them up. Those areas that retained school prayer were likely to have had constitutional or statutory requirements underlying the practices. In the East, formal requirements were eliminated, leading to compliance. But in the South, requirements were not removed and were at times supplemented, making it unlikely that the practices would be changed.[89]

After the Court's ruling, the national incidence of classroom prayers as reported by teachers decreased from 60 percent to 28 percent in 1964–1965; Bible reading decreased from 48 percent to 22 percent. It could thus be said that "the average teacher did feel the impact of the Supreme Court decision."[90] The largest number of teachers said there was no school policy on prayer or that matters were left up to them. School policies did have an effect: compared to an incidence of 40 percent in schools with no policy, only 4 percent of teachers in schools that opposed the prayers said them, but of teachers in schools favoring the prayers, 43 percent led prayers. For Bible reading, the figures were much the same. Yet teachers' own religious practices affected compliance: those who attended church more frequently were more likely to lead prayers in the classroom—both before and after the Court ruled. Conservative Protestants were most likely to have said prayers before the ruling and were least likely to comply with the Court's ruling. Jews and Catholics, who, along with liberal Protestants, were less likely to have led classroom prayer before 1963, were most likely to comply. A teacher's seniority also had an effect on compliance: the greater the seniority, the less the change in practice.

Among those who did not change their views about religious practices, there were several types of responses.[91] The "backlashers," committed to defiance of the Court's ruling, tried to bring religious activities into the schools whenever they could and took a negative stance toward the Court itself. On the other hand, the "vindicateds" were critical of "schoolhouse religion" both before the decision and afterward. Others who did not change their personal views complied with the decisions because they generally believed or led themselves to believe that they had no choice but to comply; these were the "nulists." There were also many who changed their views toward religion in the school, but not all did so in the same way. The "converts" came to believe in the Supreme Court ruling and were committed to enforcing it, while the "liberateds" softened their views about religion in the school and moved toward convergence between their own views and what the Court required. The "reverse liberateds," however, became more rather than less favorable to schoolhouse religion; they moved away from the Court's position, not toward it.

Criminal Procedure

Most of our knowledge about communication of Supreme Court decisions comes from the field of criminal justice. In the least professionalized of four police departments in medium-sized Wisconsin cities (Green Bay), the greatest proportion (more than one-third) of the officers found out initially about the *Miranda* decision from a newspaper. About 75 percent cited the newspaper as either an initial or later source, and the same proportion heard about the ruling from a superior officer. Only slightly fewer officers were exposed to the case by television, and somewhat over 60 percent heard of it in training sessions. Although a full 40 percent of the department's officers ultimately read the opinion itself, the evidence confirms that "people who have no formal connection with the judiciary may be a more important source of information than any judicial authority."[92] The newspaper was also the most common initial source in the most professional of the four departments (Madison), but more than 90 percent of the officers there were exposed to the decision in conference-and-training; roughly three-fourths heard about it from each of three sources—newspapers, a superior officer, and the attorney general. In Racine, where there was a captain of detectives on whom others relied for legal information, a high proportion of the officers received their first information about *Miranda* from superior officers—who were also the predominant overall source of information.

The greater the professionalism of the department, the larger the number of sources of information and the greater the percentage of officers who received information from training sessions. Formal law enforcement sources were stressed more in the more professionalized departments. However, none of the departments had much contact with "outside" information that might have proved helpful in understanding the decision. Professionalization did not bring increased contact with nonpolice groups, but instead tended to bring about well-developed lines of intra-departmental communication. Outside groups were listened to more frequently in the more professionalized departments, but that was because the groups furnished information that reinforced professional ideology. In all four departments, conference-and-training was rated the best source of information by the most people, with opinions as to the next best source varying. Those approving and those disapproving of the decision did not differ much in selecting the best source of information. However, those approving of the decisions were more likely to have received information at training sessions than were those who disapproved. Although professionalization affected the way *Miranda* was communicated and received, after the decision as before, "there was no real hierarchy through which binding directives regarding the implementation of the *Miranda* decision could flow." Thus *Miranda* "did not basically change the decentralized and often unsystematic communications processes used to inform police departments about innovation."[93]

In small (two- and three-officer) Wisconsin departments, the primary initial source of information about criminal justice rulings was also the newspaper—also the predominant general source of information and the one thought best. Other sources were police magazines and the attorney general's office—despite the lack of personal contact with the latter. Conferences and training sessions, attendance at which gave the officers prestige, were mentioned in connection with *Miranda* and received high ratings.[94]

Small-town police chiefs in southern Illinois and western Massachusetts interviewed in 1972 were most likely to have found out about Supreme Court decisions from other sources—bulletins and other specialized or professional literature. However, of the few chiefs who considered training programs a primary source of information about the Supreme Court, most felt they had not learned enough about the Supreme Court from such programs. In large city departments throughout the country, three types of sources of information about Court decisions predominated: the decisions themselves, specialized police publications, and the district attorney. The media were cited as a source by only about 10 percent of the departments.[95]

Small-town chiefs saw the Court's decisions—which they believed nonlawyers could understand—as the most effective means of communication, with state and local prosecutors a close second; mass media and personal friends were thought highly *in*effective means of communication. Written communications were seen by most as more effective than oral communications, although some thought a combination (training materials discussed at a conference) better still. The officers seemed to want something like a regular (monthly) bulletin or newsletter that digested cases and provided updated information for the individual officer, not just the department. They also saw the local prosecutor—in Massachusetts, along with the attorney general—as having responsibility for providing legal advice to the police. However, many officers said they were not provided sufficient material or access to it. However, differences between states can be seen in the fact that, although most Illinois chiefs did not know where the Supreme Court's decisions were available, those in Massachusetts often had copies of the decisions in their offices—and read them.

Right to Counsel

The Massachusetts and Illinois police chiefs certainly felt that the Supreme Court had affected police work, although these chiefs thought the effect had occurred primarily in large cities, not in their small towns. The Court's decisions (mainly Warren Court rulings) were thought to have improved the quality of police work. Although "old-timers" had been reluctant to "get involved" with cases, newer officers were more accustomed to the new rules and not scared by them.

Another long-term impact of the Court's rulings was on the environment in which law enforcement personnel operated. *Gideon v. Wainwright*, requiring representation of indigents at trial, played a major role in shaping this environment. It led to creation or expansion of public defender programs and, coupled with other Warren Court broad rulings on confessions and searches, to attorneys' greater persistence in pursuing criminal cases, particularly at the appeals stage. Courts interpreting *Gideon* had usually adopted a narrow view of its requirements and imposed a "variety of different lines . . . as to where the cut-off point" came for providing counsel.[96] However, a year after *Argersinger v. Hamlin* (1972), which extended the right to counsel at trial for any situations in which a jail term was imposed, most jurisdictions except for rural southern counties were complying with the Court's directive. Most locations appointed counsel even in traffic cases where imprisonment was a reasonable possibility, although they did not do so for nonserious traffic cases, which usually involve only a fine. A somewhat later study did suggest, however, that compliance with *Argersinger* had been only "token," with judges encouraging waiver of counsel and with "no coherent development of defense systems to meet the need for quality representation" that the spirit of the ruling demanded. Appointed counsel—often assigned immediately before a trial—were frequently inexperienced and not well prepared to represent their clients.[97] In the early 1980s, state funding cutbacks seriously affected both public defender agencies and reimbursement of appointed counsel. Appointed counsel resisted working without pay, and in at least one state (Missouri) judges had to impose compulsory service without compensation on attorneys so that defendants would be represented.

Even when there was an increase in appointment of counsel under *Argersinger*, staffs of public defender offices increased in only a small proportion of all counties, primarily the larger ones. This increased staffing did *not*, however, produce the expected great increase in nonguilty pleas in misdemeanor cases. Rates of guilty pleas were somewhat—but not much—lower than when counsel were not frequently present, and presence of defense counsel did not result in a greater frequency of trials. However, provision of counsel may have delayed the guilty pleas that most misdemeanor defendants intended to enter when they came to court. (More frequent case dismissals and charge-and-sentence concessions may have, however, benefited defendants.) Cases did seem more "stretched out" when defense counsel were present than when they were not. Apparently courts' administrative burdens were not affected by lawyers' actions, for misdemeanor judges did not perceive their ability to handle their caseload was being hindered by greater use of defense counsel.[98] Defense counsel—whether assigned counsel (used primarily in small counties) or public defenders (used in larger jurisdictions)—now had to help process guilty pleas. Thus the rationale of *Argersinger*—that the trial process should become more adversary in nature—was not carried out. Indeed, the Court's failure to recognize plea-bargaining before 1970 may not only have reinforced plea-bargaining, because the Court did not constrain it, but also weakened the Court's protection of the trial stage of the criminal process, as *Gideon* and *Argersinger*, among other rulings, were thought to do.[99]

Exclusionary Rule

The two most crucial Supreme Court criminal procedure decisions were *Mapp v. Ohio* (1961), imposing the exclusionary rule on the states, and *Miranda v. Arizona* (1966), on the admissibility of confessions. Questionnaire responses from police chiefs, prosecutors, defense attorneys, judges, and American Civil Liberties Union (ACLU) officials indicated that as a result of *Mapp*, search and seizure questions were raised more frequently at trial but that there had not been overall change in police effectiveness. Attitudes were reported to have altered as a result of the ruling, with a general movement toward agreement with statements that the same rules should exist for federal and state police, that the legality of searches should be broadened, that more flexible search warrants were needed, and that safety should be emphasized more and liberty less.[100] Increased police adherence to legality in searches between 1960 and 1963 was reported, with a high positive correlation between increased police education on search and seizure and adherence to legality.

Mapp also produced a substantial increase in police education, including development of courses at police academies, adult education programs, colleges, and universities. In fact, it was among the "key factors in increasing the attempts at centralization and formalization of police training procedures."[101] In New York, retraining sessions "had to be held from the very top administrator down to each of the thousands of foot patrolmen and detectives engaged in the daily basic enforcement function," with "hundreds of thousands of manhours" devoted to the task.[102] Training improved in previously nonexclusionary rule states, and the FBI increased its training of state and local officers, but the exclusionary rule did not guarantee that good police training on arrest and search would take place, with pre-*Mapp* exclusionary rule states among those doing the least. Four years after *Mapp*, training remained "very spotty in both quantity and quality."[103]

States that had a pre-*Mapp* exclusionary rule appeared to differ from those without the rule prior to 1961. Courts in the former states seem to have been *less* likely to adopt federal search and seizure precedents after *Mapp*, particularly if they had already begun to develop their own lines of precedents. Thus "where a state judiciary *anticipates* a federal rule, but with variations of its own, those variations are going to prove very hard to kill."[104] Making this conclusion problematic is that states previously adopting an exclusionary rule had seldom invoked it or had interpreted it narrowly when they did. We are thus left with "virtually no relationship between adoption and implementation of *Mapp*."[105] Nor was there a great deal of post-*Mapp* judicial action to implement the ruling. Supreme courts in eighteen states did not deal with more than two of sixteen basic search and seizure questions, and thus did not provide the law enforcement community with statements on much of what constituted an unreasonable seizure. For only three questions did two-thirds or more of the state courts rule evidence inadmissible; five of the questions were settled in a manner limiting *Mapp*'s application, in line with not uncommon explicit resistance to *Mapp* by judges, who often indicated that they had little use for it. Overall, nine states responded positively to *Mapp*, fourteen were in an intermediate category, and nine were rated negative.[106]

The most important potential effect of *Mapp* was on police actions—arrest and search warrants—where changes could have resulted from increases in particular types of crimes (guns, gambling, drugs) as well as from the decision itself. Disagreement abounds as to the decision's effects, with different studies cited on either side of the argument that the costs of the rule are too high to retain it. In the study cited most by opponents of *Mapp*, Dallin Oaks, relying primarily on data from Chicago and Cincinnati, concluded that "the data contains little support for the proposition that the exclusionary rule discourages illegal searches and seizures, but it falls short of establishing that it does not." However, in a stronger statement, he argued, "As a device for directing or deterring illegal searches and seizures by the police, the exclusionary rule is a failure." He went on to say that police conduct not leading to prosecutions was unlikely to be affected by the rule, with little deterrent effect on prosecution-oriented activity.[107]

Analysis of arrest, warrant, and disposition data for the immediate post-*Mapp* period and for later years (to allow the decision's long-term effects to be ascertained) raises doubts about these conclusions.[108] In fourteen cities without a pre-*Mapp* exclusionary rule, few search warrants had been used, but the proportion of constitutional searches, although varying from city to city, increased after the Court's decisions. Officials in large city police departments attributed the increase in search warrants primarily to the increase in narcotics traffic, with less of the change accounted for by increased numbers of police, better training, and other judicial rulings. In roughly one-third of the cities, court decisions were not thought to have had much effect on recent increases in the numbers of search warrants, but in approximately one-fourth of the cities, judicial action was thought to be a major if not the total cause. The data did suggest an interplay between increased narcotics use and judicial rulings as causes of increased warrants. Police decisions to use rather than not use search warrants turned on the existence of the exclusionary rule, but the increased use of narcotics largely explained substantial increases in use of search warrants from the late 1960s through the early 1970s. Charges dropped by police departments and prosecutors because evidence was improperly seized did not show evidence of widespread police violation of the exclusionary rule, but there was also little evidence that the rule was having a very substantial effect. It was also the case that many officers saw the exclusionary rule as creating problems, including frustration and irritation at the granting of motions to suppress evidence.

Debate about effectiveness and costs of the exclusionary rule has continued in the 1980s but still has failed to resolve the central issue. The debate has been fueled by exchanges between law professors and judges,[109] continuing suggestions by the Chief Justice and Justice Rehnquist that the rule be replaced, and two 1979 studies of the rule's effects. The General Accounting Office (GAO) reported that motions to suppress evidence under the Fourth Amendment led to exclusion of evidence in only 1.3 percent of the federal prosecutions examined; the motions, filed in less than one-fifth of the cases, were denied most of the time when they led to formal hearings; and prosecutors dropped less than one percent of cases because of search and seizure problems. A subsequent study conducted for the Senate Judiciary Committee, focusing on thirteen state jurisdictions, where the greatest effect of the rule had been alleged, also revealed a low proportion of cases dropped at the prosecution screening stage because of due process problems, with the rule having little overall impact on prosecutions.[110] Such findings may mean that the rule's opponents have exaggerated the extent to which the rule has resulted in "criminals running loose on the street because of technicalities," or that cases come to prosecutors in better shape, with fewer due process problems than earlier because police have "cleaned up their act"—an indication of the rule's effectiveness.

Confessions

If we turn our attention to *Miranda*, in the period shortly after the decision, we find that in New Haven and Washington, D.C., not all four warnings required by the decision were given in all situations at the station house and in some instances none were. An even lower rate of warning-giving occurred "on the street."[111] Warnings given at the station house did not silence all defendants for several reasons: detectives effectively used a variety of elements of psychological interrogation, those informed of their rights did not understand the warnings, or they could not take advantage of them because they did not know how to contact an attorney. Yet even when station house counsel was promptly available, many suspects talked before an attorney could arrive to assist them. Nor was this simply a result of lack of formal education. Yale University graduate students interrogated by the FBI in connection with draft-card violations were generally unaware of their *Miranda* rights until law professors called the warnings to their attention; even then, many continued to participate in the interrogations.[112]

In four Wisconsin cities (see above), police knowledge of *Miranda*'s requirements was relatively high, but the decision appeared to produce little change in the conduct gators to give warnings to suspects before interrogation were undermined by the interrogators' discretion and by their habit of giving the warnings but not following through on department policies of allowing counsel to be present at interrogations. In short, compliance was "formal, perfunctory or rhetorical" without behavioral changes. Detectives said that *Miranda* had changed the way they had to obtain evidence, particularly by forcing them to obtain it prior to beginning interrogation, but observations suggested instead that "all the departments continued to rely first on interrogations. If that failed, either because of lack of relevant information or because of a lawyer's refusal to allow questioning, only then were alternative methods relied upon."[113]

These effects were from the relatively short term. What about the longer term? For one thing, generational effects exist, with newly trained officers accustomed to the warnings from the beginning of their police service. In addition, the Burger Court's cutting back on *Miranda* might have affected the degree to which law enforcement officials applied it. Yet in 1979 prosecutors in counties with 100,000 or more population strongly supported *Miranda*, with younger prosecutors more strongly supportive than older ones. The prosecutors also supported the Burger Court's changes in requirements for compliance with *Miranda*, of which they were well aware. However, they did not think the changes significant, nor did they believe the Burger Court rulings had had "a significant, or even a moderate, effect on their decisions to prosecute." Over half reported that the Burger Court's *Miranda*-related rulings had had limited or nonexistent effects, and less than 10 percent said that their prosecutorial decisions had been significantly affected.

The greatest change came where the Supreme Court's change had been clearest—in allowing use of improperly obtained statements to impeach a defendant's credibility. Yet even on this point, less than half the prosecutors were more likely to use confessions this way. Other differences in the types of confession-related cases prosecutors were likely to pursue closely paralleled the relative clarity of the Court's rulings: the less the clarity in Burger Court rulings, the less likely the prosecutors to use a confession obtained under the circumstances covered in the Court's opinion. A factor more important than the Supreme Court's clarity affecting prosecutors' actions was local judicial standards. Because local judges either had not relaxed *their* application of *Miranda* or had become more strict since the first Burger Court ruling (1971), "the Burger Court's weakening of *Miranda* has not been duplicated at the local level."[114]

Despite all the obstacles both to communication of the Supreme Court's rulings and to compliance with those rulings that have been enumerated and discussed in this chapter, compliance with the Court's decisions does occur and those decisions have substantial impact. If that were not the case, we would hear far less objection to them. More important, without them, racial and sexual equality, freedom of speech and religion, and defendants' rights, as well as economic regulation, would not take the form in which they now exist. The resistance to implementation of those decisions serves all the more to remind us that the Supreme Court is not merely a "finder" of the law but an active policymaker.

Despite the views that many people have of the Court, which do not cast it in such a role, and despite the public's general lack of awareness of what the Court has done—even how it operates—the justices maintain a commanding presence. Other officials must at least take them into account before they act; nor has the Court, even when publicly adopting a general posture of "self-restraint," been hesitant to strike down the actions of both of its coordinate branches at the national level of government and of the state governments as well. In perhaps the most important test, attacks on the Court's major rulings have only very infrequently been successful, although the Court has at times backed off from some of its strongest positions. It is doubtful that we have "judicial supremacy" as the Supreme Court's harshest critics have argued from time to time, but we do have in the Supreme Court of the United States a body of individuals who, operating within the constraints of the nation's legal system, through both the full-dress treatment given some cases and the variety of other, less visible actions they take, regularly make policy for that system and the larger political and social system.

NOTES

1. Charles Warren, *The Supreme Court in United States History* (Boston: Little, Brown, 1922), vol. 1, p. viii.
2. Some of the material presented here, revised and updated, was first presented in Stephen L. Wasby, *The Impact of the United States Supreme Court* (Homewood, Ill.: Dorsey Press, 1970).
3. *Ableman v. Booth*, 21 How. 506 (1859); *Prigg v. Pennsylvania*, 16 Peters 539 (1842).
4. Don Fehrenbacher, *The Dred Scott Case*, pp. 454, 576.
5. Ibid., pp. 3, 449, 493.
6. Jesse Choper, *Judicial Review and the National Political Process*, pp. 231–233.
7. Warren, vol. 2, p. 358.
8. Ibid., vol. 3, p. 244. That Justices Strong and Bradley, who helped produce the second decision, were named to the Court on the day of the first decision did not help matters.
9. Merle Fainsod, Lincoln Gordon, and Joseph Palamountain, *Government and the American Economy*, pp. 540, 541.
10. Arthur M. Schlesinger, Jr., *The Politics of Upheaval* (Boston: Houghton Mifflin, 1960), p. 489.
11. Stuart Nagel and Robert Erickson, "Editorial Reaction to Supreme Court Decisions on Church and State," *Public Opinion Quarterly* 30 (Winter 1966–67):647–655; also in Nagel, *The Legal Process from a Behavioral Perspective*, pp. 285–293.
12. Chester Newland, "Press Coverage of the United States Supreme Court," *Western Political Quarterly* 17 (March 1964):15–36.
13. See Richard Claude, "The Supreme Court Nine: Judicial Responsibility and Responsiveness," in *People vs. Government: The Responsiveness of American Institutions*, ed. Leroy N. Rieselbach (Bloomington, Ind.: Indiana University Press, 1975), particularly Table 1, p. 123.

14. Edward N. Beiser, "Lawyers Judge the Warren Court," *Law & Society Review* 7 (Fall 1972):139–149.
15. Neil Milner, *The Supreme Court and Local Law Enforcement: The Impact of Miranda* (Beverly Hills, Calif.: Sage Publications, 1971).
16. Stephen L. Wasby, *Small Town Police and the Supreme Court: Hearing the Word* (Lexington, Mass: Lexington Books, 1976), p. 82.
17. Dennis C. Smith and Elinor Ostrom, "The Effects of Training and Education on Police Attitudes and Performance: A Preliminary Analysis," unpublished ms., 1973, p. 11.
18. John H. Kessel, "Public Perceptions of the Supreme Court," *Midwest Journal of Political Science* 10 (May 1966):175.
19. See Kessel (Seattle); Walter Murphy and Joseph Tanenhaus, "Public Opinion and the United States Supreme Court: Mapping of Some Prerequisites for Court Legitimation of Regime Change," in *Frontiers of Judicial Research*, eds. Joel B. Grossman and Joseph Tanenhaus (New York: John Wiley, 1969), pp. 273–303; also Walter F. Murphy, Joseph Tanenhaus, and Daniel L. Kastner, "Public Evaluation of Constitutional Courts: Alternative Explanations," Sage Professional Papers #01-045 (Beverly Hills, Calif.: Sage Publications, 1973) (1964 and 1966 SRC); Gregory Casey, "The Supreme Court and Myth: An Empirical Investigation," *Law & Society Review* 8 (Spring 1974):385–420 (Missouri); Kenneth Dolbeare, "The Public Views the Supreme Court," in *Law, Politics and the Federal Courts*, ed. Herbert Jacob (Boston: Little, Brown, 1967), pp. 194–202 (Wisconsin).
20. See Joseph Tanenhaus and Walter F. Murphy, "Patterns of Public Support for the Supreme Court: A Panel Study," *Journal of Politics* 43 (February 1981):24–39.
21. Walter F. Murphy and Joseph Tanenhaus, "The U.S. Supreme Court and Its Elite Publics," paper presented to International Political Science Association, 1970, p. 22.
22. The 1976 Wisconsin survey is reported in two unpublished papers: David Adamany, "Public and Activists' Attitudes Toward the United States Supreme Court," paper presented to American Political Science Association, 1977, and David Adamany and Joel B. Grossman, "Support for the Supreme Court as a National Policy Maker," 1982 (to appear in *Law & Policy Quarterly*), used with permission.
23. Dolbeare, "The Public Views the Supreme Court," p. 199.
24. Casey, p. 397.
25. Adamany and Grossman, p. 9.
26. Tanenhaus and Murphy, p. 29.
27. Kenneth Dolbeare, "The Supreme Court and the States: From Abstract Doctrine to Local Behavioral Conformity," in *The Impact of Supreme Court Decisions: Empirical Studies*, eds. Theodore H. Becker and Malcolm Feeley, 2nd ed. (New York: Oxford University Press, 1973), p. 203.
28. David O. Sears, Carl P. Hensler, and Leslie K. Speer, "Whites' Opposition to 'Busing': Self-Interest or Symbolic Politics," *American Political Science Review* 73 (June 1979): 382.
29. Douglas S. Gatlin, Micheal W. Giles, and Everett F. Cataldo, "Policy Support within a Target Group: The Case of School Desegregation," *American Political Science Review* 72 (September 1978):989.
30. Edward N. Muller, "A Test of a Partial Theory of Potential for Political Violence," *American Political Science Review* 66 (September 1972):940.
31. Dean Jaros and Robert Roper, "The U.S. Supreme Court: Myth, Diffuse Support, Specific Support, and Legitimacy," *American Politics Quarterly* 8 (January 1980):100.

32. Adamany and Grossman, p. 17.
33. Kenneth M. Dolbeare and Phillip E. Hammond, "The Political Party Basis of Attitudes Toward the Supreme Court," *Public Opinion Quarterly* 31 (Spring 1967):23–24.
34. Tanenhaus and Murphy, p. 36.
35. Adamany and Grossman, p. 43.
36. Ibid., p. 24.
37. Casey, pp. 398, 402.
38. Jaros and Roper, p. 95.
39. Murphy and Tanenhaus, "Public Opinion and the United States Supreme Court," p. 282; Adamany, p. 26.
40. Dolbeare, "The Public Views the Supreme Court," p. 208.
41. Kessel, p. 191.
42. Adamany and Grossman, pp. 38–39.
43. Discussion of terminology can be found in Wasby, pp. 27–42; in several of the articles in *Compliance and the Law*, eds. Samuel Krislov et al. (Beverly Hills, Calif.: Sage Publications, 1972); and in Robert V. Stover and Don W. Brown, "Understanding Compliance and Non-compliance with Law: The Contributions of Utility Theory," *Social Science Quarterly* 56 (December 1975):363–375.
44. Jon R. Bond and Charles A. Johnson, "Implementing a Permissive Policy: Hospital Abortion Services after *Roe v. Wade*," *American Journal of Political Science* 26 (February 1982):4.
45. G. Alan Tarr, *Judicial Impact and State Supreme Courts* (Lexington, Mass.: Lexington Books, 1977), pp. 54–55.
46. *Community Communications Co. v. City of Boulder, Colorado*, 102 S.Ct. 835 (1982).
47. See Henry Steadman and Joseph J. Cocozza, *Careers of the Criminally Insane* (Lexington, Mass.: Lexington Books, 1974), and Steadman and G. Keveles, "The Community Adjustment and Criminal Activity of the Baxstrom Patients:1966–1970," *American Journal of Psychiatry* 129 (1972):304–310.
48. See Roger A. Hanson and Robert E. Crew, Jr., "The Policy Impact of Reapportionment," *Law & Society Review* 8 (Fall 1973):70–93.
49. Charles A. Johnson, "The Implementation and Impact of Judicial Policies: A Heuristic Model," in *Public Law and Public Policy*, ed. John A. Gardiner (New York: Praeger, 1977), pp. 107–126.
50. John Gruhl, "Anticipatory Compliance with Supreme Court Rulings," *Polity* 14 (Winter 1981):308–309.
51. James P. Levine, "Constitutional Law and Obscene Literature: An Investigation of Bookseller Censorship Practices," in *The Impact of Supreme Court Decisions: Empirical Studies*, ed. Theodore L. Becker (New York: Oxford University Press, 1969), pp. 129–148; Harrell R. Rodgers, Jr., "Censorship Campaigns in Eighteen Cities: An Impact Analysis," *American Politics Quarterly* 2 (October 1974):376.
52. Rodgers, pp. 376, 378.
53. An earlier version of this section, which has been updated, appeared in Stephen L. Wasby, *Small Town Police and the Supreme Court*, chapter 2, pp. 25–55.
54. Richard Johnson, *The Dynamics of Compliance* (Evanston, Ill.: Northwestern University Press, 1967), p. 61.
55. Walter F. Murphy, "Lower Court Checks on Supreme Court Power," *American Political Science Review* 53 (December 1959):1017–1031; Lawrence Baum, "Implementation of Judicial Decisions: An Organizational Analysis," *American Politics Quarterly* 4 (January 1976):94.

56. John Gruhl, "State Supreme Courts and the U.S. Supreme Court's Post-Miranda Rulings," *Journal of Criminal Law & Criminology* 72 (Fall 1981):911.
57. John Gruhl, "Patterns of Compliance with U.S. Supreme Court Rulings: The Case of Libel in Federal Courts of Appeals and State Supreme Courts," *Publius* 12 (Summer 1982): 109–126; "The Libel Burden," *Columbia Journalism Review* 22 (#5, January/February 1983):27. See also Gruhl, "The Supreme Court's Impact on the Law of Libel: Compliance by Lower Federal Courts," *Western Political Quarterly* 33 (December 1980):502–519.
58. Richard Pacelle and Lawrence Baum, "Supreme Court Authority and the Judicial Hierarchy: A Study of Remands," paper presented to Midwest Political Science Association, 1982.
59. Bradley C. Canon, "Organizational Contumacy in the Transmission of Judicial Policies: The *Mapp, Escobedo, Miranda,* and *Gault* Cases," *Villanova Law Review* 20 (November 1974):69.
60. Wayne LaFave and Frank Remington, "Controlling the Police: The Judge's Role in Making and Reviewing Law Enforcement Decisions," *Michigan Law Review* 63 (April 1965): 1005.
61. Neil T. Romans, "The Role of State Supreme Courts in Judicial Policy-Making: *Escobedo, Miranda* and the Use of Judicial Impact Analysis," *Western Political Quarterly* 27 (March 1974):38–59.
62. Charles Hamilton, *The Bench and the Ballot: Southern Federal Judges and Black Voters* (New York: Oxford University Press, 1973); Kenneth N. Vines, "Southern State Supreme Courts and Race Relations," *Western Political Quarterly* 18 (March 1965):5–18.
63. J. W. Peltason, *Fifty-Eight Lonely Men: Southern Federal Judges and School Desegregation* (Urbana: University of Illinois Press, 1971 [1961]), pp. 245–246. See also Kenneth Vines, "Federal District Judges and Race Relations Cases in the South," *Journal of Politics* 26 (May 1964):337–357; Micheal W. Giles and Thomas G. Walker, "Judicial Policy-Making and Southern School Segregation," *Journal of Politics* 37 (November 1975):917–936.
64. Baum, "Implementation of Judicial Decisions," p. 95.
65. Lawrence Baum, "Lower-Court Response to Supreme Court Policies: Reconsidering a Negative Picture," *Justice System Journal* 3 (Spring 1978):208–219.
66. Alan Schechter, "Impact of Open Housing Laws on Suburban Realtors," *Urban Affairs Quarterly* 8 (June 1973):439–465.
67. Robert T. Roper and Albert P. Melone, "Does Procedural Due Process Make a Difference? A Study of Second Trials," *Judicature* 65 (September 1981):136–141.
68. Thomas E. Barth, "Perception and Acceptance of Supreme Court Decisions at the State and Local Level," *Journal of Public Law* 17 (1968):308–350.
69. See Gerald Caplan, "The Police Legal Adviser," *Journal of Criminal Law, Criminology, and Police Science* 58 (September 1967):303–309, and Frank Carrington, "Speaking for the Police," ibid., 61 (June 1970):244–279.
70. See David L. Grey, *The Supreme Court and the Mass Media* (Evanston, Ill.: Northwestern University Press, 1968).
71. Chester Newland, "Press Coverage of the United States Supreme Court," *Western Political Quarterly* 17 (March 1964):15–36.
72. William Brennan, Address at Rutgers–Newark School of Law, October 17, 1979, *Rutgers Law Review* 32 (July 1979):173–183.
73. *F.B.I. v. Abramson,* 102 S.Ct. 2054 at 2069 (1982).
74. See David W. Leslie, "The Supreme Court in the Media: A Content Analysis," paper presented to the International Communication Association, 1976, and David W. Leslie and

D. Brock Hornby, *The Supreme Court in the Media: A Theoretical and Empirical Analysis* (Final Technical Report to National Science Foundation, 1976, Grant GS 38113).

75. Harrell R. Rodgers, Jr., and Charles S. Bullock III, "Law Abidingness as a Guide to Official Decision-Making: Techniques of Neutralization," unpublished manuscript; see also Rodgers and Edward B. Lewis, "Political Support and Compliance Attitudes: A Study of Adolescents," *American Political Quarterly* 2 (January 1974):61–77; Rodgers and George Taylor, "Pre-Adult Attitudes Toward Legal Compliance," *Social Science Quarterly* 51 (December 1970):539–551; and Don W. Brown, "Cognitive Development and Willingness to Comply with Law," *American Journal of Political Science* 18 (August 1974): 583–594.
76. Bond and Johnson, pp. 13–19.
77. Stover and Brown, pp. 369–370; Harrell R. Rodgers, Jr., and Charles S. Bullock III, *Coercion to Compliance* (Lexington, Mass.: Lexington Books, 1976), p. 65.
78. Tarr, p. 199.
79. Frank Sorauf, *The Wall of Separation*, p. 287.
80. Michael Ban, "The Impact of *Mapp v. Ohio* on Police Behavior," paper presented to Midwest Political Science Association, 1973, p. 33 (study based on Boston and Cincinnati).
81. Charles A. Johnson, "Judicial Decisions and Organizational Change: Some Theoretical and Empirical Notes on State Court Decisions and State Administrative Agencies," *Law & Society Review* 14 (Fall 1979):27–56.
82. Bond and Johnson, pp. 13, 15.
83. Harold C. Fleming, "Brown and the Three R's, Race, Residence, and Resegregation," *Journal of Law & Education* 4 (January 1975):10; Earl Black, *Southern Governors and Civil Rights: Racial Segregation as a Campaign Issue in the Second Reconstruction* (Cambridge, Mass.: Harvard University Press, 1976).
84. For a discussion of the police work situation, see Neal A. Milner, "Supreme Court Effectiveness and Police Organization," *Law and Contemporary Problems* 36 (Autumn 1971):467–487.
85. Gordon Patric, "The Impact of a Court Decision: Aftermath of the McCollum Case," *Journal of Public Law* 6 (Fall 1967):455–465.
86. Frank J. Sorauf, "Zorach v. Clauson: The Impact of a Supreme Court Decision," *American Political Science Review* 53 (September 1959):777–791.
87. See Richard Johnson, *The Dynamics of Compliance* (Evanston, Ill.: Northwestern University Press, 1967). Among the other important studies are those by Donald Reich, "The Impact of Judicial Decision-Making: The School Prayer Cases," in *The Supreme Court as Policy-Maker: Three Studies on the Impact of Judicial Decisions*, ed. David Everson (Carbondale, Ill.: Public Affairs Research Bureau, Southern Illinois University, 1968), pp. 44–81; and Robert Birkby, "The Supreme Court and the Bible Belt: Tennessee Reaction to the Schempp Decision," *Midwest Journal of Political Science* 10 (August 1966): 304–319.
88. Sorauf, *The Wall of Separation*, p. 304.
89. Kenneth Dolbeare and Phillip Hammond, *The School Prayer Decisions: From Court Policy to Local Practice* (Chicago: University of Chicago Press, 1971).
90. H. Frank Way, Jr., "Survey Research on Judicial Decisions: The Prayer and Bible Reading Cases," *Western Political Quarterly* 21 (June 1968):191.
91. See William K. Muir, *Prayer in the Public Schools: Law and Attitude Change* (Chicago: University of Chicago Press, 1967).

92. Milner, *The Court and Local Law Enforcement,* p. 47.
93. Ibid., pp. 52, 226.
94. Larry Berkson, "The United States Supreme Court and Small-Town Police Officers: A Study in Communication," unpublished manuscript, 1970.
95. Data from Illinois and Massachusetts in this and the following paragraph from Stephen L. Wasby, *Small Town Police and the Supreme Court*; large-city data from a study by Bradley C. Canon, also reported in ibid.: see p. 96, and chs. 5 and 6, pp. 119–198, passim.
96. Barton L. Ingraham, "The Impact of Argersinger—One Year Later," *Law & Society Review* 8 (Summer 1975):616.
97. Sheldon Krantz et al., "The Right to Counsel in Criminal Cases: The Mandate of *Argersinger v. Hamlin,"* Summary Report (Washington, D.C.: National Institute of Law Enforcement and Criminal Justice, Law Enforcement Assistance Administration, Department of Justice, 1976), pp. 2–3.
98. Ingraham, op. cit; James J. Alfini and Patricia M. Passuth, "Case Processing in State Misdemeanor Courts: The Effect of Defense Attorney Presence," *Justice System Journal* 6 (Spring 1981):114.
99. See Milton Heumann, *Plea Bargaining* (Chicago: University of Chicago Press, 1978), p. 176, n. 22.
100. Stuart Nagel, "Testing the Effects of Excluding Illegally Seized Evidence," *Wisconsin Law Review* 1965 (Spring):283–310; also in Nagel, *The Legal Process from a Behavioral Perspective,* pp. 294–320.
101. Milner, *The Court and Local Law Enforcement,* p. 52.
102. Michael J. Murphy, "The Problem of Compliance by Police Departments," *Texas Law Review* 44 (1966):941.
103. Wayne R. LaFave, "Improving Police Performance through the Exclusionary Rule: Part II: Defining the Norms and Training the Police," *Missouri Law Review* 30 (Fall 1965): 594–595.
104. David Manwaring, "The Impact of *Mapp v. Ohio,"* in *The Supreme Court as Policy-Maker.* ed. Everson, p. 26.
105. Bradley C. Canon, "Reactions of State Supreme Courts to a U.S. Supreme Court Civil Liberties Decision," *Law & Society Review* 8 (Fall 1973):126–127.
106. Ibid.; and Canon, "Organizational Contumacy."
107. Dallin H. Oaks, "Studying the Exclusionary Rule in Search and Seizure," *University of Chicago Law Review* 37 (Summer 1970):655, 667.
108. Bradley C. Canon, "Is the Exclusionary Rule in Failing Health? Some New Data and a Plea Against a Precipitious Conclusion," *Kentucky Law Journal* 62 (1973–1974):708–709. See also Canon, "Testing the Effectiveness of Civil Liberties Policies at the State and Federal Levels: The Case of the Exclusionary Rule," *American Politics Quarterly* 5 (1977):57–82.
109. See Yale Kamisar, "Is the Exclusionary Rule an 'Illogical' or 'Unnatural' Interpretation of the Fourth Amendment?", *Judicature* 62 (August 1978):66–84; Malcolm Richard Wilkey, "The Exclusionary Rule: Why Suppress Valid Evidence?", *Judicature* 62 (November 1978):214–232; Kamisar, "The Exclusionary Rule in Historical Perspective: The Struggle to Make the Fourth Amendment More Than An Empty Blessing," *Judicature* 62 (February 1979):336–350; Wilkey, "A Call for Alternatives to the Exclusionary Rule: Let Congress and the Trial Courts Speak," *Judicature* 62 (February 1979):351–356. For an exchange on empirical evidence with respect to the rule, see Canon, "The Exclu-

sionary Rule: Have Critics Proven That It Doesn't Deter Police?", *Judicature* 62 (March 1979):398–403, and Steven R. Schlesinger, "The Exclusionary Rule: Have Proponents Proven That It Is a Deterrent to Police?", *Judicature* 62 (March 1979):404–409.

110. See "GAO: Exclusionary Rule Has Little Impact on Cases," *National Law Journal*, May 14, 1979, pp. 3, 10; Edward J. Burke, "Exclusionary Rule's Effect on Cases Called Slight," *National Law Journal*, June 11, 1979, p. 5.
111. Michael Wald et al., "Interrogations in New Haven: The Impact of Miranda," *Yale Law Journal* 76 (July 1967):1519–1648; Richard J. Medalie et al., "Custodial Police Interrogation in Our Nation's Capital: The Attempt to Implement Miranda," *Michigan Law Review* 66 (May 1968):1347–1422; Albert J. Reiss, Jr., and Donald J. Black, "Interrogation and the Criminal Process," *The Annals* 374 (November 1967):47–57.
112. John Griffiths and Richard E. Ayres, "A Postscript to the *Miranda* Project: Interrogation of Draft Protestors," *Yale Law Journal* 76 (December 1967):300–319.
113. Milner, *The Court and Local Law Enforcement*, pp. 229, 217.
114. John Gruhl and Cassia Spohn, "The Supreme Court's Post-Miranda Rulings: Impact on Local Prosecutors," *Law & Policy Quarterly* 3 (January 1981):29–54.

Table of Cases*

*All cases the names of which appear in the text are included here, as are all other important cases appearing in the notes. When the case name is not mentioned in the text, the page reference is to the notes at the end of each chapter, from which the reader can refer to the appropriate place in the text.

Index